IESUS DEUS

THE EARLY CHRISTIAN DEPICTION OF JESUS AS A MEDITERRANEAN GOD

M. DAVID LITWA

Fortress Press
Minneapolis

IESUS DEUS

The Early Christian Depiction of Jesus as a Mediterranean God

Cover photo © Foto Marburg / Art Resource, NY

Cover design: Tory Herman

Library of Congress Cataloging-in-Publication Data is available

Print ISBN: 978-1-4514-7303-2

eBook ISBN: 978-1-4514-7985-0

The paper used in this publication meets the minimum requirements of American National Standard for Information Sciences — Permanence of Paper for Printed Library Materials, ANSI Z329.48-1984.

Manufactured in the U.S.A.

This book was produced using PressBooks.com, and PDF rendering was done by PrinceXML.

To My Wife
Whom I Love

CONTENTS

Preface

The modern quest for the historical Jesus (in all its phases) is the quest for the human Christ. We are enchanted by the human Jesus in an effort, it seems, to understand our own humanness. Yet our quest demands that in many ways we read the ancient Christian sources—in which the divinity of Jesus was of supreme importance—against the grain.

If a divine Jesus is now "other" to "we historians," we must still learn to look full in the face of this other. We must learn to ask why in the very places we espy a human Jesus, early Christians witnessed the light of divinity. Admittedly, understanding the logic of Jesus' deification is no less a (post-Enlightenment) project of history—written for our purposes and governed by our interests. Nevertheless such a project seeks to understand the human through a different lens; a lens that does not make humanness dissolve as a drop of wine in an ocean of deity, but one that illumines more fully—even if through a mirror, darkly—the mystery of its nature, its needs, and its potential.

This book explores how—and by extension why—some humans in history imagined and depicted a fellow human being as divine. The "why" is perhaps more fully addressed in a companion study (*We are Being Transformed: Deification in Paul's Soteriology*). Both books explore the same basic issue: how early Christians came to assimilate and adapt larger Mediterranean discourses of deification to suit their own revelatory experiences and theological traditions. In *We are Being Transformed*, I showed how early Christians (specifically, Paul) used aspects of the discourse of deification to formulate a vision of their own eschatological destiny. In this book, I seek to describe how early Christians employed the discourse of deification to describe the divine identity of he who would become both ἀρχηγός and archetype of Christian deification: Jesus of Nazareth. For both Christians and Christ, the logic of deification is akin. Indeed, the discourse of deification in particular shows how christology can sometimes appear as soteriology writ large.

Deification is the product of the human imagination as it works itself out in speech and, in this case, the rhetorically wrought language of early Christian literature. By using the language of "deification," I cast no aspersion on the (eternal) reality of Jesus' divinity confessed by faith. Indeed, this book can be read as illustrating something of the logic of that faith in its ancient context: *Fides exhibens intellectum.*

Throughout this book I adhere to certain practices of capitalization (and de-capitalization) that require explanation. Since this book is about how Jesus was depicted as a deity up until the mid-third century, I prefer "christology" over "Christology" to avoid any post-Nicene metaphysical freight that may cling to the capital "C." A second practice requires more background. In *We Are Being Transformed*, I attempted to level the playing field between the Christian "God" and the other Mediterranean "gods" (where capital "G" suggests "true God" and lower-case "g" still carries the overtones of "false deity" or "idol") by capitalizing the word "God" throughout. It seems to me now that this practice could cause confusion, indicating that a deified individual could somehow become equal with the high God (whether Jewish or otherwise). Another way to level the playing field is, of course, to let every instance of θεός be represented by "god" with a lowercase "g." But this option too leads to misconceptions. All gods are not in fact equal. Some are high gods with universal power; others are mere daimones with local haunts and traditions. Accordingly, in this book it is my practice to refer to deities who function as supreme, singular gods as "God" (for example, Zeus, Yahweh, Philo's "Existent"), while reserving the lower-case "g" for what I call "mediate deities," or lesser members of the divine (extended) family. When the "Gods" are referred to in the plural—implicating both high Gods and minor deities—I also capitalize the "G." These spelling practices involve a judgment call on my part—a judgment for which I take full responsibility. Their purpose, at any rate, should be clear: to allow, as much as possible unbiased comparison between Christian and non-Christian sources that refer to Gods and mediate gods perceived to be equally true, present and, real.

Here I joyfully acknowledge the help of those who cared for this book while in its four-year period of gestation. Harry Gamble, a model of patient scholarship and hospitality, molded many of my premature ideas. He and other members of the faculty at the University of Virginia—including Judith Kovacs, Karl Shuve, and Jon Mikalson—provided balanced and thoughtful comments that helped these chapters take form. My faithful (and undeserved) friend Blaire French combed twice through the manuscript, healing many grammatical defects. Andy Guffey, a true companion and colleague, offered a theological and historical final checkup. Neil Elliott's thoughtful suggestions and efficient labor as editor at Fortress Press helped the book finally be born. Nevertheless, this volume could never even have been conceived without my lovely wife who for seven years of marriage has nourished me with her fellowship and financial support. Her gentle spirit of love I will treasure always.

Abbreviations

Note: Most of the abbreviations employed in this study can be found in *The SBL Handbook of Style*, ed. Patrick H. Alexander et al. (Peabody: Hendrickson, 1999), 69–153, 238–64, supplemented where necessary by *The Oxford Classical Dictionary*, ed. Simon Hornblower and Antony Spawforth, 4th ed. (Oxford: Oxford University Press, 2012), xxvi–liii. Other abbreviations are as follows:

Bibl. hist.	*Library of History* by Diodorus of Sicily
CCSA	Corpus Christianorum Series Apocryphorum
Fact. dict. mem.	*Memorable Deeds and Sayings* by Valerius Maximus
Hist.	*Histories* by Herodotus
Hist. Alex.	*History of Alexander* by Quintus Curtius
IGT	*The Infancy Gospel of Thomas*
JGRChJ	*Journal of Greco-Roman Christianity and Judaism*
Orth. fid.	*On the Orthodox Faith* by John Damascene
Vit. Philosoph.	*The Lives of Philosophers* by Diogenes Laertius

Introduction

The "Deification" of Jesus Christ

"Gods, too, are created by verse."

—Ovid, *Pont.* 4.8.55

The topic of this study is how early Christians imagined, constructed, and promoted Jesus as a deity in their literature from the first to the third centuries CE. My line of inquiry focuses on how Greco-Roman conceptions of divinity informed this construction. It is my contention that early Christians creatively applied to Jesus traits of divinity that were prevalent and commonly recognized in ancient Mediterranean culture. Historically speaking, I will refer to the Christian application of such traits to Jesus as the "deification" of Jesus Christ.

Although some Christian authors cited Tiberius's attempt to deify Jesus with a kind of curious approval, it was for them—and is still for many Christians today—a theological scandal to speak of the deification of Jesus.[1] Only a few Christians, it seems, were comfortable with the idea that Jesus became a god. Some disciples of Theodotus of Byzantium, for instance, said that Jesus became god when the Spirit descended on him at the Jordan, while others said that his deification occurred after he rose from the dead.[2] According to both Pauline and Johannine traditions, however, Jesus did not "become god," or "a god," but was originally "in the form of God" (Phil. 2:6) and "in the beginning with God" and "(a) god" himself (John 1:1). According to Celsus, an early critic of Christianity, Christians did not view as "gods" figures like Heracles and Dionysus since they had once been men (*Cels.* 3.22). Origen, his opponent, does not disagree. Christ, insofar as he is the Word incarnate, never transitioned from human to god. Although in one of her oracles, Hecate (a popular goddess associated with night and magic) once declared that Jesus' soul became immortal (i.e., deified) after his death, later Christian theologians pointedly rejected this idea

1. See Tert., *Apol.* 5.1-2; 21.14, 29-30; cf. *Spect.* 30; Eus., *Hist. eccl.* 2.2.2-6.

2. Hippolytus, *Haer.* 7.35.2.

1

(Aug., *Civ.* 19.22-23; cf. Eus., *Dem. ev.* 3.7).[3] In a sermon attributed to John Chrysostom we explicitly find the declaration that "Christ did not become god from human advancement—perish the thought. . . . [W]e preach not a human made into god (οὐκ ἄνθρωπον ἀποθεωθέντα), but confess a god made human."[4]

Despite such explicit theological resistance to Jesus' deification, however, some early Christians had few qualms about assimilating Jesus to popular deified persons. In the words of Justin Martyr,

> When we claim also that the Word, which is the first offspring of God, was born without intercourse, Jesus Christ our teacher—and that he was crucified and died and rose again and ascended into heaven—we report nothing at all novel (οὐ ... καινόν τι) beyond those said by you to be sons of Zeus. For you know how many sons of Zeus your honored poets claim there are: Hermes, the interpreting Word and teacher of all; Asclepius, who—though he was a healer—was struck by a thunderbolt and ascended into heaven; Dionysus who was torn in pieces; Heracles, who in flight from his toils committed himself to the fire; the Dioscuri, the sons of Leda; Perseus, son of Danae; and Bellerophon, who, though from human beings, [rose to heaven] on the horse Pegasus. What do we say of Ariadne, and those who, like her, are said to have become stars? What of your deceased emperors, whom you deem fit to immortalize? (*1 Apol.* 21.1-3, my trans.)

Jesus, Justin continues, is worthy of being called "son of God" on account of his wisdom (δία σοφίαν) (*1 Apol.* 22.1). He is the logos born from God like Hermes the "announcing logos." The so-called virgin birth is "in common with Perseus," and Jesus' healings are "similar to those said to have been done by Asclepius." Even Jesus' crucifixion is parallel to the sufferings of Heracles and Asclepius (*1 Apol.* 22.6).

As is natural in an apologetic text, Jesus competitively outperforms his rivals (*1 Apol.* 21, 25). Nevertheless, in Justin's very attempt "to go one up" on his opponents, he acquiesces to a deeper assimilation: Jesus not only fits the pattern of other deified heroes, he became the model for his daimonicly

---

3. The oracle is reconstructed by Gustav Wolff, *Porphyrii de philosophia ex oraculis haurienda* (Hildesheim: Georg Olms, 1962), 180–83.

4. John Chrysostom, "In illud, Memor fui dei, et delectatus sum (Ps. 76.4)," in *PG* 61.697.38–42. Cf. John Damascene, *Orth. fid.* 46:36–39.

devised competitors.[5] Thus if Justin was *theologically* opposed to the idea of Jesus' deification, he was still prepared to *apply common cultural conceptions* about what exhibited other persons as divine to establish the superior deity of his lord.[6] In arguing this way, Justin was not alone. As I hope to demonstrate in this study, many other Christian writers—including those of the New Testament—consciously or unconsciously re-inscribed divine traits of Mediterranean gods and deified figures into their discourse concerning Jesus. The result was the discursive deification of Jesus Christ.

As the adjective "discursive" indicates, the term "deification" does not mean that Jesus was thought to *become* a god (a theological statement), but that Jesus came to be *depicted* as a god (a historical judgment). Both kinds of deification are "processes" of a sort. One process is "emic" and focuses on Jesus in Christian theology (or christology), the other is "etic" and focuses on the conceptions of historical Christian communities that worshiped Jesus.[7] Although from an emic point of view, early Christians accepted the unique divinity of Jesus, from an etic perspective they also played an active role in constructing that divinity through their literary depictions of him. The poet Ovid once wrote that "gods, too, are created by verse" (*di quoque carminibus . . . fiunt*) (*Pont.* 4.8.55). What was true for other gods was also true for the god Jesus: in their gospels, epistles, apocalypses, poems, and apologetic tractates, Christians constructed what it meant for Jesus to be divine using the language, values, and concepts that were common in Greco-Roman culture.

For the historian of religion, then, the "event" of deification is not when the logos became flesh in Mary's womb, or when Jesus was transfigured, or even when he rose from the grave. Rather, the event is continually actualized in the early Christian narratives that *portray* Jesus' divine conception, transfiguration, and resurrection. The "event" of deification is thus part of church history.

5. Justin views the tales of deified men as daimonic imitations of Christ learned from Hebrew prophecy (*1 Apol.* 54, 64). On this apologetic tactic, see Annette Yoshiko Reed, "The Trickery of the Fallen Angels and the Demonic Mimesis of the Divine: Aetiology, Demonology, and Polemics in the Writings of Justin Martyr," *JECS* 12 (2004): 141–71.

6. See further Jean Pépin, "Christian Judgments on the Analogies between Christianity and Pagan Mythology," in *Mythologies*, eds. Yves Bonnefoy and Wendy Doniger, 2 vols. (Chicago: University of Chicago Press, 1991), 2:655–56.

7. "Emic constructs," according to J. W. Lett, "are descriptions and analyses conducted in terms of the conceptual schemes and categories considered meaningful by the participants in the event or situation being described and analyzed. Etic constructs are descriptions and analyses conducted in terms of the conceptual schemes and categories considered meaningful by the community of scientific [I would say "scholarly"] observers" (*The Human Enterprise: A Critical Introduction to Anthropological Theory* [Boulder, CO: Westview, 1987], 62).

Moreover, it is repeatable—it can reoccur with every fresh reading of the texts that portray Jesus as a divine being.

These textual "events" will be the focus of my study. In each chapter, I will provide a thick description of important Christian narratives that portray Jesus with the traits of typical Greco-Roman deities and deified men. I will not be offering a diachronic history of how early Christians came to perceive Jesus to be (a) god. Instead, my procedure is synchronic—focused on texts as individual "moments" of Jesus' deification in early Christian literature. The moments that I will focus on follow the course of Jesus' own life: his divine conception (ch. 1), his childhood zeal for honor (ch. 2), his miraculous benefactions (ch. 3), his epiphanic transfiguration (ch. 4), his immortalizing resurrection (ch. 5), and his reception of a divine name after his ascension (ch. 6).[8]

Two Modes of Early Christian Deification

At least two modes of deification appear in early Christian texts. The first might be called "deification through exaltation" and the second "deification through pre-existence." It appears that early Christians quickly came to depict Jesus as a preexistent divine being. He was "in the form of God" enjoying a state of equality with God (Phil. 2:6). The Apostle Paul claimed that the world was made through him (1 Cor. 8:6; cf. Col. 1:16; John 1:10). In the Johannine tradition, Jesus came to be identified with the logos who exists "in the beginning with God" (John 1:1-3). Based on such traditions, one might ask whether it is more appropriate to speak of a "*homonification*" rather than of a *deification* of Jesus. Indeed, within the cosmology envisaged by ancient Christians, it probably was less appropriate to ask, "How did a human become a deity?" than it was to ask: *cur deus homo*—"Why did a god become human?"

In a historical study, however, one cannot begin with a Christian *theologoumenon* (i.e., that there is a divine being called the "logos" or the "son" who has eternally existed alongside God and is able to be incarnated). History deals with events and ideas in a world conditioned by the categories of time and space—our world. At some point in time, a historian may grant, the logos may have become flesh, but until Jesus began manifesting his deity in first-century Galilee, his followers could not proclaim that divinity to the world. To be sure, one could examine the history of the *theological tradition* of Jesus' preexistent state and subsequent incarnation—but this is not the topic of this study.[9] My

---

8. The depiction of Jesus as a deity in his baptism has been helpfully explored by Edward Dixon, "Descending Spirit and Descending Gods: A 'Greek' Interpretation of the Spirit's 'Descent as a Dove' in Mark 1:10," *JBL* 128 (2009): 759–80.

approach assumes that at some point(s) in time, early Christians intuited that Jesus was a divine being, and in turn began in their literature to *attribute* a preexistent divinity to Jesus—and in this way to deify him.

In addition to deification by preexistence, early Christians also spoke of deification through exaltation. This is an equally Christian and equally theological way of speaking about Jesus' divinity—but one (it might be argued) more analogous to the kind of historical and literary deification I illustrate in this study. According to Romans 1:4, Jesus was "appointed" (ὁρισθέντος) son of God from (or by, ἐκ) his resurrection from the dead.[10] In another tradition, God "made" (ἐποίησεν) Jesus "lord"—apparently after his resurrection (Acts 2:36). In a third text, God "installed" (ἔθηκεν) Jesus as heir of the universe (Heb. 1:2). After his atoning death and resurrection, Jesus was exalted to God's right hand, and "became" (γενόμενος) superior to the angels by inheriting a preeminent name (vv. 3-4; cf. Phil. 2:10-11). Such appointments to so high a status (i.e., that of cosmic vice-regent who receives worship) literally represent Jesus' deification in early Christian literature. They represent, in other words, some sort of promotion of Jesus from a lower condition into a higher, divine one.

These two patterns of Christian deification (exaltation and preexistence) are juxtaposed with no hint of tension in what is perhaps our earliest christological hymn, Phil. 2:6-11. Here Jesus, "in God's form" and equal to God, becomes human (or humanoid, ἐν ὁμοιώματι ἀνθρώπων) in obedience to God. As a result of his obedience—even unto death—the human Jesus is exalted to heaven, receives "the name above every name" and is worshipped by beings on every tier of existence. In the brief compass of this passage, Jesus is both hominified and deified. He could be *hominified* because, historically speaking, some Christians as early as the 40s ce identified Jesus with a preexistent divine being endowed with God's form and glory (Phil. 2:6).[11] In the hymn, Jesus is also *deified* by being exalted, worshipped, and receiving "the name above every

9. The topic is well researched. See R. G. Hamerton-Kelly, *Pre-existence, Wisdom, and the Son of Man: A Study of the Idea of Pre-existence in the New Testament* (Cambridge: Cambridge University Press, 1973); Jürgen Habermann, *Präexistenzaussagen im Neuen Testament* (Frankfurt am Main: Bern, 1990); Karl-Josef Kuschel, *Born Before All Time? The Dispute over Christ's Origin* (New York: Crossroad, 1992), 177–395; Simon J. Gathercole, *The Pre-existent Son: Recovering the Christologies of Matthew, Mark, and Luke* (Grand Rapids, MI: Eerdmans, 2006).

10. Similarly, the author of Acts appears to connect the prophecy of Ps. 2:7 ("You are my son") to the act of resurrection—suggesting that by his resurrection, Jesus becomes God's son (Acts 13:33-4).

11. In the canonical gospels, this preexistent being is sometimes referred to as the "Son of Man." Although attacked by some (e.g., Jerome Murphy-O'Connor, "Christological Anthropology in Phil 2:6-11," *Revue Biblique* 83 [1976]: 25–50; James D. G. Dunn, *Christology in the Making: A New Testament*

name"—all of which are honors properly belonging to Yahweh (here called "the Father"). If the drama of the mini-narrative is to be retained, we must assume that Jesus apparently did not enjoy these honors before (vv. 9–11).

It is not my aim to discern which tradition of deification (preexistence or exaltation) is earlier or more original.[12] They are simply two parallel discursive strategies that early Christians used (sometimes simultaneously) in order to deify Jesus in their liturgy and literature.[13] Importantly, each strategy accords with key statements in Jewish scripture (notably Ps. 110:1; Dan. 7:13-14) that were applied and adapted to Jesus. The exegesis of these texts is not my focus in this study.[14] My concern, rather, is how early Christian literature depicts Jesus as a deity in ways intelligible and recognizable in Greco-Roman culture.

EARLY CHRISTIAN CHRISTOLOGY: RESTORING THE BALANCE

An essential aspect of my thesis is that Christians constructed a divine Jesus with traits specific to deities in *Greco-Roman* culture. It is important to make this point clear because in recent scholarship the emphasis has been placed on understanding Jesus' divinity from a solely Jewish point of view.

In his oft-cited study, *Judentum und Hellenismus*, Martin Hengel demonstrated with impressive detail that "*All of Judaism* from about the middle of the 3rd century BC must in the strict sense be called '*hellenistic Judaism*.'"[15] As he puts it in a later book: "Since after a more than three-hundred-year

Inquiry into the Origins of the Doctrine of the Incarnation, 2nd ed. [Grand Rapids, MI: Eerdmans, 1989], 114–15), preexistence in Phil. 2:6 remains the consensus view.

12. See, for instance, the developmental scheme in Otto Pfleiderer, *The Early Christian Conception of Christ: Its Significance and Value in the History of Religion* (New York: G.P. Putnam's Sons, 1905), 16–19.

13. Note the comments of Wilhelm Bousset, *Kyrios Christos*, trans. John Steely (Nashville: Abingdon, 1970), 337–38. Bousset argues that it does not matter whether Christians arrived at the divinity of Christ because they asserted his preexistence or because they viewed Christ as (at some point) promoted to deity, since the deity of Christ was originally a pre-theologized reality realized in the exalted experience of Christian worship (333–334).

14. Such exegesis can be found in any number of works on New Testament christology (a topic with a massive bibliography). For an introduction, see François Bovon, "The First Christologies: From Exaltation to Incarnation, Or From Easter to Christmas," in *Jesus Christ Today: Studies of Christology in Various Contexts*, ed. Stuart George Hall (Berlin: de Gruyter, 2009), 27–43. In the present study, I am not interested in the specific vocabulary proving Jesus' divinity or various christological titles. Although I will focus on the question of Jesus' divinity, I do not intend to prove that Jesus was god based on the predication of the word θεός to Jesus. For this project, see Murray J. Harris, *Jesus as God: The New Testament Use of Theos in Reference to Jesus* (Grand Rapids: Baker Book House, 1992).

15. "*Das gesamte Judentum* ab etwa der Mitte des 3.Jh.s. v.Chr. müsste im strengen Sinne als '*hellenistisches Judentum*' bezeichnet werden" (Hengel, *Judentum und Hellenismus: Studien zu ihrer*

history under the influence of Greek culture Palestinian Judaism can also be described as 'Hellenistic Judaism', *the term 'Hellenistic' as currently used no longer serves to make any meaningful differentiation in terms of the history of religions within the history of earliest Christianity.*[16] Naturally Hengel pointed out Jewish distinctives in the early imperial period (e.g., a focus upon Torah and apocalyptic fervor). He convincingly demonstrated, however, that Palestine had long been touched by the "spirit" (*Geist*) of Hellenistic civilization on almost every level: economically, politically, culturally, literarily, philosophically, and theologically.[17]

Given this emphasis, it comes as something of a surprise when in his *Der Sohn Gottes* (second edition, 1977), Hengel presents one of the most curt and candid attempts to cut off early christology from all Greco-Roman influence. He denied the influence of popular deified men (for example, Heracles who died a violent death), deified emperors (Octavian sent into the world as Mercury [Hor., *Od.* 1.2.41-52]), divine men (Pythagoras who incarnated Hyperborean Apollo), preexistent gnostic redeemers, and gods who appear in human disguise—indeed, virtually every Hellenistic analogue he could uncover.[18] The irony of this situation is only appreciated when one realizes that for Hengel, the earliest christology comes out of the *Palestinian* Jewish milieu—exactly the milieu that Hengel argued was *radically pervaded* by Hellenistic modes of thought. We are thus asked to believe that, despite the fact that Palestine (not to mention other centers of early Christianity) was hellenized centuries before the Christian movement, virtually no Hellenistic theological story or idea substantially affected the development of early christology.

Begegnung unter besonderer Berücksichtigung Palästinas bis zur Mitte des 2.Jh. v.Chr. WUNT 10; 3d ed. [Tübingen: Mohr Siebeck, 1988], 193, emphasis his.

16. Hengel, *The 'Hellenization' of Judaea in the First Century after Christ* (London: SCM, 1989), 53. His most recent statement about hellenization can be found in "Judaism and Hellenism Revisited," in *Theologische, historische, und biographische Skizzen. Kleine Schriften VII*, ed. Claus-Jürgen Thornton. (WUNT 253; Tübingen: Mohr Siebeck, 2010), 179–216.

17. The early hellenization of Judaism (and thus of Christianity) had already been proposed by Otto Pfleiderer (*Das Urchristenthum: seine Schriften und Lehren, in geschichtlichem Zusammenhang beschrieben* [Berlin: G. Reimer, 1887], iv–v) and Paul Wendland (*Die hellenistische-römische Kultur in ihren Beziehungen zum Judentum und Christentum*, Handbuch zum Neuen Testament I/2, 2nd ed. [Tübingen: Mohr Siebeck, 1912]). Wendland suggested two stages of Christian hellenization: an earlier (first-century) hellenization based on common concepts of popular religion (esp. demonology, miracles, and the spirit world), and a later hellenization (beginning in the mid-second century) based on the conscious integration of Greek philosophy, rhetoric, and literary culture (212–40).

18. Hengel, *Der Sohn Gottes: Die Entstehung der Christologie und die jüdisch-hellenistische Religionsgeschichte*, 2nd ed. (Tübingen: Mohr Siebeck, 1977), esp. 35–67.

By preserving christology from Hellenistic forms of thought, Hengel reinstantiated an old apologetic distinction between Jewish-Christian truth and Greek myth. In order to distinguish Jesus' story from Greco-Roman "mythos,"[19] Hengel reconstructed what he called a "firmly conjoined inner Christian-Jewish connection of tradition (*einem festgefügten innerchristlich-jüdischer Traditionszusammenhang*)" centered on the themes of a preexistent demiurgic mediator (notably, the figure of Wisdom) being sent into the world.[20] The direct sources for such a christology, Hengel believed, could only be "Jewish"—a term now implicitly used to exclude what is "Hellenistic" or Greek.[21]

Despite the tensions in Hengel's own thought, *Der Sohn Gottes* (rapidly translated into English) heralded a new trend in the study of early christology, a trend that began to focus its lens decisively—often exclusively—on Judaism. In his 1988 study, *One Lord, One God*, Larry Hurtado examined Jewish traditions of personified divine attributes, exalted patriarchs, and principal angels as (albeit ultimately insufficient) models for understanding Jesus' divinity.[22] With the same aim, Jarl Fossum examined various Jewish mystical traditions of God's image, glory, throne, and name.[23] Major studies of christology in light of Jewish angelology later came from the pens of Loren Stuckenbruck,[24] Crispin Fletcher-Louis,[25] Charles Gieschen,[26] and Darrell Hannah.[27] William Horbury studied traditions of messiahship in relation to the cult of Christ.[28] His focus

---

19. Ibid., 114 (connected tradition), 119 (distinction from "mythos").

20. In *Judentum und Hellenismus*, Hengel argued that personified, demiurgic Wisdom (who appears in Prov. 8; Sir. 24, etc.) is a product of earlier Semitic and "oriental" influence, *as well as later Hellenistic interpretation* (275–307).

21. Hengel, *Sohn Gottes*, 67.

22. Hurtado, *One God, One Lord: Early Christian Devotion and Ancient Jewish Monotheism* (Minneapolis: Fortress Press, 1988). A forerunner and apparent model for Hurtado's study was Dunn's *Christology in the Making*.

23. Jarl Fossum, *The Image of the Invisible God: Essays on the Influence of Jewish Mysticism on Early Christology* (Göttingen: Vandenhoeck & Ruprecht, 1995). Compare his earlier study *The Name of God and the Angel of the Lord: Samaritan and Jewish Concepts of Intermediation and the Origin of Gnosticism* (Tübingen: Mohr Siebeck, 1985).

24. Loren Stuckenbruck, *Angel Veneration and Christology: A Study in Early Judaism and in the Christology of the Apocalypse of John* (Tübingen: Mohr Siebeck, 1995).

25. Crispin Fletcher-Louis, *Luke-Acts: Angels, Christology and Soteriology* (Tübingen: Mohr Siebeck, 1997).

26. Charles Gieschen, *Angelomorphic Christology: Antecedents and Early Evidence* (Leiden: Brill, 1998).

27. Darrell Hannah, *Michael and Christ: Michael Traditions and Angel Christology in Early Christianity* (Tübingen: Mohr Siebeck, 1999).

on messianic figures was followed by Andrew Chester,[29] and more recently in the study *King and Messiah as Son of God* co-authored by Adela Yarbro Collins and John Collins.[30] These important and erudite works represent only the high points of a consistent scholarly tendency to focus primarily (and often solely) on Jewish *comparanda* to understand the nature and origin of Jesus' divinity.[31]

Three scholars—Fossum, Fletcher-Louis, and Hurtado—have even spoken of a new "History of Religions School"[32] that privileges Judaism as the primary (and virtually sole) context for understanding early Christianity and christology in particular.[33] Fossum's 1991 essay, "The New Religionsgeschichtliche Schule" (pregnantly subtitled "The Quest for Jewish Christology"), contrasted the concerns and methods of the "old" and "new" History of Religions Schools. "The basic difference," Fossum observed, ". . . is that the 'new' School looks *elsewhere* than the German [i.e., old] school for the materials of primitive

28. William Horbury, *Jewish Messianism and the Cult of Christ* (London: SCM, 1998), esp. 109–52. See further his essay, "The Cult of Christ and the Cult of the Saints," in *Messianism Among Jews and Christians: Twelve Biblical and Historical Studies* (London: T&T Clark, 2003), 351–80.

29. Andrew Chester, *Messiah and Exaltation: Jewish Messianic and Visionary Traditions and New Testament Christology* (Tübingen: Mohr Siebeck, 2007), 191–536.

30. Adela Yarbro Collins and John Collins, *King and Messiah as Son of God: Divine, Human, and Angelic Messianic Figures in Biblical and Related Literature* (Grand Rapids: Eerdmans, 2008).

31. Even Maurice Casey, whose book *From Jewish Prophet to Gentile God* would suggest a thorough engagement with "Gentile" materials appeals almost solely to Jewish sources (Louisville: Westminster John Knox, 1991). Recent textbooks on Christian origins that discuss Jesus' divinity also privilege a Jewish standpoint. Note, for instance, Christopher Rowland, *Christian Origins: An Account of the Setting and Character of the Most Important Messianic Sect of Judaism*, 2nd ed. (London: SPCK, 2002), 247–56. Peter Schäfer's new book, *The Jewish Jesus: How Judaism and Christianity Shaped Each Other* (Princeton, NJ: Princeton University Press, 2012), proposes that certain figures within rabbinic Judaism (e.g., David, Metatron, the Messiah, the angels, Adam) "have been assigned a place within Judaism similar to the role Jesus played in Christianity" (20). His argument, however, is not that Judaism influenced Jesus' promotion into the divine world, but the reverse: the spirit of Christianity—which deified its hero—was transferred to certain circles of rabbinic Judaism (10).

32. In *Lord Jesus Christ*, Hurtado issues something of a disclaimer when he admits that the new History of Religions school is not as localized and ideologically united as the old School, but he states nevertheless that "there is reason to describe this more recent body of work as constituting a 'new history-of-religions' effort" (12). See the remarks of Jörg Frey, "Eine neue religionsgeschichtliche Perspektive: Larry W. Hurtados *Lord Jesus Christ* und die Herausbildung der frühem Christologie," in *Reflections on the Early Christian History of Religion* (Leiden: Brill, 2013), 117–70.

33. Credit for the term "new Religionsgeschichtliche Schule" is attributed to Hengel, who used the phrase in his blurb on the back cover of Hurtado's *One Lord, One God* (see Hurtado's comments in *Lord Jesus Christ*, 11). Hurtado acknowledges his heavy debts to Hengel (Ibid., 12, n. 17), who is something of a grandfather of the "new" History of Religions School.

Christology. The German *Schule* looked to the imperial cult, the mystery religions, and Oriental religion, especially Iranian tradition," not to mention pre-Christian Gnosticism.[34] The widely acknowledged methodological errors underlying the reconstruction of a pre-Christian "Gnostic redeemer myth" have become a byword among New Testament scholars against genius gone wild.[35] Members of the "new" History of Religions School deliberately rehearse this and other errors of their predecessors to discredit attempts to go too far afield in comparing Christianity with religious movements perceived to be too foreign and "other."[36] Instead, they turn to the movement that they view as much closer to home—the "prolific mother" (to use Fossum's phrase) that (he asserts) gave birth to Gnosticism, the rabbinic movements, and Christianity—namely, Judaism.[37] Judaism is thus made the comprehensive—even exclusive—context for christology. As Fletcher-Louis writes, the "defining characteristic of the new history-of-religions school" is "an emphasis on the extent to which the *full breadth* of Christological expression is fashioned from *Jewish* raw materials."[38] Although Hurtado is more measured in his remarks, the focus and content of his recent work indicate that all the emphasis in early christology (and Jesus' deity in particular) should be placed on "the Jewish religious matrix of the Christian movement."[39]

34. Fossum, "The New Religionsgeschichtliche Schule: The Quest for Jewish Christology," *SBL Seminar Papers 1991*, ed. Eugene H. Lovering (Atlanta: Scholars, 1991), 638–46 [640]).

35. See further Carsten Colpe, *Die religionsgeschichtliche Schule: Darstellung und Kritik ihres Bildes vom gnostischen Erlösermythus* (Göttingen: Vandenhoeck & Ruprecht, 1961); Edwin M. Yamauchi, *Pre-Christian Gnosticism: A Survey of Proposed Evidences* (Grand Rapids, MI: Eerdmans, 1973); Karsten Lehmkühler, *Kultus und Theologie: Dogmatik und Exegese in der religionsgeschichtliche Schule* (Göttingen: Vandenhoeck & Ruprecht, 1996).

36. See, for example, Hurtado, "New Testament Christology: Retrospect and Prospect," *Semeia* 30 (1985): 15–28 (esp. 19–23); *Lord Jesus Christ: Devotion to Jesus in Earliest Christianity* (Grand Rapids, MI: Eerdmans, 2003), 75–76.

37. Fossum expresses some reserve about the term "Judaism," since he does not want to limit it to later Rabbinic forms of Judaism known by the same name ("New *Religionsgeschichtliche Schule*," 642–44). On p. 646 of his essay he replaces Judaism with "Late Second Temple Israelite Religion."

38. Fletcher-Louis, *Luke-Acts*, 2, my emphasis.

39. Hurtado, *Lord Jesus Christ*, 12. In this massive 653-page study of christology, Hurtado devotes four meager pages to Greco-Roman categories (74–77). Such imbalance is woefully inadequate, especially given his aim to "take due account of the historical setting and context of early Christian devotion, both the Jewish matrix . . . *and the larger historical and religious environment of the Roman period*" (25, emphasis added). His neglect of Greco-Roman *comparanda* is surprising since earlier he noted that christology "will have to be built upon a foundation composed of the best information on the complex cultural background of first-century Palestine *and the wider Hellenistic world*" (Hurtado, "New Testament Christology: A Critique of Bousset's Influence," *Theological Studies* 40 [1979]: 306–17 [317], my

Throughout his massive 2005 book *Lord Jesus Christ*, Hurtado uses "Judaism" and "Jewish" as if they excluded Hellenistic forms of thought (exactly the point that Hengel warned against, but an error foreshadowed by Hengel himself). In effect, Hurtado excludes "pagan" ideas for understanding early christology. He strongly asserts that within three or four years of his death, Jesus was worshiped and seen as "in some sense divine."[40] He is equally convinced, however, that (*contra* Wilhelm Bousset) early Christians did not deify Jesus as a result of "religious influences" from the Greco-Roman world.[41] To justify this claim, Hurtado leans on his own conservative reconstruction of Jewish monotheism.[42] After proof-texting Philo's *Embassy to Gaius* 118 ("sooner could a god change into a man than a man into a god"), Hurtado remarks that the idea of deification for a Jew is "ridiculous and blasphemous." Philo's quote, Hurtado continues,

> makes highly implausible any explanation of the Christ-devotion attested in and affirmed by, Paul as resulting from the prevalence of the notion of apotheosis in the Roman era. Though Jewish writings of the time show that principle angels and revered human figures such as Moses or Enoch could be pictured in a highly exalted status, and described in terms that can be compared with divinization, the refusal to accord any such figure cultic worship shows that we are not dealing here with a genuine apotheosis.[43]

"Devout" Jews, Hurtado continues, had an "allergic sensitivity" to deification.[44] Directing his remarks to Yarbro Collins,[45] Hurtado challenges "any scholar" who sees deification as relevant for explaining early "Christ-devotion" to

---

emphasis). In his *One Lord, One God*, he states that drawing upon "pagan religions of the Greco-Roman period" is "simply beside the point" because (i) Christ was deified early when Christianity "was thoroughly dominated by Jews and functioned as a sect of ancient Judaism," and (ii) Greco-Roman religions are not comparable because they did not uphold exclusive monotheism (6). Both points (which will be addressed below) hardly prevent fruitful comparison with Greco-Roman conceptuality, or justify exclusive attention to Jewish sources.

40. Hurtado, *How on Earth Did Jesus Become a God? Historical Questions about Earliest Devotion to Jesus* (Grand Rapids, MI: Eerdmans, 2005), 33.

41. Ibid., 37.

42. Hurtado, *Lord Jesus Christ*, 51; cf. 91.

43. Ibid., 92. For a critique of Hurtado's fixed and inflexible linkage of worship and divinity, see M. David Litwa, *We Are Being Transformed: Deification in Paul's Soteriology*, BZNW 187 (Berlin: de Gruyter, 2012), 275–81.

44. Hurtado, *Lord Jesus Christ*, 92.

provide "a cogent description of the specific process by which Christian Jews could have adopted this repellent category without realizing it."[46]

The heated language that Hurtado uses to discuss traditions of deification ("ridiculous and blasphemous"; "allergic sensitivity"; "repellent") hint at a kind of theological disgust that breathes through his normally placid prose. Such disgust, combined with a spirited attack against "pagan" influence, is consonant with a long history of Christian apologetics.[47] Michael Peppard has recently observed that, "if the old [*religionsgeschichtliche*] *Schule* breathed the air of modern liberalism, the new one is imbued with a spirit of neo-orthodoxy."[48]

Hurtado's objection that monotheism excludes deification is often taken as his strongest argument. Since in a previous study I argued at length that ancient Jewish monotheism does not conflict with early Jewish or Christian forms of deification, my comments on this issue will be brief.[49] From a historical perspective, no matter how exclusive Jewish and later Christian monotheism was, it was evidently not exclusive enough to exclude the man Jesus from the Godhead. My argument that Christians applied common Mediterranean understandings of divinity to Jesus does not, at any rate, conflict with early Jewish and Christian monotheism (the idea that all power is centralized in one divine being). It is true that Jesus' intimate association with an all-powerful, singular deity makes the Christian elevation of Jesus to divine status distinctive. It does not, however, make his deification unique in the discursive arena of the ancient Mediterranean world.[50]

---

45. Specifically her essay "The Worship of Jesus and the Imperial Cult," in *The Jewish Roots of Christological Monotheism*, ed. Carey Newman et al. (Leiden: Brill, 1999), 234–57.

46. Hurtado, *Lord Jesus Christ*, 92–93.

47. See esp. Walther Glawe, *Die Hellenisierung des Christentums in der Geschichte der Theologie von Luther bis auf die Gegenwart* (Berlin: Trowitzsch & Sohn, 1912).

48. Michael Peppard, *The Son of God in the Roman World: Divine Sonship in its Social and Political Context* (Oxford: Oxford University Press, 2011), 21. Peppard aptly notes that Hurtado's focus on the Jewish context "ignores just about everything religious going on in the Roman world" in particular "cultic practices devoted to divine humans and divine sons—heroes, ancestors, rulers, gods" (25). Cf. p. 24: "Hurtado hardly engages the gentile religious environment, which was the environment of most early Christians for whom we have evidence."

49. Litwa, *We Are Being Transformed*, 229–57; 275–81.

50. Whether or not Jesus' depiction as an ancient Mediterranean deity is actually faithful to the traditions of ancient Jewish monotheism is a theological question that I bracket in this study. For the purposes of argument, however, I am happy to grant that Christians both formed and remained faithful to their own distinctive understandings of monotheism even as they engaged in the discursive practices of deifying the first-century Jew known as Jesus of Nazareth.

Although other scholars have devoted more attention to deficiencies in Hurtado's understanding of monotheism, divinity, and worship,[51] it seems to me that the main problem with Hurtado's analysis is that his work perpetuates the old and misleading dichotomy commonly dubbed the "Judaism/Hellenism divide."[52] Although Hurtado is aware that this dividing wall has fallen,[53] his language often betrays him. He assumes, for instance, that Jews had to go out and adopt deification traditions (naturally, part of Hellenistic culture) as something external and alien to them. Hurtado fails to note that in the very cases he mentions—Moses and Enoch—deification traditions had long been adapted and integrated into Jewish tradition in a way apparently suitable to Jewish monotheism.[54]

More damagingly, Hurtado's understanding of deification is far too simplistic and constricted. It is not evident to him that his model of early Christian "binitarianism" itself is a discursive practice that names a Jewish form of deification in which a human is identified with a preexistent Prime Mediator figure. Examples of this include Enoch identified with the Son of Man (*1 En.* 70–71), Jacob identified with the firstborn of every living thing (*The Prayer of Joseph*), and Jesus identified with the logos and Wisdom of God (1 Cor. 1:30; John 1:1). To be sure, Hurtado is correct that there was a good deal of early Jewish and Christian rhetoric against beliefs and practices (such as deification) that were perceived as "other"—but he often mistakes this

51. See the reviews of *Lord Jesus Christ* by William Horbury (*JTS* 56 [2005]: 537–38) and Paula Fredriksen (*JECS* 12 [2004]: 539–41); as well as Adela Yarbro Collins, "'How on Earth did Jesus Become a God?': A Reply," in *Israel's God and Rebecca's Children: Christology and Community in Early Judaism and Christianity*, eds. David B. Capes et al. (Waco, TX: Baylor University Press, 2007), 55–66.

52. In 2001, Anders Gerdmar noted that "*the dichotomic view of Judaism and Hellenism has assumed an almost axiomatic role* in New Testament exegesis" (*Rethinking the Judaism-Hellenism Dichotomy: A Historiographical Case Study of Second Peter and Jude* [Stockholm: Almquist & Wiksell], 18, emphasis his). He is right to point out that the opposition between "Judaism" and "Hellenism" is ideological and (ultimately) Hegelian, but wrongly concludes that Hellenism was mere "varnish" for Jews. We simply do not have to decide between "varnish" and "fusion" models (328); there was, as he says, a "continuum" between Jewish and Hellenistic culture (329).

53. Hurtado, "A Critique of Bousset's Influence," 308–9; cf. Hurtado, *Lord Jesus Christ*, 23–24. Like many other scholars, he leans on Hengel's *Judentum und Hellenismus* (*Lord Jesus Christ*, 23, n. 56).

54. See further John J. Collins, "A Throne in the Heavens: Apotheosis in Pre-Christian Judaism," in *Death, Ecstasy, and Other Worldly Journeys*, eds. John J. Collins and Michael Fishbane (Albany, NY: SUNY Press, 1995), 41–56; Philip Alexander, "From Son of Adam to Second God: Transformations of the Biblical Enoch," in *Biblical Figures outside the Bible* (eds. M. E. Stone and T.A. Bergren; Harrisburg, PA: Trinity Press International, 1998), 87–122; Naomi Janowitz, *Magic in the Roman World: Pagans, Jews and Christians* (London: Routledge, 2001), 70–85; Litwa, *We Are Being Transformed*, 86–116.

rhetoric for historical reality.[55] As is known from many religious movements, the rhetoric of difference is especially intense between religious groups that share similar ideas.[56] Hurtado mistakes Jewish and Christian distrust of perceived "other" notions of deification with the historical thesis that christology could not have been tinged by shared understandings of divinity in Mediterranean culture as well as the human potential to become divine.[57]

To be fair, Hurtado's (effectively sole) focus on Judaism for understanding Jesus' deity is not outright wrong, but imbalanced. In a recent study, Gregory J. Riley warns against an "Israel-alone" model of scholarship since "both the questions asked and the answers obtained will be Israel-alone questions and answers."[58] A recent example of "Israel-alone" scholarship is the strong effort to explain a divine Jesus while maintaining a rigorously exclusive form of Jewish monotheism.[59] Fascinated by this question, Hurtado attempts to preserve early Christian monotheism by redescribing it as "binitarian" (in apparent analogy to "trinitarian" monotheism in later Christian orthodoxy).[60] Richard Bauckham, a strident proponent of early Christian monotheism, strongly maintains Jesus' "unique divine identity" because he shares Yahweh's ultimate power and demiurgic ability.[61] In the same school of thought, Chris Tilling has recently argued that Jesus is divine for Paul because his relation to believers closely corresponds to the relation of Yahweh to Israel as it is depicted in the Hebrew Bible.[62]

Although these scholars have done much to make Jesus' divinity comprehensible in terms of ancient Judaism, in the process they have more

---

55. Hurtado, *How on Earth*, 45.

56. See on this point John G. Gager, *Kingdom and Community: The Social World of Early Christianity* (Englewood Cliffs, NJ: Prentice-Hall, 1975), 82–8; Gerd Theissen, *A Theory of Primitive Christian Religion* (London: SCM, 1999), 44–49.

57. Hurtado, *How on Earth*, 43.

58. Gregory J. Riley, *The River of God: A New History of Christian Origins* (New York: HarperSanFrancisco, 2001), 5; complete discussion on 6–14.

59. Hurtado, for instance, begins his study of early Christian christology with the question, "How did the early Christians accommodate the veneration of the exalted Jesus alongside God while continuing to see themselves as loyal to the fundamental emphasis of their ancestral tradition on one God . . . ?" (*One Lord, One God*, 2). See further Paul Rainbow, "Jewish Monotheism as the Matrix for New Testament Christology" *NovT* 33 (1991): 78–91.

60. Hurtado, *One Lord, One God*, 93–124, esp. 114; Hurtado, "The Binitarian Shape of Early Christian Worship," in *Jewish Roots of Christological Monotheism*, 187–213.

61. Richard Bauckham, *Jesus and the God of Israel: God Crucified and Other Studies on the New Testament's Christology of Divine Identity* (Grand Rapids, MI: Eerdmans, 2008), 1–59.

62. Chris Tilling, *Paul's Divine Christology*, WUNT 2/323 (Tubingen: Mohr Siebeck, 2012).

or less neglected Christianity's broader (Greco-Roman) environment and thus larger questions that help us understand (to adapt one of Hurtado's book titles) "how on earth Jesus became a god." To be sure, Hurtado is right to oppose an evolutionary model of Jesus' deification that came about relatively late as a result of increasing Gentile majorities in early Christian communities. He associates this theory with Bousset, an imposing representative of the "old" History of Religions School.[63] Regrettably, Hurtado appears to implicitly follow Bousset in associating a Gentile majority with increased hellenization.[64] It is this view (namely, a gradual hellenization of Christianity through the influx of Gentiles) that in recent years has been shown to be fundamentally wrong.[65] Christianity was born from a Jewish mother who was already hellenized.[66] The socio-cultural phenomenon of hellenization was not something that infiltrated later as a foreign body after Christianity ceased to be a primarily Jewish movement.[67] In

63. Hurtado, *How on Earth*, 14–16. For a description of the (old) History of Religions School, see Gerd Lüdemann and Martin Schröder, *Die religionsgeschichtliche Schule in Göttingen: Eine Dokumentation* (Göttingen: Vandenhoeck & Ruprecht, 1987); Lüdemann, "Die 'Religionsgeschichtliche Schule' und die Neutestamentliche Wissenschaft," in *Die "Religionsgeschichtliche Schule": Facetten eines theologischen Umbruchs*, ed. Gerd Lüdemann (Frankfurt am Main: Peter Lang, 1996), 9–22; Gerald Seelig, *Religionsgeschichtliche Methode in Vergangenheit und Gegenwart: Studien zur Geschichte und Methode des religionsgeschichtlichen Vergleichs in der neutestamentlichen Wissenschaft* (Leipzig: Evangelische Verlagsanstalt, 2001); William Baird, *History of New Testament Research*, vol. 2, *From Jonathan Edwards to Rudolf Bultmann* (Minneapolis: Fortress Press, 2003), 238–53.

64. In *One Lord, One God*, for instance, Hurtado felt capable of bypassing Greco-Roman traditions because the earliest Christianity was "dominated by Jews and functioned as a sect of ancient Judaism" (6). He assumes, apparently, that examining Greco-Roman traditions is only appropriate when early churches gradually become Gentile. The same assumptions appear in the preface to the second edition to *One Lord, One God* (ix).

65. Besides Hengel's *Judentum und Hellenismus*, see his shorter study on *The 'Hellenization' of Judaea*. A sampling of significant later studies includes: David L. Balch, Everett Ferguson, and Wayne A. Meeks, eds., *Greeks, Romans, and Christians: Essays in Honor of Abraham J. Malherbe* (Minneapolis: Fortress Press, 1990); Pieter W. van der Horst, *Hellenism-Judaism-Christianity: Essays on Their Interaction* (Kampen: Kok Pharos, 1994); Erich S. Gruen, *Heritage and Hellenism: The Reinvention of Jewish Tradition* (Berkeley: University of California Press, 1998), 335; Lee I. Levine, *Judaism and Hellenism in Antiquity: Conflict or Confluence?* (Seattle: University of Washington Press, 1998), 3–32; John J. Collins and Gregory Sterling, *Hellenism in the Land of Israel* (Notre Dame, IN: University of Notre Dame Press, 2001), 343; Troels Engberg-Pedersen, ed. *Paul Beyond the Judaism/Hellenism Divide* (Louisville: Westminster John Knox, 2001); Tessa Rajak, *The Jewish Dialogue with Greece and Rome: Studies in Cultural and Social Interaction* (Leiden: Brill, 2001), esp. 355–72; 447–62; Gruen, "Hebraism and Hellenism," in *The Oxford Handbook of Hellenic Studies*, eds. George Boys-Stones et al. (Oxford: Oxford University Press, 2009), 129–39.

66. Compare Hurtado, who rejects a Judaism "corrupted or paganized" before the Christian era (preface to the second edition of *One Lord, One God*, x).

the time of Jesus himself, Palestinian Jews had thoroughly adopted and adapted Greek ideas (including theological ones) to such an extent that in many cases what appears to be a distinctly "Jewish" notion is in fact a "Greco-Jewish" cultural hybrid.[68]

JUDAISM AS BUFFER

In his book, *The 'Hellenization' of Judea*, Hengel writes, "We must stop attaching either negative or positive connotations to the question of 'Hellenistic' influence . . . Judaism and Christianity, indeed our whole Western world, have become what they are as a result of both the Old Testament *and* the Greek tradition."[69] Why then, one can ask, did Hengel in *Der Sohn Gottes* seek to cut off Greek and Roman influence from early christology? Why in the general tendency of the "new" *Religionsgeschichtliche Schule* are Greco-Roman sources regularly downplayed or ignored? One can only speculate on the potential answers to this question, but Jonathan Z. Smith has given the outlines of what seems in part to be a possible response: Judaism is being used by scholars to insulate Christianity from its so-called "pagan" environment.[70] Hengel put it this way: "no direct pagan influence [on early Christianity] that is not mediated by Judaism ... can be proved."[71]

67. Philip Alexander, "Hellenism and Hellenization as Problematic Historiographical Categories," in *Paul Beyond*, 63–80, esp. 69; Antonio, Piñero, "On the Hellenization of Christianity" in *Flores Florentino: Dead Sea Scrolls and Other Early Jewish Studies*, ed. Anthony Hilhorst et al. (Leiden: Brill, 2007), 667–83, esp. 682–83; Luther H. Martin in "The Hellenisation of Judaeo-Christian Faith" *Religion and Theology* 12 (2005): 1–19, esp. 13.

68. On hellenistic culture and its spread in the ancient Mediterranean, see Momigliano, *Alien Wisdom: The Limits of Hellenization* (Cambridge: Cambridge University Press, 1975); Jonathan A. Goldstein, *Semites, Iranians, Greeks, and Romans: Studies in their Interactions* (Atlanta: Scholars Press, 1990); Yaacov Shavit, *Athens in Jerusalem: Classical Antiquity and Hellenism in the Making of the Modern Secular Jew*, trans. Chaya Naor and Niki Werner (London: Littman Library of Jewish Civilization, 1997); Alain Le Boulluec, "Hellenism and Christianity," in *Greek Thought: A Guide to Classical Knowledge*, eds. Jacque Brunschwig and Geoffrey E. R. Lloyd (Cambridge: Belknap, 2000), 858–69; Erik Nis Ostenfeld, *Greek Romans and Roman Greeks: Studies on Cultural Interaction* (Aarhus: Aarhus University Press, 2002); Jonathan M. Hall, *Hellenicity: Between Ethnicity and Culture* (Chicago: University of Chicago, 2002), 220–26; Erich Gruen, "Greeks and non Greeks," in *The Cambridge Companion to the Hellenistic World*, ed. Glenn R. Bugh (Cambridge: Cambridge University Press, 2006), 295–314; Andrew Wallace-Hadrill, *Rome's Cultural Revolution* (Cambridge: Cambridge University Press, 2008), 3–28; Susan Stephens, "Hellenistic Culture," in *Oxford Handbook of Hellenic Studies*, 86–97.

69. Hengel, *The 'Hellenization' of Judaea*, 53.

70. J. Z. Smith, *Drudgery Divine* (Chicago: Chicago University Press, 1990), esp. 54–84.

Although historically both Judaism and "paganism" served as polemical "others" to Christianity, we have already seen Fossum characterizing Judaism as early Christianity's "mother." Even before Fossum's essay, Alan Segal had depicted early Judaism and Christianity as sisters.[72] In fact, the current mainstream position in scholarship seems to be that when Christianity was at its most tender age, it *was* Jewish plain and simple, and therefore Judaism *could not* be other.[73]

The importance of this point becomes clear when we note Hengel's bold but influential dating for a divine Christ. According to him, Christians were worshiping a divine Jesus within twenty years of his death, at a point in time, he insisted, *when Christianity was almost entirely an intra-Jewish movement.*[74] If this is the case, then the divinity of Jesus could not be a Hellenistic or "pagan" idea, and the old Deist charge that Jesus' divinity (which ultimately gave rise to a Trinitarian conception of the Godhead) was adopted from "pagan" theological notions, falls to pieces. Jesus' deity was in fact a *Jewish* idea, and the Jews (like the Deists, exemplars of rational and approved religion) were monotheists. In this formulation, the "pagan" threat to the orthodox understanding of a divine Jesus is neutralized on what seems to be purely historical grounds. What shields early christology is precisely *Judaism*—even if early christology transcended Jewish categories,[75] and Judaism was later finally sloughed off as an "other"

---

71. Hengel, "Das früheste Christentum als eine jüdische messianische und universalistische Bewegung," in *Judaica, Hellenistica et Christiana, Kleine Schriften II* WUNT 109; (Tübingen: Mohr Siebeck, 1999), 200–18,(216). Hengel immediately adds that "pagan" influences were assumed by Judaism and creatively used to strengthen Jewish identity. The concession is helpful, but Hengel uses it mainly to neutralize "pagan"—which he equates with "foreign"—influence. He portrays Judaism as the great strainer or purifier of pagan culture. The paganism that goes through Judaism is no longer paganism, and thus no longer a threat.

72. Alan Segal, *Rebecca's Children: Judaism and Christianity in the Roman World* (Cambridge, MA: Harvard University Press, 1986).

73. Hengel stated this position lucidly: "[E]arly Christianity was almost wholly dependent on Jewish thought and tradition. . . . In other words, early Christianity is essentially 'Jewish,' a messianic, eschatological, enthusiastic, and universalist form of Judaism" ("A Gentile in the Wilderness," in *Kleine Schriften VII*, 532-45 (542). In another essay, Hengel states: "das Urchristentum ... *ganz* aus jüdischem Boden hervorging, d.h. ohne Einschränkung" ("Das früheste Christentum," 200). Here he makes clear that his thesis directly opposes the Religionsgeschichtliche Schule, which posited "extrem verschiedenen Wurzeln" for early Christianity (*ibid.* 201).

74. Hengel, *Sohn Gottes*, 11; cf. 92. See his earlier essay "Christologie und neutestamentliche Chronologie: Zu einer Aporie in der Geschichte des Urchristentums," in *Neues Testament und Geschichte: Historisches Geschehen und Deutung im Neuen Testament*, eds. Heinrich Baltensweiler and Bo Reicke (Zürich: Theologischer Verlag, 1972), 43–67.

in the fourth century when Jesus' relation to God received precise creedal definition.[76]

Despite the apparent cogency of this position, it seems to me that Hengel and his heirs in early christology have fused a demographic point—that most early Christians were Jews—with a historical and cultural conclusion—that early Christology must have been developed from solely Jewish ideas (where "Jewish" is again assumed to exclude the "Hellenistic"—or as they commonly say—"pagan" other). As I have already pointed out, Hengel's own arguments asserting the early hellenization of Judea completely undercut this line of reasoning. The so-called Jewish ideas about divinity were already hellenized when Christianity arose, and thus to mentally isolate an early Jewish from a hellenistic christology is misleading. Add to this the inconsistency of Hengel who used extraordinarily late depictions of Jewish numina (e.g., the figure of Enoch-Metatron in *Sefer Hekhalot* or *3 En.*) to shed light on early christology, while rigorously excluding even late first-century Greco-Roman sources on *chronological* grounds.[77] In light of current trends, one can only strive to make this Hengel agree with the Hengel who elsewhere claimed: "First of all we must be concerned with the historical connections, which are more complicated and more complex than our labels, clichés and pigeon-holes, but at the same time also with a real understanding and an evaluation which does justice to the past and is no longer one-sided and tendentious."[78]

THESIS

In an effort to balance the one-sidedness of current scholarship on early christology, this book proposes that early Christians did in fact use and adapt

---

75. Hurtado, *One Lord, One God*, 93–128. Cf. Hengel: "The fundamental teaching of the church was built on basically Jewish foundations. This does not mean that Christianity and Judaism are the same; certainly not. The differences are at once fundamental and necessary" ("A Gentile in the Wilderness," 542).

76. The so-called "parting of the ways" between Judaism and Christianity is variously dated by scholars and depends on the geographical area that one studies. James Dunn dated the "clear-cut and final" parting to 135 CE (*The Parting of the Ways Between Christianity and Judaism and their Significance for the Character of Christianity* [London: SCM, 1991], 238, 243). Since then, authors who have explored the interaction of Jews and Christians up until the Middle Ages have questioned any "clear-cut and final" parting. See esp. Adam H. Becker and Annette Yoshiko Reed, *The Ways that Never Parted: Jews and Christians in Late Antiquity and the Early Middle Ages* (Tübingen: Mohr Siebeck, 2003).

77. Hengel, *Sohn Gottes*, 73–76 (Metatron), 45, 50, 53–4 (chronological exclusion of Greco-Roman sources). Further instances and rationale in Smith, *Drudgery*, 43–6.

78. Hengel,'Hellenization' of Judaea, 53.

widespread Hellenistic conceptions about divinity in order to understand and depict the divine status of Jesus.

The slipperiness of many terms in this thesis require immediate clarification. Throughout, I use the adjective "Hellenistic" in a cultural sense. It is not designed to exclude Judaism, but rather (as often) to characterize the form that Judaism took in the first century. As a synonym of "Hellenistic," I will use the commonly employed global term "Greco-Roman." Although "Greco-Roman" (like the more politically charged word "pagan") is commonly used by scholars to exclude what is "Jewish" and "Christian," I will argue that certain "Greco-Roman" conceptions of deity were perceived by early Jews and Christians as proper to their own traditions. In order to partially mitigate the polarizing force of the term "Greco-Roman," however, I will often employ as a synonym the adjective "Mediterranean"—since few would dispute that early Judaism and Christianity were Mediterranean religious phenomena.

To be clear, I consider ancient Judaism to be the primary matrix of early Christianity, but I refuse to play a zero-sum game wherein the triumph of the Greeks means that the Jews lose, and *vice versa*. Scholars of a past era—for their own political reasons—underscored Greco-Roman influence to the detriment of the Jewish thought world.[79] Today, scholars balk at the idea that Christianity was a syncretistic faith (Hermann Gunkel) or a kind of Greek mystery religion (Richard Reitzenstein).[80] History indeed indicates that Christianity grew out of Judaism and from Judaism received its most direct and decisive stamp. Nonetheless, I contend that ancient Judaism(s) (implicitly or explicitly viewed as separate from the Greco-Roman world) should not be treated as the *sole* matrix informing Jesus' literary promotion to divine status. Ancient Judaism was a living Mediterranean religion engaged in active conversation and negotiation with larger religious currents of its time. If Judaism in the first century was an obviously distinctive religion, many Jews still shared *views of deity* surprisingly

79. Briefly documented by Gerdmar, *Judaism-Hellenism Dichotomy*, 16–17. See also Susannah Heschel "Jewish Studies as Counterhistory," in *Insider/Outsider: American Jewish & Multiculturalism*, ed. D. Biale et al. (Berkeley: University of California Press,1998), 101–15 (esp. 105–6; 110–11). She notes that in the twentieth century American academy, "Judaism was presented as an effort not to undermine Christianity but to contribute to its understanding and reinforce its hegemony" (103).

80. Hermann Gunkel, *Zum religionsgeschichtlichen Verständnis des Neuen Testaments* (Göttingen: Vandenhoeck and Ruprecht 1903). For Gunkel "the influence of foreign religions" came through Judaism (*durch das Judentum*) (1), and Judaism itself was "very strongly syncretistically determined" (*sehr stark synkretistisch gestimmt gewesen*) (69). Necessary definition and correctives for the category of "syncretism" are provided by Henning Paulsen, "Synkretismus im Urchristentum und im Neuen Testament," in *Zur Literatur und Geschichte des frühem Christentums: Gesammelte Aufsätze*, ed. Ute E. Eisen, WUNT 99 (Tübingen: Mohr Siebeck, 1997), 301–9.

similar to other Mediterranean peoples of the time.[81] It was these pervasive, cultural notions of deity that early Christians appropriated and adapted to describe the divine identity of their lord.

My argument asserts *not* that early Christians *borrowed* their divine christology from Hellenistic theology, but that certain conceptions of deity were part of the "preunderstanding" of Hellenistic culture—a culture in which Jews and Christians already participated. Ancient Jews and Christians, even if they assumed an oppositional stance toward the dominant (Hellenistic) culture, were still enmeshed in the ideational world of the οἰκουμένη. No big ugly epistemological ditch removed them from the basic cosmological, anthropological, and theological assumptions of their time—many of which were simply taken for granted.[82] Such assumptions formed not so much the *content* of thought for ancient Mediterranean peoples as its *framework*. They were the loom on which the warp and woof of thought were woven; they formed a set of givens shaping how the world and the gods were perceived. One of these assumptions was the notion that a mortal, weak human being could on occasion be promoted to the immortality of the "strong ones" called "gods." If actual cases of deification were rare, traditions of deification were not. They were the stuff of heroic epic, lyric song, ancient mythology, cultic hymns, Hellenistic novels, and popular plays all over the first-century Mediterranean world.[83] Such discourses were part of mainstream, urban culture to which most early Christians belonged. If Christians were socialized in predominantly Greco-Roman environments, it is no surprise that they employed and adapted common traits of deities and deified men to exalt their lord to divine status.

In formulating this thesis, I acknowledge that the perceived uniqueness of Jesus was part of the reality of early Christian experience and discourse.[84] Uniqueness, in this sense, is an expression of value. Out of their devotion to Jesus, early Christians depicted his divinity as unique and thus superior to any competitor. This desire "to go one up" on one's rivals is part of the dynamics of a missionary religion seeking to expand its influence in a diverse

---

81. Litwa, *We Are Being Transformed*, 50–56.

82. George H. van Kooten, "Christianity in the Graeco-Roman World: Socio-political, Philosophical, and Religious Interactions Up to the Edict of Milan (CE 313)," in *The Routledge Companion to Early Christian Thought* (ed. D. Jeffrey Bingham; London: Routledge, 2010), 3–37.

83. For a survey of deification in the Greco-Roman world, see Litwa, *We Are Being Transformed*, 58–85.

84. For the importance of experience in early Christianity, see Luke Timothy Johnson, *Religious Experience in Early Christianity: A Missing Dimension in New Testament Studies* (Minneapolis: Fortress Press, 1998).

religious marketplace.[85] As vigorous competitors who viewed truth as a zero-sum game, Christians like Justin Martyr sometimes built bridges of conceptual similarity with their opponents, and then quickly rearranged the blocks to create walls of perceived superiority. Schematically speaking, Jesus and "x" could be depicted as similar with regard to trait "y," provided that Jesus was also different in aspect "z" and thus superior. To use an economic analogy, Christians modified the design of many competing products on the market (i.e., other divine and deified individuals), and—after more rigorous and widespread advertisement—presented these modified religious ideas under their own trademark. In the days before copyright, such competitive assimilation was rife and effective in the marketplace of ideas. No one in the ancient Mediterranean world could claim ownership of the meaning of deity. With relative ease, Christians could exploit basic agreements on the notions of godhood to portray the superior and exclusive divinity of Jesus.[86] In sum, the emic observation that Christians perceived Jesus' deity to be unique does not annul the etic point that they deified Jesus in their literature.

DEIFICATION: BEYOND ΘΕΙΟΣ ἈΝΗΡ

Although I focus on ideas of divinity in the Greco-Roman world, I abandon the attempt to depict Jesus as a "divine man" (θεῖος ἀνήρ).[87] As a scholarly concept, the "divine man" has come under continual fire in the last thirty years.[88] The

85. For the competitive nature of Christianity, see Leif E. Vaage, ed., *Religious Rivalries in the Early Roman Empire and the Rise of Christianity* (Waterloo, Ont.: Wilfrid Laurier University Press, 2006); van Kooten, "Christianity in the Graeco-Roman World," 21–24.

86. For the economic model of religion, see Rodney Stark, "Economics of Religion," in *The Blackwell Companion to the Study of Religion*, ed. Robert A. Segal (Malden, MA: Blackwell, 2006), 47–67.

87. For a survey of the θεῖος ἀνήρ paradigm in scholarship with bibliography, see Hans Dieter Betz, "Gottmensch II," in *Reallexikon für Antike und Christentum*, eds. Theodor Klauser et al. (Stuttgart: Anton Hiersemann, 1982), cols. 234–312; David S. du Toit, *Theios Anthropos: Zur Verwendung von θεῖος ἄνθρωπος und sinnverwandten Ausdrücken in der Literatur der Kaiserzeit*, WUNT 2/91 (Tübingen: Mohr Siebeck, 1997), 2–39; Wilhelm Geerlings, "Die θεῖος ἀνήρ-Vorstellung der 'Religionsgeschichtlichen Schule' und ihre Kritik," in *Gottmenschen: Konzepte existentieller Grenzüberschreitung im Altertum*, eds. Gerhard Binder et al. (Trier: Wissenschaftlicher Verlag, 2003), 121–132; Thomas Paulsen, "Verherrlichung und Verspottung. Die Gestalt des 'Gottmenschen' bei Philostrat und Lukian," in ibid. 97–120.

88. Note, for example, Carl Holladay, *Theios Aner in Hellenistic-Judaism: A Critique of the Use of This Category in New Testament Christology* (Missoula, MT: Scholars, 1977); Barry Blackburn, *Theios Anēr and the Markan Miracle Traditions: A Critique of the theios Anēr Concept as an Interpretive Background of the Miracle Traditions Used by Mark* (Tübingen: Mohr [Siebeck], 1991); Aage Pilgaard, "The Hellenistic Theios Aner—A Model for Early Christian Christology?" in *The New Testament and Hellenistic Judaism*,

chief problem, it seems, is that the category is simply too vague.[89] "Divine" (θεῖος) has an appallingly broad signification in ancient discourse.[90] Applied to kings, it can refer to divine origin; for heralds, it can mean divine protection; and for poets, divine inspiration. In many cases, however, the adjective amounts to nothing more than "grand" or "magnificent."[91] There are cases where θεῖος is applied merely as an epithet of honor. According to Homer, the "divine" (θεῖος) can even describe salt (Il. 9.214).

Accordingly, the "divine man" (whether viewed as a historical personage or as a scholarly construct) is typically not necessarily or even usually a god. He is simply a cut above the common herd of humanity—somehow wise, inspired, great, or beyond the measure of normal human capabilities.[92] Typically, he is a mediator, a liminal being ambiguously ranked between humans and gods. In modern terms, he is a holy man, or shaman.[93] Apollonius of Tyana—the paradigmatic "divine man"—although formally heroized and given a shrine by

eds. P. Borgen and S. Giversen (Aahrus: Aahrus University Press, 1995), 101–22; Erkki Koskenniemi, "Apollonius of Tyana: A Typical Θεῖος Ἀνήρ?" *JBL* 117 (1998): 455–67; du Toit, *Theios Anthropos*. Dieter Zeller's response to du Toit ("The θεῖα φύσις of Hippocrates and Other 'Divine Men,'" in *Early Christianity and Classical Culture: Comparative Studies in Honor of Abraham J. Malherbe*, eds., John T. Fitzgerald; Thomas H. Olbricht, and L. Michael White [Leiden, Brill, 2003], 49–70) falls short of a rehabilitation of the θεῖος ἀνήρ.

89. Ian W. Scott, depending on the work of W. von Martitz (*TDNT* 8:338–40) and du Toit (*Theios Anthropos*, 401–2), points out that θεῖος ἀνήρ "never did serve, for ancient writers, as a technical term for the kind of divine man to which scholars usually apply it ("Is Philo's Moses a Divine Man?" *Studia Philonica Annual* 14 [2002]: 87–111 [89]).

90. See Jean van Camp and Paul Canart, *Le sens du mot theios chez Platon* (Louvain: University of Louvain, 1956); Hermann Steinthal, "Platons anthropologische Theologie—aus der Ferne betrachtet," in *Geschichte-Tradition-Reflexion: Festschrift für Martin Hengel*, ed. Hubert Cancik, 3 vols. (Tübingen: Mohr Siebeck, 1996), 233–50 (239–40). On the meaning of θεῖος, in addition to δαιμόνιος and θεσπέσιος, see esp. du Toit, *Theios Anthropos*. In general, du Toit thinks that a θεῖος ἀνήρ is typically a guarantor of a particular intellectual tradition. Alternatively, θεῖος functions as a characterizing adjective, which underscores the special piety of the person in question (Ibid., 402).

91. Ludwig Bieler, ΘΕΙΟΣ ΑΝΗΡ: *Das Bild des 'Göttlichen Menschen' in Spätantike und Frühchristentum*, 2 vols. (Darmstadt: Wissenschaftliche Buchgesellschaft, 1967), 10–12.

92. Aristotle remarked that whenever the Spartans "very much admire someone, they say he is a divine man (σεῖος [= θεῖος] ἀνήρ)" (*Nic. eth.* 7.1, 1145a29).

93. Bieler, ΘΕΙΟΣ ΑΝΗΡ, 18–20. For Christ as a shaman, see Pieter F. Craffert, *The Life of a Galilean Shaman: Jesus of Nazareth in Anthropological-Historical Perspective* (Eugene, OR: Cascade, 2008). I am prepared to admit, with Talbert, that the categories of the "divine man" and the "deified man" sometimes merged (*What is a Gospel? The Genres of the Canonical Gospels* [Minneapolis: Fortress Press, 1977], 35–38, citing Luc., *Cyn.* 13). It seems to me, however, that whereas a "divine man" is a more or less vague category not recognized by the ancients, they would have been familiar with a deified individual as a type of lesser deity.

Caracalla in the early third century (Cass. Dio, *Rom. Hist.* 78.18.4) —is never deified in the way that Jesus was deified, nor does he become the focus of a worshiping community.[94]

To speak of Jesus as "deified" is to say something different than that Jesus was a "divine man" or modeled on the divine man. The deified Jesus had (in the minds of early Christians) decisively crossed the threshold of heaven, and entered into the category of "god"/θεός.[95] Deification, as recent research has indicated, is not to be understood in solely essentialist terms.[96] Divinity in the ancient world is a kind of status. The status of (a) god (even a god who is or was human), however, is not ambiguous like the status of a "divine man." In other words, there were certain distinctive qualities in the ancient world that made it clear that one possessed a divine status. Chief among these were immortality and ruling power. Since I have discussed these traits at length elsewhere, I will not delve into them here.[97] What I turn to now are representative studies (old and new) that have attempted to understand Jesus' divinity using the *comparanda* of Greco-Roman gods and deified men.

History of Research

Despite Hurtado's attempt to "set aside [Bousset's] *Kyrios Christos* as an account of the development of Christ devotion," Bousset's study retains many valuable insights for understanding the origins of Jesus' divinity.[98] The German scholar successfully showed that Jesus' title "lord" (κύριος) was an established cult title for gods and deified heroes in Egypt and Syria.[99] He then claimed that the "belief in the deity of Jesus grew out of the Kyrios cult."[100] Bousset explicitly

94. Lactantius's question remains apposite: "Why does no one worship Apollonius as a god?" (*Inst.* 5.3.8).

95. For god/θεός as a distinct category in ancient thought, see D. S. Levene, "Defining the Divine in Rome," *TAPA* 142 (2012): 41–82.

96. See, for example, Simon Price, "Gods and Emperors: The Greek Language of the Roman Imperial Cult," *Journal of Hellenic Studies* 54 (1984): 79–95; Ittai Gradel, *Emperor Worship and Roman Religion* (Oxford: Clarendon, 2002), 25–26.

97. Litwa, *We Are Being Transformed*, 37–57. Compare Albert Henrichs, "What is a Greek God?" in *The Gods of Ancient Greece: Identities and Transformations*, eds. Jan N. Bremmer and Andrew Erskine (Edinburgh: Edinburgh University Press, 2010), 19–39.

98. Hurtado, *Lord Jesus Christ*, 23. I agree with Hurtado that Bousset erred in many of his methods and assumptions. But if Hurtado intended his *Lord Jesus Christ* to replace *Kyrios Christos*, he has not succeeded. Whatever the faults of his study, Bousset's attention to both Greco-Roman and Jewish sources if anything indicates a much more balanced approach.

99. Bousset, *Kyrios Christos*, 138–46. In making this observation, Bousset does not ignore the contribution of Judaism to Jesus' deification. He points out that the deity of Jesus was already assumed in

called this process a "deification" (*Vergottung*).[101] As in other cultic contexts, he believed that Jesus' deification was realized in worship.[102] Early Christians honored Christ as a god long before becoming comfortable with calling him "god" in a direct way.[103] Bousset denied that Christians began calling Jesus θεός in response to the larger culture. Nonetheless they were affected by ancient cults in which one-time human beings were worshiped as θεοί.[104] With the development of the Kyrios cult, then, "Christianity paid tribute to its time and its milieu."[105]

In 1933, Stephan Lösch directly studied the deity of Jesus in light of ancient traditions of deification.[106] Lösch focused initially on the traditions of self-deifying kings, demonstrating how repugnant they were to Jews (and Greeks) in antiquity.[107] In his second part, Lösch tried to undermine the divinity of emperors by claiming that all "good" emperors used a formula to reject divine honors granted them by the peoples of the eastern Mediterranean—in particular, as Lösche portrayed them, the boisterous and erratic Egyptians who still maintained the ceremony of the Ptolemaic court.[108] Lösch concluded that (1) Greco-Roman traditions of apotheosis are universally rejected in the New Testament[109] because (2) the new religion was rooted in Jewish tradition (*von jüdischen Boden ausnimmt die neue Religion ihren Ausgang*).[110]

The argument is indeed familiar, but there are several problems with it. First of all, focusing on traditions of self-deifying kings is highly selective—as if these (universally hated) rulers were somehow models of how deification worked in the ancient world. Second, Lösch ignores the fact that the "formula" of rejecting divine honors was often a formality that in practice denied none of the standard divine cult given to living emperors since the time of Augustus.

Christian apocalyptic thought: Christ, the "Son of Man," was the judge of the living and the dead. This was the power that only a god could wield.

100. Ibid., 331.

101. Ibid., 317. German text: *Kyrios Christos: Geschichte des Christusglaubens von den Anfängen des Christentums bis Irenaeus* (Göttingen: Vandenhoeck & Ruprecht, 1921), 246.

102. Bousset, *Kyrios Christos* (ET), 330, 327.

103. Ibid., 318–27.

104. Ibid., 330.

105. Ibid., 331.

106. Stephan Lösch, *Deitas Jesu und antike Apotheose: Ein Beitrag zur Exegese und Religionsgeschichte* (Rottenburg: Bader, 1933).

107. Ibid., 10–38.

108. Ibid., 47–67.

109. Ibid., 46, 129–30.

110. Ibid., 129.

Lösch's emphasis on the difference between east and west in the bestowal of divine honors (fawning Greeks and rational Romans) has been thoroughly revised in recent scholarship.[111] As to Lösch's conclusion, it is in fact what he had assumed all along: monotheistic Judaism, the protective buffer of Christianity, saves Christians from pagan influence when the new religion grows up in the Hellenistic world.[112] Regrettably, Lösch's conclusion seems to be based in part on his own imperialistic attitudes and theological biases. The provincial worship of the emperor, he believed, was servile, the "naïve error of primitives," a "delusional idea of those who yet sit in darkness and the shadow of death."[113]

In 1937, Friedrich Pfister published a study that argued for "unique points of agreement" between the figures of Heracles and Christ.[114] Pfister was concerned to demonstrate parallels in the birth narratives, youth, temptations, mature deeds, deaths, and ascensions of the two figures. He pointed out that both Heracles and Jesus suffer throughout their lives and undergo a violent death. Nevertheless, both receive heavenly exaltation as a kind of reward (Phil. 2:9; cf. Ps.-Apollod., *Bibl.* 2.73). Both go to hell and back (1 Pet. 3:19; Sen., *Herc. Fur.* 893), and are said to conquer death (1 Cor. 15:54-55; [Sen.], *Herc. Oet.* 1955). In their ascent, both heroes disappear in a cloud (Acts 1:9; Ps.-Apollod., *Bibl.* 2.160). Pfister finds many other tantalizing similarities, such as the death announcement "it is finished" (τετέλεσται, John 19:30; *peractum est*, [Sen.], *Oet.* 1476). Although Pfister was roundly and rightly criticized for his unmitigated parallelomania (sometimes merely listing painfully trite similarities), his basic thesis remains: Heracles' death and apotheosis could and did serve as a cultural model for the deification of Jesus Christ.[115]

In his article "The 'Divine Hero' Christology in the New Testament," Wilfred L. Knox argued that in Rom. 1:4, Paul "described Jesus in terms which represented Him in very much the same light as some of the most popular cult-

---

111. Gradel, *Emperor Worship*, esp.162–250.

112. Lösch, *Deitas Jesu*, 1–5.

113. Ibid., 129–130.

114. Friedrich Pfister, "Herakles und Christus," *ARW* 34 (1937): 42–60 (46).

115. For sharp criticism of Pfister see H. J. Rose, "Herakles and the Gospels," *HTR* 31 (1938): 113–142. Rose attributed the Heracles-Christ parallels to "popular methods of thought and forms of imagination" (141). Arnold Toynbee traced them to "folk-memory" (*A Study of History*, 12 vols. [London: Oxford University Press, 1939], 6:475). See further Marcel Simon, *Hercule et le Christianisme* (Strasbourg: University of Strasbourg, 1955), 47–74; David E. Aune, "Heracles and Christ: Heracles Imagery in the Christology of Early Christianity," in *Greeks, Romans, and Christians: Essays in Honor of Abraham J. Malherbe*, 3–19; van Kooten, "Christianity in the Graeco-Roman World," 25–29.

figures of the hellenistic world, an active deity who was partly human and partly divine." These "popular cult-figures" were the sons of Zeus who "earned their immortality by the services they rendered to humankind."[116] The language of certain Pauline passages (Rom. 1:3-4; Phil. 2:6-11; Col. 1:15-20) "show a close affinity with the descriptions and panegyrics" of deified figures like Heracles, Dionysus, and Asclepius. Although Knox was able to point to some verbal parallels (e.g., between Phil. 2:6-11 and Plut., *Fort. virt. Alex.* 330d),[117] he resisted the idea of conscious borrowing.[118] To explain the overlap, he appealed to "the use of a common stock of ideas, ultimately religious, but adopted by rhetoric and popular philosophy, and carried over into the liturgical and homiletic language of the hellenistic world, including that of the Church."[119]

In the 1970s, Charles Talbert argued that Christians used the "mythology of the immortals" (i.e., deified individuals) to develop their christology. Immortals, according to Talbert, were originally human beings but were made into gods by a transformation or ascension bestowing the "same honors as the eternals [i.e., the pre-established gods]." Literary examples include Osiris, Heracles, Asclepius, Aristaeus, Aeneas, Romulus, and Moses.[120] Eventually the mythology of the immortals attached to historical figures such as Alexander the Great, Augustus, Empedocles, Apollonius of Tyana, and Peregrinus. Talbert pointed out several structural analogies between Jesus and the immortals. "Hellenistic Jewish Christianity," he said, presented four constitutive ideas: (1) Jesus became lord and Christ at his "resurrection/exaltation/ascension" (Acts 2:36; 13:33; Rom. 1:3-4), (2) Jesus had a divine father, (3) Jesus was qualified to be Messiah not only by physical descent but by his benefactions bestowed on the sick and suffering (e.g., Mark 10:46-52), and (4) Jesus may have been a preexistent divinity (cf. Mark 12:6).[121] Talbert claimed that the "average Mediterranean man-in-the-street who was confronted by such a christological pattern" would assume that Jesus was "being portrayed as an immortal." He added that "Jesus' ascent to heaven, like that of the other immortals, is constitutive for his new status." Christ's heavenly existence is "a new type of

---

116. Wilfred L. Knox, "The 'Divine Hero' Christology in the New Testament," *HTR* 41 (1948): 229–49 (231).

117. Ibid., 237.

118. Ibid., 247.

119. Ibid., 242. See Knox's earlier work, *Some Hellenistic Elements in Primitive Christianity* (London: Oxford University Press, 1944), where he refuses to separate Palestinian and "hellenistic" Judaism (2).

120. Talbert, *What is a Gospel?* 27–30. Talbert covers much of the same ground in "The Concept of the Immortals in Mediterranean Antiquity," *JBL* 94 (1975): 419–36.

121. Talbert, *What is a Gospel?* 39.

existence different from that of mortal men." From heaven, Jesus can radiate virtue and beneficence to his devotees.[122] Talbert concluded that the Synoptic Gospels employed the mythology of the immortals as the frame for their stories of Jesus.[123]

In more recent years, increasing interest in ruler cult and emperor worship has resulted in some important comparisons with Jesus' deity. Yarbro Collins, for instance, argues that "the imperial cult was a catalyst in the origin of the worship of Jesus."[124] The ruler cult was part of the "prior cultural experience" of ancient Mediterranean peoples—including those in Palestine.[125] This prior cultural experience in turn shaped the early Christian experience of the risen Christ. Yarbro Collins goes so far as to conclude that the early followers of Jesus "adapted non-Jewish religious traditions deliberately and consciously as a way of formulating a culturally meaningful system of belief and life."[126] The strongest parallel to the worship of an exalted human being after death is the Roman emperor.[127] Unlike Jesus, however, Roman rulers were typically honored when alive and able to reciprocate with benefactions. Still, "such worship of living beings may have provided a provocative incentive to followers of Jesus to offer veneration to the one human being who truly deserved it and whose worship was legitimated by the will of the one true God."[128]

Although I employ the above works dedicated to viewing Jesus' divinity in a broader Mediterranean framework, my study attempts to (1) provide a fuller picture of Jesus' deification by treating every major stage of his recorded life, and (2) provide more in-depth and rigorous comparisons of Jesus' deity with other divine and deified figures in the ancient Mediterranean world.

---

122. Ibid.

123. Ibid., 40–42.

124. Yarbo Collins, "Worship of Jesus and the Imperial Cult," 251.

125. Ibid., 241. For emperor worship in Palestine, see Monika Bernett, *Der Kaiserkult in Judäa unter den Herodiern und Römern*, WUNT 203 (Tübingen: Mohr Siebeck, 2007).

126. Yarbo Collins, "Worship of Jesus and the Imperial Cult," 242.

127. Ibid., 248

128. Ibid., 249. For further studies on the structural affinities between the worship of Jesus and the imperial cult, see, for example, Larry J. Kreitzer, *Striking New Images: Roman Imperial Coinage and the New Testament World* (Sheffield: Sheffield Academic Press, 1996), esp. ch. 2; Jeffrey Brodd and Jonathan L. Reed, eds., *Rome and Religion: A Cross-Disciplinary Dialogue on the Imperial Cult* (Atlanta: Society of Biblical Literature, 2011).

THEORY OF COMPARISON

Although Judaism's influence on Christianity now seems obvious to most, the theologically charged history of interpretation of Christianity in Greco-Roman culture calls for a more sophisticated theory of comparison and of cultural influence.[129] In his many essays, J. Z. Smith has provided a method and a model of comparison for religious studies. His greatest contribution, perhaps, is his sophisticated interfacing of traditional historical and literary models with anthropological approaches.[130] In this study I will follow a generally Smithian theory of comparison, which I briefly sketch here.[131]

In his two classic essays, "Adde Parvum Parvo Magnus Acervus Erit,"[132] and "In Comparison a Magic Dwells,"[133] Smith maps out a "paradigm for comparison."[134] He isolates four ideal types: (1) the ethnographic, (2) the encyclopedic, (3) the morphological, and (4) the evolutionary. The ethnographic and encyclopedic he quickly disposes of as unusable,[135] so I will focus on the morphological and evolutionary approaches.

Morphological comparison has been called "synthetic," "structural," "synchronic," or "phenomenological."[136] It presents phenomena in "a typological series" that is "fundamentally ahistorical."[137] That is to say, patterned relationships posited between phenomena are logical and formal rather than temporal.[138] "If a series is proposed, it will deal with the movement from the

---

129. On comparison in religious studies, see Michael L. White, and John T. Fitzgerald. "Quod est Comparandum: The Problem of Parallels," in *Early Christianity and Classical Culture: Comparative Studies in Honor of Abraham J. Malherbe*, 13–40; Paul Roscoe, "The Comparative Method," in *The Blackwell Companion to the Study of Religion*, 25–46.

130. See, for instance, J.Z. Smith, "What a Difference a Difference Makes," in *Relating Religion: Essays in the Study of Religion* (Chicago: University of Chicago Press, 2004), 250–302.

131. Smith's essays, as any reader of them knows, cannot be boiled down to a summary or a few main points without forsaking the depth of his discursive practice, the richness of his suggestive comments, and the many "eureka"-type insights embedded in his prose. It goes without saying that my attempt at a clear summary will simplify Smith's discussion.

132. Smith, "Adde Parvum Parvo Magnus Acervus Erit," in *Map is Not Territory: Studies in the History of Religions* (Chicago: University of Chicago Press, 1978), 240–264. The essay was originally published in 1971.

133. Smith, "In Comparison a Magic Dwells," in *Imagining Religion: From Babylon to Jonestown* (Chicago: University of Chicago Press, 1982), 19–35.

134. Ibid., 22.

135. Ibid., 24; Smith, "Adde Parvum," 248–49.

136. Smith, "Adde Parvum," 254.

137. Ibid., 256. Smith adds, "The type is by definition ahistorical, yet it stands in a complex relationship to the historical" (257).

138. Ibid., 258.

simple to the complex, from the perfect manifestation to the fractured."[139] The evolutionary approach, in turn, attempts to structure phenomena in a diachronic scheme manifesting logical development, and often relations of (historical) cause and effect.[140]

Smith is right to think that imposing an evolutionary scheme on phenomena that appear on a scale from simple to complex is "illegitimate"[141]—a fact disqualifying the evolutionary approach. But Smith, due to training and disposition, is not wholly satisfied with pure morphology (an approach more closely associated with his teacher, Mircea Eliade). He is aware, I think, that it is wrong to identify an *evolutionary* approach with *historical* comparison plain and simple. History need not assume a biological model of gradual mutation through multiple generations of reproduction. Thus although Smith often opposes the morphological and historical as ideal types of comparison, in practice morphology need not exclude categories of space and time (the bases of history).[142]

In "A Magic Dwells," Smith himself turns to discuss a historical way of comparison "within the morphological mode."[143] His example of historical-morphological comparison is drawn from a school that stands at the beginning of modern, systematic scholarly comparison: the "Pan-Babylonian school." It is perhaps not wise, however, to stress the "Pan-Babylonian" character of this kind of comparison in order, as Smith says, not to "drive usually calm scholars to a frenzy of vituperation."[144] As Smith himself notes, the methods of this school have been mined and refined for over a century and thus are not the intellectual property of any one movement. The basic pattern of comparison—drawn from the work of Alfred Jeremias—is as follows. Comparison, Jeremias posited, is based on neither borrowing nor (the ahistorical concept of) the psychic unity of humankind. Rather, Jeremias based comparisons on structural similarities of thought based on shared language and culture.[145] In this way, Smith thinks, one

139. Ibid., 258.

140. Smith, "In Comparison a Magic Dwells," 24.

141. Smith, "Adde Parvum," 260.

142. Smith, "In Comparison a Magic Dwells," 25. Smith tends to associate traditional historical approaches with the search for causation by contiguity and/or association of ideas, people, or phenomena. Appealing to causation, he implies, is an appeal to "magic," not science (21–22). Nonetheless, Smith is aware that there are more sophisticated ways of imagining a historical connection. In "Adde Parvum," for instance, Smith admits that there is a dialectic between type and history (257).

143. Smith, "In Comparison a Magic Dwells," 26.

144. Ibid..

145. Ibid., 26–28. Specifically, Jeremias distinguished between a worldview, a cultural system, and "a linguistic manifestation of the interaction of these two" (28). I am simplifying matters by placing all three

can "ground comparison and patterns in a historical process."[146] Comparison, in other words, requires a third term: a larger culture that offers generally agreed-upon understandings of divinity that can be instantiated by two or more independent religious texts or movements.[147]

Admittedly, this model of comparison leans upon a term hotly contested among current anthropologists, namely "culture."[148] My purpose in this study is not to provide a universally accepted definition of the term, but to offer clarity on what it means here. Often definitions of culture emphasize either shared knowledge or shared practice. I confess my focus on ideas. Accordingly, in this study, "culture" refers to a system of inherited and socially constructed patterns of thought by which people communicate, perpetuate, and develop their various bodies of knowledge. Specifically, I focus on knowledge about the nature and character of the divine. Such knowledge can be learned through conscious instruction and adaptation but also by the more indirect means of socialization.[149] As a result of socialization, people who belong to a particular

factors under the umbrella of "culture." Worldview is based on culture (and cannot be separated from its cultural instantiation), and language is one of the chief *exempla* of culture, helping to define the character of thought.

146. Ibid., 29.

147. Smith, *Drudgery Divine*, 99. Smith best exemplifies this mode of comparison in the last chapter of *Drudgery Divine* ("On Comparing Settings," 116–43). Here he compares early Christianity and the mystery cults with reference to his generic pattern of "locative" versus "utopian" religion. He posits that Christianity in its Late Antique phase showed many locative features analogous to the Late Antique versions of the cults of Attis and Cybele. I would argue that many of those locative analogies are based on a shared intellectual culture.

148. On the history and complexity of the term "culture" with special reference to the Greco-Roman world, see Wallace-Hadrill, *Rome's Cultural Revolution*, 28–37. On the development of the term, and its use in a postmodern context, see esp. Kathryn Tanner, *Theories of Culture: A New Agenda for Theology* (Minneapolis: Fortress Press, 1997), 3–58.

149. Joan E. Grusec and Paul D. Hastings define socialization broadly as "the way in which individuals are assisted in becoming members of one or more social groups." They underscore "assist" because socialized individuals are active in their own socialization process and selective in what they accept. "Socialization," they observe, "involves a variety of outcomes, including the acquisition of rules, roles, standards, and values across the social, emotional, cognitive, and personal domains. Some outcomes are deliberately hoped for on the part of agents of socialization while others may be unintended side effects." Socialization, they assert, can also come about in many ways (they mention modeling, proactive techniques, routines, and rituals), and continues throughout life ("Introduction," in *Handbook of Socialization: Theory and Research*, eds. Joan Grusec and Paul Hastings [New York: Guilford, 2006], 1–9 [1–2]). For a classic discussion, see Peter L. Berger and Thomas Luckmann, *The Social Construction of Reality: A Treatise in the Sociology of Knowledge* (New York: Doubleday, 1966), 119–59.

culture could share a set of assumptions about the nature of divinity and experience it in a similar way.[150]

I do not claim that there was one, single monoculture in the ancient Mediterranean world. It is more accurate to think of the ancient Mediterranean as a multicultural society with many competing religious ideas and ideologies.[151] Nevertheless, there is still a sense in which the many lands of the ancient Mediterranean basin—as they were politically unified by a system of imperial government—represented a cultural οἰκουμένη in which, as Tacitus says, "all things were connected" (*cuncta inter se conexa*) (*Ann.* 1.9).[152] In the thick of diversity, in other words, there remained a dominant cultural ethos privileging the values, art, language, rationality, and theological ideas of ancient Greece. Mainstream Hellenistic culture was so assertive that to a certain extent it captured the Roman conquerors who subsequently became its sponsors.[153] In the famous line of Horace: "Conquered Greece her conqueror subdued (*Graecia capta ferum victorem cepit*), and Rome grew polished, who till then was rude" (*Ep.* 2.1.156-57, trans. J. Conington).[154]

The case of Rome shows that adopting Hellenistic culture does not necessarily imply a top-down imposition of Hellenism as happened (or was reported to have happened) in Judea in the time of Antiochus Epiphanes.[155] For

150. My notion of cultural influence adds nothing new to scholarship. It merely fleshes out the commonly accepted (even banal) idea that people experience reality in the grooves cut by culture (that is, by being socialized in a particular culture). Hurtado, for instance, asks, "How could there be any group or individuals not shaped in various ways by the cultural setting in which they live?" (*Lord Jesus Christ*, 74–75; cf. his "New Testament Christology: Retrospect and Prospect," 22).

151. See most recently Mary T. Boatwright, *Peoples of the Roman World* (Cambridge: Cambridge University Press, 2012) (with bibliography).

152. Cf. Polyb., *Hist.* 1.3.3-4: "Previously [prior to 220 BCE] the doings of the world had been, so to say, dispersed, as they were held together by no unity of initiative, results, or locality; but ever since this date history has come together as if it was part of one body (οἷον εἰ σωματοειδῆ συμβαίνει), and the affairs of Italy and Africa have been interwoven (συμπλέκεσθαι) with those of Greece and Asia, the movement of all things leading up to one goal (πρὸς ἕν γίνεσθαι τέλος τὴν ἀναφορὰν ἁπάντων)."

153. See further Tim Whitmarsh, "Greece and Rome," in *The Oxford Handbook of Hellenic Studies*, 114–28; Whitmarsh, "Hellenism," in *The Oxford Handbook of Roman Studies*, eds. Alessandro Barchiesi and Walter Scheidel (Oxford: Oxford University Press, 2009), 728–47 (with bibliography).

154. Josephus claimed that Hellenes and Jews are distinguished from one another more in terms of geography than by practices (ἐπιτηδεύματα) (*Ap.* 2.121-23). He also insisted that Greeks borrowed heavily from Jewish traditions and practices.

155. In judging this episode, one must give equal weight to the Hellenizing activity of Jews themselves (noted with scorn in 1 Macc 1:11-15). On hellenization during the time of the Maccabees, note Momigliano, *Alien Wisdom*, 101–11; Susan Sherwin-White and Amélie Kuhrt, *From Samarkhand to Sardis: A New Approach to the Seleucid Empire* (Berkeley: University of California, 1993), 141–87; and

centuries, the peoples of the eastern Mediterranean (including Jews) had been absorbing, appropriating, and internalizing Hellenistic culture for their own ends.[156] At no point did Jews and Christians fuse with Greek culture and so lose their identity. Instead, they entered into a vigorous process of reciprocal exchange on all levels—social, material, and intellectual.[157] We can call the end result a kind of cultural "hybridity" provided that we understand that distinct cultures were not lost or transformed beyond recognition in a syncretistic melting pot.[158] Rather, members of different cultures mutually assimilated to one another while continuously constructing differences in practice and thought. Jews in particular were eager to construct and maintain their own perceived distinctives out of their deep sense of cultural pride.[159] A similar pride and sense of distinction manifested itself in the self-proclaimed τρίτον γένος, or "third race" of the Christians.[160]

especially John J. Collins, *Jewish Cult and Hellenistic Culture: Essays on the Jewish Encounter with Hellenism and Roman Rule* (Leiden: Brill, 2005), 29–40.

156. "Romanization" instead of "hellenization" has recently come into vogue in classical circles, although not always with clarity. For discussion see J. C. Barrett, "Romanization: A Critical Comment," in *Dialogues in Roman Imperialism: Power, Discourse, and Discrepant Experience in the Roman Empire*, ed. D. J. Mattingly, Journal of Roman Archaeology Supplementary Series (Portsmouth, RI: JRA, 1997), 51–64; D. Mattingly, "Vulgar and Weak 'Romanization,' or Time for a Paradigm Shift?" *Journal of Roman Archaeology* 15 (2002): 536–40; Janet Huskinson, ed., *Experiencing Rome: Culture, Identity, and Power in the Roman Empire* (London: Routledge, 2000), 20–23, 56–60, 269–71; Wallace-Hadrill, *Rome's Cultural Revolution*, 9–14.

157. For a model of reciprocal cultural exchange, see Hartmut Böhme et al., eds., *Transformation: Ein Konzept zur Erforschung kulturellen Wandels* (Munich: Wilhelm Fink, 2011), esp. 39–56.

158. For cultural hybridization as selective adaptation and negotiation see Peter Burke, *Cultural Hybridity* (Cambridge: Polity, 2009). See also Ray Laurence and Joanne Berry, eds., *Cultural Identity in the Roman Empire* (London: Routledge, 1998).

159. For Judaism in the Greco-Roman world, see John Barclay, *Jews in the Mediterranean Diaspora: From Alexander to Trajan (323 BCE–117 CE)* (Berkeley: University of California, 1999); Barclay, *Negotiating Diaspora: Jewish Strategies in the Roman Empire* (Edinburgh: T&T Clark, 2004); John J. Collins, *Between Athens and Jerusalem: Jewish Identity in the Hellenistic Diaspora*, 2nd ed. (Grand Rapids, MI: Eerdmans, 2000); Margaret Williams, "Jews and Jewish Communities in the Roman Empire," in *Experiencing Rome*, 305–33; Jack T. Sanders, "Establishing Social Distance Between Christians and Both Jews and Pagans," in *Handbook of Early Christianity: Social Science Approaches*, eds. Anthony J. Blasi et al. (Lanham, MD: AltaMira, 2002), 361–84; Erich Gruen, *Diaspora: Jews Amidst Greeks and Romans* (Cambridge: Harvard University Press, 2002); C. Bakhos, *Ancient Judaism in its Hellenistic Context* (Leiden: Brill, 2005).

160. On early Christian identity, see Gillian Clark, *Christianity and Roman Society* (Cambridge: Cambridge University Press, 2004); Judith M. Lieu, *Neither Jew Nor Greek? Constructing Early Christian*

PRINCIPLES OF COMPARISON

Consequently, when I compare concepts of divinity, my intention is never to dissolve distinctively Christian ideas like a drop of wine flung into an ocean of Hellenism. The first rule of comparison is that *comparison never means identity*. In the words of Smith, "Comparison requires the postulation of difference as the grounds of its being interesting (rather than tautological)."[161]

Conversely, comparison assumes that no phenomena are strictly speaking "unique."[162] "'Uniqueness' is absolute," writes Smith, "and, therefore, forbids comparison by virtue of its very assertion."[163]All phenomena can be classed, and classed together, based on perceived similarities.

Similarities, in my approach, are rooted in the matrix of a shared culture, not direct causation between thinkers, texts, or words. Large distances of space and time and yawning gaps in the historical record make constructing causative relations almost impossible and more often jejune. The lines that I draw between texts do not portray genetic relations but analogical patterns of thought. Texts that long predate Christian sources (such as Homer and Hesiod) are employed chiefly because of their pivotal role in the curriculum of *paideia* during the infancy of Christianity.[164]

Finally, sound comparisons must consider both similarities and differences. Differences make comparisons sharper and more interesting; similarities make them more productive and enlightening. To focus on pure similarity is parallelomania;[165] to focus on pure difference is apologetics.[166] If in this study I

Identity (London: T&T Clark, 2002); Lieu, *Christian Identity in the Jewish and Graeco-Roman World* (Oxford: Oxford University Press, 2004).

161. Smith, "In Comparison a Magic Dwells," 35; cf. Smith, *To Take Place: Toward Theory in Ritual* (Chicago: University of Chicago Press, 1987), 14.

162. In common English usage, "unique" can sometimes mean "strikingly distinctive" or "extraordinary." Here, however, I am using "unique" in its absolute sense as "one of a kind" or *sui generis*. For the employment and criticism of this sort of uniqueness in scholarship, see Smith, *Drudgery Divine*, 36–46.

163. Ibid., 116.

164. Heraclitus in the first century CE says, "From the very first age of life, the foolishness of infants just beginning to learn is nurtured on the teaching given in his [Homer's] school. One might almost say that his poems are our baby clothes, and we nourish our minds by draughts of his milk" (*Homeric Problems* 1.5; cf. Plato, *Resp.* 377b-c; Callimachus, *Epigr.* 49; Philo, *Virt.* 178; Ps. Clem., *Hom.* 4.18-19.). See further Dennis Ronald MacDonald, *Christianizing Homer:* The Odyssey, *Plato, and* The Acts of Andrew (Oxford: Oxford University Press, 1994), 17–34; Simon Price, *Religions of the Ancient Greeks* (Cambridge: Cambridge University Press, 1999), 129; Raffaella Cribiore, *Gymnastics of the Mind: Greek Education in Hellenistic and Roman Egypt* (Oxford: Oxford University Press, 2001), 178–80, 194–205; Beryl Rawson, *Children and Childhood in Roman Italy* (Oxford: Oxford University Press, 2003), 168–69.

tend to underscore aspectual similarities between Christian and Greco-Roman conceptions of deity, it is because the hoary tradition of Christian apologetics and apologetic scholarship that precedes me (both in the ancient and modern worlds) has long trumpeted the differences. This study is thus an attempt to restore balance in contemporary historical scholarship on the meaning and cultural context of Jesus' divinity.

CONCLUSION

Smith emphasizes that "Comparison provides the means by which *we* [scholars] 're-vision' phenomena as *our* data in order to solve *our* theoretical problems."[167] In an earlier study he even professed that the phenomenon of religion as a whole "is solely the creation of the scholar's study. It is created for the scholar's analytic purposes by his imaginative acts of comparison and generalization. Religion has no independent existence apart from the academy."[168] Based on such statements, it would seem that for Smith comparison in the field of religious studies is a matter of scholarly construction pure and simple. In his view, that is, comparison does not bring together two phenomena which once existed "out there," but two constructions (or reconstructions) that solely exist in the academic community and between the scholar's ears.

Assuming the correctness of this reading, I must confess that I am no pure disciple of Smith. I come to the table unapologetically as a historian and philosophical realist. I am willing, in other words, to admit that two phenomena in the past can be similar or different due to real historical processes, and not simply because they are brought together and gauged in the scholar's mind for his or her intellectual ends.[169] Texts do represent ideas and give us a window into ancient culture. This stance hardly signifies a return to the old paradigm of "objective" history or historicism. It is, rather, an admission that subjectivity and objectivity are always finely intertwined in scholarly discourse.[170] I admit that when I compare historical patterns of thought, those patterns—along with their posited similarities and differences—have first been constructed in the

165. For "parallelomania," see Samuel Sandmel, "Parallelomania," *JBL* 81 (1962): 1–13.

166. Smith, *Relating Religion*, 275; Smith, *Drudgery Divine*, 116.

167. Smith, *Drudgery Divine*, 52. Cf. also Smith, "In Comparison a Magic Dwells," 21.

168. Ibid., xi.

169. Smith, *Drudgery Divine*, 51–52, 115.

170. Most historians, have absorbed the lessons of postmodernism even if they have refused to enter the cage of pure subjectivity (Beth Sheppard, *The Craft of History and the Study of the New Testament* [Atlanta: SBL, 2012], 164–69). See also the historiographical comments of Craffert, *Life of a Galilean Shaman*, 3–34.

"lab," so to speak, of the scholar's mind. As a scholar, I am happy to admit that the academy is my context in which I provide thick descriptions of historical phenomena for the purposes of comparison. In composing my thick descriptions, I have inevitably shaped the data to suit my comparative purposes. My particular reconstruction, as well as the details my comparison, can and should be challenged by other reconfigurations and interpretations of the data in the academic community. In the end, we may not discover "what really happened" (von Ranke's *wie es eigentlich gewesen*), but with keen attention and perseverance we can still find plausible (and real!) connections between ideas and events that generate new and deeper understandings of how on earth Jesus became a god.

"Not through Semen, Surely"

Luke and Plutarch on Divine Birth

"For what is born from god is a god"
(τὸ γὰρ ἐκ θεοῦ γεννηθὲν θεός ἐστιν)
—Ptolemy in Iren., *Haer.* 1.8.5

Introduction

The philosopher Celsus, in one of the first attempts to compare Christ with other ancient Mediterranean heroes, points out that Jesus is not alone in his divine conception.[1] Ancient stories (παλαιοὶ μῦθοι) also attributed a divine begetting (θείαν σποράν) to Perseus, Amphion, Aeacus, and Minos. These are men who demonstrated their divine origin by their truly great and wondrous works (Orig., *Cels.* 1.67). Earlier in Origen's *Contra Celsum*, Celsus even pokes fun at the Christian birth narrative, depicting it as a run-of-the-mill Mediterranean legend: "Was Jesus' mother beautiful, and did God have sex (ἐμίγνυτο) with her due to her beauty, although according to nature God does not love a perishable body (οὐ φεφυκὼς ἐρᾶν φθαρτοῦ σώματος)? It is not reasonable (οὐδ' εἰκὸς ἦν) that God lusted for her—she being neither rich nor royal—since nobody—not even her neighbors—knew her" (1.39; cf. Justin, *Dial.* 67).[2]

---

1. The phrase "divine conception" is preferred over "virgin birth" since it puts the focus on Jesus and the divine agency to which he owes his origin.

2. See further John Granger Cook, *The Interpretation of the New Testament in Greco-Roman Paganism* (Tübingen: Mohr Siebeck, 2000), 28–31.

Although speaking of Jesus' divine conception means wading into a theological maelstrom, it is necessary to discuss this first element of Jesus' biography in order to form a complete picture of the strategies that early Christians used to depict Jesus' divine status in their literature. The possibilities of comparison are vast. In this chapter, however, I focus on the nearly contemporary accounts of Jesus' divine conception in Luke (1:26–38) and Plato's divine conception in Plutarch's *Table Talk* (717e–718b; cf. *Num* 4). Since the comparative road is well-trodden, I prepare the way with some well-needed clarifications. Comparisons of divine conceptions have—since the days of Celsus—repeatedly run aground because they have attempted to make (or strongly imply) genetic links between the divine birth of Jesus and other Mediterranean gods and heroes.[3] In the "Greek" world (so it is thought), divine conception is literal and common (as seen, for instance, in the cases of Heracles, Dionysus, Perseus, and so on), whereas in the "Jewish" world, divine conception is infrequent and figurative.[4] Although the Israelite king (Ps. 2:7; 1 Sam. 7:14), collective Israel (Exod. 4:22; Deut. 14:1; Hos. 11:1), and the righteous man (Sir. 4:10; Wisd. of Sol. 2:18) are all called "sons of god" in ancient Jewish literature, this is usually understood figuratively.[5] Thus many interpreters—and not a few

---

3. For a survey of older literature, see Josef Hasenfuss, "Die Jungfrauengeburt in der Religionsgeschichte," in *Jungfrauengeburt gestern und heute*, eds., Hermann Josef Brosch and Josef Hasenfuss (Essen: Driewer, 1969), 11–21. Rudolf Bultmann stated that Matthew's account of Jesus' birth "was first added in the transformation in Hellenism, where the idea of the generation of a king or a hero from a virgin by the godhead was widespread" (*History of the Synoptic Tradition*, trans. John Marsh, 2nd ed. [New York: Harper & Row, 1968], 291–92). More recently, Gerd Lüdemann has stated, "The notion that Jesus was fathered by the Holy Spirit and born of a virgin derives from the reinterpretation which was being given, indeed which had to be given, to the title 'son of God' at the moment when Hellenistic Jewish Christianity was making Jesus as Son of God at home in a Hellenistic environment" (*Virgin Birth? The Real Story of Mary and Her Son Jesus*, trans. John Bowden [Harrisburg, PA: Trinity, 1998], 75–76). Most arguments of this sort *imply* genetic links rather than trace them directly. Robert Funk, for instance, states, "Ancient literature abounds with infancy narratives about famous men. These narratives characteristically underscore in various ways how the divine, or the gods, participated in the generation and protection of these heroes" ("Birth and Infancy Stories," in *The Acts of Jesus: The Search for the Authentic Deeds of Jesus* [New York: HarperSanFrancisco, 1998]), 501–2. On 497–507, he includes the birth stories of Alexander the Great, Apollonius of Tyana, and Plato as self-evident parallels to the divine birth of Jesus.

4. Examples of Greco-Roman divine conceptions are catalogued and briefly discussed in Pfleiderer, *The Early Christian Conception*, 33–35; and Knox, *Hellenistic Elements*, 22–25. Beverly Ann Bow discusses at length miraculous births in the Jewish tradition ("The Story of Jesus' Birth: A Pagan and Jewish Affair," PhD diss., University of Iowa, 1995], 19–330).

5. Even striking phrases such as, "today I have begotten you" (Ps. 2:7) and "from the womb before the morning star I begot you" (Ps. 109:3, LXX) have not broken this consensus.

critics of Christianity—have deduced that early Christians must have borrowed a tradition of divine birth from Greco-Roman sources, either as a result of their own gradual hellenization or in a secondary attempt to render the gospel persuasive to gentiles.

In response, Christian apologists throughout the ages have come armed with ways to present Jesus' divine conception as unique. One apologetic strategy uses Judaism as a buffer to protect Jesus' earliest birth accounts from the "pagan" environment. In a classic essay, for instance, Martin Dibelius argued that divine conception through pneuma (or "spirit") (Luke 1:35) was a "theologoumenon" (i.e., a theological statement) already present in "hellenistic Judaism" (as seen in Philo and Paul).[6] Dibelius then contrasted a *Jewish* theologoumenon with a "*pagan*" "myth."[7] According to this great form critic, Luke's story of Jesus' divine conception does not borrow from "pagan" myth, but simply adapts an essentially Jewish idea (the "*hellenistic-*Jewish" now being muted).[8] Dibelius was willing to grant that the notion of a god's congress with a virgin probably stemmed from Egyptian royal mythology[9] but was careful to emphasize that this "Egyptian theology" (now no longer a "myth") was already integrated into Hellenistic Judaism.[10] Thus Luke did not need to go outside Judaism to speak of Jesus' divine conception.

The political implications of Dibelius's attempt to save divine conception for Judaism become clear later. When he traces out the development of divine conception in Christianity, he includes a "Fall" myth. Later Christian traditions of Jesus' divine conception, that is, succumb to borrowing from "pagan" mentality.[11] Such borrowing is illustrated by later texts that speak of the *manner* of Jesus' conception. Sometimes the "Word" enters Mary's womb. In other cases, an angel enters her—or even Christ in the form of an angel. The

---

6. Dibelius, "Jungfrauensohn und Krippenkind. Untersuchungen zur Geburtsgeschichte Jesu im Lukas-Evangelium," in *Botschaft und Geschichte: Gesammelte Aufsätze von Martin Dibelius* [Tübingen: Mohr Siebeck, 1932], 1.33. In his curt formulation: "*aus der Vorstellung wurde die Legende*" (39). Analogies for this process (i.e., the development of a legend from a theologoumenon) include the actual description of Jesus' resurrection (first found in the *Gos. Pet.*) expanded from bare statements (e.g., "He is risen!"), as well as the harrowing of hell—mentioned in 1 Pet. 4:6—growing into colorful legends in the second century (36–38).

7. Ibid., 35, 39.

8. Ibid., 35.

9. Ibid., 41, n. 66.

10. Ibid., 41–42.

11. Dibelius briefly discusses the putatively paganized birth traditions of *Prot. Jas.* 11.2, *Ascen. Isa.* 11:1-16; *Odes Sol.* 19.8; *Sib. Or.* 8.456-79, as well as passages from the *Ep. Apos.*, *Pist. Soph.*, and *Ps.-Matt.* (ibid., 47–52).

penetration of Mary by a divine entity (however that is "conceived") indicates, for Dibelius, a mythical mindset. The "ecclesiasticizing" (*Verkirchlichung*) of this myth, Dibelius says, occurred in the fourth century when it was taught that Mary conceived through her ear.[12]

The essentially apologetic dichotomy of "myth" versus "theology" colors Dibelius's conclusion. Although later Christian tradition was infected with myth, the "chaste beauty" of the Lucan legend (derived from a Jewish theologoumenon) is never made into a "pagan" "mythologoumenon."[13] Indeed, Dibelius concluded that there are no "pagan" elements in Luke 1:26-38 at all. It remains a virgin account, just like Mary herself.[14]

To leap to a more recent example of Judaism used as a "buffer" to protect Christianity from "paganism," I turn to N. T. Wright. Although an unlikely bedfellow with Dibelius, Wright's apologetic attempt to maintain the stiff competition of "Jewish" versus "pagan" tradition remains similar. The "setting" of the divine birth in both Matthew and Luke is "Jewish," as indicated by the "verbal and narratival allusions to and echoes of the Septuagint."[15] Luke has a "very Jewish point," namely that Christ's birth challenges "pagan" power (in this case, Caesar). "This fits," Wright says, "with Luke's whole emphasis: the (very Jewish) gospel is for the whole world, of which Jesus is now the Lord."[16] At the same time, Wright admits that there is nothing in Judaism to suggest a virgin birth—for the Messiah or anyone else.[17] "The only conceivable parallels are

---

12. Ibid., 52. For conception through the ear, see Katarzyna Urbaniak-Walczak, *Die conceptio per aurem: Untersuchungen zum Marienbild in Ägypten unter besonderer Berücksichtigung der Malereien in El-Bagawat* (Altenberge: Oros, 1992).

13. Dibelius, "Jungfrauensohn und Krippenkind," 52.

14. Dibelius had to admit that the tradition in which the father abstains from sex to guarantee the truly divine origin of the child (cf. Diog. Laert. *Vit. Philosoph.* 3.2; Plut., *Alex.* 2.2) is a pagan motif with no Jewish intermediary. But this motif is only found in Matthew (1:25).

15. Marcus Borg and N. T. Wright, *The Meaning of Jesus: Two Visions* (New York: HarperSanFrancisco, 1999), 174. A similar argument was made a century ago by G. H. Box, "Gospel Narratives of the Nativity and the Alleged Influence of Heathen Ideas," *ZNW* 6 (1905): 80–101.

16. Ibid., 175.

17. Jews did apparently know of the divine begetting of the Messiah (1QSa 2:11-12, based on Ps. 2:7), but this begetting is usually taken in a figurative sense, and does not occur through a virgin. See Otto Michel and Otto Betz, "Von Gott gezeugt," in *Judentum, Urchristentum, Kirche: Festschrift für Joachim Jeremias*, ed. Walther Eltester [Berlin: Alfred Töpelmann, 1964], 3–23. According to Gerhard Delling, "The idea of divine generation seems to be incompatible with the OT belief in God" ("παρθένος," *TDNT* 5:832). More recently Robert Menzies has commented that the creative spirit in Luke 1:35 is "quite uncommon to the Jewish thought-world of Luke's day" (*The Development of Early Christian Pneumatology with Special Reference to Luke-Acts* (Sheffield: Sheffield Academic, 1991), 122.

pagan ones." But there cannot be any genetic relation between these "pagan" parallels and Luke's account because Luke's story is so "fiercely Jewish."[18]

Such attempts to isolate Luke's narrative of divine conception from the larger Mediterranean culture remain unconvincing. Few scholars today are prepared to assert (with Dibelius) an entirely Jewish (even if "hellenistic" Jewish) origin for Luke's account of divine conception.[19] Paul's statement that Isaac was born according to spirit (κατὰ πνεῦμα, Gal. 4:29) does not indicate that he was born without a human father. Philo's statement that God impregnated the matriarchs through "the divine seeds" (τὰ θεῖα σπέρματα) (Cher. 46) is an allegory about God fertilizing the soul with the seed of blessedness (σπέρμα . . . εὐδαιμονίας) (Cher. 49). The product is not a child, but virtues (ἀρεταί)—virtues that the matriarchs themselves represent. The notion that Philo knew a Jewish tradition of literal divine conception that he subsequently allegorized has the convincing power of what it is—speculation. There is, it seems, no "hellenistic Jewish" precedent for Jesus' divine conception.

Even fewer scholars are prepared to take Wright's path and depict "Jewish" and "pagan" in such openly oppositional ways. Such language perpetuates the old (and mistaken) Judaism/Hellenism divide, and is no longer acceptable in mainstream scholarship. That said, many scholars are content to perpetuate a binary between "Judaism" and "Hellenism," provided that it is done in more circumspect and clandestine ways. One such way is to deny that there is any "precise parallel" between Jewish and Mediterranean stories of divine conception. The great Roman Catholic scholar Raymond Brown speaks for many when he states that "there is no clear example of *virginal* conception in world or pagan religions [*sic*] that plausibly could have given first-century Jewish Christians the idea of the virginal conception of Jesus."[20] In this way, Christian scholars can still secure the uniqueness (thus revelatory quality, thus

---

18. Borg and Wright, *Meaning of Jesus*, 176.

19. Raymond Brown (among others) rightly notes that Isa. 7:14 was interpreted with reference to the virginal conception only after this tradition had become known (*The Birth of the Messiah: A Commentary on the Infancy Narratives in Matthew and Luke* [Garden City, NJ: Doubleday, 1977], 524). Cf. his *The Virginal Conception and Bodily Resurrection of Jesus* (New York: Paulist, 1973), 15–16, 63.

20. Brown, *Birth of the Messiah*, 523; cf. Brown, *Virginal Conception*, 65. Similar conclusions in Alphons Steinmann, *Die Jungfrauengeburt und die vergleichende Religionsgeschichte* (Paderborn: Ferdinand Schöningh, 1919), 33; C. E. B. Cranfield, "Some Reflections on the Subject of the Virgin Birth," *SJT* 41 (1988): 177–89 (181); Robert Gromacki, *The Virgin Birth: A Biblical Study of the Deity of Jesus Christ*, 2nd ed. (Grand Rapids, MI: Kregal, 2002), 210–215. The phrasing of Hasenfuss is worth quoting: "Comparative History of Religions has not compared anything as dignified (*Ebenbürtiges*) as the birth of the Lord from divine pneuma through the virgin mother Mary" ("Jungfrauengeburt," 22).

truth) of Christian belief. Indeed, the presumed uniqueness of the Christian story of divine conception threatens to undermine comparison as such.

But Brown's statement that "there is no exact parallel" between Jesus' divine conception and that of other heroes and gods in the ancient Mediterranean—though often repeated—is founded (it seems to me) on a misunderstanding of the very nature of comparison.[21] The first rule of comparison is that it *does not assert identity*. As a result, there is *never* an "*exact*" parallel.[22] Difference will always remain in comparison if the comparison is going to work (and if it is going to be interesting). Consequently, we need not search for an "exact parallel" between divine birth stories to speak of their similarities due to common cultural conceptions.

In the theologically charged arena of comparative religions, one needs to forsake both the search for genetic links (many of which are banal and at any rate historically impossible to prove) as well as the religiously motivated attempt to sever those links. As some have pointed out, it is not that the author of Luke *borrowed* from the stories of Perseus, Heracles, or Minos to present his idea of divine conception. Stories of divine conception were cultural common coin in the ancient Mediterranean world and could be imagined in philosophically and theologically sophisticated ways.[23]

Luke, no unsophisticated literary artist, expressed the "mechanics" of divine birth in subtle and theologically sensitive language. In the passage commonly known as the "Annunciation" (Luke 1:26-38), Gabriel announces to Mary that she will have a son. Surprisingly, the young (but betrothed!) girl asks a

---

21. Brown, *Virginal Conception*, 62.

22. I recognize that there is some ambiguity in Brown's notion of "exact parallel." Although it need not mean "identical" it still suggests a kind of similitude that borders on equivalence. It seems to me that Brown used the ambiguity of his expression to good rhetorical effect.

23. Dieter Zeller also denies any Christian borrowing from Greek tales, since both Jews and "cultured pagans" resisted "sexually colored myths." Nevertheless Luke wrote in a "horizon of thought" (*Denkhorizont*), that was both "Jewish-Christian and hellenistic." Yet only the "hellenistic" side of this *Denkhorizont*, for Zeller, appeals to a divine conception ("Religionsgeschichtliche Erwägungen zum 'Sohn Gottes' in den Kindheitsgeschichten," in *Neues Testament und hellenistische Umwelt*, Bonner Biblische Beiträge 150 [Hamburg: Philo, 2006], 94). For similar formulations, see Robert Miller, *Born Divine: The Births of Jesus & Other Sons of God* (Santa Rosa, CA: Polebridge, 2003), 134, cf. 238–39; Andrew Welburn, *Myth of the Nativity: The Virgin Birth Re-examined* (Edinburgh: Floris Books, 2006), 148; Heikki Räisänen, "Begotten by the Holy Spirit," in *Sacred Marriages: The Divine-Human Sexual Metaphor from Sumer to Early Christianity*, ed. Martti Nissinen and Risto Uro [Winona Lake, IN: Eisenbrauns, 2008], 333); Andrew T. Lincoln, "'Born of the Virgin Mary': Creedal Affirmation and Critical Reading," in *Christology and Scripture: Interdisciplinary Perspectives*, ed. Lincoln and Angus Paddison (London: T&T Clark, 2007), 94–95.

rather awkward question: "How will this be—since I do not know a man?" (1:34).[24] Such a question puts a nervous smile on the face of the reader since it could easily function as an innocent lead-in to a discourse on divine sex education. Gabriel is in a delicate situation, since he is now forced to explain to an adolescent girl exactly where divine babies come from. Thankfully, Luke provides him with a tactful and poetically pleasing response:

> holy spirit (πνεῦμα ἅγιον) will come upon you (ἐπελεύσεται ἐπὶ σὲ), and power of the Most High (δύναμις ὑψίστου) will overshadow you (ἐπισκιάσει σοι)—and so (διὸ καὶ) the child to be born will be called holy (ἅγιον), son of god (υἱὸς θεοῦ). (Luke 1:35)

Such delicate and indeterminate theological language allowed Luke to present his narrative of Jesus' divine birth as both plausible and reliable history, and thus to distance himself from stories of sexual divine conception that he deemed mythical (with the sense of *untrue*) and unworthy of Yahweh.[25]

Since the beginning, Christian apologists and conservative commentators have pointed out the non-sexual nature of conception in Luke.[26] As it turns out, Luke shared with philosophers of his day a theological presupposition that still remains prevalent: God (or the gods) do not have sex (since sex involves passion and passion is perceived to be an evil). Celsus, as we have seen, bases this point on a Platonic maxim: "by nature, God does not love [or feel sexual attraction for] a perishable body" (οὐ φεφυκὼς ἐρᾶν φθαρτοῦ σώματος) (*Cels.* 1.39). When in other ancient stories the gods are depicted as enjoying sexual

---

24. On the narrative logic of this question, see Jane Schaberg, *The Illegitimacy of Jesus: A Feminist Theological Interpretation of the Infancy Narratives*, expanded ed. (Sheffield: Sheffield Phoenix, 2006), 84–85; David T. Landry, "Narrative Logic in the Annunciation to Mary (Luke 1:26-38)," *JBL* 114 (1995): 65–79.

25. To be sure, Yahweh in Luke's account does make overtures (via a messenger) to a young, nubile, virgin woman. Nevertheless Mary's sexual ripeness is not at issue as in Greek divine birth traditions (see further Giulia Sissa, *Greek Virginity* [Cambridge, MA: Harvard University Press, 1990]). Mary the virgin is Mary chaste and pure (a fact especially emphasized later in the *Prot. Jas.*) (see further Mary Foskett, *A Virgin Conceived: Mary and Classical Representations of Virginity* [Bloomington: Indiana University Press, 2002], 141–64, esp. 162–64). She is a clean vessel, safe for interaction with divine pneuma (cf. Philo, *Cher.* 49). See further Todd Klutz, "The Value of Being Virginal: Mary and Anna in the Lukan Infancy Prologue," in *The Birth of Jesus: Biblical and Theological Reflections*, ed. George J. Brooke (Edinburgh: T&T Clark, 2000), 71–88 (80). Mary's humility, low social status, and obedience also distinguish her from the typically noble and privileged women who bear divine children in Greek stories.

26. Brown, *Virginal Conception*, 62; Schweitzer, "πνεῦμα," *TDNT* 6:397; Joseph A. Fitzmyer "Virginal Conception of Jesus in the New Testament," *TS* 34 (1973): 541–75 (565–66, n. 84).

intercourse, such accounts are perceived to take on a legendary, mythical aura. Christian apologists throughout the ages have taken it upon themselves to expose these mythical elements with relish.

According to Justin Martyr, for instance, the Word, the "first offspring of god" (πρῶτον γέννημα τοῦ θεοῦ), was born "without sexual union" (ἄνευ ἐπιμιξίας) (1 Apol. 21), "not through intercourse (οὐ διὰ συνουσίας) but through power (διὰ δυνάμεως)" (§33). A venerable line of patristic and medieval commentators have beat this same drum, and it suffices to fast-forward to the modern period. Writing in 1919, Alphons Steinmann summed up the prevailing sentiment among theologians and theological exegetes of his time:

> Although holy Scripture expressly allows Christ's divine origin and through this shows that he is in no way inferior to the heroes and famous men of the pagans (der Heiden), still it anxiously ensures that this splendor not be darkened by any blemish (Makel). One reads not of amatory adventures (galanten Abenteuern), of the disgraceful amours of a god (schimpflichem Liebesglühen), of sensual lusts (sinnlichen Lüsten), or of tasteless transformations into a bull, a dragon, a snake, a shower of gold, et sim. Rather, everything is connected to the Spirit of God, to the holy and chaste (keuschen) Spirit. In general, pagan miraculous births have to do with a perhaps miraculous, but always a physical (physische) begetting. The father of the hero is not removed but replaced by a god.[27]

Although less colorfully expressed, Brown essentially emphasizes the same point: "These [extrabiblical] 'parallels' consistently involve a type of hieros gamos where a divine male, in human or other form, impregnates a woman, either through normal sexual intercourse or through some substitute form of penetration."[28] Thus in one fell swoop, Brown eliminates as parallels not only Zeus bedding with Semele, but also the famous golden drops impregnating Danaë.[29]

---

27. Steinmann in Brosch and Hasenfuss Jungfrauengeburt, 32–33, emphasis in original. Steinmann concludes, "Paganism was lost in sensual notions, in mythological concepts, in vague speculations about the wandering of souls or purely political expectations of a deliverer, which support no comparison with the presentation of the Gospels" (41).

28. Brown, Birth of the Messiah, 523. Brown's distinctive language reappears in the collaborative study Mary in the New Testament, ed. Raymond Brown (Philadelphia: Fortress Press, 1978), 121.

29. Divine beings having sex with mortal women is, interestingly, part of Jewish lore (cf. Gen. 6:1-4). The Testament of Reuben makes clear that the "sons of god" (here called "Watchers") "were transformed

Luke's theologically tactful avoidance of sexual language, however, does not remove him from his culture's presuppositions about divine conception. The Platonist philosopher and biographer Plutarch (c. 50–120 CE), Luke's contemporary, uses like language and a similar pattern of thought when he speaks of divine conception (*Quaest. conv.* 717e-718b; *Numa* 4).[30] Careful comparison with Plutarch will indicate, I believe, that Luke was thoroughly in step with the culture of other sensitive literary men of his day who eschewed the crass anthropomorphism of a divine-human sexual encounter in an attempt to construct a historically and theologically plausible account of divine conception.

COMPARISON WITH PLUTARCH

In Plutarch's *Table Talk*, Tyndares the Lacedaemonian remarks that begetting (τὸ γεννῶν) seems opposed to divine incorruptibility (τῷ ἀφθάρτῳ) (8.1 [= *Mor.* 717e-f]) because it involves change (μεταβολή) and passion (πάθος) in God. This logic goes back to Plato's famous models (τύποι) for theology, the first of which being that God is good, and second, that God does not change (*Resp.* 380d-381e). Tyndares goes on to make a remark derived from Plato's *Timaeus*: "I take courage when I hear Plato himself [say concerning] the father and maker of the world (κόσμου) and other born beings (καὶ τῶν ἄλλων γεννητῶν)—whom he calls the unborn and eternal God—[that beings born of God] do not come to be through seed (οὐ διὰ σπέρματος) surely, but by another power of god (ἄλλη δὲ δυνάμει τοῦ θεοῦ), who engendered (ἐντεκόντος) in matter the productive principle [or generative beginning] (γόνιμον ἀρχήν) by which it [the world and the things made in it] suffered passion and changed" (8.1 [*Mor.* 718a]).[31]

The theological language is tactful and careful—and for good reason. In his treatise to an unlearned prince (*Princ. inerud.* 5) Plutarch says, "For it is neither probable nor fitting that God is, as some philosophers [i.e., the Stoics] say, mingled with matter." For Plutarch, as for Celsus, the imperishable God does not love a perishable body and cannot be mixed with it. Thus it is not God who

---

into human males" and appeared to women who were already married (5:5-6). For more on this episode, see John J. Collins, "The Sons of God and the Daughters of Men," in *Sacred Marriages*, 259–274.

30. Plutarch's *Table Talk* was composed between 99–116 ce. It was during this time also that Plutarch was writing his *Lives*. The historical setting of the *Table Talk*, however, is earlier—going as far back as the 60s CE (Plutarch's student days) (Frieda Klotz and Katerina Oikonomopoulou, eds., *The Philosopher's Banquet: Plutarch's* Table Talk *in the Intellectual Culture of the Roman Empire* [Oxford: Oxford University Press, 2011], 4).

31. My translation. Translations of Plutarch and Luke that follow, unless otherwise noted, are my own.

directly interacts with matter, but God's power. God's power—a term used to defer God's (sexual) presence—is made the means of his generative activity.

Plutarch illustrates the generative activity of this "other power of God" (ἄλλῃ δυνάμει τοῦ θεοῦ) by a humorous quote from Sophocles: "the crisscrossing of the winds (κἀνέμων διέξοδοι) escapes the notice of the hen, except when she lets fall a chick (παρῇ τόκος)!" The idea here is that the hen is not made pregnant by male seed but by a more subtle power transmitted in or by the winds.[32] The word for "wind" that Plutarch uses is ἄνεμος, whereas in his *Life of Numa*, he uses the more flexible term πνεῦμα ("wind"/"breath" /"spirit"). The linguistic overlap between Luke and Plutarch—both of whom use δύναμις and πνεῦμα in their accounts of divine conception—invites a closer investigation of their conceptual similarity.[33]

THE LIFE OF NUMA

In the fourth chapter of his *Life of Numa*,[34] Plutarch passes on the common tradition that Numa (Rome's second king and lawgiver) had a "divine marriage" (γάμων θείων) with the nymph (i.e., lesser goddess) Egeria, and from her learned divine laws and rites (τὰ θεῖα) (4.1-3).[35] Although the language of "divine marriage" could easily excite the vituperative outcry of a parallel-buster ("The skirts are lifted! Behold *hieros gamos*!") it is important to see how Plutarch treats this detail. Although as a *historical writer*, he feels obliged to pass on this Roman tradition, Plutarch the late first-century *Platonist* and *man of learning* presents a reaction of mild disgust.[36] Although he finds it reasonable that God (τὸν θεόν) loves human beings (φιλάνθρωπον), and especially joins company

32. Cf. Arist., *Hist. an.* 541a27; 560b14; Virg., *Georg.* 3.274-75; Varro, *Rust.* 2.1.19; Pliny, *Nat.* 2.116; 10.102, 166; Ael. *Nat. an.* 17.15; Lact., *Inst.* 4.12.2. The idea is scoffed at in Lucian, *Tox.* 38; *Vera hist.* 1.22. See further Conway Zirkle, "Animals Impregnated by the Wind," *Isis* 25 (1936): 95–130.

33. Most commentators merely cite Plutarch's *Table Talk* as an apparent parallel to Luke's account of divine conception, with no discussion. An exception is Hans Dieter Betz, "Credibility and Credulity in Plutarch's Life of Numa Pompilius," in *Reading Religions in the Ancient World: Essays Presented to Robert McQueen Grant on his 90th Birthday*, ed. David Aune and Robin Darling Young (Leiden: Brill, 2007), 52–54. Compare also Talbert, "Jesus' Birth in Luke and the Nature of Religious Language," in *Reading Luke-Acts in its Mediterranean Milieu* (Leiden: Brill, 2003), 79–90 (esp. 88).

34. For a general introduction to the *Life of Numa*, see Robert Lamberton, Plutarch (New Haven, CT: Yale University Press, 2001), 87–91.

35. For the divinity and cult of nymphs, see *OCD*[4], "Nymphs," 1027.

36. In *The Fortune of the Romans*, Plutarch calls the story of Numa's association with Egeria "rather mythical" (μυθωδέστερον), and argues that it is more likely that Numa had Good Fortune (personified: ἀγαθή Τύχη; non-personified: εὐτυχία) as his true companion, counselor, and colleague (§9 [*Mor.* 321b-322c]).

with people who are good (ἀγαθός), religiously correct (ὅσιος), and temperate (σώφρονος), he cringes to think that "a god and daimon" would engage in fellowship and gratification (κοινωνία καὶ χάρις) with a human body, however lovely.[37] Consequently, Plutarch—as a man sensitive to the symbolic truth of ancient tradition—tries to find a way to hold together both divine-human love, and proper respect (εὐσέβεια) for a transcendent deity.

He turns to Egyptian theology. The "Egyptians," he says, "not unpersuasively assume this distinction: that *with a woman* (γυναικὶ μέν), it is not impossible for a pneuma of a God (πνεῦμα . . . θεοῦ) to draw near (πλησιάσαι) and engender (ἐντεκεῖν) certain principles of generation (ἀρχὰς γενέσεως), but *with a man* (ἀνδρὶ δέ), there is no mingling with a god (σύμμιξις πρὸς θεὸν) nor bodily association (ὁμιλία σώματος)" (*Num* 4.4).

The best way to construe this text is to let Plutarch interpret Plutarch. "A God's pneuma" (πνεῦμα . . . θεοῦ) in the *Life of Numa* is analogous to the "other power of God" mentioned in *Table Talk*. The results of power and pneuma, we note, are the same: the engendering (ἐντίκτω—the verb used in both *Quaest. conv.* 718a and *Num.* 4.4) of "principles of generation" (ἀρχὰς γενέσεως, *Num.* 4.4), or a productive principle (γόνιμον ἀρχήν, *Quaest. conv.* 718a). Pneuma and power are evidently linked for Plutarch; they are, furthermore, sophisticated terms that do not imply a sexual encounter.

We must understand why Plutarch says that—according to Egyptian theology—divine pneuma can interact with a woman but *not with a man*. It is important for Plutarch to be clear on this point, because his comments appear in a biography of Numa—a *man* who (according to tradition) had a peculiar relation with a goddess. To help explain this passage, we can again draw on *Table Talk* as an illuminating parallel discussion. In *Table Talk* 718b, the Egyptians are said generally to "allow association (ὁμιλίαν) with a mortal woman and a male god [to produce divine conception]. On the contrary, they would not think that a mortal *male* could impart to a female divinity the principle of birth and pregnancy, because they posit (τίθεσθαι) that the substances (τὰς οὐσίας) of the gods consist of air (ἀέρι) and breaths (πνεύμασιν), and of currents of heat and moisture."[38]

For Egyptians, then, pneuma—called the "pneuma of god (θεοῦ)" in *Numa* 4.4 —is a kind of divine "stuff" (οὐσία) associated with the basic elements of air, heat, and moisture. In his *On Isis and Osiris*, Plutarch observes that for

---

37. Brown was thus wrong to say that in *Numa* 4, Plutarch "argues . . . that a man ought to be able *to have intercourse* with a goddess" (*Virginal Conception*, 62, n. 104, emphasis his).

38. The word οὐσίας is a correction for the MS reading θυσίας ("sacrifices").

Egyptians, Zeus-Amon himself is identified with πνεῦμα (365d).[39] It is unclear exactly how much of this Egyptian theology has undergone an *interpretatio Graeca*. The identity between the high God and pneuma—as well as the association of pneuma with fire and air—bears a significant resemblance to Stoic theology. According to Chrysippus, for example, the essence of God (ἡ τοῦ θεοῦ οὐσία) is an intelligent and fiery pneuma (πνεῦμα νοερὸν καὶ πυρῶδες) (*SVF* 2.1009). According to Alexander of Aphrodisias, the Stoics understand God to be "an intelligent and eternal pneuma" (*Mixt.* 224.32-225.4= *SVF* 2.310). Pneuma, in other words, embodies the reality of God (who for Stoics, is also called "Logos" and "Zeus"), as it is spread throughout the universe.

Whatever the exact relation between Stoic and Egyptian theology, however, the point is relatively clear: pneuma can fertilize flesh, but flesh cannot impregnate pneuma. Divine reality (the active principle) can make humans bear children (in particular, "passive" human females), but humans (even if "active" human males) cannot make a god (or rather goddess) conceive.[40] This is a basic principle of theological "physics" as it were: divine pneuma can make a woman pregnant, but human men cannot return the favor! Evidently, then, the Egyptians—and Plutarch—would consider the stories of Demeter and Iasion (Hom., *Od.* 5.125-28; Hes., *Theog.* 969-70), Anchises and Aphrodite (*Hom. Hymn Aphr.* 74-167), as well as Eos and Tithonus (*Hom. Hymn Aphr.* 218-25) untrue. "With a man," Plutarch apparently concedes to the Egyptians, "there is no mingling with god (σύμμιξις πρὸς θεὸν) nor bodily association (ὁμιλία σώματος)." This assertion should not be taken to imply that Plutarch accepts ordinary bodily sex (σύμμιξις) with a *male* god and a *female* human. He has already made clear that any "drawing near" (πλησιάζω) between god and woman is mediated through (a neuter) pneuma. The pneuma of God (πνεῦμα θεοῦ), as we see in *Numa* 4.4, draws near to engender the principles of generation.

---

39. Δία μὲν γὰρ Αἰγύπτιοι τὸ πνεῦμα καλοῦσιν. Cf. Diod. Sic., *Bibl.* 1.12.2: "[The Egyptians] call vital breath (πνεῦμα) 'Zeus' (Δία)." For further remarks on Egyptian theology, see Andrew Welburn, *Myth of the Nativity*, 145.

40. In *Quaest. conv.* 718a, Plutarch writes that the power of God engenders the generative principle in *matter* (ὕλη), which the Stoics consider to be a passive principle, generally associated with the female. See A. A. Long, *Hellenistic Philosophy: Stoics, Epicureans, Sceptics*, 2nd ed. (Berkeley: University of California, 1986), 153–56. According to ancient medical science, women's bodies were more "porous" and thus more penetrable than men's bodies, making them more susceptible to the entrance and effects of πνεῦμα (Dale Martin, *The Corinthian Body* [New Haven, CT: Yale University Press, 1995], 242). On ancient views of conception, see Craffert, *Life of a Galilean Shaman*, 368–77.

To be sure, pneumatic proximity does not signify a completely *incorporeal* liaison, since πνεῦμα in the first century was not usually taken to refer to an incorporeal entity (as seen for instance among the Stoics).[41] Nevertheless, the "drawing near" of pneuma to a woman is entirely non-anthropomorphic. The pneuma, if a kind of body, is not a *human* body. When Plutarch speaks of a pneuma interacting with a woman, he is not assuming that a god in a male body has sex with a female.

Nonetheless, in *Numa* 4 Plutarch does not want the Egyptian prohibition of all σύμμιξις between a *male* and a divinity to mean that there is no *possibility* of love between a god and men in general. "To the contrary, it would be fitting for there to be love (φιλίαν) in a god for a human being (πρὸς ἄνθρωπον), as well as what is called eros (ἔρωτα)—which is based on this (i.e., φιλία)." The eros spoken of here does not lead to bodily sex but to moral virtue. It is, as Plutarch says, naturally engendered for the care of human character and virtue (ἤθους καὶ ἀρετῆς) (4.4).

It is important to understand the Platonic background of what we might call Plutarch's "moral eros." In Plato's *Symposium*, Socrates defines eros in this way: "eros (ὁ ἔρως) is wanting to possess the good forever" (τοῦ τὸ ἀγαθὸν αὑτῷ εἶναι ἀεί) (206a11-12). The action of lovers is "engendering in beauty" (τόκος ἐν καλῷ) (206b7-8). On the level of the body, "engendering" (τόκος) is the union (συνουσία) of a man and a woman (206c5-6). But other people conceive in their *soul*, and they beget "wisdom and the rest of virtue" (φρόνησίν τε καὶ τὴν ἄλλην ἀρετήν) (209a3-4). The most beautiful part of wisdom "deals with the proper ordering of cities and households" (ἡ περὶ τὰ τῶν πόλεών τε καὶ οἰκήσεων διακόσμησις) and is called "moderation and justice" (σωφροσύνη τε καὶ δικαιοσύνη) (a6-8).[42] The engendering of these virtues occurs in the soul. When a young man meets a soul that is "beautiful and noble and well-formed," he begins to teem with "ideas and arguments about virtue" (209c; cf. *Phaedr.* 246e-253c). Those who beget virtue beget children who are not mortal but immortal. Plato specifically singles out lawgivers like Lycurgus and Solon as those who have created the very constitutions in which virtue can be fostered and operate (*Symp.* 209d-e). These are the sorts of figures who have

---

41. A point often made by Troels Engberg-Pedersen. See, for example, his *Cosmology and the Self: The Material Spirit* (Oxford: Oxford University Press, 2010), 8–74.

42. According to Plato, someone can be pregnant with these virtues while being ἤθεος (209b1). This word means "an unmarried youth." In several passages it is paired with πάρθενος ("virgin"; see Hom., *Il.* 22.127; Herod., *Hist.* 3.48, cf. Plut., *Thes.*15.1).

seen truly divine Beauty, and thus beget true virtue (ἀρετὴν ἀληθῆ). It is this kind of man who is loved by God (θεοφιλής) (212a-b).

In tune with this moral vision of divine-human eros, Plutarch explains tales of gods loving particular men. Phorbas, Hyacinthus, and Admetus were said to be the beloveds (ἐρωμένους) of Apollo (Num 4.5).[43] One could take this in a sexual sense. Plutarch, however—as a Platonist and sympathetic student of Greek tradition—spiritualizes the eros. Those loved by Apollo are taught Apollo's special virtue: poetry and music.[44] This leads Plutarch to speak of other examples of this type: Pan loved the songs of Pindar, Asclepius loved the tragedian Sophocles, and the poet Hesiod dallied with the Muses (Num 4.6).[45] These were certainly not sexual relationships. What this eros produced was not children but immortal poems.

But Plutarch is not satisfied with poets. If gods dallied with poets to produce poems, he asks, should we disbelieve that "the divine (τὸ δαιμόνιον) was in the habit of conversing to the same effect with Zaleucus, Minos, Zoroaster, Numa and Lycurgus who piloted kingdoms and established constitutions (βασιλείας κυβερνῶσι καὶ πολιτείας διακοσμοῦσιν)?" (Num 4.7).[46] The phraseology here is reminiscent of Plato's Symposium (209a6-7), where Plato says that the most beautiful part of wisdom "deals with the proper ordering of cities and households" (ἡ περὶ τὰ τῶν πόλεών τε καὶ οἰκήσεων διακόσμησις) (a6-8), and lists the lawgivers Lycurgus and Solon as examples (209d-e). Lycurgus (the Spartan lawgiver) is an important figure for Plutarch, since he is the parallel with Numa in this set of Plutarch's Parallel Lives. For both Plato and Plutarch, these ancient lawgivers are as divine as any human could hope to be. These are the men specially loved by God, and so became pregnant with divine ideas. But these heroes were pregnant with far more than poems; they bore immortal virtue. As legislators, they formed the characters of whole nations that came after them.

To say that such men had erotic relations with God(s) does not—for Plutarch at least—imply anything about bodily sex. Rather it is a way of

---

43. The mention of Apollo is important to Plutarch because of the tradition of Plato's birth from Apollo. See below.

44. In Betz's interpretation of Plutarch, "the Delphic Apollo is to be regarded as the highest god of all, as intellect (νοῦς), law and world order (λόγος, νόμος). Thus, Apollo is also the ultimate guardian of truth, including both the oracle of the Pythia and all scientific enterprise" ("Credibility," 43). For Apollo the one and indivisible god, see Plut., E Delph. 393b-d.

45. Cf. Hes., Theog. 29-33, esp. 31-32: "they [the Muses] breathed into me (ἐνέπνευσαν δέ μοι) divine song."

46. For Zaleucus, lawgiver of Italian Locri Epizephyrii, see OCD⁴, "Zaleucus,"1586.

pointing out the source of their virtue. Numa and Lycurgus did not produce virtue out of their own means or ability. Virtue is divine and had to come from a divine source. So, to use the metaphor of Plato in the *Symposium*, these lawgivers were made pregnant by gods. They were made pregnant not in their bodies, but in their souls. What they conceived was, as Plutarch makes clear, the finest teaching (διδασκαλία), and exhortation toward the best things for humankind (παραινέσει τῶν βελτίστων). These "best things," as we know from Plato's *Symposium*, are the virtues of moderation and justice.

In this way Plutarch bring us back to Numa who in his "divine marriage" with Egeria was said to produce τὰ θεῖα—namely, divine virtue, order, law, and ritual for the Roman people. Numa proves that gods can fruitfully interact with (in this case, male) humans to produce—not children—but a new and productive way of life. This is the result of a "divine marriage" (γάμος θεῖος) and "more sacred companionship" (σεμνότερα ὁμιλία), which Plutarch does not—as is clear from the context—conceive of in a sexual way. Indeed, Plutarch is savvy enough to know that the myth of Numa's "relationship" with Egeria probably arose as a political ploy to legitimate Numa's reforms among the Roman *plebs* (*Numa* 8.3-6). But even if there is a touch of political machination in the old tradition, Plutarch is sensitive to the deeper meaning of divine-human eros.

PNEUMATIC PREGNANCY

Let us return to the relationship of the πνεῦμα θεοῦ and women, specifically. As we saw in *Numa* 4.4, Plutarch concurs with the Egyptians that "with a woman, it is not impossible for a pneuma of god (πνεῦμα . . . θεοῦ) to draw near and engender (ἐντεκεῖν) certain principles of generation (ἀρχὰς γενέσεως)." The ambiguity of πνεῦμα (breath? wind? spirit?) is important, and it makes apt Plutarch's analogy of the wind impregnating the hen in *Table Talk* 718a. In both cases, the motion of air was felt to be a good analogy for how the divine comes into contact with a human female in order to make her pregnant.[47] Wind is invisible, but its effects are powerful. Even more importantly, wind is not anthropomorphic. It does not take any shape at all. Thus wind or breath cannot make contact with the human body in a crude, sexual way.[48]

---

47. According to Aeschylus, the family (γένος) of the Danaids—and specifically Epaphus, son of Ino—was generated "from the contact and in-breathing of Zeus" (ἐξ ἐπαφῆς κἀξ ἐπιπνοίας Διός) (*Suppl.* 16-18, 41-45). In this play, the whole land rejoices at Epaphus's birth with the cry: "This is indeed the son of life-begetting Zeus" (φυσιζόου γένος τόδε Ζηνός ἐστιν ἀληθῶς) (581–585). Cf. Aesch., *Prom.* 849-51, where Zeus, touching Io by his "hand, which produces no fear" (ἐπαφῶν ἀταρβεῖ χειρὶ) and "only touching her" (θιγὼν μόνον), causes her to give birth to "black Epaphus" (τέξεις κελαινὸν Ἔπαφον), who has his name from the manner in which Zeus engendered him (i.e., by touch, ἐπαφή).

As a result, pneuma's contact with a woman is a type of productive, yet non-sexual touch. The character Tyndares approaches this point later in *Table Talk*: "And I do not find it strange," he says, "if it is not by a physical approach (πλησιάζων), like a man's (ὥσπερ ἄνθρωπος), but by other forms—and *through* other forms—of contact and touch (ἀλλ' ἑτέραις τισὶν ἁφαῖς δι' ἑτέρων καὶ ψαύσεσι) that a god alters (τρέπει) mortal nature and makes it pregnant (ὑποπίμπλησι) with a more divine offspring (θειοτέρας γονῆς)" (718a). Here Plutarch uses the same verb (πλησιάζω) to speak of the "approach" of god to a woman as he does in *Numa* 4.4. This connection leads one to think that the "other forms of contact or touch" he mentions are specifically pneumatic. The pneuma of god makes contact with a woman not like a human being (ὥσπερ ἄνθρωπος), but like a breath or a wind subtly "caressing" the human body. If it is assumed that the pneuma enters the female body (which need not occur through the vagina), it is not unlike the subtle pneumatic penetration hinted at in Luke 1:35 (πνεῦμα ἅγιον ἐπελεύσεται ἐπὶ σέ).[49]

To sum up the matter so far: Plutarch's explanation (in both *Mor.* 717e–718b and *Numa* 4) of divine conception is a carefully worded and sophisticated account of how it can occur without saying anything impure or unworthy of God (i.e., that he changes form and suffers passion). Plutarch, an educated member of a literary elite, is clearly uncomfortable with crassly anthropomorphized gods having sex with mortal women. For him, such stories were not theologically correct and thus not credible. Speaking of divine conception in terms of pneuma was a philosophically respectable—because non-sexual—way of relating the mystery of divine conception in the late first century CE.

Speaking circumspectly about this topic is important to Plutarch because the comments in *Table Talk* are occasioned by the divine conception of no

---

48. Brown notes that, "To the ancients . . . the invisible movement of the wind had a divine and mysterious quality. In primitive thought the wind was described as God's breath" (*The Gospel According to John [i-xii]*, 2 vols., AB 29 [Garden City, NJ: Doubleday, 1966], 1:131). Cf. also Zirkle, "Animals Impregnated by the Wind," 126.

49. C. K. Barrett overstates the case when he says, "There is no suggestion of physical contact or action of any sort in the NT [birth narratives]" (*The Holy Spirit and the Gospel Tradition* [London: SPCK, 1966], 7). Neither are the actions of the holy pneuma necessarily "non-material" (8). According to Theodotus, a second-century Valentinian Christian, "the phrase, 'and the power of the Most High will overshadow you' [Luke 1:35b], manifests the shaping of God (τὴν μόρφωσιν . . . τοῦ θεοῦ), which he imprinted onto the body (ἣν ἐνετύπωσεν τῷ σώμα<τι>) of the Virgin" (Clement of Alexandria, *Exc. Theod.* 60). See further Sjef van Tilborg and Patrick Chatelion Counet, *Jesus' Appearances and Disappearances in Luke 24* (Leiden: Brill, 2000), 241–43.

less than Plato himself. The literary setting for the dinner conversation in this passage is in fact the celebration of Plato's birthday. Accordingly, Florus, another dialogue partner, remarks that "those who ascribe Plato's generation to Apollo say nothing, I think, that shames the god, since this man has been fashioned on our behalf through Socrates (just as another Chiron [the benevolent centaur]) as a doctor for greater passions and diseases" (717d-e).

According to a tradition circulated soon after Plato's death, Plato was thought to be son of the god Apollo.[50] Thus by a strange twist of fate, Platonists found themselves in a situation in which their founder explicitly taught that gods (1) do not have passions, and (2) do not change (Resp. 380d-381e), despite the fact that a god was involved with Perictione (Plato's mother) to produce the revered philosopher himself! In light of this situation, Plutarch must tread carefully if he is going to maintain Platonist tradition (which eschews myths of anthropomorphic gods having sex with human women) and simultaneously honor his divinely conceived master.[51]

Plutarch shows himself prudent in every way. He knew well the story that Zeus begot Alexander by impregnating his mother Olympias in the form of a snake (Plut., Alex. 2.5-3.2). This myth was more or less transferred to Augustus by Asclepias of Mendes (in Suet., Div. Aug. 94.4), who said that Augustus's divine father (like Plato's) was Apollo.[52] In contrast to these tales, Plutarch avoids any implication that Apollo appeared in anthropomorphic (or theriomorphic) form to have sex with Perictione.[53] He has Florus merely mention "the vision (ὄψεως) which is said (λεγομένης) to have appeared to Ariston, Plato's father, in his sleep, which spoke and forbade him to have intercourse with his wife, or to touch her, for ten months" (Quaest. conv. 717e). Plutarch expresses some

---

50. Diogenes Laertius traces the tradition to three written sources: Clearchus's Encomium on Plato, Anaxilides's On Philosophers, and Speusippus's Plato's Funeral Feast (Vit. Philosoph. 3.2). Speusippus was Plato's nephew and successor in the Academy. The evidence is collected and commented on in Alice Swift Riginos, Platonica: The Anecdotes Concerning the Life and Writings of Plato (Leiden: Brill, 1976), 9–17, 29–32. She concludes that "the main elements of Plato's Apollonian birth seem to go back to the first generation of Plato's students. The story, circulated by those seeking to glorify the philosopher, may have originated during Plato's own lifetime" (13).

51. Räisänen, apparently under the influence of Delling ("παρθένος," TDNT 5:830), states that Plutarch "rejects" the "tale of Plato's begetting by Apollo . . . because he finds it incompatible with the immutability of God" ("Begotten by the Holy Spirit," 334). The language here is too brusque. Plutarch does not reject the story of Plato's divine conception; he reinterprets it in a de-sexualized way suitable to his concept of God.

52. For this topos, see Robin S. Lorsch, "Augustus' Conception and the Heroic Tradition," Latomus 56 (1997): 790–99.

53. Pace Barrett, The Holy Spirit, 7.

distance from this myth by his guarded use of λεγομένης. Matthew was less hesitant about a similar dream vision, in which an angel informs Joseph that Jesus is God's offspring (born from holy pneuma).[54] Consequently, Joseph does not touch Mary until she has given birth (Matt. 1:20-25). In both cases, the purpose for such a story is similar: the purely divine origin of the child is secured (cf. *Prot. Jas.* 19:3—20:3).

Yet how exactly, for Plutarch, would Apollo have been the efficient cause for Perictione's pregnancy? Plutarch's answer in *Table Talk* has already been discussed, and we have only to give it final summary here. First, (a) god cannot have sex with a woman because that involves a change to a mortal form and a consequent depreciation of the divine (incorruptible) nature. But if a god cannot change his own form, he can still change (τρέπει) and make pregnant a mortal woman. He does so by "other forms of contact or touch"—namely, by divine power (*Quaest. conv.* 718a) and pneuma (*Num* 4.4). God does not have to come as a man to make a woman bloom and bear fruit. He can work like the winds—blowing where he wishes—to generate the divine child.[55]

EXCURSUS: PNEUMATIC BIRTH IN JOHN'S GOSPEL

Interestingly, Plutarch's description of divine begetting resembles the language that John's gospel uses to expound spiritual birth.[56] According to John, one must be "born from above" (ἄνωθεν), which apparently means the same as being "born from pneuma" (γεννηθῇ ἐξ . . . πνεύματος) (John 3:3, 5).[57] The pneuma

---

54. See further Gerard Mussies, "Joseph's Dream (Matt 1,18-23) and Comparable Stories," in *Text and Testimony: Essays on New Testament and Apocryphal Literature in Honour of A. F. Klijn* (Kampen: J. H. Kok, 1988), 177–186.

55. At the end of his discussion in *Table Talk*, Plutarch adds that "the Egyptians say that Apis is brought to birth by a touch of the moon" (718b; cf. *Is. Os.* 368c; Herodotus, *Hist.* 3.28). At this point, however, Plutarch cannot go along with the Egyptians. He distances himself from this theory with a quote from Euripides: καὶ οὐκ ἐμός ὁ μῦθος ("and not mine the tale!").

56. The key Johannine texts about spiritual birth (with bibliography) can be found in Maarten J. J. Menken, "'Born of God' or 'Begotten by God'? A Translation Problem in the Johannine Writings," *NovT* 51 (2009): 352–68. Menken automatically—and wrongly in my view—assumes that Johannine imagery of rebirth is purely metaphorical. He also incorrectly de-feminizes the imagery (God begets but does not give birth because he is a "father"), thus limiting its potential. A more reliable discussion of the Johannine texts in their historical context is Dietrich Rusam, *Die Gemeinschaft der Kinder Gottes: Das Motiv der Gotteskindschaft und die Gemeinden der johanneischen Briefe* (Stuttgart: Kohlhammer, 1993), 111–14, 118, 121–22.

57. For the meaning of ἄνωθεν, see especially Jeffrey A. Trumbower, *Born from Above: The Anthropology of the Gospel of John* (Tübingen: Mohr Siebeck, 1992), 69.

here is evidently the pneuma of God, and the phrase "born from a holy pneuma" is the same phrase used to describe Jesus' birth in Matthew (1:20).

John, like Plutarch, can also speak of pneuma in the broader sense of "wind" or "breath": "The wind (τὸ πνεῦμα) blows where it chooses, and you hear the sound of it, but you do not know where it comes from or where it goes. So it is with everyone who has been born of the spirit (ὁ γεγεννημένος ἐκ τοῦ πνεύματος)" (3:8). In this verse, the divine pneuma acts like the natural pneuma (or wind). It interacts with the human world by a subtle, delicate form of touch. This time, however, God's pneuma does not make a human woman pregnant, but of itself gives birth to special (heavenly—or divine?) human beings.

John's late first century discussion of birth through pneuma avoids, like that of Plutarch and Luke, crass anthropomorphic elements. Nicodemus, Jesus' earthly minded interlocutor, had earlier thought of reentering his mother's womb (v. 4). For such physicalist thinking, Jesus rebukes him: "If I have told you about earthly things and you do not believe, how can you believe if I tell you about heavenly things (τὰ ἐπουράνια)?" (v. 12).[58]

Earlier in John's Gospel we learn that the children of god are "born, not of blood [i.e., biologically] or of the will of the flesh [i.e., sexual desire] or of the will of a man [again, sexual desire, or possibly the act of adoption], but from God (ἐκ θεοῦ ἐγεννήθησαν)" (1:12-13).[59] The image here is different from Plutarch's or Luke's theory of divine conception, and ultimately more daring. In John 1:12-13, God's pneuma does not make a woman pregnant to produce a son; God himself gives birth directly. He gives birth to one divine son (the "Word") apparently by speaking (1:1). The other (divine?) children are born from (ἐκ) God himself.[60] Brown notes that the "crude realism" of divine begetting "is even more brutal" in 1 John 3:9, "where it is said that one begotten by God has God's *seed* [or sperm, σπέρμα] abiding in him."[61] The comment of Ernst Haenchen on John 1:12-13 is revealing: "Taken literally, these words express the virgin birth for all Christians."[62]

---

58. Cf. Plato's contrast between Aphrodite πάνδημος and Aphrodite οὐράνιος in *Symp.* 181b.

59. John F. McHugh takes all three negatives as denying a notion of birth through "sexual congress" (*A Critical and Exegetical Commentary on John 1–4*, ed. Graham Stanton [London: T&T Clark, 2009], 47). See further Trumbower, *Born from Above*, 71–75; Jan G. van der Watt, *Family of the King: Dynamics of Metaphor in the Gospel According to John* (Leiden: Brill, 2000), 183–84.

60. That ἐκ connotes source is indicated by the contrast in 1:13, "not from (ἐκ) bloods, nor from (ἐκ) the will of the flesh nor from (ἐκ) the will of a man." See van der Watt, *Family of the King*, 180–82.

61. Brown, *Gospel According to John*, 1:138, emphasis in original.

Are those born from (or of) God divine? Commentators commonly avoid this question. Jan G. van der Watt notes that birth determines both status and identity.[63] Most commentators (including van der Watt) commenting on these Johannine passages, however, speak of changed identity in a social or vaguely "spiritual" sense: the children of God become part of God's spiritual family. Adoption language, it seems, works just as well to express this—but John (deliberately?) avoids the Pauline language of υἱοθεσία. Instead, he uses the imagery of physical birth from God. Physical birth involves more than a change of status; it is a change—indeed the creation—of a new nature. Accordingly Otto Pfleiderer (less timid than many modern commentators) spoke of "divine birth" in John producing a "relation of essence" (Wesensverwandtschaft)—what we might call a "genetic relationship"—between humans and God.[64] This interpretation, if daring, deserves fuller exploration.[65]

COMPARISON WITH LUKE

For Luke, God's pneuma and power were operative much earlier in Jesus' life—indeed, they were present at the moment of his conception (1:35). Luke 1:35 is a fascinating verse, since it expounds, in poetic parallelism, the means of divine conception. To quote it again: "holy pneuma will come upon you

62. Ernst Haenchen, John 1: A Commentary on the Gospel of John Chapters 1–6, eds. Robert Funk and Ulrich Busse, trans. Robert Funk, Hermeneia (Philadelphia: Fortress Press, 1984), 118. John's image of being born anew (or from above) through pneuma may be a baptismal image. John 3:5 mentions being born "from water and the pneuma." Jesus' reception of the spirit at his baptism (Mark 1:9-11, par.) may, according to some Christians, have been the time when he was thought to become (or be adopted as) son of God. All three Synoptic Gospels agree (with minor variation) that when Jesus was baptized, he heard a voice saying, "This is my beloved son, in whom I am well pleased" (σὺ εἶ ὁ υἱός μου ὁ ἀγαπητός, ἐν σοὶ εὐδόκησα). The "Western" text (Codex Bezae, along with the majority of Old Latin MSS) of Luke 3:22, supported by Justin, Origen, Hilarius, and Augustine, as well as Acts 13:33, contains the full quote of Ps. 2:7: "Today I have begotten you."

63. van der Watt, Family of the King, 175, 180.

64. Otto Pfleiderer, Das Urchristentum seine Schriften und Lehren im geschichtlichen Zusammenhang, 2nd ed., 2 vols. (Berlin: Georg Reimer, 1902), 2:492–93.

65. To be sure, in early Christian tradition, Jesus becomes son of God at various points of his career (apparently with no felt contradiction). Our earliest witness, Romans 1:4, has Jesus' appointment to sonship occur at his resurrection/ascension. Paul passes on the tradition (apparently with slight adaptation) that Jesus was appointed son "in power according to the pneuma of holiness (ἐν δυνάμει κατὰ πνεῦμα ἁγιωσύνης) from the resurrection of the dead (ἐξ ἀναστάσεως νεκρῶν)." Here, as most commentators point out, both divine power and pneuma are used to speak of the act by which Jesus is made son. The act, however, is not a begetting from the pneuma, but an appointment (ὁρίζω) "according to" pneuma, or "in terms of" the pneuma of holiness. For more on Rom. 1:4, see J. D. G. Dunn, Romans 1–8, WBC 38a (Nashville: Thomas Nelson, 1988), 14–15.

(πνεῦμα ἅγιον ἐπελεύσεται ἐπὶ σὲ), and power of the Most High will overshadow you (δύναμις ὑψίστου ἐπισκιάσει σοι)."[66]

Importantly, both Luke and Plutarch use the language of pneuma and power to speak of divine conception. For Plutarch, it is "not impossible for a pneuma of God (πνεῦμα . . . θεοῦ) to approach a woman and engender certain productive principles" (*Num* 4); and it is "by a different power of god (ἄλλη . . . δυνάμει τοῦ θεοῦ) that God engendered in matter its productive principle" (*Quaest. conv.* 718a).[67] For both authors, the pneuma and power are specifically thought to be divine. Luke's "holy pneuma" is a divine entity, as is Plutarch's πνεῦμα θεοῦ. Likewise, Luke's δύναμις ὑψίστου ("power of [the] Most High") is parallel to Plutarch's δύναμις τοῦ θεοῦ ("power of God").[68]

The similarity of language may be related to a third factor. When Aristotle speaks of pneuma in his account of divine conception, he also employs the term δύναμις. According to the Stagirite, pneuma is said to contain δύναμις (*Gen. an.* 736a28) and to allow the semen to perform its function. Specifically, the δύναμις within the semen "sets" (συνίστησιν, 739a18) the secretion (περίττωμα) of the female allowing for the formation of the child.[69] Such technical usage of pneuma and δύναμις in the context of conception may suggest that Luke and Plutarch—even if they spoke of divine, not natural conceptions—still drew upon the scientific or quasi-scientific resonance of these terms.

Such linguistic concurrence does not mean that divine pneuma and power have exactly the same connotation in Luke and Plutarch.[70] In their accounts of divine conception, however, they function in similar ways. In both authors, divine "pneuma" and "power" are physically indeterminate ways to speak of divine action. But it is this very indeterminacy that serves to exclude sexual interpretations of divine conception. For both authors, pneuma and power are not technical terms referring to seed, or something that causes pregnancy. In Luke, they are words that are often coupled to speak of any powerful action of

66. For other places where πνεῦμα and δύναμις are conjoined, see Luke 4:14; Acts 1:8; 6:8; 10:38, and the comments below.

67. Philo also highlights the importance of divine power in miraculous birth. Speaking of the birth of Isaac from the ninety-year-old Sarah, he says, "It is not owing to the faculty of conception that a barren woman should bear a son, but rather to the operation of divine power" (*QG* 3.18; cf. 3.56).

68. For Aristotle, pneuma—although the productive agent in male seed (*Gen. an.* 736b39)—is naturalistic (being "hot air," [θερμὸς ἀήρ, 736a]). Nevertheless, Aristotelian pneuma is still possibly "divine" since it contains a divine element (an aether-like substance that is the productive principle) (736b39–737a8). On pneuma and semen, see further Martin, *Corinthian Body*, 201–02.

69. See further Aristotle *Gen. an.* 740b30–741a3; 741b37–742a16.

70. For the relation of pneuma and power in Luke, see Menzies, *Pneumatology*, 124–28.

God (Luke 1:17; Acts 10:38).[71] The closest Lukan parallel to 1:35 is Acts 1:8 (cf. 24:48-49), where power (δύναμις) is received and holy pneuma comes upon (ἐπέρχομαι) the apostles, so that they can preach the gospel. (Here, incidentally, there is no objection to the idea that the pneuma *entered* the apostles and filled them, allowing them to preach in different tongues.[72])

As *applied* to birth, however, Luke's use of pneuma and power fulfill a similar function as they do in Plutarch. Pneuma—in the elevated sense of "spirit"—can be used to refer to a non-sexual, non-anthropomorphic divine reality. Thus to use "pneuma" instead of simply "God" is a safe way of talking about spiritual—yet productive—contact between the divine and a mortal female while preserving Yahweh's—and Apollo's—dignified distance and lack of passion.

Furthermore, to speak of divine conception through *power* (δύναμις) carries a ring of theological respectability. Power is a basic trait of divinity in the Mediterranean world.[73] It expresses the reality and activity of God in the world, even if the deity in mind far transcends common human modes of conception. As a vague term, moreover, "power" is a safe way to speak about a god's non-anthropomorphic interactions with a human female.

In sum, both Luke and Plutarch effectively speak of divine pneuma and power as the efficient cause of pregnancy without hinting at perceived theologically crass features such as metamorphosis into a male body, penetration by a divine penis, and the ejaculation of divine seed into the womb.

The verbs expressing the *means* of divine conception reinforce this conclusion. When citing the Egyptian theory of divine conception, Plutarch uses the verb πλησιάζω (*Num* 4.4). The most basic meaning of this verb—related to the adjective πλήσιος ("near")—is simply "to draw near." But πλησιάζω can also indicate a sexual relationship, and Plutarch often uses it in this sense (e.g., *Thes.* 19.2; *Sol.* 20.2; *Cim.* 4.5).[74] Nevertheless, a sexual interpretation of this verb in *Numa* 4.4 (as well as *Quaest. conv.* 718a) is not appropriate because the pneuma does not have a male body with which to engage the female in a sexual way. When Plutarch (through Tyndares) seeks

---

71. Other examples in Foskett, *A Virgin Conceived*, 204, n.14.

72. Foskett observes that "the sending of the prophetic Spirit is quite a physical phenomenon." She concludes with reference to Luke's birth account: "Mary will be overcome by divine power. She will conceive at the initiative of the divine will and by the activities of its Spirit. . . . Through the Holy Spirit and the *dynamis* of the Most High, Mary's body will soon become a site of sacred, procreative activity" (ibid., 122).

73. Litwa, *We Are Being Transformed*, 46–57; Henrichs, "What is a Greek God?" 36–37.

74. *LSJ* 1420, s.v. "πλησιάζω," II.3.

to go beyond the Egyptian theory of divine conception, he avoids πλησιάζω—likely because of its sexual overtones—and speaks of "other forms . . . of contact and touch" (ἑτέραις τισὶν ἀφαῖς . . . καὶ ψαύσεσι) (*Quaest. conv.* 718a).

Plutarch's other verb of conception is ἐντίκτω, to "generate in." Of almost a dozen uses, only one (*Tiberius and Gaius Gracchus* 17.2) is literal. Plutarch prefers a metaphorical usage, as in *On Superstition* 165b, where certain judgments and assumptions "give birth" (ἐκτίκτουσι) to diseases and passions in the soul just like maggots and worms. Accordingly, the verb does not seem to require any notion of bodily union. It is a general—and thus safe—verb to describe divine generation.

The author of Luke's Gospel makes equally skillful use of "kosher" verbs to describe divine conception. "Pneuma of god," he says, "*will come upon* (ἐπελεύσεται) you [Mary]" (1:35).[75] The verb ἐπέρχομαι, although it may carry "the notion of onrushing, overpowering vitality,"[76] need not imply crude sexual contact. It is used literally in Luke 11:22 and Acts 14:19, but also in a more extended way to speak of the "oncoming" of fear (Luke 21:26) or threats (Acts 8:24; 13:40). It does not mean "mount," for which the Greeks used ἐποχεύω (e.g., Arist. *Gen. an.* 741a31) or ἐπιβαίνω (Philo, *Somn.* 1.200).[77] But it does not exclude physical contact either.

More interesting is Luke's second verb: "the power of the Most High *will overshadow* (ἐπισκιάζεται) you." In the early twentieth century, both Hans Leisegang and Eduard Norden suggested that a sex act was involved, or at least implied by ἐπισκιάζω.[78] Later, David Daube argued for an allusion to Ruth 3:9, where Ruth propositioned Boaz with a (so Daube) sexual metaphor: "Spread your wing over (περιβαλεῖς τὸ πτερύγιόν σου ἐπὶ) your maidservant."[79] Both

75. Luke's use of this verb in 1:35 has the cadence of Isa. 32:15 (LXX): ἕως ἂν ἐπέλθῃ ἐφ᾽ ὑμᾶς πνεῦμα ἀφ᾽ ὑψηλοῦ ("until spirit from on high comes upon you"). But here "spirit" occasions the fertility of the land, not a person. In my view, Luke is probably not "drawing attention to the Greek text of Isa 32:15" and thus calling up eschatological associations (*pace* John Nolland, *Luke 1–9:20*, WBC 35a [Dallas: Word Books, 1989], 54). For other LXX combinations of ἐπέρχομαι with pneuma, see Num. 5:14; Job 1:19; 4:15.

76. Schaberg, *Illegitimacy*, 105.

77. Schaberg notes one instance of ἐπέρχομαι "in what looks like a (violent) sexual context," namely Hos. 10:11 LXX: "I [God] will come upon (ἐπελεύσομαι) the fairest part of her neck; I will mount (ἐπιβιβῶ) Ephraim." She admits, however, that "this one text is not enough evidence for us to hold that sexual sense is intended in Luke 1:35" (ibid., 106).

78. Hans Leisegang, *Pneuma hagion: der Ursprung des Geistbegriffs der synoptischen Evangelien aus der griechischen Mystik* (Leipzig: Hinrichs, 1922), 25–29; Eduard Norden, *Die Geburt des Kindes: Geschichte einer religiösen Idee* (3rd printing; Darmstadt: Wissenschaftliche Buchgesellschaft, 1958), 93–95.

interpretations proved unconvincing to most.[80] Literally, ἐπισκιάζω signifies the flickering of a shadow over another person (Acts 5:15). Commentators often point to Exod. 40:35 (LXX), and Luke 9:34 (cf. Mark 9:7; Matt. 17:5), respectively, where the glory cloud of Yahweh overshadowed (ἐπεσκίαζεν) the Tent of Meeting and Christ on the mount of transfiguration.[81]Although the "overshadowing" metaphor does not entirely exclude a physical element, it avoids a crudely sexual notion of Yahweh's contact with Mary.[82] Indeed, I would argue that Luke's "overshadowing" language is an artful way of talking about Plutarch's "other forms of contact or touch."[83]

THE APPEAL TO CREATION

The hovering imagery associated with ἐπισκιάζειν (and possibly ἐπέρχομαι) has been taken as an echo of the creation story where the πνεῦμα θεοῦ (LXX) is "carried over" (ἐπεφέρετο) the waters (Gen. 1:2; cf. Ps. 33:6; Jth. 16:14; 2 Bar. 21:4; Ps. 104:30).[84] Brown, for instance, comments, "the Spirit that comes upon Mary is closer to the Spirit of God that hovered over the waters before creation in Gen 1:2. The earth was void and without form when that Spirit appeared; just so Mary's womb was a void until through the Spirit God filled it with a child who was His Son."[85]

Although in Genesis 1:2 God is not impregnating a primordial soup, he is preparing a new birth of sorts for the world. Soon he will call the land to emerge from the waters, and on it will teem all cattle, reptiles, trees, fruit, and so on. If Luke's "overshadow you" is a genuine intertext recalling the creation story,

79. David Daube, *The New Testament and Rabbinic Judaism* (London: Athlone, 1956), 32–36.

80. For criticism of Leisegang and Norden, see Dibelius, "Jungfrauengeburt," 19–22, esp. 22, n. 33. For criticism of Daube, see Schaberg, *Illegitimacy*, 108.

81. For the verb's use in Philo, see *Her.* 265; *Somn.* 1.119.

82. There is no reason to suppose that both ἐπέρχομαι and ἐπισκιάζω are "figurative expressions" that have nothing to do with physical contact (*pace* Fitzmyer, "Virginal Conception," 569).

83. Some kind of physical touch is implied in later Christian interpretations of Jesus' divine conception. In *Prot. Jas.*, Mary will conceive "by means of the divine *logos*" (11.5; cf. Justin Martyr, *1 Apol.* 33). H. R. Smid notes an Armenian variant that locates Mary's ear as the entrance point for the penetrating Word (*Protoevangelium Iacobi: A Commentary* [Assen: Van Gorcum, 1956], 84). This idea appears later in the late fifth-century Christian epic poet Dracontius (*De laudibus dei* 2.89-90). For the Logos flying directly into the womb of Mary, see *Sib. Or.* 8.469-72; *Ep. Apos.* 14. Tertullian believed that "a divine ray of light glided down into her [Mary], and descending was made concrete as flesh in her womb" (*Apol.* 21; cf. Herodotus, *Hist.* 3.28; Plut., *Is. Os.* 368c; *Quaest. conv.* 718b).

84. For the creative power of πνεῦμα, see Ps. 33:6; Jth. 16:14; 2 Bar. 21:4, 23:5; Ps. 10:30; Ps. 104:30; Wisd. of Sol. 1:7; 12:1. For life-giving spirit, see Ezek. 37:14; Job 27:3; 33:4; Rom. 8:11; John 20:22.

85. Brown, *Birth of the Messiah*, 314. Schaberg opposes an allusion to creation (*Illegitimacy*, 112–13).

he is showing that Yahweh's pneumatic production of Jesus in Mary's womb is less like human procreation than direct creation. The pneuma of God does not mount Mary; he more delicately hovers over her like the primordial pneuma, engendering something new within her.

Interestingly, an appeal to creation is also used by Plutarch to explain the logic of divine begetting. Naturally, Plutarch does not appeal to Genesis, but to his own (Platonic) creation story, the *Timaeus*. "I take courage," says Tyndares, "when I hear Plato himself [say concerning] the Father and Maker of the world (κόσμου) and other born beings (καὶ τῶν ἄλλων γεννητῶν) . . . [that beings born of God] do not come to be through seed (οὐ διὰ σπέρματος), surely, but by another power of God (ἄλλῃ δὲ δυνάμει τοῦ θεοῦ), who engendered (ἐντεκόντος) in matter a productive principle" (*Mor.* 718a).

The reference to the "Maker and Father of the world" is citation of perhaps the most frequently quoted passage in the *Timaeus*: "Now to find the M*aker and Father of this world* is hard enough, but to declare him to all is impossible" (28e, my emphasis). The world's "Maker and Father" refers to the creator God. If God is going to father a child, Plutarch reasons, he will act as he did to make the world. Plato's creator God does not procreate by injecting sperm in a woman's womb; he creates something new within her by a more subtle form of contact. This (implicit or explicit) appeal to a creator God is yet another strategy that both Luke and Plutarch use to avoid the crass anthropomorphism of sexual contact.

RESULTS

Let me summarize the comparison and my argument thus far. Judging from the language of Celsus, among the cultured elite of the second century a sexual act between (a) god and a woman was viewed as both theologically incorrect and physically defiling. It was theologically incorrect because a god would not desire a physical body. It was physically defiling because, at least in this time period, a woman's body (in particular her genitals) were viewed as a source of pollution (*Cels.* 6.73). But if it was viewed as questionable for a god to have sexual contact with a woman, it was not viewed as inherently problematic that a woman could conceive with a god through "other forms of contact or touch."

Both Luke and Plutarch, as late first-century historians, share many of these theological assumptions and sensibilities.[86] Accordingly, they reject a

86. For Plutarch's status and education, see C. P. Jones, *Plutarch and Rome* (Oxford: Clarendon, 1971), 8–10; 39–47. Luke's social status is admittedly more difficult to determine. From the text of *Luke-Acts* itself, Fitzmyer remarks that the author "is obviously a rather well educated person, a writer of no little

crassly anthropomorphic and sexual understanding of divine conception. Even so, they do not reject the *possibility* of such a conception for their respective protagonists (Plato and Jesus). Both historians apparently receive their stories of divine conception from previous tradition.[87] As creative writers, both probably improve upon these traditions in order to make them theologically sophisticated, plausible, and thus acceptable to the cultured reader of their day.[88]

This is not an argument that Luke "borrowed" from Plutarch or from Greek myth in general. Luke attached a story of divine conception to his Gospel not because he succumbed to "hellenization" or was attempting to address Greeks. Wright is right on this point: Luke's birth narratives radiate the rhetorical aura of Septuagintal ("Jewish") history. The similarities between Luke and Plutarch—if we attribute them to anything—are due not to genetic relation, but to a shared intellectual culture. It was a common set of (generally Platonic) theological and historical conceptions that shaped what would be appropriate and plausible in a story of divine conception.[89]

MYTH AND HISTORY

The issue of historical plausibility is worth emphasizing. Both Luke and Plutarch, it seems, were working with similar assumptions about myth and history. For both, tales of anthropomorphic gods mating with human women could only be "mythical" (i.e., not historically true). (So, I might add, would stories about "sons of god" mating with human women in Genesis 6.)[90]

merit, acquainted with both OT literary traditions . . . and Hellenistic literary techniques" (*The Gospel According to Luke: Introduction, Translation and Notes*, 2 vols., AB 28–28a [Garden City, NJ: Doubleday, 1981–85], 1:35). According to François Bovon, "The cultivated language [of Luke] indicates that the author's roots are in one of the higher strata of society, and that the author had a good education encompassing Greek rhetoric as well as Jewish methods of exegesis" (*Luke 1: A Commentary on the Gospel of Luke 1:1—9:50*, trans. Christine M. Thomas, ed. Helmut Koester, Hermeneia [Minneapolis: Fortress Press, 2002], 8).

87. For Luke inheriting a narrative of the annunciation to Mary, see Bovon, *Luke 1*, 47–48.

88. I do not claim that Luke was a philosopher or had a Platonic conception of God. I do argue, however, that he had all the cultural resources available to him to develop a story of divine conception credible to the cultural elite of his day.

89. So Frederick W. Danker, who denies that Luke directly borrows from Mediterranean myths. Danker errs, however, when he asserts that only *non*-Jewish authors would "readily recognize that the singular parentage of Jesus provides him with a claim to excellence that was accorded" to other divinely conceived gods and demigods (*Jesus and the New Age: A Commentary on St. Luke's Gospel*, rev. ed. [Philadelphia: Fortress Press, 1988], 39).

90. The distinction between myth and history is old, appearing in an influential passage of Thucydides, *Hist.* 1.22.4, "Perhaps the lack of the mythical (τὸ μὴ μυθῶδες) from my narrative will seem

Nevertheless, both Plutarch and Luke craft stories of divine begetting that are refined and sophisticated enough to be taken as "history" as it was understood in the first century. From our perspective, however, what makes "history" is not necessarily "the facts" objectively perceived, but a culturally informed framework of plausibility about what *could* happen. Although few educated persons in the late first century CE might believe that gods take on male bodies and ejaculate semen into female vaginas, it was apparently credible that a wind/breath/spirit of god could "come upon" a woman in some indeterminate sense, and by divine power create a child in her womb.[91]

Despite these commonalities, Luke and Plutarch portray very different styles of engagement with popular (Greek) traditions. Plutarch, for his part, realizes that there are things in Greek myth that are hopelessly crude and unredeemable. To use his own words, sometimes "myth brashly despises what is likely" (*Thes.* 1.3). At other times it is useless and shameful (*Is. Os.* 12 [*Mor.* 355d]; 20 [*Mor.* 358e]). But Plutarch does not for these reasons eschew all myth. Rather, he skillfully rationalizes and moralizes it in line with Platonic philosophy (which he considers to be the most ancient wisdom).[92] In cultic myth (e.g., the myth of Isis and Osiris), Plutarch assumes that truth is contained symbolically. As he puts it in *The Daimon of Socrates*, even "what is mythic gropes in some fashion after truth" (589f–590a). Of specifically Egyptian mythology, Plutarch says that it contains "dim, faint effluvia of the truth" (λεπταί τινες ἀπόρροιαι καὶ ἀμυδραὶ τῆς ἀληθείας). Nevertheless, a man needs "a sleuth-like (ἰχνηλάτου) mind" to track those truths, a mind "which can draw important conclusions from tiny scraps of evidence" (*Amat.* 762a). Alas, Plutarch never lays out or employs a single theory of interpreting myths. In general, one can say that he does not treat them as factual statements (λόγοι). Rather, he adopts "out of each what is appropriate (τὸ πρόσφορον), on the principle of likeness" (*Is. Os.* 374e).[93] In the myth of Plato's divine conception,

---

displeasing to my listeners. But as many who wish to examine the clear account of what happened (τῶν τε γενομένων τὸ σαφές) . . . for these to judge my history beneficial will be satisfactory." For Strabo—writing in the first century—τὸ μυθῶδες designates "material which is old, false, and monstrous" (τὰ παλαιὰ καὶ ψευδῆ καὶ τερατώδη) (*Geog.* 11.5.3).

91. Today one might still argue that the Lucan and Plutarchian versions of divine conception are fundamentally mythic. The point is that in the ancient world, to quote Margaret Mitchell: "the historicity of μῦθοι [myths] or διηγήματα [narratives] [is] based upon the criterion of πιθανότης [persuasiveness]" ("Origen, Celsus and Lucian on the 'Dénouement of the Drama' of the Gospels," in *Reading Religions in the Ancient World*, 218).

92. Peter van Nuffelen, *Rethinking the Gods: Philosophical Readings of Religion in the Post-Hellenistic Period* (Cambridge: Cambridge University Press, 2011), 49, 70.

what is rationally and morally appropriate for Plutarch is that Plato was (and is) the son of a god. Plato, as Plutarch notes, proved this by his character and virtue.

Luke, on the other hand, engages not Greek but Hebrew myth. He skillfully uses the stories of Sarah (Gen. 18:1-15; 21:1-7) and Hannah (2 Sam. 1–2)—among other Hebrew Bible texts—to weave together two tales of wondrous conception (those of Jesus and John the Baptist). The Baptist—not Heracles or Perseus—is Luke's direct *comparandum* in the birth narratives (Luke 1–2), and Jesus both imitates (i.e., is shown as similar) and emulates (i.e., is shown as superior to) him. Even with regard to divine conception without a human father (Luke 1:34-35), there is no direct allusion to Greek myth. This does not mean that Luke did not *in*directly emulate these tales. (Luke, an educated man, presumably had a general knowledge of the many stories of divine birth in classical tradition.)[94] Nevertheless, Luke's refusal to directly engage the Greek "other" reminds us of an important point: Luke the late first-century historian was also a Christian apologist. Although he lived in a broadly Greco-Roman culture—and was thus unable to escape its influence—for religious (and other) reasons, he chose to identify with the stories and traditions of the Jewish subculture.[95] For Luke even to gesture toward "Greek" stories in any direct way would have hindered his apologetic aim: to portray Christ as the uniquely divine savior and lord of the world. By not mentioning the other Greek tales of divine conception, Luke declared not only their falsity, but their insignificance.[96]

THE QUESTION OF DEIFICATION

Even if Luke chose not to engage directly with other Mediterranean stories of divine conception, we should not conclude that Luke was not on some level

93. For further observations on Plutarch and myth, see Lamberton, *Plutarch*, 49–50; P. R. Hardie, "Plutarch and the Interpretation of Myth," *ANRW* 33.6:4743–4787; Christopher Pelling, *Plutarch and History: Eighteen Studies* (Swansea: Classical Press of Wales, 2002), 171–96; Luc Brisson, *How Philosophers Saved Myths: Allegorical Interpretation and Classical Mythology*, trans. Catherin Tihanyi (Chicago: University of Chicago, 2004), 63–71.

94. For Christian knowledge of such traditions, see Justin Martyr, *1 Apol* 22.5; Tert., *Apol.* 21.14; Clement of Alexandria, *Protrep.* 32–33.

95. To argue this point, I do not need to enter the debate about whether Luke was ethnically Jewish or a Gentile "God-fearer" (for which see Fitzmyer, *Luke*, 41–47).

96. Indeed, for most who hear Luke's "Christmas story" (Luke 1–2) in ecclesial settings, the memory of all the other divinely conceived sons of God has vanished. On the uniqueness of Jesus' divine conception, cf. John Dominic Crossan, *The Birth of Christianity: Discovering What Happened in the Years Immediately After the Execution of Jesus* (New York: HarperSanFrancisco, 1998), 27–29.

shaped by what divine conception meant in Mediterranean culture. Here we arrive at the essential point for the purposes of this study, namely how Luke—by recounting a sophisticated tale of Jesus' divine conception—ascribed to him a widely recognized divine trait, in this case, a *divine origin*.[97]

It is difficult to deny that a divine conception in Greco-Roman culture hinted at the divinity of the child. The fact of having a divine father entails some "natural" (as opposed to purely metaphorical or attributed) divinity for the offspring.[98] Apuleius, when he treats the birth of Plato, for instance, comments that the philosopher, "being of such a nature (*talis*) and originating from such great beginnings (*de talibus*), . . . not only excelled the virtues of heroes (*heroum virtutibus*), but also became equal to the powers of the gods (*aequiperavit divum potestatibus*)" (*De Platone* 1.2). Divine conception signified a divine status. It could even suggest the presence of a divine nature (Philostratus, *Vita Apoll.* 1.6).[99] Neither Luke nor Plutarch, however, mentions a divine φύσις for their heroes. Although both authors might assume some ontological implications for divine conception, they do not expand on this point.[100]

It is important, however, to understand divine conception as part of a larger pattern of ascribing divinity to someone in Mediterranean culture. Historians and literary critics of the ancient world realized that in order of importance as well as time, typically it was *works*, not birth that proved deity. Divine conception, that is, was viewed as secondary, as something typically *read back* into the lives of great men. In the mind of Celsus, for instance, it is the "great and wondrous works" (ἔργα μεγάλα καὶ θαυμαστά) of heroes that demonstrated (ἐπέδειξαν) that the myths of their divine conception are

---

97. Bovon, *Luke 1*, 47. Marina Warner opines, "In the pre-Christian Roman empire virgin birth was a shorthand symbol, commonly used to designate a man's divinity" (*Alone of All Her Sex: The Myth and the Cult of the Virgin Mary* [New York: Knopf, 1976], 34).

98. Fitzmyer argues that "Luke does not intend that Jesus should be recognized as God's son merely in the adoptive sense . . . his explicit relation of the title to the conception of Jesus connotes much more" (*Luke*, 207). According to Bovon, "God takes the place of the human father through the working of his spirit, so that 'Son of the Most High' (v. 32) is now to be understood in the literal sense" (*Luke 1*, 44).

99. Cf. Ael., *Var. hist.* 4.17; Aelius Aristides, *Or.* 5.31.13. See further Zeller, "θεῖα φύσις"54–62, esp. 61.

100. According to Joel B. Green, however, Luke is "moving toward a more ontological (and not only functional) understanding of Jesus' sonship" (*The Gospel of Luke*, NICNT [Grand Rapids, MI: Eerdmans, 1997], 91).

not unconvincing (μὴ ἀπίθανοι) (Orig., *Cels.* 1.67).[101] Origen agrees with the connection of works and divinity, using the example of Plato himself:

> ... as for instance even Plato, born from Amphictione [another name for Plato's mother], when [his father] Ariston was prevented from coupling with her until she gave birth to the child sown from Apollo. But these are truly myths. People were motivated to invent such a story about a man whom they considered to be greater than the common herd (μείζονα τῶν πολλῶν), one who had wisdom and power (ἔχοντα σοφίαν καὶ δύναμιν), and who received from superior and more divine seeds (ἀπὸ κρειττόνων καὶ θειοτέρων σπερμάτων) the beginning of the composition of the body, seeing that this fits those greater than human nature (μείζοσιν ἢ κατὰ ἄνθρωπον). (*Cels.* 1.37, my trans.)

Plutarch was also willing to admit the secondary nature of divine conception for Theseus and Romulus (*Thes.* 2.1; 6.1; *Rom.* 4.2). In the case of Plato, however, he is loathe to affirm that Plato's divine conception was invented. Nevertheless, Plato had proved his divinity primarily from his beneficent deeds. In *Table Talk*, Florus says that Apollo made Plato *a greater physician than Asclepius* (Apollo's other divine son). Asclepius, after all, only healed ailments of the body, while Plato healed (and continues to heal) those of the soul (*Quaest. conv.* 717d-e).[102] For this reason, Tyndares breaks in, it is suitable to celebrate Plato with the Homeric line: "He seemed the scion not of mortal man, but of a god!" (*Il.* 24.258).

Plutarch's attitude toward Plato's origin shows that if divine conception was secondary to divine works, *it was not for this reason insignificant.* In the ancient world, it was not for every hero and ruler that a myth of divine conception was devised. Only the greatest men and philosophers received such an honor; and only those whom their votaries wanted to see as unambiguously—even uniquely—divine. This ancient Mediterranean convention applies, to a greater or lesser degree, for the Lucan Jesus, whose divine origin is celebrated with festival and gift giving even to this day.

---

101. Cf. Aulus Gellius, who comments on Scipio Africanus that "it was far more because of his exploits (*ex rebus gestis*) than because of that prodigy [his miraculous conception] that he too was believed to be a man of divine excellence (*virum . . . virtutis divinae*)" (*Noct. att.* 6.1.5).

102. For Hippocrates as having a divine nature as the basis for his medical advances, see Zeller, "θεῖα φύσις," 62–68.

Conclusion

I conclude that Luke's story of Jesus' divine conception was one important way for him to ascribe a divine status to his master and lord in ancient Mediterranean culture. The birth narratives show that for Luke, Jesus did not *become* divine. Nor did Luke imagine that he could ascribe any real, "ontological" divinity to Christ. For Luke, the divinity of Jesus was a theological truth, a truth that he illustrated by portraying Jesus' divine conception in a careful, theologically sensitive way. Luke did not create this tradition, but he did present it in a sophisticated, historically plausible form. In this way, then, Luke sought to secure what Plutarch devised for his own master: a theologically credible account of divine conception, together with a historically plausible discussion of divine–human contact which combined to authenticate the status of his hero. In short, to use the language of this study, Luke crafted a plausible and enduring account of the deification of Jesus Christ.

2

"From Where Was this Child Born?"

Divine Children and the Infancy Gospel of Thomas

"As flies to wanton boys, are we to gods;
they kill us for their sport."

—SHAKESPEARE, *KING LEAR* 4.1,

LINES 36-37

INTRODUCTION

The Infancy Gospel of Thomas (IGT) "was one of the most popular of the early Christian apocrypha down through the ages."[1] Few other Christian narratives are as fast-paced, compact, memorable, and entertaining as the tales of Jesus

---

1. Bart D. Ehrman and Zlatko Pleše, *The Apocryphal Gospels: Texts and Translations* (Oxford: Oxford University Press, 2011), 3. Ehrman and Pleše reprint a text that is "essentially" the longer text printed by Constantin von Tischendorf in the nineteenth century—what has become the *textus receptus* for this document (7). Tony Burke (*De Infantia Iesu: Evangelium Thomae Graece*, CCSA 17 [Turnhout: Brepols, 2010]) and Reidar Aasgaard (*The Childhood of Jesus: Decoding the Apocryphal Infancy Gospel of Thomas* [Eugene, OR: Cascade Books, 2009]) argue that a better text is presented in the eleventh-century Jerusalem manuscript *Sabaiticus gr. 259* (known as Gs). This is the text that I will follow here, as it is printed in Burke, *Infantia Iesu*, 302–337. For additional childhood traditions from other manuscripts, see Ehrman and Pleše, *Apocryphal Gospels*, 25–29, 73–193. The probable date and provenance of IGT is Syria in the early to mid-second century CE. As in the New Testament, it is impossible to recover the "original" text of IGT. For further introduction to IGT, see esp. Burke and Aasgaard (cited above); J. K. Elliot, *The Apocryphal New Testament* (Oxford: Clarendon, 1993), 68–83; R. F. Hock, *The Infancy Gospels of James and Thomas* (Santa Rosa, CA: Polebridge, 1995), 84–146; Hans-Josef Klauck, *Apocryphal Gospels: An Introduction*, trans. Brian McNeil (London: T&T Clark, 2003), 73–78.

from age five to twelve.[2] The character of Jesus in IGT remains, however, an enigma. Although a sometimes sweet and playful child, he is also a killer. When provoked, he can become impatient and angry. Sometimes his wrath can flare up to the point of cursing. What follows is death. The slayings can seem arbitrary. Once, Jesus curses and kills another boy merely for bumping into him (4:1-2). After another young boy falls from a roof and dies, Jesus raises him—not for the benefit of the child or his anguished parents—but to defend his own honor. After the boy testifies that Jesus did not push him off the roof, Jesus commands him, "Fall asleep!"—and (apparently) the boy dies twice (9:1-3). In the schoolroom, when a teacher bids Jesus, "Say alpha!" Jesus answers peremptorily: "You tell me first what the beta is, and I shall tell you what the alpha is." When the indignant teacher hits Jesus, Jesus curses him so that he falls over and dies (13:1-2). Such miracles, in the words of Tony Burke, "have been called 'ridiculous' and 'immoral,' 'puerile, or malevolent and cruel,' 'anstössige und abstossende,' or just plain 'crude.'"[3] It is no surprise, then, that the Jesus of IGT has been accused of being an "*enfant terrible* who seldom acts in a Christian way!"[4]

Yet if Jesus "seldom acts in a Christian way," it is difficult to claim that he acts like the (or a) Christian god either. This is even more problematic, since the author of this Gospel seems intent on establishing Jesus' divine identity. The emphasis is variously expressed. In 4:1, after people see that Jesus killed a small boy, they cry out, "From where was this child born, since his word becomes deed?" Later, Jesus' teacher Zacchaeus asks, "Perhaps this child existed before the creation of the world?" (7:2). He confesses that he does not know whether Jesus is "a god or an angel"—although to settle for an "angel" seems to underestimate both his powerful deeds and mysterious wisdom (7:4). Jesus himself professes his preexistence in chapter 6:6 of IGT. And, given the overall thrust of the document, it is fair to say that Jesus is represented as a divine being throughout.[5]

2. IGT ends with the boy Jesus in the temple (cf. Luke 2:41-52). Bradly S. Billings has recently argued that in this episode Jesus is presented as the "superior and successor to the deified Augustus" ("'At the Age of 12': The Boy Jesus in the Temple [Luke 2:41-52], the Emperor Augustus, and the Social Setting of the Third Gospel," *JTS* 60 [2009]: 70-89).

3. Burke, *Infantia Iesu*, viii–ix. The embarrassment and disgust scholars have felt in the face of such acts is well catalogued in Burke's "History of Scholarship" (*Infantia Iesu*, 45–126). The title of Gd (another MS tradition of IGT) is instructive: "Concerning the shocking (ἐξαισίων) and hair-raising (φρικτῶν) wonders which our Lord Jesus Christ did as a child."

4. The remark stems from Elliott, *Apocryphal New Testament*, 68, and is oft-quoted.

5. So Hurtado (who cites Tischendorf's longer text): "At several points the child Jesus openly declares his transcendent status and heavenly origins (6.5-7, 10; 8.2); several other times others wonder at him and pose the likelihood that he is no ordinary mortal but instead a divine child (7.4-5, 11; 17.4; 18.3). This is

But if the storyteller(s) of IGT wanted to illustrate Jesus' divine identity, why would they portray him as a (sometimes) arbitrary, mischievous problem child? This would seem to be a "very naïve or crude" and "unsophisticated" way to portray Jesus' divinity, in the words of Larry Hurtado.[6] But these are modern value judgments and do not accord with ancient perceptions of divinity. One might argue from the biblical tradition (as Marcion did) that the God of the Old Testament is rather violent, angry, and arbitrary in his punishments! And indeed, Jesus does possess the central trait of the God of Genesis: creation by word alone.

Nevertheless the deep structure of Jesus' character has been at least equally shaped by popular Mediterranean conceptions of deity, including divine children.[7] Tales of the gods and heroes were widespread in ancient Mediterranean culture. It is no surprise, then, that in Christian tales about Jesus, elements and thought patterns from the dominant culture would emerge. The pattern common to both Jesus and other young divinities is, I will argue, a peremptory and destructive defense of divine honor.

PREVIOUS RESEARCH

Before I defend this thesis, let me turn briefly to consider other ways of understanding and comparing the dangerous and powerful divine child of IGT. In an important study, Tony Burke situates IGT (1) in terms of Greco-Roman depictions of children, especially of future famous men, and (2) in the context of Jewish holy men, including Israelite prophets and rabbinic wonder workers. In accordance with the first thesis, he argues that Jesus in IGT is portrayed as an ideal child, a *puer senex*. In accordance with the second thesis, he argues that the most relevant *comparanda* for the divine child are not Greco-Roman deities, but full-grown figures like Elijah and Elisha, Honi the Circle-Drawer, and Hanina ben Dosa.[8]

---

clearly the main premise and point of the compilation. In one sense, of course, this is a version of the familiar Christian belief that Jesus is divine" (*Lord Jesus Christ,* 450–51).

6. Ibid., 451. John Meier's description of IGT is even more lurid: "The portrait of this sinister superboy belongs more in a horror movie than a gospel" (*The Roots of the Problem and the Person,* vol. 1, *A Marginal Jew: Rethinking the Historical Jesus,* 4 vols. [New York: Doubleday, 1991], 115).

7. For child gods in general, see Martin P. Nilsson, *The Minoan-Mycenaean Religion and its Survival in Greek Religion,* 2nd ed. (Lund: C.W.K. Gleerup, 1968), 533–83. Albert Henrichs treats divine children in Callimachus ("Gods in Action: The Poetics of Divine Performance in the *Hymns* of Callimachus," in *Callimachus,* ed. M. A. Harder et al. (Groningen: Egbert Forsten, 1993], 127–48 [140–42]). Corinne Ondine Pache's *Baby and Child Heroes in Ancient Greece* (Urbana: University of Illinois, 2004) treats very young (mostly infant) heroes who play mostly passive roles as opposed to active child gods.

Although illuminating in some respects, there are several problems with Burke's argument. First of all, the irascible, destructive, peremptory Jesus of IGT is far from being an ideal child. Rather, he consistently shocks and appalls his father Joseph, his teachers, and the crowds—not to mention the readers of IGT (both ancient and modern). If by "ideal child" Burke means that Jesus is being presented as a child who acts like an *adult*, this point does not explain Jesus' violent behavior.

As to Jewish holy men, these individuals do not correspond to the enormity of Jesus as he is presented in IGT. Although ancient Jewish miracle workers and prophets occasionally embodied divine power, they never claimed to *be* divine or the right to be *worshiped* as (a) god. The Jesus of IGT, in contrast, proclaims his own preexistence. His acts show his divine origin. People do not know if he is a god or an angel (not a typical question asked of a Jewish holy man). They ask what womb Jesus came from, thinking he cannot be "earthborn" (γηγενής) (7:2). In response to his deeds of power, people fall down and worship him (9:3), worship that Jesus evidently accepts. These acts and statements indicate that Jesus is no mere holy man (or holy child). In fact, the astounding power of his deeds seems directly framed to draw us beyond the holy-man traditions.

What we see in IGT, I contend, is a pattern of manifest divinity much closer to the logic of John's Gospel: Jesus' deeds are signs that demonstrate his divinity. In the case of IGT, however, Jesus is a *child*, and some of his deeds are destructive. And—in spite of all the bitter polemics in John—this gospel does not portray Jesus performing a sign that harms people.[9] Nor is the serenity of John's Jesus ever broken by fits of anger or acts of mischief. To understand the Jesus

8. Burke, "The Infancy Gospel of Thomas: The Text, its Origins, and its Transmission," (PhD diss., University of Toronto, 2001), 309–313. In another article, Burke includes "Luke-Acts' portrayal of the apostles" as some of the "most vivid parallels" for Jesus in IGT. For example, Peter brings about the deaths of Ananias and Sapphira (Acts 5:1-11), and Paul blinds Elymas (Acts 13:6-11) ("'Social Viewing' of Children in the Childhood Stories of Jesus," in *Children in Late Ancient Christianity*, eds. Cornelia B. Horn and Robert R. Phenix [Tübingen: Mohr Siebeck, 2009], 29–44 [41]). But Ananias and Sapphira die for their own lies, and Elymas is considered to be a false and wicked prophet. Their sufferings are not analogous to the arbitrary and vindictive harm inflicted by Jesus in IGT.

9. The same applies to the Synoptics. Burke's attempt to imply otherwise is strained ("The Infancy Gospel of Thomas," 312; cf. "Social Viewing," 41). True, Jesus does curse the fig tree (Mark 11:12-22 and par.), but a tree is not a human being! Burke claims that Jesus curses disbelieving towns (e.g., Luke 10:13-15). But in this text, Jesus only laments in light of their future punishment. The statement that Jesus permits his disciples to curse cities and individuals is misleading (Matt. 10:11-15; Luke 9:5; 10:10-12). In these texts, no cursing is mentioned, only the threat of future divine punishment. When Jesus becomes angry, it is out of zeal for his Father's house (John 2:14-17), or his indignation is directed against the hard hearts of the Pharisees (Mark 3:5; cf. 7:6-13; 8:17-21).

of IGT, then, we need more than holy men and more than the divine Jesus of John's Gospel.

To be fair, it seems that Burke soft-pedals Jesus' divinity because he struggles against older readings which discovered a "Gnostic" (i.e., docetic) and thus a non-human Christ in IGT.[10] Yet his almost exclusive underlining of Jesus' humanity swings the pendulum too far to the other side.

Reidar Aasgaard's *The Childhood of Jesus* is another impressive and welcome study of IGT.[11] Far from highlighting the *puer senex* motif, Aasgaard sees Jesus' mischievous and childish character in IGT as stemming from the fact *that he is a child*. Naturally, Aasgaard admits that Jesus is more than a mere child: he is a *divine* child; in him divinity and humanity are combined. Nevertheless, Aasgaard moves Jesus' foibles and deviant character traits decisively to the *human* side of the ledger. Thus, it is as one who is "far too human" that Jesus appears "emotionally imbalanced and outraged without due reason." It is Jesus the human child who "corrects and ridicules his teachers" and "provokes spectators by claiming to be co-existent with God" (an odd claim for a little boy).[12] In this light, IGT ends up being "very much a story about ordinary children living in an ordinary village environment."[13]

Although an interesting approach, Aasgaard's interpretation has the same limitation as Burke's: it takes the focus off the very point IGT seems most to want to highlight—the *exceptionality* of Jesus—and specifically his divine status. We cannot attribute Jesus' roguish and even spiteful character to his pre-pubescent humanity. There is more at work here. In the words of Joseph to Zacchaeus in IGT: "Do not regard him [Jesus] to be a human in miniature, brother" (6:3).[14]

In contrast to the studies of Burke and Aasgaard, Lucie Paulissen's recent essay rightly asserts that a—perhaps the—key point in IGT is recognizing Jesus' divine nature. Jesus' divine nature, moreover, is manifested in both his acts of weal and woe.[15] I disagree with Paulissen, however, that the balance of Jesus'

---

10. Burke, "Infancy Gospel," iii, 405; Burke, *Infantia Iesu*, 221, 269; Burke, "Social Viewing," 40.

11. See also Aasgaard's article "Uncovering Children's Culture in Late Antiquity: The Testimony of the *Infancy Gospel of Thomas*," in *Children in Late Ancient Christianity*, 1–28.

12. Aasgaard, *Childhood of Jesus*, 86.

13. Ibid., 101.

14. Cf. *The Gospel of Pseudo-Matthew* 18: "And Jesus said to them [his parents]: 'Do not be afraid, and do not consider me to be a child, for I am and always have been perfect." Cf. Thomas Wiedemann, *Adults and Children in the Roman Empire* (London: Routledge, 1989), 51.

15. Paulissen, "Jésus enfant divin: Processus de reconnaissance dans L'Évangile de l'Enfance selon Thomas," *Revue de Philosophie Ancienne* 22 (2004): 17–28 (24).

acts is positive, that his punishments are ultimately salvific, and that the surprise and shock he causes is pedagogical.[16] The ferocity and ambiguity of Jesus' character are not compensated by his acts of benevolence. One must face head-on the disturbing character of Jesus in this gospel. Attempts to tame the wild child remain unsatisfying.

In what follows, I will argue that we can understand the wild divinity of Jesus by comparing it to other tales of child divinities in ancient Mediterranean culture.[17] By comparing Jesus with other child gods, we can (1) put proper emphasis on the divinity of Jesus in IGT, (2) understand why that divinity could be destructive, and (3) comprehend why stories of Jesus' dangerous divinity made sense to the early Christians who heard and handed them on.

COMPARISON OF CHILD GODS

JESUS AND HERACLES

The story of Jesus killing his teacher has an interesting analogue in the story of the young Heracles and his teacher Linus. Heracles, one of the most popular gods in the Greco-Roman world, was the son of Zeus and Alcmene. As young prince of Thebes, Heracles had only the finest of teachers. His music instructor was Linus, no less than the brother of Orpheus. But Heracles was no natural on the lyre, and he needed discipline. As was the custom in ancient education, Linus strikes the young Heracles for messing up his notes.[18] In response, the son of Zeus is instantly enraged; he grabs his lyre and cracks it over Linus's head, killing him instantly (Ps.-Apollod., *Bibl.* 2.4.9; cf. Paus., *Descr.* 9.29.9; Ael., *Var. hist.* 3.32; Diod., *Bibl.* 3.67).[19] Heracles's (adopted) father Amphitryon then sends the boy to the cattle farm to avoid any more mishaps. In quarantine, Heracles

16. Paulissen, "Jésus enfant divin," 19, 21–23

17. For a recent overview and comparison of "Jewish" and "Greco-Roman" infancy narratives, see Andrés García Serrano, *The Presentation in the Temple: The Narrative Function of Lk 2:22-39 in Luke-Acts,* Analecta Biblica 197 (Rome: Gregorian & Biblical Press, 2012), 87–145.

18. For pedagogical punishment in the ancient world, see Mark Golden, *Children and Childhood in Classical Athens* (Baltimore: Johns Hopkins University Press, 1990), 64–65; Richard Saller, "Corporal Punishment, Authority, and Obedience in the Roman Household," in *Marriage, Divorce, and Children in Ancient Rome,* ed. Beryl Rawson (Oxford: Clarendon, 1991), 144–165 (esp. 163–64); John K. Evans, *War, Women and Children in Ancient Rome* (London: Routledge: 1991), 169–70.

19. For artistic depictions of the attack, see *Lexicon Iconographicum Mythologiae Classicae (LIMC)* (Zurich: Artemis 1981–), IV.2 Nrs. 1667, 1668, 1671, 1673. In these images, Heracles attacks Linus with a broken stool. Further description and commentary on these and other portrayals can be found in ibid. vol. IV.1.833-834. For further discussion and images, see Frank Brommer, *Herakles II: Die unkanonischen*

shows no remorse or sense of wrongdoing. As a god—in this case, a divine child—Heracles has simply defended his honor.

Jesus displays a similar attitude with his first teacher Zacchaeus (IGT 6). According to procedure, Zacchaeus writes out the alphabet, voices the letters, and asks Jesus to repeat after him. When Jesus does not respond, he seems to be either refractory or a dullard. Zacchaeus then hits him on the head. Jesus becomes angry and says to his teacher: "I want to teach you rather than be taught by you. For I know the letters that you are teaching much more accurately than you" (v. 8).

Jesus' interactions with his second teacher are hardly improved. As already mentioned, when Jesus responds peremptorily, the teacher strikes him, earning a curse and instant death (13:1-2). At this point, Joseph, Jesus' (adopted) father, despairs of controlling the child except through quarantine. He instructs Mary: "Don't let him [Jesus] go outside the house lest those who annoy him end up dead" (v. 3).

JESUS AND HERMES

Another popular divine child of the ancient world is the god Hermes in the Homeric *Hymn to Hermes*—and no child god is more of a rogue.[20] From the very first day of his birth, this παῖδα πολύτροπον ("wily child," *Hom. Hymn Herm.* 13) reveals his mischievous character: he is a wheedling (αἱμυλομήτην) trickster and a thief (ληϊστῆρα) (14). To establish his marvelous and glorious deeds (κλυτὰ ἔργα) (16), he steals the cattle of Apollo, craftily leading them off backwards, wearing leafy shoes that obscure his tracks. When called to account, Hermes lies on oath to Apollo and then even to his father Zeus. The high god thunders with laughter, the deed is disclosed, and the divine half-brothers are reconciled by a mutual exchange of honors. Hermes, like Jesus, shows his divine character even as a child. His aim is to receive honor from the gods and worship from human beings—the same worship that Apollo receives (172-73).

There is a particular linguistic point of similarity between IGT and the Homeric *Hymn to Hermes*. It is mentioned on two occasions in IGT that Jesus' word became deed (4:1; 17:2). The saying seems to relate Jesus to the Jewish

---

Taten des Helden (Darmstadt: Wissenschaftliche Buchgesellschaft, 1984), 6–7; and Raimund Wünsche, *Herakles Herkules* (Munich: Staatliche Antikensammlungen, 2003), 47–51.

20. For an introduction to the Homeric *Hymn to Hermes*, see Jenny Strauss Clay, *The Politics of Olympus: Form and Meaning in the Major Homeric Hymns*, 2nd edition (London: Bristol, 2006), 95–151; Athanassios Vergados, *The Homeric Hymn to Hermes: Introduction, Text, and Commentary*, Texte und Kommentare 41 (Berlin: Walter de Gruyter, 2012), 1–159.

creator in Genesis 1. Yet the god whose word mixes with deed also resonates in the Greek ear. In the *Hymn to Hermes*, we read the following lines:

> As when a swift thought pierces through the breast
> Of a man whom dense cares whirl about,
> And then beams whirl from his eyes:
> So was glorious Hermes devising word and deed at once
> (ὡς ἅμ' ἔπος τε καὶ ἔργον ἐμήδετο κύδιμος Ἑρμῆς) (43-46).[21]

In this chapter, however, I stress not verbal similarity, but fundamental parallels in mentality shared by Greek divinities and the divine Jesus. That mentality is summed up in the zeal for divine *honor* (τίμη), a basic character trait possessed by virtually all Greco-Roman deities (*Il.* 9.498). As Aphrodite relates in Euripides's *Hippolytus:*

> I honor (πρεσβεύω) those who respect my powers,
> But I overthrow those who are haughty [or "think big"] towards me.
> For there is this characteristic even in the race of gods,
> They rejoice (χαίρουσι) in being honored (τιμώμενοι) by human beings. (lines 5-8)[22]

When the gods do not receive the honor that is their due—even from those who are innocent of moral wrongdoing—they lash out in rage. That rage can touch not just one offender, but a group of people connected with the offender. Often

---

21. Josef-Klauck, *Apocryphal Gospels*, 77. Cf. Hom., *Il.* 19.242; Ap. Rhod., *Arg.* 4.103; Call., *Hymns* 1.55-57 (ἐφράσσαο πάντα τέλεια [spoken of Zeus]). Nicholas Richardson believes that ἅμ' ἔπος ἅμ ἔργον was proverbial ("no sooner said than done") (*Three Homeric Hymns* [Cambridge: Cambridge University Press, 2010], 160). For further references and bibliography, see Vergados, *The Homeric Hymn to Hermes*, 266. Later, Hermes the messenger of the gods was assimilated to god's creative Logos (Justin Martyr, *1 Apol.* 21).

22. The god Dionysus too "wishes to have honors (τιμάς) from all people" (Eur., *Bacc.* 208), and "enjoys being honored" (τέρπεται τιμώμενος, 321). Outside the theater, we observe the same attitude. Ps.-Hippocrates (*Aer.* 22.9) says that gods "rejoice (χαίρουσι) in being honored (τιμώμενοι) and wondered at (θαυμαζόμενοι)." See further Jon Mikalson, *Honor Thy Gods: Popular Religion in Greek Tragedy*(Chapel Hill: University of North Carolina Press, 1991), 183–202. Ritoók Zsigmond points out that gods rejoice in their κῦδος, or glory (*Il.* 1.405; 5.905-906; 8.51; 11.81) ("Die Götter und der Ruhm," in *Religio Graeco-Romana: Festschrift für Walter Pötscher*, ed. Joachim Dalfen et al. [Graz: F. Berger & Söhne, 1993], 51–56). For the glory (κῦδος, κλέος) of Hermes, see Dominique Jaillard, *Configurations d'Hermès: une "théogonie hermaïque"* (Liège: Centre international d'étude de la religion grecque antique, 2007), 76–83.

the anger seems arbitrary, because at times the offender appears to dishonor the god purely by accident. Those who threaten divine honor are punished—often in extreme ways.

Like the gods in Greek stories, Jesus—when his honor is violated—strives to protect it by punishing his antagonist(s). When he is honored, on the other hand, he responds with benefaction. He helps those he views as akin to him (his father, mother and brother). Those who annoy him and dishonor him (such as the teacher who strikes him) are liable to chastisement and even death.

We return to Hermes to illustrate this dynamic of dishonor and destruction. In the Homeric *Hymn*, Hermes meets a nameless old man when driving away Apollo's cattle.[23] The god addresses the old man to ensure—by promise and possible threat—that the man will tell nothing of what he has seen (87-93). The speechless senior seems compliant. Yet when Apollo later approaches and asks the man if he has seen a cattle-rustler, the old man prattles about a young child with a wand who drove the cattle backwards across the plain (190-212). Hermes's secret is revealed. The trickster god has been out-tricked. Oddly, however, the old man never receives his comeuppance.

This is not the case in Ovid's adaptation of the story (*Met.* 2.687-707).[24] Here the old man is called "Battus," meaning "stammerer," or possibly "chatterbox."[25] When Mercury (the Latin Hermes) coaxes him to keep silent about the theft of cattle with the reward of a cow, Battus says, "Proceed! You're safe; that stone will tell sooner than I."[26] Mercury heads off, but soon returns

---

23. For a commentary on this episode, see Richardson, *Three Homeric Hymns*, 168–170; 183–86; Vergados, *Homeric Hymn to Hermes*, 297–307.

24. Scholars are divided as to whether the Homeric *Hymn to Hermes* creates or adapts the story of the old man. At any rate, Ovid does not seem to be directly dependent on the *Hymn to Hermes* for his story, but rather on the Hellenistic author Nicander, whose account of Battus is reflected in Antoninus Liberalis, *Met.* 23. Here Battus strides out to meet Hermes and demands a bribe for silence. The Scholiast to Antoninus indicates that this version of the tale goes back to Hesiod (Clay, *Politics*, 114, n. 65). According to Vergados, the Battus of Nicander and the Old Man of the Homeric Hymn should "be treated as two distinct characters, each having a different function in the story in which he appears (though this does not preclude that the *Hermes* poet may have drawn on the story of Battus …): the speechless Old Man proves later during his meeting with Apollo to be simply an idle talker. Battus, on the other hand, is a perjurer, tested by Hermes who has to assume a different guise, and is bent on profit" (*Homeric Hymn to Hermes*, 298). For general treatments of this episode in Ovid, see Victor Castellani, "Two Divine Scandals: Ovid Met. 2.680ff and 4.171ff and His Sources," *TAPA* 110 (1980): 37–50; and A. M. Keith, *The Play of Fictions: Studies in Ovid's* Metamorphoses *Book 2* (Ann Arbor: University of Michigan Press, 1992), 95–115.

25. For the meaning of "Battus," see Franz Bömer, *P. Ovidius Naso Metamorphosen Kommentar*, 7 vols. (Heidelberg: Carl Winter, 1969), 1:401–02.

in a different build and guise to test Battus. "Good fellow," he says, "help me; if you've seen some cattle hereabouts, speak up, they're stolen; and you shall have a cow and bull, a pair." The old man replies, "There on yon hill they'll be"—and there they were. Mercury laughed. "You rogue, so you betray me to myself, me to myself, I say!"—and he changes Battus into a stone that cannot speak. Mercury has been dishonored. The punishment comes swift and without remorse.[27]

Two other examples from classical literature illustrate the pattern of dishonor and divine punishment with important additions. First is the story of Actaeon and Diana. Again, Ovid well tells the tale (*Met.* 3.131-255).[28] Actaeon, while hunting in the forest, accidentally stumbles on a cave where the virgin goddess Diana (Greek Artemis) is bathing. Although his intentions were not evil, Actaeon saw much more than he should have. Diana, the virgin goddess, is shamed and dishonored. In a flash of rage, she splashes water on Actaeon's face and utters this curse: "Now tell you saw me here naked without my clothes, if you can tell at all!" Immediately Actaeon is metamorphosed into a stag, and is promptly torn apart by his own hunting dogs. Any Xenophanes or Plato would immediately cry foul against divine injustice, and Ovid shows himself aware of how cruel Actaeon's punishment is: "The fault," says the narrator, "was fortune's and no guilt that day. For what guilt can it be to lose one's way (*quod enim scelus error habebat*)?" (3.141-142).[29] And yet there is a logic to the curse. At the end of the story, Ovid notes that some praised Diana's action "as proper to her

---

26. Here and in the translations of Ovid that follow I use the lively rendition of A.D. Melville, *Ovid: Metamorphoses* (Oxford: Oxford University Press, 1986), 45.

27. Castellani paints Mercury in very dark colors: "Not only is the Ovidian Mercury guilty of the traditional cattle theft; he also gravely compounds his felony with what we might call conversion of goods, with bribery, with entrapment, and finally with a lethal sort of practical joke. He even incidentally breaks a promise of his own, namely to award a bull and cow for information. Worst of all, however, must be the gross hypocrisy of his punishing anyone else for anything" ("Two Divine Scandals," 44).

28. For Actaeon in art, see Françoise Frontisi-Ducroux, *L'homme-cerf et la femme-araignée: Figures grecques de la métamorphose* (Paris: Gallimard, 2003), 95–143; Richard Buxton, *Forms of Astonishment: Greek Myths of Metamorphosis* (Oxford: Oxford University Press, 2009), 99–105.

29. In other traditions, Actaeon's guilt is played up. He is made to boast that he is a better hunter than Artemis (Eur., *Bacc.* 339-40; cf. Diod. Sic., *Bibl.* 4.81.4). Such explanations may have been introduced to justify his punishment. Later, Ovid will assimilate himself to Actaeon with regard to his own involuntary fault against Augustus: "Unwitting (*inscius*) was Actaeon when he beheld Diana unclothed; none the less he became the prey of his own hounds. Clearly, among the gods (*in superis*), even ill-fortune (*fortuna*) must be atoned for, nor is mischance (*veniam*) an excuse when a deity is wronged (*laeso numine*)" (*Trist.* 2.103-108). For further comments, see Bömer, *Kommentar*, 1:488–89.

severe virginity" (254-255). Diana had acted to defend her honor. The death of a human being paled in comparison to the preservation of divine dignity.[30]

A story with which to compare Diana's divine attitude occurs in IGT chapter 4. Here Jesus, while walking along the road, is bumped on his shoulder by another young boy. Though it is a very common occurrence on a crowded road, a pure accident—and only a slight detriment to Jesus' honor—the deed has deadly consequences. Jesus immediately blurts out: "Cursed be your ruling power!" Instantly the boy falls and dies. The parents of the dead child protest to Joseph, who asks Jesus, "Why do you say such things?" Jesus, far from showing remorse, responds by blinding his accusers (5:1). Again, there is no expression of regret. At this point, Jesus' opponents start to realize who they are dealing with. Anyone who dishonors Jesus must be prepared to meet instant ire. In these stories, Jesus shows his divine power and divine character (4:1). He has no compassion on those whom he kills and blinds. He ruthlessly exercises divine justice on those who dishonor his divinity. Jesus the child god could easily fall under the same Platonic criticism of injustice as Diana (*Resp.* 377d-378e).[31] But Platonic theology is not popular theology.

IGT AND POPULAR GRECO-ROMAN THEOLOGY

It is worth dwelling on this point for a moment. Christian apologists who ridiculed Greek gods for acting childishly were typically well-educated members of the elite.[32] If we take them as representative, we get the false impression that the average Christian in the ancient world viewed God as an incorporeal, ineffable, serene, and supremely just being in radical contrast to the embodied, blustering, competitive, honor-loving gods of the Greeks and Romans.

But the gods of popular theology do not play by human moral rules. They are less immoral than amoral—or rather, "supra-moral." Their vast power and prestige puts them in a category above human beings. Thus they do not abide

---

30. Cf. Karl Galinsky, *Ovid's Metamorphoses: An Introduction to the Basic Aspects* (Oxford: Blackwell, 1975), 66–67. In a similar story recounted by Callimachus, Tieresias loses his eyesight for accidently espying Athena naked (*Hymn. lav. Pall.* 68-82).

31. In his *Republic*, Plato places justice (or rather the form of Justice) above the gods. This makes both gods and humans subject to Justice (a moral absolute that can be perceived by both divine and human minds). This is a development distinctive to Plato, and should not be taken as representative of how most Greeks (that is non-philosophers) thought about the gods in the ancient world.

32. Take, for instance Gregory of Nazianzus: "The 'gods' . . . worshipped by the pagans have no need of *us* to accuse them. They stand convicted by their own theologians of being affected by evil emotions, of being quarrelsome, of being brimful of mischief in all its varieties" (*Or.* 31.16).

by (or rather are not limited by) human moral conventions. Therefore to accuse a god of injustice is to misunderstand what a god is: neither just nor unjust, but something above human justice—like a force of nature.[33]

Thus *the very fact* that both Diana and Jesus are oblivious to what on the human level are rather obvious moral violations manifests not their inhumanity (traditionally, the gods *never cared* to be human or to share human emotions), but their divinity. This understanding of divinity puts the focus squarely on *power*, arguably the central trait of Mediterranean deities. This power is essentially amoral. When this amoral power is joined to an anthropomorphic deity (such as Diana or Jesus), the personified power has a basic concern: not to do justice—but *to defend its own honor*. And it will defend its honor at any cost. Those who pay that cost are sometimes careless human beings with no chance of knowing who they are dealing with—until it is too late.

JESUS AND DIONYSUS

In a final comparison, I focus on the figure of Dionysus in Euripides's *Bacchae*. The Dionysus of this play is relatively young. Only recently has he crossed to Greece from Asia where he had grown up as the nursling of nymphs in Nysa of Arabia (Diod., *Bibl.* 3.64.3–65.8). In Greece he appears as a pretty boy from Lydia with long golden locks. The god arrives with a group of devoted female followers from Asia to bring his new religious rites to Thebes. He comes to his own (Dionysus had a Theban mother [Semele], though he is son of the high God Zeus), but his own do not receive him. King Pentheus (Dionysus's cousin) arrests the young man as a religious charlatan and disturber of the peace. Dionysus has broken rules of reason and order. Pentheus enters as an authority to enforce the law. Little does the king know that the mysterious young fop is a god. Although the Lydian miraculously escapes from prison, Pentheus persists in his desire to persecute him and his devoted female followers (the maenads). The consequences are predictable, but gruesome. A maddened Pentheus is dismembered by his own mother, and Dionysus shows no pity. In the end, the god punishes the whole family of Pentheus, though their guilt is unequal. Cadmus and Harmonia, grandparents of Pentheus and Dionysus, are to be turned into serpents. Agave (Pentheus's mother), Ino, and Autonoe (Actaeon's mother) are banished from Thebes. Attempts to lessen the punishments are futile. Standing above his human family at the end of the play, Dionysus silences all the complaints of his grandfather with the words: "I am a god! I was outraged by you! (πρὸς ὑμῶν θεὸς γεγὼς ὑβριζόμην)" (1347).[34] Here clearly punitive

---

33. Cf. the fierce God of Job in the Hebrew Bible, who appears from a whirlwind (chs. 38–41).

miracles lead to a recognition of divinity. In the line of the chorus: "Pentheus is destroyed by the son of Echion / O Lord Bromios, you are revealed as a great god (θεὸς φαίνῃ μέγας)" (1030-31; cf. 992-96, 1011-16).[35]

In IGT, we view another honor-demanding deity interacting with humans ignorant of his divine status—with sometimes frightful results. Take, for instance, the story of Jesus and Annas's son (IGT 2). Here we find the young Jesus busily collecting water into pools and making clay sparrows on the Sabbath. The acts are clearly felt to be wrong (or at least against convention) in Jesus' society. Joseph accordingly rebukes Jesus, asking, "Why do you do this on the Sabbath?" (2:4) Jesus retains his composure, clapping his hands, making the clay birds fly. Another boy, the son of Annas the high priest, then approaches Jesus and asks the same question: "Why do you do this on the Sabbath?" Annas's son then takes a willow branch and breaks up the pools Jesus had made. When Jesus sees this, he loses his temper. He says to the boy, "Your fruit be without root, and your shoot withered like a branch let off by a strong wind!" Immediately the son of Annas withers away (3:2-3).

Here we have an authority figure—an older boy, young son of the high priest—who takes a disobedient Jesus to task. He has already seen signs of Jesus' divinity (the animated clay birds), but he persists. He accuses Jesus of breaking convention, even divine law—and the accusation is true. Annas's son then uses force to undo the dangerous work of Jesus, teaching him a lesson. But the lesson is his to learn. He is literally desiccated. The account ends with a remorseless silence.[36]

What do we make of these honor-defending acts of Dionysus and Jesus? As in popular Greek tales of the gods, Jesus and Dionysus seem to belong to a world above human morality. Both gods are young. Both gods wield divine power and demand divine honor. When they are dishonored by their own people, they manifest divine wrath at great human expense. Other humans learn

---

34. The story is reminiscent of how the young Dionysus dealt with Lycurgus, impious leader of the Thracians (Diod. Sic., *Bibl. hist.* 3.65.2-5). For another popular story of Dionysus who takes wild vengeance on his kidnappers see the Homeric *Hymn to Bacchus* 7 (cf. Ovid, *Met.* 3.582-691; Ps.-Apollod., *Bibl.* 3.5.3; Hyg., *Fab.* 134). In this story, Dionysus is specifically said to be a youth or a boy (νεηνίῃ ἀνδρὶ ἐοικὼς / πρωθήβῃ [*Hymn Bacc.* 7.3-4]; *puerum* [Ovid, *Met.* 3.607]; *impubis* [Hyg., *Fab.* 134]).

35. Cf. Ovid who relates the story of Bacchus turning the impious daughters of Minyas into bats: "Then truly was the divinity of Bacchus (*Bacchi . . . numen*) acknowledged throughout all Thebes" (*Met.* 4.416).

36. It is instructive to compare this episode with the gospel trial scenes before Annas the (adult) priest. Here we find a Jesus taciturn and suffering in his trial (John 18:13, 19-24). When Jesus talks back to Annas, he receives a blow to the face. In IGT, the tables have turned: Annas's son dishonors Jesus and is destroyed.

by example and fall into line. This is no ordinary young rogue. This is a god demanding honor at any human cost.

If Dionysus and Jesus had come with all their divine glory, people would have known to honor them. In IGT and the *Bacchae*, however, the human form veils the divine power. People are subject to mistaken perceptions. Technically, Pentheus is within his rights when he arrests a young disturber of the peace. Likewise, a son of the high priest is under some obligation to defend the institution of the Sabbath. Yet these reasonable human actions have deadly consequences. Dionysus is no Lydian dandy, and Jesus is more than a kid with chutzpah. They are gods. Those who dishonor them learn the hard way.

One might argue, however, that the god Jesus is in the end much kinder than Diana or Dionysus. He does, after all, heal some he formerly harmed (8:1-2; cf. 14:4).[37] But a god who heals is hardly unusual in the Hellenistic world—especially if reparations have been made. The very opening scene of the *Iliad* presents us with Apollo letting loose the arrows of plague against the Achaeans for the sin of Agamemnon who dishonored Apollo's priest. But when reparations are made, the plague is removed (*Il.* 1.1-100). Another famous example is the lyric poet Stesichorus. Plato tells us (*Phaedr.* 243a; cf. Dio Chrys., *Or.* 11.40-41) that Stesichorus once dishonored the divine Helen in his poems, and was blinded as a result. Yet when he sung a reparatory "palinode" in honor of Helen, he was healed. The principle is clear: dishonor leads to wrath, and honor to benefaction.

A similar pattern emerges in IGT. Zacchaeus dishonors Jesus by smacking him on the head. Jesus rebukes him, and teaches him a lesson. Zacchaeus then sings his own palinode, repenting and honoring the divinity of the child. "The child is simply not earth-born . . . ," he says. "Perhaps this child existed before the making of the world? What kind of womb bore him? What kind of mother raised him? I don't know. Alas, brother, he bewilders me!" (7:2). Zacchaeus has learned from his mistakes. He announces, if querulously, the true identity of Jesus. Pleased, the god Jesus responds with benefaction by healing "all those who had fallen under his curse" (8:1-2). Who exactly is healed is never made clear. All the same, a principle is established: just as the gods punish more than the guilty, so an act of true repentance can lead them to heal more than the innocent.

---

37. There is significant ambiguity as to who exactly is healed. It is not stated that everyone he has killed or maimed since the beginning becomes well.

CONCLUSION

According to Reidar Aasgaard, the Jesus of IGT is "true God and true child."[38] Indeed, some of the very character traits that make Jesus a child also make him a god. That is, Jesus as a rancorous, unpredictable, pitiless defender of his own honor is just as much a god as he is a child. And this is the way that he transcends childhood. Leslie Beaumont notes, "it is possible for a male god to be a child if he both embraces and yet transcends the nature of childhood."[39]

IGT gives a glimpse of how a variety of Christians (not just the uneducated majority) thought about divinity in the period of Christianity's own infancy. It indicates that some Christians and their non-Christian neighbors may not have had radically different conceptions of what a god was. Barring obvious differences about the number of gods and their peculiar personalities, young gods in early Christianity and Greco-Roman folklore possess a similar zeal for honor. Sometimes, as we have learned, this zeal can kill.

I conclude that Jesus the "unChristian" *enfant terrible* in IGT is not to be written off as the fancy of a theological simpleton thrilling an audience that is also "not theologically astute."[40] Rather, IGT makes an important theological statement about the divine identity of Jesus. Jesus is not divine solely in an exalted, philosophical sense. The spell of the Logos could only bewitch a very small circle of Christian elites in the second century (such as Justin Martyr and his students). In IGT, we find a Jesus who is divine according to different canons, the canons of popular Mediterranean theology. Jesus the honor-demanding child ends up looking like—at least for the story-teller(s) of IGT—a fairly typical Greco-Roman god.

By pointing out the similarities in the conception of divinity, I do not want to make a (tedious) argument about Christian "borrowing" from the larger culture, involving a "paganization" or "hellenization" of Christian thought (as if a touch of Greek thought somehow made Christianity impure). No, the Christian storytellers who told and retold the tales of Jesus' childhood would have been oblivious, I think, to having "borrowed" elements or patterns of thought from the larger culture. They probably would have openly denied that

---

38. Aasgaard, *Childhood of Jesus*, 216.

39. Leslie Beaumont, "Mythological Childhood: A Male Preserve? An Interpretation of Classical Athenian Iconography in its Socio-historical Context," *Annual of the British School at Athens* 90 (1995): 339–361 (359).

40. Here I borrow the language of Paul Allan Mirecki, who believes that IGT was "not read as a serious theological tractate" (542), and that its audience was "not theologically astute." These judgments, I think, tell us more about Mirecki's own theological biases than IGT itself ("Thomas, the Infancy Gospel of" in *ABD* 6.542–543).

their god had anything to do with Dionysus.[41] IGT retains a strong Jewish local color but is simultaneously a good example of a kind of "embedded hellenization" that would not necessarily have been recognized by contemporary Jews and Christians as hellenization at all. In IGT, then, Christian storytellers quite innocently depicted Jesus with the acts and attitudes of a Mediterranean divinity. Historically speaking, that is what he was.

Having come to a similar conclusion long ago, Ludwig Conrady argued that the author of IGT adopted a "pagan" conception of god.[42] He claimed that Jesus' miracles have a "purely pagan nature, since they lack all ethical content and announce themselves as pure displays" and "bare instances of magic." The Jesus of IGT, Conrady concluded, is an "entirely pagan god-child" (der volle heidnische Götterknabe).[43]

A hundred and ten years after Conrady wrote his article, scholars cannot so easily distinguish what is "pagan" from what is Jewish and/or Christian in the Greco-Roman world—at least when it comes to the question of divinity. Simply because an author (or storyteller) seems to have painted the young Jesus in the colors of popular Mediterranean deities does not mean that the author presented a Jesus any more "pagan" than Christian. What we have in IGT, it seems, is a Christian storyteller (or group of them) who found Jesus' childhood (essentially ignored in the canonical gospels) a blank canvas. How storytellers painted on this canvas is therefore revealing, and it was only natural that they should depict Jesus' divine status in accordance with their own conceptions of the divine, using models furnished by the larger culture.

This argument in no way diminishes the *Jewish* character of Jesus' deity. Indeed there are parallels between the honor-loving character of Greece's gods and the jealous god Yahweh. That oracle of Deuteronomy could have been spoken by any number of hellenistic deities: "I kill and I make alive" (32:39). The point is that such distinctions between ancient "Greek" and "Jewish"

---

41. The Athenian proverb "nothing to do with Dionysus" (οὐδὲν πρὸς τὸν Διόνυσον) is recorded by the Sophist Zenobius. See further A. W. Pickard-Cambridge, *Dithyramb Tragedy and Comedy* (Oxford: Clarendon, 1962), 294–95; J. Winkler and F. I. Zeitlin, eds., *Nothing to Do with Dionysus: Athenian Drama in its Social Setting* (Princeton, NJ: Princeton University Press, 1990), 3.

42. Ludwig Conrady, "Das Thomasevangelium: Ein wissenschaftlicher Versuch," *Theologische Studien und Kritiken* 76 (1903): 377–459 (400). Cf. Philipp Vielhauer, who wrote that the material in IGT is "not Christian, but pagan." Vielhauer drew on stories of divine children as *comparanda*, but limited himself to Buddhist and Indian tales. His views on the pagan origin of IGT are partially driven by his judgment that the stories of this gospel are crass and vulgar (*Geschichte der urchristlichen Literatur: Einleitung in das Neue Testament, die Apokryphen und die Apostolischen Väter* [Berlin: Walter de Gruyter, 1975], 676–77).

43. Conrady, "Das Thomasevangelium," 401.

understandings of the divine, at least for the storytellers of IGT, may be overblown. Both Jews and Christians had long lived in the Hellenistic world—which is neither properly "Greek" nor "Jewish" (or at least cannot be neatly spliced into these elements). If the average uneducated Mediterranean person was going to understand and accept the child Jesus as a god, it is no surprise that he or she would accept a Jesus depicted in the theological colors of the larger culture.

When we compare both the *acts* and the *attitudes* of divinity, we arrive decisively at this conclusion: IGT presents Jesus as a rather typical Greco-Roman deity: a god who (1) is zealous for his own honor, (2) acts to honor those who honor him, and in turn (3) blasts those who dishonor him. In the Greek world, anyone who dishonored the gods could expect a knee-jerk explosion of divine wrath. Dishonored gods were passionate and could become violently angry. Such was Jesus. Consequently, the short temper and destructive power of this *enfant terrible* is no enigma for those in tune with the pervasive influence of Mediterranean culture on popular Christian tales. In the second century, and far into late antiquity, the old gods of Greece and Rome had not died. Their love of honor and violent attempt to defend it had been reborn in the child of Bethlehem.

3

Deus est iuvare

Miracle, Morals, and Euergetism in Origen's Contra Celsum

Culcianus, Governor of Egypt: "Was Christ god?"
Phileas: "Yes."

Culcianus: "What has convinced you that he was god?"

Phileas: "He restored sight to the blind and hearing to the deaf, healed lepers and raised the dead to life, made the dumb speak, and cured the infirmities of many."
—*Acta Phileae 4.3*[1]

INTRODUCTION

The divinity of Jesus, in comparison to the divinity of various other Mediterranean deities, is a pervasive theme in Origen's *Contra Celsum*.[2] The third-century CE. Alexandrian theologian expends enormous intellectual energy proving Christ's divinity over against popular gods like Heracles, Asclepius, and Dionysus. Such an oppositional stance might seem to support the common view that the *Contra Celsum* assumes a purely *contra gentes* ("against the [pagan] nations") mentality.[3] Upon closer examination, however, Origen and Celsus

---

1. H. Musurillo, *The Acts of the Christian Martyrs* (Oxford: Clarendon, 1972), 349. Musurillo assigns the Greek text to a date "not long after the actual martyrdom [of Phileas]" in 306 ce (i.e., between 320–35).

2. For a recent introduction to the *Contra Celsum*, see Horacio E. Lona, *Die 'wahre Lehre' des Kelsos* (Freiburg: Herder, 2005), 1–69. It is a late work of Origen, composed shortly prior to his death in the mid-third century CE. Origen was responding to Celsus's work *True Doctrine*, which most scholars date to the late 170s CE. For a slightly later dating (ca. 200), see Jeffrey W. Hargis, *Against the Christians: The Rise of Early Anti-Christian Polemic* (New York: Peter Lang, 1999), 20–24.

employ strikingly similar notions of divinity as well as what deeds and qualities deify human beings. These commonalities indicate that both Christian apologist and anti-Christian critic were tapping into conceptions of deity and deification that were common coin in the ancient Mediterranean world. The common conception I explore in this chapter is summed up in Pliny the Elder's phrase *deus est iuvare*, roughly "divinity signifies benefaction."[4]

DEITY AND BENEFACTION

Although ancient Mediterranean religions obviously featured a wide spectrum of divinities who displayed numerous qualities and powers, there was widespread consensus on what made gods and deified humans divine. It was a display of power, and particularly power to bestow benefits (e.g., to liberate from oppression, to protect against danger, or to heal disease).[5] Abundant references from classical authors and inscriptions establish this point.

In the fifth century BCE, the sophist Prodicus of Ceos is reported to have said that "those things that benefit (*ea quae prodessent*) human life are held to be in the number of the gods" (Cic., *Nat. d.* 1.118), or simply that "that which benefits (ὠφελοῦν) life is considered god" (Sext. Emp., *Math.* 9.18, 52).[6] At this stage, "the things that benefit" were not necessarily thought to be personal gods. Instead, goods like grain and oil were deified.

Perseus, a disciple of Zeno of Citium, presented a similar view: things "that nourish and benefit us were the first to be considered gods and honored as such." He adds, however, that later it was "the *discoverers* of foods and shelter and the other practical arts" that were deified (my emphasis). The names of the

---

3. As noted by Guy Stroumsa, "Celsus, Origen, and the Nature of Religion," in *Discorsi di Verita: Paganesimo, Giudaismo e Cristianesimo a confronto nel Contro Celso di Origene*, ed. Lorenzo Perrone (Rome: Institutum Patristicum Augustinianum, 1998), 81–96 (81).

4. In full: *deus est mortali iuvare mortalem* ("Divinity is a mortal aiding a mortal") (*Nat.* 2.18-19). I do not pretend to be using the phrase in the same sense as Pliny; rather, it illustrates a principle.

5. The gods were known as δοτῆρες ἐάων ("givers of good things") since Homer (*Od.* 8.325; cf. Hes., *Theog.* 46, 111, 633, 664; cf. Hom. *Hymn Merc.* 18.12; Hom. *Hymn. Vest.* 29.8). See on this topic Marek Winiarczyk, *Euhemeros von Messene: Leben, Werk und Nachwirkung* (Munich: Saur, 2002), 43–50, with bibliography and notes. For deity and power, see above, ch. 1, n. 73.

6. Cf. Minucius Felix, *Oct.* 21.2. On the theory of Prodicus, see W. Nestle, *Vom Mythos zum Logos: die Selbstentfaltung des griechischen Denkens von Homer bis auf die Sophistik und Sokrates*, 2nd ed. (Stuttgart: A. Kröner, 1975), 351–55; W. K. C. Guthrie, *A History of Greek Philosophy*, 6 vols. (Cambridge: University of Cambridge Press, 1962), 3:238–42. Further literature in Winiarczyk, *Bibliographie zum antiken Atheismus* (Bonn: R. Habelt, 1994), 81–83.

gods, such as Demeter and Dionysus, were the names of these benefactors.[7] For Perseus, in other words, not only the benefits (such as grain and wine) are divine, but also the (originally human) culture heroes who bring those benefits. In Cicero's succinct description: "people have deified those persons who have made some discovery of great utility for civilized life" (*aliqua magna utilitas ad vitae cultum*) (*Nat. d.* 1.38). This logic presages an important development in ancient theories of deification and the origin of the gods.

Beginning in 277 BCE, Perseus worked in the royal court of the Macedonian king Antigonus Gonatas. This is the same Macedonian court where some decades earlier Euhemerus of Messene may have been active.[8] Euhemerus's work, the *Sacred Chronicle* (Ἱερὰ Ἀναγραφή) embedded an originally philosophical hypothesis about deification into a popular romance. The *Sacred Chronicle* includes a fictional travelogue wherein a legendary explorer arrives at a mythical island on the Indian Ocean called "Panchaia." There in the temple of Zeus Triphylia, the hero of the tale sees a golden stele recounting the deeds of Zeus. Long ago Zeus himself, an ancient king, had set up this stele, recording on it the deeds of his father and grandfather Uranus and Cronus (or Saturn). Later, Zeus's son Hermes added the deeds of Apollo and Artemis.[9]

Most of the *Sacred Chronicle* seems to have been focused on relating the history of these ancient kings (now gods). Uranus and Cronus were deified after their deaths for their benefactions. Zeus was the first to institute a cult for himself.[10] This God, as every Greek knew, was the greatest of gods, the Father of gods and men. If he was once a man, the implication was that all the Greek gods in Zeus's family (commonly known as the "Olympians") were also historical human beings. Unlike other kings who had come and gone, these kings were culture heroes who were deified on account of their beneficent deeds. In the summary of Diodorus of Sicily: "Because of their benefactions (εὐεργεσίας) to people, they [the benefactors] received immortal honor and reputation, as did Heracles, Dionysus, Aristaeus, and the others similar to these."[11]

---

7. Perseus's views are recorded by Philodemus, *Piet.* ch. 9 (translated in Guthrie, *History of Greek Philosophy*, 3:238).

8. A. Henrichs, "Two Doxographical Notes: Democritus and Prodicus on Religion," *HSCP* 79 (1975): 107–23. For the intellectual context of Euhemerus, see Winiarczyk, *Euhemeros*, 30–74.

9. Winiarczyk, *Euhemeri Messenii Reliquae* (Stuttgart: Teubner, 1991), T 37 = Diod. Sic., *Bibl. hist.* 5.46.7.

10. Winiarczyk, *Euhemeros*, 73.

This logic was not totally foreign to Greek theology before Euhemerus. Deified mortals (like Heracles and Dionysus) had always formed a subtype of deities (namely, deified benefactors) (*SVF* 2.1009 = Ps.-Plut. *Plac. Phil.* 880c). Euhemerus merely extended the bounds of that subtype to encompass Olympians like Zeus and Hera. Euhemerus never implied that the eternal and immortal gods like the sun, moon, and stars had ever been human beings.[12] It is thus erroneous to conclude that Euhemerus denied the reality of divinity, even though he finds himself in several catalogues of arch-atheists.[13]

By the first century BCE, euhemeristic historians like Diodorus of Sicily had converted the story of the *Sacred Chronicle* into a theological master narrative. All mythology was historicized such that all anthropomorphic gods became ancient mortal benefactors and culture heroes. Like other Hellenistic historians, Diodorus applied Euhemerism to non-Greek gods as well. According to Philo of Byblos (c. 70–160 CE), for instance, the Phoenicians and Egyptians "considered as greatest gods those men who had made discoveries valuable for life's necessities or those who had in some way benefited their nations. Since they considered these men as benefactors and sources of many blessings, they worshiped them as gods even after they passed on."[14]

In the period relevant to early Christianity, Euhemerism was taken in at least two directions: (1) a "Skeptical-Academic" variety that questioned the divinity of all anthropomorphic gods (since they were only human benefactors) and (2) a Stoic Euhemerism that stressed the motives for apotheosis and accepted the idea that mortals could rightly be deified for their benefactions (*SVF* 1.488).[15] Origen, as we will find out, places himself along the Stoic trajectory of Euhemerism. Thus in explaining popular notions of the divine, I will lean more heavily on Stoic sources.

11. Winiarczyk, *Euhemeri Messenii Reliquae* T25.9-12 = Diod. Sic., *Bib. hist.*, 6.1.1-2 from Eus., *Prep. Ev.* 2.2.52-53. Cf. ibid. frag. 23: "Euhemerus said that those considered gods (θεούς) were once powerful human beings (δυνατούς . . . ἀνθρώπους), and for this reason deified (θεοποιηθέντας) by others" (= Sext. Emp., *Math.* 9.51). For benefaction and euhemerism in Diodorus, see Kenneth S. Sacks, *Diodorus Siculus and the First Century* (Princeton, NJ: Princeton University Press, 1990), 55–82.

12. Winiarczyk, *Euhemeri Messenii Reliquae* T25 = Diod. Sic. *Bibl. hist.* 6.1.1 ; Cf. Varro, *Ant. Rer. Div.*, fr. 32 Cardauns; Cic., *Leg.* 2.19; Plut., *Pelop.* 16.5. For further comments on Euhemerus's eternal gods, see A. I. Baumgarten, "Euhemerus' Eternal Gods: or, How Not To Be Embarrassed by Greek Mythology," in *Classical Studies in Honor of D. Sohlberg*, ed. R. Katzoff et al. (Ramat Gan: Bar-Ilan University Press, 1996), 91–103. Cf. also Winiarczyk, *Euhemeros*, 28–29, 108, and the sources he cites on 146, n. 42.

13. Winiarczyk, *Euhemeros*, 12, n. 4.

14. Philo, *The Phoenician History*, prologue. I use the edition of Harold Attridge and Robert Oden (Washington, DC: Catholic Biblical Association of America, 1981). Cf. Cic., *Nat. d.* 1.101; Winiarczyk, *Euhemeros*, 147-57.

According to the Stoic Chrysippus, the gods are beneficial (εὐεργετικούς) and kindly to human beings (φιλανθρώπους) (*SVF* 2.1115 = Plut. *Stoic. rep.* 1051e). A later Stoic, Antipater of Tarsus (died c. 130 BCE), included the adjective εὐποιητική ("providing benefits") in his definition of divinity (*SVF* 3.33-34 = Plut., *Stoic. rep.* 1051f). According to Balbus, the Stoic in Cicero's *On the Nature of the Gods*, "human ways and general custom have made it a practice to raise into heaven through renown and gratitude men who are distinguished by their benefits (*beneficiis excellentis*)" such as Heracles, Asclepius, and Dionysus (*Nat d.* 2.62; cf. 1.121).[16] Likewise Seneca, the first-century Stoic, writes to Nero: "He who carries himself in accordance with the gods' nature, who is beneficent (*beneficus*), generous and uses his power for the better—does he not hold a place closest (*proximum*) to these [the gods]?" (*Clem* 1.19.9).

The historian Quintus Curtius (first century CE) recounts a story told about Alexander the Great wherein a Scythian envoy challenges the Macedonian king: "if you are a god, you ought to confer benefits on mortals" (*si deus es, tribuere mortalibus beneficia debes*) (*Hist. Alex.* 7.8.11).[17] Plutarch puts into the mouth of Pericles: "We don't see them [the gods] but on account of the honors which they receive and the good things they bestow on us (τοῖς ἀγαθοῖς ἃ παρέχουσιν) we judge them to be immortal [i.e., divine]" (*Per.* 8.6).[18] Those who deprive the gods of their power to benefit contradict common sense (Plut., *Stoic. rep.* 1052b).[19] "Delight in bestowing benefits (χαίροντα εὐεργεσίας)," says

15. Harry Y. Gamble, "Euhemerism and Christology in Origen: *Contra Celsum* 3,22-43," *VC* 33 (1979): 12–29 (14). Both approaches, he notes, are manifest in Cicero's *Nat. d* (skeptical: 3.39-41; 45-50; 1.38; Stoic: 2.62; 1.38-39) (14, n. 7).

16. For further references, see Arthur Stanley Pease, *M. Tulli Ciceronis De Natura Deorum*, 2 vols. (New York: Arno, 1979), 2:698–700. A balanced article on Heracles and his importance for early Christianity is provided by David Aune, "Heracles and Christ" in *Greeks, Romans, and Christians*, 3–19. Cf. Emma Stafford, "Herakles Between Gods and Heroes," in *The Gods of Ancient Greece: Identities and Transformations*, eds. Jan N. Bremmer and Andrew Erskine (Edinburgh: Edinburgh University Press, 2010), 228–44; Stafford, *Herakles* (London: Routledge, 2012). For Asclepius as a popular hero and savior, see Howard Clark Kee, *Miracle in the Early Christian World: A Study in Sociohistorical Method* (New Haven, CT: Yale University Press, 1983), 83–104.

17. The Scythian's comment well sums up the argument of Philo, the Jewish exegete who argues that Gaius Caligula is not a god because he does not grant godlike benefactions to his subjects (*Legat.* 81-116; cf. *Spec Leg.* 4.186-88).

18. Plutarch attributes the quote to Stesimbrotos of Thasos, a contemporary of Pericles and eyewitness (*FGH* 107 F9, T2).

19. Harmful gods were acknowledged (the Penalties, the Furies, Ares, etc.). But gods who made the transition from humanity to divinity are universally acknowledged as beneficial: "there are [gods who were] born human but were honored because of their benefactions for the common life (τὸ διὰ τὰς εἰς

the orator Dio Chrysostom (late first century CE), is "a trait which approaches most nearly to the nature of the gods (ἐγγυτάτω τῆς τῶν θεῶν φύσεως)" (Or. 2.26; cf. 32.15). Similarly, the Stoic Epictetus (second century CE) affirmed, "what has power to confer the greatest advantage (ὠφελείας) is divine (θεῖόν)," and consequently "we even worship (προσκυνοῦμεν) those [beneficent] persons [such as Caesar] as gods (ὡς θεοὺς)" (Diatr. 4.1.60-61).[20]

We find the same logic of deification assimilated by Jewish authors—even if they looked askance at Greco-Roman traditions of deification. According to Ps.-Aristeas, the way to become a god is to invent something useful for human life (τι πρὸς τὸ ζῆν αὐτοῖς χρήσιμον) (Ep. §135). Likewise for Philo of Alexandria, "beneficence is the peculiar property of a god" (θεοῦ δὲ τὸ εὐεργετεῖν ἴδιον) (Mut. 129), and the "proper" (κύριον) name of the power called "god" is "Benefactress" (εὐεργέτις) (QE 2.68). Philo's example of a deified human is Heracles, who "purged the earth and the sea, undergoing trials of endurance most necessary and profitable (ὠφελιμωτάτους) for all humankind in order to destroy things which are mischievous and baneful" (Legat. 81; cf. 90). Consequently Heracles and the other deified men, "received and still receive admiration for the benefits for which we admire them, and were judged worthy of worship and the highest [i.e., divine] honors" (Legat. 86).[21]

This basic, widespread notion—that beneficent power proves divinity—accords well with Celsus's conception of deity in the Contra Celsum. A god, he says, above all ought to provide benefactions for all people (πάντας ἀνθρώπους εὐεργετεῖν) (Cels. 2.20; cf. 2.33; 3.22). The benefits, as we learn from the context, are conceived as those typical of civic benefactors and culture heroes like Heracles (the provision of grain, the founding of cities, and so on). As the preceding discussion indicates, Celsus is not describing his idiosyncratic theory about divinity, but employing a conception basic to

---

τὸν κοινὸν βίον εὐεργεσίας ἐκτετιμημένον)" (Ps.-Plut., Plac. philos. 880c). The key examples cited are those whom Celsus also chose: Heracles, the Dioscuri, and Dionysus.

20. Cf. Diod. Sic., Bibl. hist. 1.13.1.

21. For the concept of euergetism in Judaism and the New Testament, see F. W. Danker, Benefactor: Epigraphic Study of a Graeco-Roman and New Testament Semantic Field (St. Louis: Clayton, 1982); Danker, "Graeco-Roman Cultural Accommodation in the Christology of Luke-Acts," in SBL Seminar Papers 1983, ed. Kent Harold Richards (Chico, CA: Scholars, 1983), 391–414; Rajak, "Benefactors in the Greco-Jewish Diaspora," in The Jewish Dialogue with Greece and Rome: Studies in Cultural and Social Interaction (Leiden: Brill, 2001), 373–92; George van Kooten, "Pagan, Jewish and Christian Philanthropy in Antiquity: A Pseudo-Clementine Keyword in Context," in The Pseudo-Clementines, ed. Jan Bremmer (Leuven: Peeters, 2010), 36–58, esp. 56–57; Susan Sorek, Remembered for Good: A Jewish Benefaction System in Ancient Palestine (Sheffield: Sheffield Phoenix, 2010).

Mediterranean religious thought. To be recognized as a god—to be deified—one must provide benefaction to aid human beings. For the purposes of this chapter, I will call this logic of deification "deifying euergetism."[22]

CELSUS AND THE CRITERION OF DEIFYING EUERGETISM

Applying the criterion of deifying euergetism, Celsus denies that Jesus was divine. Apart from the charge that Jesus was arrogant and a liar (*Cels.* 2.7)—and thus guilty of positive harm—Celsus claims that Jesus performed nothing advantageous for human life. The case is proved by comparison. Whereas the demigods Perseus, Amphion, Aeacus, and Minos performed "great and truly wonderful works on behalf of (ὑπὲρ) humankind" (1.67), and the gods Heracles, Asclepius, the Dioscuri, and Dionysus performed many "noble acts for the benefit of human beings" (γενναῖα ὑπὲρ ἀνθρώπων) (3.22), Jesus displayed no "word or deed that is excellent or wonderful (τί καλὸν ἢ θαυμάσιον ἔργῳ ἢ λόγῳ)" (1.67). In fact, Jesus showed himself to be miserable and powerless, particularly in his death. During his last night on earth, Jesus was so helpless that he could not even persuade or reform his own disciples—all of whom abandoned or betrayed him (2.39). More disturbingly, Jesus predicted the betrayal of Judas, which seemed to goad on the treachery itself.[23] Celsus sarcastically concludes that "a god led his own disciples . . . so far astray that they became impious and wicked" (2.20). Jesus' evil influence on his disciples establishes, says Celsus, that Jesus was a mere human being and a fraud, since "a god above all ought to have done good to all people" (2.20).

---

22. By the adjective "deifying," I am assuming that there is a form of euergetism—what we might call civic euergetism (e.g., the rich providing food at festivals as part of their civic obligation)—which is not necessarily deifying. For a broad introduction to euergetism, see C. Spicq, "La philanthropie hellénistique, vertu divine et royale," *Studia Theologica* 12 (1958): 169–91, esp. 173–91; R. Le Déaut, "ΦΙΛΑΝΘΡΩΠΙΑ dans la littérature grecques jusqu'au Nouveau Testament," in *Mélanges Eugène Tisserant*, ed. E. Tisserant, 7 vols. (Vatican City: Biblioteca Apostolica Vatican, 1964), 1:255–94, esp. 279–94; P. Gauthier, *Les cités grecques et leur bienfaiteurs* (Athens: Ecole française d'Athènes, 1985); Paul Veyne, *Bread and Circuses: Historical Sociology and Political Pluralism*, ed. Oswyn Murray and Brian Pearce; London: Penguin, 1990), esp. 5–19; G. M. Rogers, "Demosthenes of Oenoanda and Models of Euergetism," *JRS* 81 (1991): 91–100; Maria Kantiréa, *Les dieux et les dieux augustes: Le culte impérial en Grèce sous les Julio-claudiens et les Flaviens* (Athens: Center for Hellenic and Roman Antiquity, 2007), 21–87.

23. Note in particular the account of John's Gospel: "After he [Judas] received the piece of bread [from Jesus],Satan entered into him. Jesus said to him, 'Do quickly what you are going to do' . . . So, after receiving the piece of bread, he immediately went out" (13:27, 30). Inhabitation by Satan is a Johannine interpretation.

Yet Jesus' failure to reform his own disciples was not, according to Celsus, the end of Jesus' weakness and shame. Christ wept pathetically in the garden of Gethsemane (2.24)—though a real god would have despised opposition and mocked calamity (2.33). Dionysus, for instance, was able to free himself from his chains and laugh at his captors (Eur., *Bacc.* 576-642).[24] Jesus, by contrast, proved unable to free himself from his bonds (*Cels.* 2.34).[25] Celsus adds that those who condemned Jesus did not suffer the penalty of Pentheus (madness and dismemberment). Jesus, though he knew his fate, was unable to avoid the despicable death of the cross (2.17). Crucifixion is the acme of weakness. God on a cross is an oxymoron, since—as even a later Christian apologist admits—"feebleness is not a feature of a god" (Lact., *Inst.* 1.16.16).[26]

Twisting the knife, Celsus observes that Jesus' death howl (Mark 15:37) was supremely pathetic (*Cels.* 2.58). Such a cowardly demise could not inspire posterity or motivate the virtue of courage (ἀνδρία) so important in Greco-Roman culture. How could Jesus be an example for martyrs if he died so wretchedly (2.38)? How could Jesus be immortal if he died? Even after his putative resurrection, Celsus declares, Jesus hid himself and did not manifest his power to his murderers (2.63). All this weakness and cowardice was, in Mediterranean culture, the very opposite of divinity. In Celsus's language: "No one gives a proof of a god or son of a god by such signs . . . nor by such disreputable evidence" (2.30).[27]

ORIGEN'S RESPONSE

Instead of disagreeing with Celsus about the nature of divinity, Origen mounts his counterattack by assuming the importance of deifying euergetism. Jesus, contrary to what Celsus thinks, displayed divine power that bestowed (and continues to bestow) benefits on people in the Mediterranean world.[28] Origen's first strategy is to point to Jesus' *miracles* as manifestations of divine power (cf.

24. For Dionysus's escape from prison and its afterlife, see John B. Weaver, *Plots of Epiphany: Prison-Escape in Acts of the Apostles*, BZNW 131 (Berlin: Walter de Gruyter, 2004), esp. 44–51; cf. 59–60.

25. Origen's rebuttal actually supports Celsus's case: he boasts that Peter's chains fell off in Acts 12, and that Paul's chains fell off in Acts 16. Here the disciples of Jesus appear better than the master himself.

26. Cf. Seneca: "If you see someone wretched, be sure that he is mortal (*hominem scias*)" (*Herc. fur.* 463).

27. See further John Cook, *The Interpretation of the New Testament in Greco-Roman Paganism*, Studien und Texte zu Antike und Christentum (Tübingen: Mohr Siebeck, 2000), 40–5, 53–61.

28. For the word εὐεργετέω applied to Jesus and connected to his ministry of exorcism, see Acts 10:38 (applied to rulers in Luke 22:25; cf. Philost., *Vit. Ap.* 8.7). For a modern treatment of Jesus as benefactor in the Gospels and Paul, see Luke Timothy Johnson, *Among the Gentiles: Greco-Roman Religion and Christianity* (New Haven, CT: Yale University Press, 2009), 142–57.

Lact., *Inst.* 4.15.6-25). "Jesus," he says, "showed himself among the Jews to be 'divine power' (θεοῦ δύναμις) by the miracles that he did" (*Cels.* 2.9, cf. 1 Cor. 1:24). The miracles are noble deeds because they benefit the entire human community. "The noble action (γενναῖον) of Jesus consists in this," Origen retorts, "that to this day people whom God wills are cured by his name" (2.33). These cures Origen later calls the "token" (σύμβολον) of Jesus' divinity (3.33). In *Contra Celsum* 2.48, Origen affirms that Jesus "healed the lame and the blind, for which reason we regard him as . . . son of God [i.e., divine]."[29]

Although all kinds of cures were involved, Origen particularly emphasizes deliverance from daimonic possession. "But the creator of the universe himself," he says, "by means of the persuasive power of his miraculous utterances, showed Jesus to be worthy of [divine] honor, not only to the men who were willing to welcome him, but also to daimones and other invisible powers; to the present day these appear either to fear the name of Jesus as superior to them, or to accept him in reverence as their lawful ruler" (3.36). Exorcisms performed in Jesus' name demonstrated, according to Origen, that Jesus was more divine than the powerful daimones (among whom Christians placed the traditional Greek gods). Yet exorcism was not only a display of power, but also of benefaction, since it liberated those who were possessed. Just as the miracles of Moses are "divine" (θεῖα) by virtue of their power to benefit, so the miracles of Jesus that brought "the preservation [or salvation] of souls" (σωτηρίαν ψυχῶν) demonstrated his deity (2.50).[30]

Nevertheless, the problem with Jesus' miracles—as Origen himself realized—was that they were not fundamentally distinct from the miracles so often performed by other thaumaturges roaming the Mediterranean world. Origen confesses in his *Commentary on John* that "in the time of our Lord

---

29. For the connection of miracles and divinity in the ancient world, see O. Weinreich, *Antike Heilungswunder* (Giessen: Töpelmann, 1909); Weinreich, *Neue Urkunden zur Sarapisreligion* (Tübingen: Mohr Siebeck, 1919), 13–18; A. D. Nock, *Conversion: The Old and the New in Religion from Alexander the Great to Augustine of Hippo* (Oxford: Clarendon, 1933), 83–93; Nock, *Essays on Religion and the Ancient World*, 2 vols. (Cambridge, MA: Harvard University Press, 1972), 1:327–28 and n. 107; H. S. Versnel, ed., *Faith, Hope and Worship: Aspects of Religious Mentality in the Ancient World* (Leiden: Brill, 1981), 53–62; Ramsay MacMullen, *Paganism in the Roman Empire* (New Haven, CT: Yale University Press, 1981), 96, 191, nn.1–2; MacMullen, *Christianizing the Roman Empire* (New Haven, CT: Yale University Press, 1984), see index, *s.v.* "miracle." Much useful comparative material is provided by Wendy Cotter, *Miracles in Greco-Roman Antiquity: A Sourcebook for the Study of New Testament Miracles* (London: Routledge, 1999).

30. For further discussion of miracles in *Cels.*, see Michel Fédou, *Christianisme et religions païennes dans le Contra Celse d'Origène* (Paris: Beauchesne, 1988), 396–415; Michael Fiedrowicz, ed., *Origenes: Contra Celsum, Gegen Celsus*, trans. Claudia Barthold, 3 vols. (Freiburg: Herder, 2011), 1:58–61.

miracles were able to bring people to faith, but as time passed they did not preserve their demonstrative power, and were suspected to be myths" (2.204; cf. Lact., *Inst.* 5.3.7-21). Celsus, for his part, views Jesus' miracles as run-of-the-mill displays of magic—proof that Jesus could *coax* the divine, not that he *was* divine.[31]

In consequence, Origen attempts to distinguish miracles from magic. Part of his strategy is to ignore the pure "shock and awe" wonders of Jesus. He does not mention, for instance, Jesus' stilling of the sea or the multiplication of the loaves.[32] The miracles that Origen prefers are the miracles with obvious benefit—namely, healings. By these wonders, Origen tries to prove that Jesus is divine, and more divine than the daimones whom magicians control.

Nevertheless, Origen knows that—though he can prove Jesus divine by *beneficent* miracles—he cannot by this method prove that Jesus is *uniquely* divine. The popular god Asclepius, for instance, was viewed as divine for healing the lame and the paralyzed (Justin Martyr, *1 Apol.* 22).[33] In order to trump Asclepius, Origen needed to go beyond the miracles—and beyond the popular understanding of deifying euergetism.[34]

FROM MIRACLES TO MORALS

Origen admits that healing people, discovering the cultivation of staple foods, and saving a city from harm are all significant benefits. Nevertheless the supreme advantages, he asserts, are *moral* and come from moral benefactors.[35] In most Hellenistic religions, the gods were not entangled in a human moral framework or expected to live by human moral conventions.[36] Nevertheless, it

31. For ancient magic, see esp. Fritz Graf, *Magic in the Ancient World* (Cambridge, MA: Harvard University Press, 1997); Paul Mirecki and Marvin Meyer, eds., *Magic and Ritual in the Ancient World* (Leiden: Brill, 2002); Gideon Bohak, *Ancient Jewish Magic: A History* (Cambridge: Cambridge University Press, 2008).

32. Such miracles, it would seem, were temporary measures designed to persuade people about Jesus' teachings (cf. *Cels.* 8.47).

33. For further testimonies, see Ludwig and Emma Edelstein, eds., *Asclepius: A Collection and Interpretation of the Testimonies*, 2 vols. (New York: Arno, 1975), 1:§§239-47. A more recent introduction to Asclepius (with full archaeological detail) can be found in Thomas Lehmann, ed., *Wunderheilungen in der Antike: Von Asklepios zu Felix Medicus* (Oberhausen: Athena, 2006).

34. On the conflict between Christ and Asclepius, see Harold Remus, *Pagan-Christian Conflict over Miracle in the Second Century* (Cambridge, MA: Philadelphia Patristic Foundation, 1983), 97-135.

35. On the argument from morality, see Fiedrowicz, *Contra Celsum, Gegen Celsus*, 1:107-109.

36. The same is generally true in Roman religion. See J. H. W. G. Liebeschuetz, *Continuity and Change in Roman Religion* (Oxford: Clarendon, 1979), 39-54.

became increasingly common—especially among philosophical circles—to see moral virtue as a truly divine characteristic.[37] As Euripides says through the mouth of (the god!) Heracles:

> I do not believe the gods are fond of unlawful sexual liaisons
> Or that they love to bind chains on hands.
> I never thought it worthy, nor will I be convinced that
> One god is tyrant of another by nature
> For god, if he is truly god, lacks nothing. (*Herc.* 1341-46, my trans.)

A generation after Euripides, Plato gave moral theology a firmer (philosophical) basis. In his *Republic*, he demanded that poetic theology follow certain patterns (τύποι).[38] The first and most important pattern is that a God "must always be represented as he is"—namely as a being who is good (*Resp.* 379b-c). The second guideline is that God does not change, and thus does not lie (*Resp.* 380d-383a).

For Plato, the supremely divine goods are also the four cardinal virtues: wisdom (φρόνησις), temperance (σωφροσύνη), justice (δικαιοσύνη), and courage (ἀνδρεία) (*Leg.* 1.631b2-d6). Non-moral goods—things that Greeks expected from their gods like health, strength, and wealth—Plato viewed as lesser, merely "human" goods. In his *Laws*, Plato says that the gods supremely possess the four cardinal virtues.[39] Indeed, what "sets Plato's gods apart from the gods of popular belief," writes Jon Mikalson,

> . . . is their concern for justice, not only for that part of justice that concerns the gods ('proper respect' and 'religious correctness') which was equally a concern of popular religion, but also for that part of justice that involves other human beings. And not for just

37. Xenophanes is arguably the first to offer a theology guided by human moral sensibilities. Nevertheless, his criticism of the gods' morality in Homer and Hesiod does not amount to a full-scale wedding of theology and ethics. For the fragments and commentary, see J. H. Lesher, ed., *Xenophanes of Colophon: Fragments* (Toronto: University of Toronto Press, 1992), 22–23; 47–77.

38. Celsus is almost certainly aware of the Platonic "patterns" of theology, since he directly uses them in *Cels.* 4.65, 4.18.

39. Sound-thinking (σωφροσύνη, 906b1), wisdom (φρόνησις, 906b1), courage (ἀνρεία, 900e), and justice (δικαιοσύνη, 906a8). This point is noted by Richard Bodéüs, *Aristotle and the Theology of the Living Immortals*, trans. Jan Edward Garrett (Albany: State University of New York, 2000), 121.

some parts of the latter, but for all of it. For Plato, of course, the gods in so promoting justice and punishing injustice in human affairs were also *showing benevolence* to humans because, in the Platonic vision, whatever humans might think at the moment, the practice of justice in both divine and human affairs led to the best life and the acquisition of 'the good things' here and hereafter . . .[40]

By implication, the true benefits a (Platonic) god bestows on human beings are moral: the power to reason and its consequence: the life of virtue.

HERACLES

Cynics and Stoics adopted and adapted Platonic theology by emphasizing that divine virtue was, properly speaking, moral virtue. As a consequence, truly divine benefactions had to be *moral*. We see this development in the philosophical appropriation of Heracles, whose motley stories were well known in the ancient Mediterranean. For instance, a fragment from Herodorus (a contemporary of Socrates) allegorizes Heracles's adventure to obtain the golden apples of the Hesperides. In this story, the hero, draped with the lion skin and wielding his famous club, must overcome the serpent guarding the fruit. For Herodorus, all these elements are symbolized and morally transvalued. The serpent is "the variegated reasoning of bitter passion" (τὸν πολυποίκιλον τῆς πικρᾶς ἐπιθυμίας λογισμόν), the club is philosophy (φιλοσοφία), and the lion skin is Heracles's "noble mind" (γενναῖον φρόνημα). The three apples are three virtues, "not growing angry (τὸ μὴ ὀργίζεσθαι), not loving money (τὸ μὴ φιλαργυρεῖν), and not loving pleasure (τὸ μὴ φιληδονεῖν)." "For through the club of his enduring soul and the skin of his most bold and temperate reasoning (τοῦ θρασυτάτου σώφρονος λογισμοῦ), he [Heracles] overcame the earthly contest of worthless passion, and philosophized even unto death" (*FGH* 31 frg. 14).[41]

Antisthenes, a disciple of Socrates, wrote three books on Heracles—one of which with the significant title: *Heracles: Concerning Reason or Force* (Diog.

---

40. Jon Mikalson, *Greek Popular Religion in Greek Philosophy* (Oxford: Oxford University Press, 2010), 240–41, emphasis added.

41. See further Ragnar Höistad, *Cynic Hero and Cynic King: Studies in the Cynic Conception of Man* (Lund: C. Bloms Boktryckeri, 1948), 30–33. See also Abraham Malherbe, "Herakles," in *RAC*, eds. Carsten Colpe et al., 24 vols. (Stuttgart: Anton Hiersemann, 1988), 14:560–62; Litwa, *We Are Being Transformed*, 197–98; Aune, "Heracles," 8; Emma Stafford, "Vice or Virtue? Herakles and the Art of Allegory," in *Herakles and Hercules: Exploring a Graeco-Roman Divinity*, eds. Louis Rawlings and Hugh Bowden (Swansea: Classical Press of Wales, 2005), 71–96; Stafford, *Herakles*, 123–29.

Laert., *Vit. philosoph.* 6.16-17, cf. 2.61). He seems to have suggested that Heracles learned virtue from Chiron, the benevolent centaur. Probably drawing on Heracles as an example, he defined toil (or suffering, i.e., πόνος) as a good, and the end of ethics as life according to virtue (Diog. Laert., *Vit. philosoph.* 6.104-105).[42]

The Cynic tradition later made ample use of Heracles as a moral model. Diogenes of Sinope claimed that his own life of toil and resistance to pleasure was the same sort of life that Heracles lived (Diog. Laert., *Vit. philosoph.* 6.70-71).[43] In the *Cynic Epistles*, Pseudo-Diogenes declares that the mind (φρόνημα) of Heracles was "mightier than every turn of fortune" (*Ep.* 26). Dio Chrysostom places a eulogy of Heracles in the mouth of Diogenes with the message that the moral labors of Heracles are far more impressive than the athletic feats of the Isthmian Games (*Or.* 8.27-28, 30). For Philo, as we have seen, Heracles was a model of patient endurance of suffering (*Prob.* 120). According to Epictetus, Heracles travelled the world to cast out violence and introduce the well-ordered (εὐνομίην) life. He believed that Zeus was his own father and looked to him in all that he did (*Diatr.* 3.24.13-16). Heracles was "son of God," we learn from Dio Chrysostom, not genetically, but because of his proper moral training (*Or.* 4.29, 31).[44] It was as a friend of God and in obedience to God that Heracles "went about clearing away wickedness (ἀδικία) and lawlessness (ἀνομία)" and "introducing justice (δικαιοσύνη) and right religion (ὁσιότης)" (*Diatr.* 2.16.44; 3.26.32; cf. 1.6.30-36; 4.10.11).[45]

Heracles the teacher of virtue also appears in Heraclitus's *Homeric Problems* (first century CE). "Heracles," he says, "should be thought of not as someone so trained in bodily power that he was the strongest man of his time, but as a sensible man (ἀνήρ ἔμφρων) and an initiate of heavenly wisdom (σοφίας οὐρανίου μύστης) who brought to light philosophy (ἐφώτισε τὴν φιλοσοφίαν) which had been plunged into the depths of fog . . . as the most learned Stoics agree" (33:1). He then allegorizes Heracles's labors: "The boar which he overcame is the common incontinence of men; the lion is the indiscriminate rush towards improper goals; in the same way, by fettering irrational passions he gave rise to the belief that he had fettered the violent bull. He banished

---

42. Hoïstad, *Cynic Hero*, 35–37; H. D. Rankin, *Anthisthenes Sokratikos* (Amsterdam: Adolf M. Hakkert, 1986), 101–106.

43. Hoïstad, *Cynic Hero*, 47. Cf. Luc., *Vit. auct.* 8.

44. Cf. Diog. Laert., *Vita Philosoph.* 6.70-71.

45. Hoïstad, *Cynic Hero*, 61.

cowardice also from the world, in the shape of the hind of Ceryneia" (33:3-9, trans. Russell and Konstan).[46]

ORIGEN AND STOICIZING THEORIES OF DEIFICATION

When the Platonist Celsus underscores the "many noble acts (γενναῖα)" of "the Dioscuri, Heracles, Asclepius, and Dionysus," he does not highlight the specifically moral worth of these benefits (*Cels.* 3.22). Failure to emphasize true virtue leaves him open to attack. Origen, seeing the weakness in Celsus's argument, follows a Cynic and Stoicizing trajectory of euergetism: the only truly deifying benefits (i.e., those worthy of a god) are moral.[47]

By emphasizing the ethics of euergetism, Origen attacks Celsus's prime *exempla* of deification through benefaction. For Origen, Heracles—as well as Asclepius and Dionysus—are disqualified from deification because (1) they were immoral in their personal lives, and (2) as putative gods, their powers manifested immoral effects.[48] Heracles, for instance, was morally disqualified from being a god since he was "licentious" during his life on earth, and served a woman (3.22).[49] Dionysus, in turn, was "frenzied" and "clad in feminine clothing" (3.22).[50] Asclepius, however, was a harder case, since the only major *faux pas* mentioned for this hero (which in fact gets him electrocuted) is raising the dead.[51] But this was a pastime of Jesus himself (Mark 5:21-43; Luke 7:11-17; John 11:1-45).[52] As a god, furthermore, Asclepius had a clean record as a healer at various cult centers and even had a reputation as one who promoted moral ideals. As Emma and Ludwig Edelstein observe,

> Not only did he sift his patients by refusing to help those whom he
> did not deem worthy of help, not only did he himself follow the

---

46. For Heracles as a moral exemplar in Cicero, see *Fin.* 2.118-19; *Offic.* 3.25.

47. For morality and truth in Origen, see Christiana Reemts, *Vernunftgemässer Glaube: Die Begründung des Christentums in der Schrift des Origenes gegen Celsus* (Bonn: Borengässer, 1998), 198–203.

48. Gamble, "Euhemerism," 23. For this strategy in other apologists, see Athenagoras, *Legat.* 29; Clement of Alexandria, *Protrep.* 2.22-23, 26-28, 30; Lactantius, *Inst.* 1.19.7; as well as Lautaro Roig Lanzillotta, "Christian Apologists and Greek Gods," in *The Gods of Ancient Greece*, 442–64 (esp. 448–57).

49. Cf. Lactantius, *Inst.* 1.9.1.

50. Origen's male chauvinism is particularly patent here. Cf. Lucian, *Deor. conc.* 4.

51. Edelstein and Edelstein, *Asclepius*, 1.§§66-93.

52. A positive, though cursory comparison of Jesus and Asclepius is offered by Johannes L. P. Wolmarans, "Asclepius and Jesus of Nazareth," *Acta Patristica et Byzantina* 7 (1996): 117–127. The myths of both Asclepius and Jesus, he argues, were "produced by a similar vision of the world, a similar frame of reference" (120). Differences are traced to minor Christian refinements and the Jewish local color of the Jesus stories.

highest moral standards, he even expected those who came to him to strive for perfection as it was envisaged by the philosophers. For in contrast to the outward purity of ceremonies and rites he desired for them the inner purity of the heart. It was Asclepius on whose temple at Epidaurus the words were inscribed: "Pure must be he who enters the fragrant temple; purity means to think nothing but holy thoughts." Besides, the god expected his patients, after they had been healed by him, to lead a better life in the future than they had done before, he urged them [sic]: "Enter a good man, leave a better one."[53]

Origen must admit that Asclepius's power to heal and to foretell the future are effective for gaining devotees (3.24). Pressing his attack, however, Origen claims that Asclepius's healings are morally indifferent and thus have no real worth. For the Alexandrian apologist, "there is nothing divine (μηδὲν θεῖον) about the healing of Asclepius" (3.25).

Origen could better besmirch the reputation of Asclepius's father Apollo. The Pythian oracle, Origen claims, is morally skewed—a fact that undercuts the divinity of its author (3.25). Apollo, for instance, commanded that Aristeas the Proconnesian be worshipped as a god because he "both vanished so miraculously from men and again clearly appeared, and a long time afterwards visited many parts of the world and related amazing tales" (3.26). But the oracle was wrong to announce the divinity of such a man, says Origen, since Aristeas had no moral effect on posterity (3.27-28, 31). The same applies to the famous Abaris riding his arrow, and especially to the boxer Cleomedes. After Cleomedes demolished a building (killing several children), he escaped stoning by jumping into a chest in the temple of Athena. When people pried opened the chest, Cleomedes had disappeared. Though Apollo ordered that Cleomedes be worshiped as a hero, Origen declares that Cleomedes's behavior shows "no evidence of divinity." What was the point, Origen asks, of god or providence making Cleomedes disappear? There was no true—that is, *moral*—benefit; thus both the disappearance and Apollo's oracle were not worthy of a god (3.33).

In *Contra Celsum* 3.34, Origen summarizes his main point: the divinity of Celsus's deified men (Heracles, and so on) is vacuous because it produced no real (read: *moral*) benefit for humanity (μηδὲν ὠφεληκότας τὸ τῶν ἀνθρώπων γένος). Lumping Greek gods and heroes together, Origen concludes that they were not free from the antitheses of the cardinal virtues: licentiousness, unrighteousness, folly, and cowardice (*Cels.* 3.42). For Origen, the criterion

---

53. Edelstein and Edelstein, *Asclepius*, 2.126–27. Cf. Aristid., *Or.* 28.132K.

of divinity is not just deifying euergetism, but what I will call "ethical euergetism."[54]

JESUS AND ETHICAL EUERGETISM

Only Jesus, according to Origen, fulfills the model of ethical euergetism in both his life and death. In his life, Jesus demonstrates his divinity through acts of moral reformation. In his death, Jesus bravely sacrifices himself to provide the ultimate benefit: the kingdom of heaven. By describing Jesus in these terms, Origen attempts to redefine Jesus as a moral benefactor and culture hero. As in the Cynic-Stoic depiction of Heracles, it is Jesus' moral benefits that ensure his deity.

Origen does not dispute that Solon or Minos devised law codes beneficial to the human race, thus lending credence to their divine origin. What he disputes is that such men provided a benefaction as profound and long-lasting as Jesus. Jesus' good deed, Origen states, is the conversion of thousands "from countless evils" and the implantation of virtue (he mentions specifically meekness, tranquility, and love of humankind) (1.67). Origen is confident that in this respect Jesus outshines all of Celsus's deified competitors. "Let Celsus's Jew," Origen challenges, "show us not many, nor even a few, but just one man of the same type as Jesus, who by the power within him (μετὰ τῆς ἐν αὐτῷ δυνάμεως) introduced a system of doctrines which benefited the human race (βιωφελῆ) and converted it from the flood of sins" (2.8).[55] "[E]ven to this day," he says, "the power (δύναμις) of Jesus brings about conversion and moral reformation" (1.43; cf. 3.33). This beneficent and moral power of Jesus is what constituted Jesus' divinity. As Origen later rephrases it: "His [Jesus'] divinity (θειότης) is testified by great numbers of churches, which consist of people converted from the flood of sins" (1.47; cf. Tert., Apol. 21.30-31). Later, "the churches of people who have been benefited (αἱ τῶν ὠφελουμένων ἐκκλησίαι)," along with Christ's wisdom and gift of rationality are portrayed as "proofs of Jesus' divinity" (θειότης) (3.33).

In short, Origen declares that Jesus excelled all those deified by virtue—precisely by his surpassing (moral!) virtue. In his own words, "Jesus is far, far superior to everyone who for his virtue (διὰ τὴν ἀρετήν) is called

---

54. Cf. Eugene Gallagher, *Divine Man or Magician?* (Atlanta: Scholars Press, 1982), 139, and *passim*. Origen is not the only ancient author to deny someone divinity based on moral criteria. Seneca in his farce *Apocolocyntosis of the Divine Claudius* denies that Claudius is divine because he killed so many close relations (§11).

55. "Celsus' Jew" is a character that Celsus uses (appearing in *Cels.* 2-3) to criticize the Christian movement.

a son of God, since he is as it were the source and origin of such virtues" (*Cels.* 1.57). Although Origen attempts to portray Jesus as unique, he asserts this uniqueness on the basis of a commonly accepted philosophical idea. Stated crudely, Origen's deified hero trumps other deified heroes by being preeminently the source of what was thought to deify: virtue.[56]

The supreme moral benefit that Jesus gives, Origen makes clear, is the ability to attain the four cardinal virtues. Jesus made people "become controlled instead of licentious—or at least making progress in self control (σωφροσύνην)." He made people "just instead of unjust, or making progress toward justice (δικαιοσύνην), . . . wise instead of stupid, or on the road to wisdom (φρόνησιν)," and finally "brave (ἀνδρεῖοι) and bold" (2.79). Jesus is thus a paragon of Platonic virtue, the true image of the ultimate and exclusive source of benefaction: the Good.

But does a Platonic god die? Death, one would have to say, remains a paradoxical manifestation of Jesus' divinity in Mediterranean culture. Nevertheless the way that Origen construes the meaning of Jesus' death makes it amenable to common conceptions of divine power. The power of Jesus, Origen thought, was not fundamentally different than the power of Greek heroes and deified men—it was simply greater.

The key is to realize that Jesus' divine power was hidden behind a veil of weakness. Celsus scorns Jesus for choosing tax collectors and "sailors" to spread his message. But the weakness of the teachers, Origen retorts, shows all the more the divine power of the teaching (1.62; cf. 3.39). The argument sounds Pauline: "when I am weak, then I am powerful" (2 Cor. 12:10). But this logic can also be found in Greco-Roman culture. In the *Bacchae*, Dionysus exercised his power from an initial chosen position of weakness and inferiority. He appeared as an effeminate Lydian teenager and allowed himself to be chained and mocked (Eur., *Bacc.* 434–518). Just so, Jesus allowed himself to be bound and ridiculed, while giving ample demonstration of his power (e.g., by the earthquake, eclipse, and the rending of the temple veil coincident with his death; Matt. 27:45-56, par.). By a simple self-identification, according to the Gospel of John, Jesus was able to knock down all those who came to arrest him (18:6).

Yet the greatest demonstration of paradoxical power was Jesus' death itself. Origen must admit that it is not proper—or even conceivable—for a god to die. Yet he qualifies Jesus' death by affirming that what died was only Jesus'

---

56. Origen also claims that due to "their purity of character, surpassing human nature," judges in the Old Testament were called "gods" by "traditional Jewish usage" (*Cels.* 4.31; Ex 22:27 LXX).

body—not the divinity that inhabited Jesus (2.9). Thus whatever indignities the body of Jesus underwent did not besmirch his divinity, which took up residence *in* his body. In the words of Eugene Gallagher, "Origen's concept of Jesus as a 'composite being' [body plus divine Logos] allows him to attribute those statements which give evidence of an anguished and suffering human being to 'the supposedly human Jesus' while attributing others to the Logos."[57] The divine Logos within Jesus was not affected by Jesus' death, but bore it patiently. The soul of Jesus interwoven with the Logos could thus still be a moral exemplar. As Origen remarks,

> The things that were done to Jesus, in so far as they are understood to apply to the divine element in him, are pious, and not in conflict with the accepted notion of God. But in so far as he was a man, who more than anyone else was adorned by sublime participation in the very Logos and wisdom himself, he endured as a wise and perfect man what must be endured by a man who does all in his power on behalf of the entire race of human beings and of rational beings as well. There is nothing objectionable in the fact that a man died, and in that his death should not only be given as an example of the way to die for the sake of religion, but also should effect a beginning and an advance in the overthrow of the evil one, the devil, who dominated the whole earth. (*Cels.* 7.17)

Origen immediately turns to the beneficial aspect of Jesus' death. By defeating the devil, Jesus' demise proved "beneficial to all" (τῷ παντὶ χρήσιμον) (2.23). Jesus' silent passivity during the trial, for Origen, does not disprove his deity. Rather, Jesus is an example of one who died "willingly for religion" and—like Dionysus in the *Bacchae*—showed how to "despise people" who laugh and mock at piety.[58] Jesus was a true example of courage, because he suffered *for others* (2.34, cf. 42), and it is not disgraceful to endure sufferings for others' benefit (2.38). Most importantly, Jesus died "for the common good of humankind" (κατὰ τὸ κοινωνικόν) (2.44); and his resurrection "produced a greater benefit" (μείζονα εἰργάσατο) than the world had ever known—eternal life (2.58).

Origen even goes so far as to claim that Jesus benefited his murderers. If Jesus had appeared to those who killed him—as Celsus wanted—they would have been struck blind like the men of Sodom (Gen. 19:11). By *not* appearing

---

57. Gallagher, *Divine Man or Magician*, 125.

58. Cf. Remus (semi-divine brother of Romulus), who was said to maintain an "orderly silence" (εὐκόσμος σιώπη) at his trial, which would likely lead to his death (Dion. Hal., *Ant. Rom.* 1.81.3).

to them, Jesus showed them the benefit of mercy. Jesus was not weak, but by hiding his divine power (δύναμιν . . . θείαν) he proved to be a beneficent god (2.67).

Origen's overarching point is not that weakness is power or that power is weakness, but that *apparent* weakness guarantees the authenticity of divine power. In this way, Origen accepts the Greco-Roman logic of divinity: *power manifests godhood.* The power was there for those with eyes to see it. Power concealed was all the more effective if it benefitted and transformed those who experienced it.

CONCLUSION

Half a century after Origen, the Christian apologist Arnobius asks,

> Is he [Christ] not worthy to be called a god by us (*dignus a nobis est . . . deus dici*) and felt to be a god (*deusque sentiri*) on account of the favor or such great benefits (*tantorum ob munerum gratiam*)? For if *you* [non-Christians] have enrolled Liber [Dionysus] among the gods because he discovered the use of wine, and Ceres the use of bread, Aesculapius the use of medicines, Minerva the use of oil, Triptolemus plowing, and (finally) Hercules because he conquered and restrained beasts, thieves, and the many-headed hydra—with how many honors should we endow him who removed us from great errors by putting truth in our lap . . . who has pointed out to us what is especially fruitful and salvific for the human race—namely what, who, how vast, and how great God is—who allowed us to grasp and understand—and even taught us—his depths and unspeakable heights . . . So then, ought we not to consider Christ a god (*deus*), and to bestow upon him all the worship due to his divinity—or else whatever can be conceived as greatest of all? Ought we not to consider Christ a god—he from whom we have received for a long time such great goods while we live, and from whom we expect (when the day comes) greater benefits? (1.38-39, my trans.)[59]

Arnobius acknowledges that Jesus was human, but claims that "on account of the many gifts (*donis*) which have come from him to us, he ought to be called and addressed as god (*deus dici appellarique deberet*)" (1.42, cf. 44-46). The basic

---

59. For background on Arnobius, see Michael Simmons, *Arnobius of Sicca: Religious Conflict and Competition in the Age of Diocletian* (Oxford: Clarendon, 1995), 229-42.

message is clear: Jesus' benefactions proved his divinity. Classically, Arnobius "goes one up" on his opponents by declaring that Jesus' benefits were the first to reveal the nature of deity. From "the kindliness of his deeds" (*ex operum benignitate*), he says, people were "taught to surmise what a true god is (*quid esset deus verus iam addiscerent suspicari*)" (1.47). The argument discloses how educated Christians shared Mediterranean theological ideas (deeds demonstrate divinity) while simultaneously trying to play the game of one-upmanship: Jesus is not only the best of benefactors, but the *only* true benefactor and source of benefaction. He shows not only that he is a god, but of what true godhood consists.

Almost four hundred years before Arnobius we hear from the lips of Lucretius this encomium of Epicurus:

> Who in strength of mind is worthy to compose a poem to match the dignity of the subject and of such discoveries? Who can with words alone mold praises to match his merits—he who left behind so many sought-after benefits created by his mind? No one, I think, born from a mortal body will be able. For if we must speak as the recognized dignity of the subject itself demands—he [Epicurus] was a god, noble Memmius!—this one who first discovered the principle of life which is now called 'wisdom,' who by his ingenuity moved life from such great billows and such vast darkness into so tranquil and placid a light! Compare the old divine discoveries of others, for we are told that Ceres provided grain for mortals and Liber the liquid of the vine-born drink. Still without these benefits, life could have remained, as we are told that even now other peoples live. But one cannot live well without a pure heart (*puro pectore*). Thus all the more rightly does he appear to us to be a god from whom still today among great peoples the sweet solaces of life, spread abroad, soothe human souls. But if you will suppose that the deeds of Hercules rival his, you will stray very far from true reason. For how does the great Nemean jaw, that terrible gaping of the lion, harm us? Or the bristling Arcadian boar? What in the end can the Cretan bull or the Lernean hydra fortified with venomous snakes do to us? . . . But unless the heart is purged (*pergatumst pectus*), what battles and perils then will work their way into us against our will? How many bitter cares of desire will divide an anxious person! How many fears besides! What arrogant acts, morally foul and over-bold! How many disasters will arise! What luxury and idleness! And so he who

subjugated all these things, and drove them from the mind by words not weapons—will it not be fitting that this man be counted worthy of the rank of gods (*numero divom dignarier esse*)? (*Rerum Nat.* 5.1-51, my trans.; cf. Cic. *Nat. d.* 1.16.43)

Here we find another insider's report about a human being who by his benefits is proved to be divine. Again we see the game of one-upmanship. The benefits of Epicurus are better than Ceres, Liber, and Hercules. The reason why they are better, we learn, is because they are moral. They purge the heart from its infections. They do away with internal fears, anxieties, arrogance, and sloth that worm their way into the human soul. Because he freed people from these passions, Epicurus—who models the victory over all the wild beasts of the soul—is worthy to join the gods.

Between these thinkers we find Origen—considered one of the greatest Christian theologians—dealing with the same logic and strategies of deification. Origen similarly taught that Jesus is divine because he "brings us the benefits of the Father" (τοῦ πατρὸς εὐεργεσίας) (*Cels.* 3.34).[60] Jesus' benefits were better than those of Dionysus, Asclepius, and Heracles because they were distinctly moral and have an enduring effect. Those Christians who experienced those benefits—external and internal, temporary and eternal, natural and supernatural—could rightfully attest to Jesus' godhood. His power over nature, over the human body, over daimones, and over death proved that he was not simply a man but (a) god worthy of divine honor.[61]

Celsus denies that Jesus is divine, while Origen argues that he was—but both use a similar euergetistic criterion. The difference between Origen and Celsus is not that Origen denies the logic of euergetism as "pagan" and false, but that he relies on a particular philosophical appropriation of euergetism with its emphasis on *moral* virtue as the true beneficence.[62] For Origen, true divinity is *moral* divinity, and thus true euergetism is *ethical* euergetism. This is a distinctive and rhetorically effective argument in Origen's apologetic arsenal. His philosophical fine-tuning of euergetism manifests an underlying similarity. The *rationale* of divinity remains similar for both Origen and Celsus—power,

---

60. Cf. 2.42: "Jesus confirmed the truth of what he claimed to do by the benefits (δι' ὧν ὠφέλησε) which he brought to his adherents."

61. Gamble, "Euhemerism," 26.

62. Ibid., 26, n. 32. Gamble concludes that Origen's argument is "an apologetical *tour de force* because it works within the traditional category of apotheosis, but in such a way as to meet the problems which the critically-minded discovered in this type of piety" (29).

and specifically *beneficent* power, expresses deity. Christians and non-Christians could thus agree on the fundamental principle: *deus est iuvare*.

To be sure, Origen never states that Jesus was *deified* because of his moral benefits. These benefits are the proof of his *antecedent* deity, not the grounds for his future (or postmortem) transformation into god. Yet this same reasoning was maintained before by the votaries of Heracles, Asclepius, and Dionysus. These gods were not *made* divine by their benefactions; rather their benefactions proved them *already* to be sons of god, born of the high God Zeus and (in the case of Asclepius) Apollo. For his own part, Origen accepts this common strategy of deification and applies it *a fortiori* to his own lord.

Admittedly, Origen's audience in the *Contra Celsum* shaped the form of his argument. From his preface, he indicates that he speaks to those without faith in Christ or to the weak in faith (*pref.* 6). To the strong in faith, presumably, Origen would not need to prove Jesus' divinity. He could merely expound it—as he so richly does in his exegetical and theological works. Yet in arguing for Jesus' divinity, Origen never apologizes for using the criterion of euergetism. Though he attempts to moralize it, he shows no sign that the criterion is flawed or embarrassing to him. Far from being defunct, euergetism meets its fulfillment in Jesus.

Thus despite Origen's promotion of Jesus to *sui generis* status, historically speaking Jesus' divinity was not "unique" in the Mediterranean world.[63] If it was, it would not even have been understandable—let alone convincing—to anyone in that world. For Origen, there were ways (mostly metaphysical) of describing Jesus' deity to highlight its distinctive nature. From the standpoint of euergetism, however, Jesus' godhood was greater in *degree* rather than different in *kind*. By the basic principles woven into his argument, then, Origen shows that Jesus—though he surpasses "all the distinguished [and deified] men that have ever lived" (1.30)—is still comparable to them.

When compared with Cynic and Stoic counterparts, however, Origen's understanding of Jesus' divinity does prove distinctive. For Stoics and like-minded Cynics, the moral virtue of Heracles demonstrated his divinity. It did not, however, make him the source and center of divinity or the exclusive model for living the divine mode of life. Origen, by contrast, not only roots

---

63. *Pace* Reemts, who bases the uniqueness of Jesus' divinity on Origen's metaphysics of the incarnation (*Vernunftgemässer Glaube*, 165–74). A singular metaphysics, however, only establishes distinctiveness, not uniqueness. There were several theories of incarnation in the ancient world; Origen's view is only one (Christian) variant. On the question of uniqueness, see further Fiedrowicz, *Origenes: Contra Celsum*, 1:103–4.

Jesus' divinity in ethical euergetism, he makes Jesus the focus and chief conduit of divinity. He is the focal point of divinity because he is the unique source of good and advantage for the human race. Origen expresses this difference by saying that Jesus is "the source and origin" of the virtues (*Cels.* 1.57).

As the focal point and conduit of divinity, Jesus is the sole archetype for the divine way of life. When facing the likes of Heracles, Origen emphasizes Jesus' distinctive deity. Nevertheless even Origen assumes that Jesus' divinity is not in fact exclusive. Those who share Jesus' way of life partake of his divinity—though in a lesser, derived sense. The deifying power of ethical euergetism extends to those made divine like Christ. Jesus' example taught Christians (in Stoic language) "the life closest to the life of God" (τὸ παραπλήσιον τῷ ζῆν τοῦ θεοῦ ζῆν) (*Cels.* 2.45). Stated Platonically, Jesus allowed Christians to live according to the ideal of assimilation to God (ὁμοίωσις θεῷ) (Plat., *Theaet.* 176b). In this line of thought, moral reformation (or virtue) deifies not only Jesus, but also those who follow Jesus' example of beneficence. In a masterful passage of the *Contra Celsum*, Origen writes that from the time of Christ "human and divine nature began to be woven together (θεία καὶ ἀνθρωπίνη συνυφαίνεσθαι φύσις), so that by fellowship with what is more divine (τῇ πρὸς τὸ θειότερον κοινωνίᾳ) human nature might become divine (θεία)—not only in Jesus—but also in all those who, after believing, take up the life which Jesus taught" (3.28).[64]

---

64. For the deification of Christians in Origen, see Norman Russell, *The Doctrine of Deification in the Greek Patristic Tradition* (Oxford: Oxford University Press, 2004), 140–54.

4

"Light Was That Godhead"
Transfiguration as Epiphany

Another evangelist testifies: 'His face shone like the sun, and his garments became white like the light,' showing them that he was himself the God who, in the Psalmist's words, 'wraps himself in light as in a mantle.'

———GREGORY PALAMAS, THE TRIADS,

2.3.18

INTRODUCTION

Scholars have sometimes pressed a basic difference between the Synoptic and the Johannine Gospels on the question of Jesus' divinity. To adapt a phrase of Rudolf Bultmann, John's Jesus is a translucent figure through whom divinity gleams.[1] The divinity of the Synoptic Jesus—at least to modern historical critics—seems more dim. The Synoptic Gospels are often mined by historical Jesus scholars to reconstruct Jesus as an apocalyptic prophet, sage, rabbi, Cynic, revolutionary (and so on)—all of whom are seen as human figures. The language and themes of the Synoptic writers indicate that demonstrating the divinity of Jesus was not their central concern. Jesus' titles "son of man" and "son of god," are multivalent and complex, and do not automatically amount

---

1. Rudolf Bultmann, *Theology of the New Testament*, 2 vols. (New York: Scribner, 1951–1955), 2.42.

111

to the meaning of "god" or "divine being." The idea that Jesus' divinity is implied in many Synoptic stories may be true (e.g., the forgiveness of sins, the healings, the stilling of the sea), but ambiguity remains and results in the notorious indecisiveness of the Synoptic disciples themselves: "*Who then is this?*" (Mark 4:41).[2]

The story of Jesus' transfiguration, however, throws a question mark against the mere humanity of Jesus. This story—shared by all Synoptic writers—uses language and imagery that recall epiphanies of gods and goddesses in the ancient Mediterranean world. In the transfiguration, we find a human undergoing metamorphosis, shining with a divine aura, being proclaimed a son of God, all the while evoking the extreme terror of his disciples and gestures of worship. Given the general cultural expectations of divine appearances in the Mediterranean world, I contend, such a story would have indicated that Jesus was a divine being—indeed, a god clothed in human flesh. The aim of this chapter is to unpack these cultural expectations by comparing the transfiguration with other epiphanies from both Greek and Jewish sources.

Although elements from all three Synoptic accounts of the transfiguration will be discussed, for simplicity I will quote in full only the Markan account (taken by most to be the earliest as well as the model for the Lukan and Matthean versions). In the immediately preceding context Jesus proclaims, "Truly I say to you that there are some standing here who will certainly not taste death until they see the kingdom of God arrive in power."

> Then, after six days, Jesus takes alongside Peter and James and John and leads them up a high mountain alone by themselves. And he was metamorphosed before them! And his clothes became dazzling—extremely white—like no launderer on earth could bleach them And there appeared to them Elijah and Moses, and they were conversing with Jesus. Then in response Peter says to Jesus, "Rabbi, it is well for us to be here. Now let us construct three tents—one for you, one for Moses, and one for Elijah." He did not know how to respond, since they were terrified out of their minds. Then a cloud appeared, overshadowing them. And there was a voice from the cloud: "This is my beloved son—hear him!" And suddenly, having

---

2. On the divinity of Christ in the Synoptics, see Daniel M. Doriani, "The Deity of Christ in the Synoptic Gospels," *JETS* 37 (1994): 333–50; Eugene Boring, "Markan Christology: God-language for Jesus?" *NTS* 45 (1999): 451–71. Sigurd Grindheim focuses on this issue in his *Christology in the Synoptic Gospels: God or God's Servant?* (London: T&T Clark, 2012).

looked around, they no longer saw anyone except Jesus alone with them. (Mark 9:1-8, my trans.)

The Second Evangelist may have been the first writer to situate the transfiguration in Jesus' ministry.[3] Literarily speaking, Mark makes the transfiguration a kind of fulcrum for his book. Peter has just confessed that Jesus is the Messiah (or anointed ruler) (8:29). On the Mount of Transfiguration this kingly status is dazzlingly revealed. The way that Mark describes the metamorphosis, however, indicates that a more-than-human messiahship is portrayed. The metamorphosis of Jesus is an epiphany of a divine being.[4]

3. Bultmann's theory that the transfiguration "was originally a resurrection story" (*History of the Synoptic Tradition*, trans. John Marsh, rev. ed. [New York: Harper & Row, 1968], 259) turned on its head the view of Eduard Meyer (*Ursprung und Anfänge des Christentums*, 5th ed. [Stuttgart: J.G. Cotta, 1921–1923], 1:153–56) and Adolf von Harnack (Die Verklärungsgeschichte Jesus, der Bericht des Paulus (1 Kor. 15,3ff) und die beiden Christusvisionen des Petrus, *Sitzungsberichte der Preussischen Akademie der Wissenschaften* 34 [1922]: 62–80), who believed that the transfiguration was a historical vision during Jesus' lifetime, which became the basis for the later Easter appearances. In the 1950s, C. H. Dodd criticized Bultmann's view on form critical grounds ("The Appearances of the Risen Christ: An Essay in Form-Criticism of the Gospels," in *Studies in the Gospel: Essays in Memory of F. L. H. Lightfoot*, ed. D. Nineham [Oxford: Basil Blackwell, 1955], 9–35 [25]). Redeploying some of Dodd's arguments, Robert Stein further undermined the theory of the transfiguration as a retrojected resurrection ("Is the Transfiguration [Mark 9:2-8] a Misplaced Resurrection-Account?" *JBL* 95 [1976]: 79–96). Neither Dodd nor Stein, however, returned to the vision theory of Meyer and Harnack. The reasons are fairly clear. It is difficult to develop a plausible account of the vision as a historical event in the life of Jesus, or as a psychological event in the life of his disciples. Historians have an innate skepticism of supernatural events and lack a framework with which to explain how unearthly experiences could have occurred in Jesus' lifetime (see further Donald Evans, "Academic Scepticism, Spiritual Reality, and Transfiguration," in *The Glory of Christ in the New Testament*, eds. L. D. Hurst and N. T. Wright [Oxford: Clarendon, 1987], 175–86). Those who hunt for a historical kernel beneath the transfiguration have offered both wild speculation (Morton Smith, *Clement of Alexandria and a Secret Gospel of Mark* [Cambridge, MA: Harvard University Press, 1973], 243–44), and trivial historicism (Jerome Murphy-O'Connor, "What Really Happened at the Transfiguration?" *BRev* 3 [1987]: 8–21). Recently, John Pilch has sketched a cultural and psychological framework for understanding the transfiguration as a historical (even if subjective) event (*Flights of the Soul: Visions, Heavenly Journeys, and Peak Experiences in the Biblical World* [Grand Rapids, MI: Eerdmans, 2011], 124–45). From my perspective, however, the transfiguration narrative is better received as theology, and specifically a theological foreshadowing of the resurrection. See further Robert J. Miller, "Historicizing the Transhistorical: The Transfiguration Narrative (Mark 9:2-8; Matt 17:1-8; Luke 9:28-36)," *Forum* 10 (1994): 219–48, esp. 244–47.

4. According to Henrichs, epiphany is a "litmus test for divinity, and at the same time an opportunity to put one's divinity to effective use" ("What is a Greek God?" in *The Gods of Ancient Greece*, 34).

THE MEANING OF EPIPHANY

In a classic article, Friedrich Pfister delimited three uses of the Greek word ἐπιφάνεια (epiphany): (1) "the personal, visible appearance of a superhuman being to an awake person," (2) an appearance in a dream, and (3) the manifestation (*Offenbarung*) of a god in general.[5] Pfister was rightly vague about the figure revealed in an epiphany: a "superhuman" person could imply a god, hero, a daimonic being, and so on. The same ambiguity occurs in Jewish literature, where angelophanies and theophanies often share similar characteristics (e.g. Dan. 10:5-21). By introducing the voice from the cloud ("This is my beloved son!" 9:7), however, Mark reveals that the transformed Jesus was more than an angel and higher than glorified saints (i.e., Moses and Elijah).[6] The account indicates that Jesus was revealed specifically as a deity—akin but subordinate to Yahweh (the presumed "father"). In accordance with this emphasis, I will limit my usage of "epiphany" to mean the visible

---

5. Friedrich Pfister, "Epiphanie," in PWSup 4. cols. 277–78 (1924). For a historical overview of Mediterranean epiphanies, see Robin Lane Fox, *Pagans and Christians* (New York: Knopf, 1987), 102–67; 700–711. H. S. Versnel underscores the ambiguous nature of a god's presence in ancient epiphanies ("What Did Ancient Man See When He Saw A God? Some Reflections on Greco-Roman Epiphany," in *Effigies Dei: Essays on the History of Religions*, ed. Dirk van der Plas [Leiden: Brill, 1987], 42–55. Although ἐπιφάνεια does often refer to divine aid, Versnel criticizes Dieter Lührmann ("Epiphaneia. Zur Bedeutungsgeschichte eine griechischen Wortes," in *Tradition und Glaube*, ed. G. Jeremias et al. [Göttingen: Vandenhoeck & Ruprecht, 1971], 185–99) for limiting epiphany to a god's salvific actions. See further on this point Andrew Y. Lau, *Manifest in Flesh: The Epiphany Christology of the Pastoral Epistles*, WUNT 2/86 (Tübingen: Mohr Siebeck, 1996), 179–225. Fritz Graf notes that epiphanies are visions that can be mediated through ritual and story ("Epiphany," in *Brill's New Pauly: Encyclopedia of the Ancient World*, eds. Hubert Cancik and Helmuth Schneider [Leiden: Brill, 2004], 4:1122). For epiphany in theater, see Christian Wildberg, *Hyperesie und Epiphanie: Ein Versuch über die Bedeutung der Götter in den Dramen des Euripides* (Munich: C. H. Beck, 2002), 113–72. For epiphany in the New Testament, see Margaret Mitchell, "Epiphanic Evolutions in Earliest Christianity," *ICS* 29 (2004): 183–204; F. E. Brenk, "Greek Epiphanies and Paul on the Road to Damaskos," in *The Notion of 'Religion' in Comparative Research*, ed. U. Bianchi (Rome: L'Erma di Bretschneider, 1994), 415–24; Jan Bremmer, "Close Encounters of the Third Kind: Heliodorus in the Temple and Paul on the Road to Damascus," in *Greek Religion and Culture, the Bible and the Ancient Near East* (Leiden: Brill, 2008), 215–33. For epiphany mediated through cult images, see Verity Platt, *Facing the Gods: Epiphany and Representation in Graeco-Roman Art, Literature and Religion* (Cambridge: Cambridge University Press, 2011).

6. *Pace* Andrew Chester who see Jesus as taking on "the form of an angelic figure" (*Messiah and Exaltation: Jewish Messianic and Visionary Traditions and New Testament Christology* [Tübingen: Mohr Siebeck, 2007], 98). It is possible to call the transfiguration a "Christophany" (Elpidius Pax, *ΕΠΙΦΑΝΕΙΑ. Eine religionsgeschichtliche Beitrag zur biblischen Theologie* [Munich: Karl Zink, 1955], 171–72), provided that one admits an overlap between christophany and theophany.

appearance of a *specifically divine being*. In my discussion, then, epiphany amounts to theophany.[7]

HISTORY OF RESEARCH

Viewing the transfiguration as an epiphany is not new. In fact, the dominant approach to the transfiguration in the patristic era was to understand it "as an epiphany of the essential deity of Christ."[8] John McGuckin, who wrote a monograph substantiating this point, quotes Clement of Alexandria as a prominent example: "The Lord who ascended the mountain . . . laid bare the power proceeding from him . . . displaying this power as god in flesh" (θεὸς ἐν σαρκίῳ τὴν δύναμιν ἐνδεικνύμενος) (*Strom.* 6.16.140.3).

In Late Antiquity, the "Greeks" or "Hellenes" were constructed as the socio-cultural "other" to Christians.[9] When, in the nineteenth century, "Hellenism" was made the cultural foil of "Judaism," Hellenism and Christianity could join forces.[10] The (Christian) transfiguration became a witness to a

---

7. My understanding of epiphany differs from Marco Frenschkowski (*Offenbarung und Epiphanie: Die verborgene Epiphanie in Spätantike und frühem Christentum*, 2 vols. [Tübingen: Mohr Siebeck, 1997]), who discusses the phenomenon of "hidden epiphany" (*verborgene Epiphanie*). The *verborgene Epiphanie* is not the manifestation of a god to a human being, but an "unrecognized presence (*unerkannte Präsenz*) of a numen (*des Numens*)" who need not be a god (2.5). I consider the transfiguration story to be a literary epiphany (as opposed to an epiphany occurring in history or as part of a historical ritual), and will compare it with other epiphanies in literature below. I agree with Jean-Pierre Vernant that there is no "single standard scenario" for epiphany, even if some aspects of divine presence show recurrent features (*Mortals and Immortals* [Princeton, NJ: Princeton University Press, 1991], 42). To think of an epiphany as a "type-scene" is too restrictive. On the other hand, Alexander Stevens's refusal to define epiphany because divine presence itself disrupts human categorization seems excessive ("Telling Presences. Narrating Divine Epiphany in Homer and Beyond," PhD diss., University of Cambridge, 2002, see esp. 52–53). There is a difference between the indeterminate nature of epiphanies in epiphanic narratives and later historical and etic analyses of those epiphanies. We can admit *both* that the appearances of gods are elusive, *and* that they are marked by certain thematic elements.

8. John McGuckin, *The Transfiguration of Christ in Scripture and Tradition* (Lewiston, NY: Edwin Mellen, 1986), 1, cf. 110. For McGuckin himself, Jesus' transfiguration in Mark "is a theophany by virtue of the fact that it has emanated directly from the divine Kabod" (65).

9. E.g., Eus., *Praep. ev.* 1.5.10-12. "Christianity is neither Hellenism nor Judaism" (ὁ Χριστιανισμός οὔτε Ἑλληνισμὸς ὢν οὔτε Ἰουδαϊσμός) (§12). See further Glen Bowersock, *Hellenism in Late Antiquity* (Ann Arbor: University of Michigan Press, 1990), 9–13; Aaron P. Johnson, *Ethnicity and Argument in Eusebius' Praepartio Evangelica* (Oxford: Oxford University Press, 2006); Anthony Kaldellis, *Hellenism in Byzantium: The Transformations of Greek Identity and the Reception of the Classical Tradition* (Cambridge: Cambridge University Press, 2007), 120–72; Claudia Rapp, "Hellenic Identity, *Romanitas*, and Christianity in Byzantium," in *Hellenisms: Culture, Identity, and Ethnicity from Antiquity to Modernity*, ed. Katerina Zacharia (Burlington, VT: Ashgate, 2008), 127–47, esp. 138–39.

"hellenistic" revelation of Jesus' divinity.[11] This understanding of the transfiguration was maintained well into the twentieth century. Bultmann, for example, described Mark's transfiguration story as a "theophany."[12] Ferdinand Hahn read it as a disclosure of Jesus' divine nature,[13] and Hans-Peter Müller argued that the transfiguration is an adapted theophany report.[14] All these scholars assumed that the transfiguration was theophanic because it was "hellenistic."

Since Hellenism and Judaism were constructed as cultural others, assuming a "Jewish" framework of the transfiguration produced radically different interpretations. The significance of the switch from a Hellenistic to a Jewish backdrop is portended in the work of Ernst Lohmeyer. Originally, Lohmeyer attempted to explain the transfiguration by Greco-Roman analogues. The verb of transfiguration (μεταμορφόω, Mark 9:2), he thought, indicated that Jesus was transformed from his own earthly corporeality into a heavenly figure of light.[15] The transfiguration of Jesus is thus a fragment of (or motif from) a Hellenistic myth of a "heavenly epiphany" transferred to Jesus.[16] "Jesus is a divine being come down from heaven who on earth has assumed human form and once before a small circle of intimate disciples reveals his original divinity through his transformation."[17]

---

10. See further Matthias Lutz-Bachmann, "Hellenisierung des Christentums?" in *Spätantike und Christentum: Beiträge zur Religions- und Geistesgeschichte der griechisch-römischen Kultur und Zivilisation der Kaiserzeit*, eds. Carsten Colpe et al. (Berlin: Akademie, 1992), 77–98; James I. Porter, "Hellenism and Modernity," in *The Oxford Handbook of Hellenic Studies*, ed. George Boys-Stones et al. (Oxford: Oxford University Press, 2009), 7–18.

11. Noted by Siegfried Schulz, as quoted by Howard Clark Kee, "The Transfiguration in Mark: Epiphany or Apocalyptic Vision?" in *Understanding the Sacred Text: Essays in Honor of Morton S. Enslin on the Hebrew Bible and Christian Beginnings*, ed. John Reumann (Valley Forge, PA: Judson, 1972), 135–52 (137).

12. Bultmann, *History of the Synoptic Tradition*, 259–61.

13. Ferdinand Hahn, *The Titles of Jesus in Christology*, trans. Harold Knight and George Ogg (New York: World Publishing, 1969), 300–302, 334–37.

14. Hans-Peter Müller, "Die Verklärung Jesu: Eine motivgeschichtliche Studie," *ZNW* 51 (1960): 56–64.

15. Ernst Lohmeyer, "Die Verklärung Jesu nach dem Markus-Evangelium," *ZNW* 21 (1922): 185–215 (203).

16. Ibid., 203, 205.

17. Ibid., 205. "*Jesus ist ein vom Himmel herabgekommenes göttliches Wesen, das auf Erden menschliche Gestalt angenommen und einmal vor dem kleinen Kreise der vertrauten Jünger durch die Verwandlung in himmlische Lichtgestalt seine ursprüngliche Göttlichkeit offenbart hat.*" Lohmeyer's understanding of the transfiguration is more complex than this summary would suggest. Behind the transfiguration are actually two stories: (1) a Jewish tale describing the appearance of Moses and Elijah, culminating in a

Nevertheless, in his later commentary on Mark, Lohmeyer exchanged wholesale a "Hellenistic" for an "apocalyptic" interpretation of the transfiguration. Quite suddenly all "Hellenistic" ideas about revealed divinity disappear from his explanation. In a footnote, Lohmeyer quietly notes that since the motif of transformation is grounded in apocalyptic expectation, it is unnecessary to draw on Hellenistic models as he did earlier.[18]

Lohmeyer's *volte-face* foreshadowed later divisions in scholarship. In his article on μεταμορφόω, J. Behm assured scholars that the "miracle of transformation from an earthly form into a supraterrestrial, which is denoted by the radiance of the garments (also the countenance in Mt. and Lk.), has nothing whatever to do with metamorphosis in the Hellenistic sense but suggests the context of apocalyptic ideas."[19] Adopting this line of thought, Howard Clark Kee openly pitted the transfiguration-as-epiphany reading against a "proleptic" and "apocalyptic" vision of Jesus as "kingly Son of man."[20] For Kee, the transfiguration is an apocalyptic vision. Therefore, Jesus' metamorphosis is not a manifestation of Jesus' divinity, but a proleptic vision of the glorification of the righteous.[21] Following this line of interpretation, Barry Blackburn claimed that it is "difficult to prove that any given element in the traditions used by Mark represents an assimilation of the portrait of Jesus to distinctively Hellenistic/pagan traditions."[22] After selecting a solely Jewish background informed by the story of Moses' glorification and the apocalyptic expectation of transformation,

---

cloud-theophany (Mark 9:4-8), and (2) a fragment from a Hellenistic myth describing the metamorphosis of Jesus into a figure of light (vv. 2-3). Both stories have different origins and ends (205–06). The essence (*Kern*) of the story is Jewish (212). But the Hellenistic myth of metamorphosis was added to make the Jewish story understandable to a Hellenistic audience (213).

18. For the "apocalyptic" background of the transfiguration, Lohmeyer cites the standard texts: 2 Bar. 51:10, 12; 4 Ezra 7:97; Dan. 12:3 (*Das Evangelium des Markus*, Meyer Kommentar 2 [Göttingen: Vandenhoeck & Ruprecht, 1967], 174–75, n. 7). Here he also eschews his theory of Jewish story (vv. 4-8) plus Hellenistic myth of metamorphosis (vv. 2-3). Even so, Lohmeyer still asserted that μεταμορφόω designates the "change from human to divine form" (*den Wandel von menschlicher zu göttlicher Gestalt*), and that the story of transfiguration belongs to "the style of an epiphany-narrative (*Epiphanie-Erzählung*)." The epiphany is especially signaled by the supernaturally white garments—typical of divine figures (174–75). See also Wolfgang Geber, "Metamorphose," *TZ* 23 (1967): 385–95.

19. Behm, *TDNT* 4:758.

20. Kee, "Apocalyptic Vision," 138; 149–150.

21. Ibid., 143–44. Glorification, it should be noted, is assumed to be inherently different than deification.

22. Barry Blackburn, *Theios Anēr and the Markan Miracle Traditions: A Critique of the Theios Anēr Concept as an Interpretive Background of the Miracle Traditions Used by Mark*, WUNT 2/40 (Tübingen: Mohr Siebeck, 1991), 263.

Blackburn could "see nothing" in the transfiguration account "that points to speculation about the θεία φύσις [divine nature] of the earthly Jesus."[23]

More recently, John Paul Heil's monograph on the transfiguration still opposes a "Jewish" framework to a "hellenistic" or epiphanic reading. Heil offers a "narrative-critical perspective" on the transfiguration focused on Jewish sources.[24] He recognizes that the transfiguration fits the category of epiphany. Nevertheless he uses the term only as a literary genre of his own derivation, explicitly eschewing "the hellenistic concept of divinization."[25]

In general, recent commentaries have preferred Jewish as opposed to Greek intertexts to elucidate the transfiguration. For instance, Joel Marcus—although he notes that the various backgrounds "do not have to be mutually exclusive"—prefers traditions about Moses, the Feast of Tabernacles, and royal pageantry as "the most important backgrounds" for understanding the transfiguration.[26] The other settings (including divine epiphany) are present but portrayed as "more distant."[27]

A few voices, however, still defend an epiphanic reading of the transfiguration. According to Dieter Zeller, for example, Mark's transfiguration story plays the same role as Hellenistic epiphanies—the revelation of preexistent divinity.[28] Distinctively, however, Jesus does not return to his celestial

---

23. Ibid., 123–24.

24. John Paul Heil, *The Transfiguration of Jesus: Narrative Meaning and Function of Mark 9:2-8, Matt 17:1-8 and Luke 9:28-36, 22* (Rome: Biblical Pontifical Institute, 2000).

25. Ibid., 35, n. 2. Agustín del Agua makes a case for the transfiguration as a midrash (which for del Agua signifies a mode of interpretation, rather than a literary genre) on various scriptural stories (Moses' shining face, the Feast of Tabernacles, the Glory Cloud in Exodus). These midrashic (or "derashic") traditions are shot through with apocalyptic motifs ("The Narrative of the Transfiguration as a Derashic Scenification of a Faith Confession [Mark 9.2-8 PAR]," *NTS* 39 [1993]: 340–54). Dorothy Lee's recent study focuses on the "theology, symbolism and spirituality" of the transfiguration in a biblical framework (*Transfiguration: New Century Theology* [London: Continuum, 2004], 2). Neither author shows interest in reading the transfiguration stories in light of their larger Mediterranean milieu.

26. Marcus, *Mark 8-16*, 2 vols., AB 27–27a (New York: Doubleday, 2000–2009), 2:1117.

27. Ibid., 1118. In making this remark, Marcus shows his concern to preserve the distinctives of Markan theology. Stories of transforming gods remind him of Docetism, leading him to remark, "There is no indication within the Markan story . . . that Jesus is merely masquerading as a human being, as gods and angels [*sic*] do in Greco-Roman epiphany stories" (1117). Marcus also denies that the transfiguration is the moment of Jesus' deification in Mark's narrative (1117–18). In his earlier discussion in *The Way of the Lord: Christological Exegesis of the Old Testament in the Gospel of Mark* (Louisville: Westminster John Knox, 1992), Marcus was more open to the divine implications of Jesus as "Son of God" (proclaimed in Mark 9:7) (90–92). He adds, however, that because Elijah is placed before Moses in Mark 9:4, "Mark's readers are not to understand Jesus in precisely the same way as Philo understands Moses, as a man divinized because of his virtue and therefore made immortal" (92).

homeland, but to his earthly state.[29] Dennis MacDonald has compared the transfiguration with Odysseus's "transfiguration" before his son Telemachus in book 16 of the *Odyssey*. Here Odysseus's changed clothes and skin cause Telemachus immediately to conclude: "surely you are some god who rules the vaulting skies!" (182). Telemachus even offers "gifts of hammered gold" to appease the god (184–85).[30] For Crispin Fletcher-Louis, the transfiguration presents a "theophanic Christology." He cites some fragmentary evidence from Qumran (4Q374 [frg. 2 col. ii]; 4Q377 [frg. 2, recto, col. ii]) that depicts Moses as "a real divine presence" and "covered by the theophanic cloud."[31] By analogy, Christ is no less a "divine presence" in the transfiguration, and should be judged "divine."[32] Here, interestingly, Fletcher-Louis uses Jewish texts to arrive at some rather "Hellenistic" conclusions.[33]

For scholars who assume an opposition between epiphanic ("Greek") and apocalyptic ("Jewish") readings, Adela Yarbro Collins proposes an irenic solution. She notes that Mark's first readers probably came from a mix of both Jewish and Gentile backgrounds. (This is true whether or not Mark was written in Rome, Syria, or elsewhere.) It is reasonable to suppose, then, that from the very beginning, the transfiguration story would have recalled both the (Jewish)

28. Dieter Zeller, "La métamorphose de Jésus comme épiphanie (Mc 9, 2-8)," in *L'Évangile Exploré: Mélanges offerts à Simon Légasse*, ed. Alain Marchadour (Paris: Éditions du Cerf, 1996), 167–86 (179, 185).

29. Ibid., 181.

30. Dennis MacDonald, *The Homeric Epics and the Gospel of Mark* (New Haven, CT: Yale University Press, 2000), 92–96. Candida R. Moss comments that "all the elements of Mark 9:2-10 which MacDonald views as Homeric parallels are characteristic of Hellenistic epiphanies in general" ("The Transfiguration: An Exercise in Markan Accommodation," *BibInt* 12:1 [2004]: 83). MacDonald recognizes this: "This pattern of revelation-fear-sacrifice was stock" (*Homeric Epics*, 93); "Epiphanies were common in ancient literature, and several of these motifs are topoi, such as luminescent clothing, trembling, and offering gifts or establishing cult" (95).

31. Crispin Fletcher-Louis, "The Revelation of the Sacral Son of Man: The Genre, History of Religions Context and the Meaning of the Transfiguration," in *Auferstehung-Resurrection*, eds. Friedrich Avemarie and Hermann Lichtenberger, WUNT 135 (Tübingen: Mohr Siebeck, 2001), 247–300 (251–52).

32. Ibid., 253–54. Cf. his discussion in *Luke-Acts: Angels, Christology and Soteriology* (Tübingen: Mohr Siebeck, 1997), 38–50, which ably applies the insights of Michael Mach, "Christus Mutans: Zur Bedeutung der 'Verklärung Jesu' im Wechsel von jüdischer Messianität zur neutestamentlichen Christologie," in *Messiah and Christos: Studies in the Jewish Origins of Christianity*, ed. Ithamar Gruenwald et al. (Tübingen: Mohr Siebeck, 1992), 177–98.

33. Similarly Alan Segal interpreted the transfiguration as a Mosaic vision of Jesus as God's Glory, and specifically, "the principal angel of God." This is another epiphanic reading of the transfiguration based entirely on Jewish sources (*Life After Death: A History of the Afterlife in the Religions of the West* [New York: Doubleday, 2004], 464–65).

eschatological transformation of the righteous and (Greek) epiphanies of various deities.[34] We cannot assume that the author of Mark was unaware of the double entendre of the transfiguration account. In fact, it is a credit to his literary artistry that he could craft a story that would resonate with both audiences.

In tune with this understanding, Candida R. Moss divides her recent account of the transfiguration into "Jewish motifs" and "Hellenistic motifs."[35] The separate motifs correspond to different audiences: "For those more familiar with Greek religious practices and thought he [Mark] uses the epiphany motif to explain the significance of Jesus' undisclosed identity. For those better acquainted with Jewish motifs he utilizes contemporary thought about Moses and Elijah to anticipate the future resurrection and glorification of God's Son." Recognizing that a "Jewish" versus a "Greek" audience appears too neat, however, Moss adds the disclaimer that "not all of the gospel's first-century audience can be divided into these two groups. There would have been many, such as the evangelist himself, who were familiar with both Jewish biblical and non-biblical traditions and Greek epiphany stories. Many more, no doubt, would have fallen somewhere on a spectrum in between."[36]

THESIS

It seems to me that Moss's comment provides the way forward for research on the transfiguration, since it refuses to construct at the outset an opposition between "Jewish"/ "Hellenistic" and "apocalyptic"/"epiphanic" readings. Even if there were a "Jewish" versus a "Greek" way of reading the transfiguration, it seems to me that hellenized peoples in the ancient world (including the author of Mark) would not necessarily have recognized certain theophanic elements as specifically Greek *or* Jewish. Elements like blinding light, terror, and the response of worship were cultural common coin in the ancient Mediterranean

---

34. Adela Yarbro Collins, "Mark and His Readers: The Son of God Among Jews," *HTR* 92:4 (1999): 393–408 (393); Yarbo Collins, "Mark and His Readers: The Son of God Among Greeks and Romans," *HTR* 93:2 (2000): 85–100 (90–92).

35. Moss, "Transfiguration: An Exercise," 72–85.

36. Ibid., 88–89. Simon Lee also acknowledges that the transfiguration can be understood from multiple frameworks and does not oppose a Mosaic background to "Hellenistic metamorphosis stories by gods [*sic*]" (*Jesus' Transfiguration and the Believer's Transformation: A Study of the Transfiguration and Its Development in Early Christian Writings*, WUNT 2/265 [Tübingen: Mohr Siebeck, 2009], 9–10). He ultimately prefers, however, "the epiphany with metamorphosis" framework (38). Armand Puig i Tàrrech ("The Glory on the Mountain: The Episode of the Transfiguration of Jesus," *NTS* 58 [2012]: 151–72) cuts the Gordian knot by depreciating the significance of both apocalyptic and epiphanic contexts.

world. As a result, both "Jewish" and "Greek" readers would have viewed them as signaling the presence of divinity.

Let me develop this thesis with reference to concrete examples. Above I defined epiphany as "the visible appearance of a specifically divine being" and commented that this definition of epiphany amounts to theophany. Theophany is a recognized category in Jewish studies.[37] The appearances of Yahweh in many texts show clear markers that manifest his divinity. In Ezekiel 1:26-28, Yahweh appears anthropomorphically in a luminous cloud with an upper body of amber and a lower body of fire. In *1 Enoch* 14, Yahweh (called "the Great Glory") appears with apparel "like the appearance of the sun and whiter than much snow." His face is so bright that no human or angel dares to look at it (vv. 20-21). In Daniel 7:9, Yahweh ("the Ancient One") sits on a throne with a garment white as snow and a fire streaming before him. Repeatedly, we see the same theophanic markers appear: gleaming garments, supernatural light, fire, and a cloud. These are narrative symbols that Jews used to speak of the divinity of Yahweh, and the divinity of those beings associated with the divine world (such as angels, sons of God, and other Jewish numina).[38]

These theophanic symbols are not, however, unique to Judaism. Brilliant light imagery, for instance, is perhaps the most common signal of a theophany in ancient Mediterranean literature.[39] In the Homeric *Hymn to Apollo*, for instance, the god reveals himself in a profusion of flashing sparks, with a blaze

---

37. For an overview with bibliography of older sources, see Theodore Hiebert, "Theophany in the OT," in *ABD* 6:505–11. More recent studies (also covering NT literature) include Jeffrey J. Niehaus, *God at Sinai: Covenant and Theophany in the Bible and Ancient Near East* (Carlisle, UK: Paternoster, 1995); Fletcher-Louis, *Luke-Acts*; Charles Gieschen, *Angelomorphic Christology: Antecedents and Early Evidence* (Leiden: Brill, 1998); Darrell Hannah, *Michael and Christ: Michael Traditions and Angel Christology in Early Christianity* (Tübingen: Mohr Siebeck, 1999); J. Andrew Dearman, "Theophany, Anthropomorphism, and the *Imago Dei*: Some Observations about the Incarnation in the Light of the Old Testament," in *The Incarnation: An Interdisciplinary Symposium on the Incarnation of the Son of God*, ed. Stephen T. Davis et al. (Oxford: Oxford University Press, 2002), 31–46; Esther Hamori, *"When Gods were Men": The Embodied God in Biblical and Near Eastern Literature* (Berlin: Walter de Gruyter, 2008).

38. For "other Jewish numina," see Litwa, *We Are Being Transformed*, 231–39; 266–73. Yarbro Collins, among many other interpreters, notes that shiny white clothing is indicative of "heavenly beings" in general—including angels and glorified saints ("Son of God Among Jews," 400). I am more comfortable with calling these "heavenly beings" divine, provided that one understands that for Jews these beings participate in the divinity of the primal deity, Yahweh, and are not independent gods.

39. For light as a feature of epiphany, see Dieter Bremer, "Die Epiphanie des Gottes in den homerische Hymnen und Platons Gottesbegriff," *ZRGG* 27 (1975): 1–21 (5–8); Walter Burkert, "From Epiphany to Cult Statue," in *What is a God? Studies in the Nature of Greek Divinity*, ed. Alan B. Lloyd (Swansea: Classical Press of Wales, 1997), 15–30.

reaching to heaven, a blaze that fills with radiance the whole town of Crisa (440-445; cf. Hom., *Il.* 4.75-79). In a poem of Hesiod, Heracles sees the god Ares light up the entire grove and altar of Pagasaian Apollo, "and the shining from his eyes was like fire" (*Scut.* 70-72). Other examples can be multiplied.

Importantly, white or shining garments (as in Mark 9:3) are also a recurrent sign of divinity in a variety of ancient Mediterranean religious texts. In the Homeric hymn celebrating Apollo, for example, "gleamings" (μαρμαρυγαί) emerge from the god's well-woven chiton (202-203).[40] Similarly, the god Asclepius-Imuthes is "clothed in brilliant linen garments" (λαμπραῖς ἠμφιεσμένος ὀθόναις) (Oxyrh. Pap 1381).[41] In the Homeric *Hymn to Aphrodite*, the goddess appears before Anchises in a hidden guise, but the signs of her divinity still shine through her mortal form. She wears "glittering garments" (εἵματα σιγαλόεντα), and clothes herself with a robe brighter than a ray of fire (πέπλον . . . φαεινότερον πυρὸς αὐγῆς) (85-86).[42]

Since gleaming garments are used as symbols of divinity in the literary depictions of both Greek and Jewish theophanies, it would be facile to think of these theophanic traits as *either* Hellenistic *or* Jewish. The Jews did not borrow these symbols from the Greeks, nor did Hellenes plagiarize the Hebrew Scriptures. Such symbols were not the proper possession of any particular ethnicity or subculture in the Mediterranean world. From Spain to Palestine, they formed a kind of *koine* signifying manifest divinity.[43]

Consequently, even though I am glad to agree with Yarbro Collins that Jews would have read the transfiguration with different nuances than other hellenized peoples, I am (like Moss) uncomfortable with thinking of "Greco-Roman" peoples and "Jews" as if they belonged to separate compartments or interpretive communities. There are some ways in which, I believe, both "Jews" and "Greeks" living in ancient Mediterranean culture thought in surprisingly similar ways. One of those ways regards epiphanic traits that signal the presence of divinity. By framing my approach this way, I hope in some measure to

---

40. Cf. *Hom. Hymn Ven.* 5.84-87.

41. The text of this papyrus (second century CE) can be found in Edelstein and Edelstein, *Asclepius* 1.§331. See also Eur., *Bacchae* 1083, 1329; Porph., *Vit. Plot.* 68; Herodotus, *Hist.* 6.117; Rev 1.10.

42. Cf. also Hera's veil, "bright as the sun" in Hom., *Il.* 14.183-85.

43. Cf. Nanno Marinatos and Dimitris Kyrtatas: "The phenomenon [of epiphany] was part of a shared culture and, therefore, anticipated and widely accepted . . . The New Testament authors . . . were actually quite at home with the customary views of their pagan and Jewish contemporaries [about divine manifestations]" ("Epiphany: Concept Ambiguous, Experience Elusive," *ICS* 29 [2004]: 227-34 [233-34]).

overcome the (still lingering) Judaism/Hellenism divide surrounding the interpretation of the transfiguration.

The aim of my comparative analysis, then, is to depict the Markan transfiguration as a divine epiphany without submerging its distinctively Jewish color in a swarm of Greco-Roman parallels. I contend that one can view the transfiguration story as an epiphany equally "Jewish" and "Greco-Roman." To accomplish this task, I will orient my comparative texts around the figure of Moses.

THE ROLE OF MOSES

Recent commentators have stressed that the best background for understanding the Markan transfiguration is the story of Moses' ascent up Mount Sinai (Exod. 24 and 34).[44] This argument is borne out by the following considerations: (1) Jesus, like Moses, ascends a mountain (Exod. 24:9, 12–13, 15, 18; 34:4; Mark 9:2b), (2) the revelation on the mountain occurs after a six-day period (Mark 9:2 and Exod. 24:16), (3) Jesus, like Moses, ascends with three named individuals (Exod. 24:1, 9; Mark 9:2a), (4) the theophany on the mountain is signaled by the presence of a cloud of glory (Exod. 24:15-16; 34:5; Mark 9:7), (5) a voice comes from the cloud (Exod. 24:15-16, 18; Mark 9:7a), (6) Jesus is glorified in a way similar to Moses (Exod. 34:29, 35; Mark 9:3),[45] and (7) Aaron as well as the elders fear approaching the glorified Moses just as the disciples cower before Jesus (Exod. 34:30; Mark 9:6). What we see in Mark's transfiguration account, then, is a thoroughgoing adaptation and transformation of Moses' Sinai experience.

This Mosaic background is sometimes taken as evidence against those who view the transfiguration as a manifestation of Jesus' divinity. Jesus, as we learn from the mysterious voice ("This is my beloved son; hear him!"; Mark 9:7) is the (human) prophet like Moses (Deut. 18:15). His sonship is a "Jewish" sonship signifying close relation to Yahweh (cf. Gen. 22:2), not deity.

In his *The Way of the Lord*, however, Marcus questioned the mere humanity of Jesus in his Mosaic reading of the transfiguration. Drawing on Ezekiel the Tragedian's *Exagoge* (68-82), Marcus pointed out that Moses' ascent of Sinai was associated with his kingship, and specifically God's kingship.[46]

---

44. Both chapters in Exodus are rightly appealed to since they are often conflated in later Jewish literature (see, e.g., *L.A.B.* 11:5-12:1; *Deut. Rabb.* 3.12). See also Joachim Gnilka, *Das Evangelium nach Markus: 2 Teilband Mk 8,27—16,20*, EKK II/2 (Zurich: Benziger, 1979), 32; R. T. France, *The Gospel of Mark: A Commentary on the Greek Text* (Grand Rapids, MI: Eerdmans, 2002), 348; Dale Allison, *The New Moses: A Matthean Typology* (Minneapolis: Fortress Press, 1993), 243–48; Joel Marcus, *Mark 8–16*, 2.1114; Yarbro Collins, *Mark: A Commentary*, Hermeneia (Minneapolis: Fortress Press, 2007), 417.

45. Note Matt. 17:2 and Luke 9:29 for the glorification specifically of Jesus' face.

Mark's transfiguration account is associated with the coming of God's kingdom (Mark 9:1), and the declaration "This is my beloved son!" is also an echo of royal traditions (Ps. 2:7).[47] Instead of opposing kingship and godhood, Marcus remained open to the idea that royalty and divinity were linked. He observed, for instance, how Philo strongly associated "god" and "king" in the *Life of Moses* (e.g., 1.155-58). In the end, however, Marcus hesitated to draw a strong conclusion. Although "son of God" in Mark 9:7 attributes a status to Jesus "that transcends the human" and bestows a "unique familial likeness to God," it gives Jesus an identity that only "*approaches* the category of divinity."[48]

The royal traditions, I believe, allow for a more definite conclusion about Jesus' divinity in the transfiguration account. Marcus is correct that both Moses in the *Exagoge* and Jesus in Mark 9:2-8 are being depicted in kingly terms. This point is significant, as Andrew Erskine explains, "for a majority of the thousand years or so of documented Greek religion (roughly from Homer to the 'triumph' of Christianity), rulers, whether kings or Roman emperors, are found being accorded divine status."[49] Indeed, royalty and deity during this period can be plotted on a single spectrum, since the decisive factor defining deity—power—is also the central trait of kings.[50] Ancient Jews are not exceptions to this view (note, e.g., Ps. 45:7).[51] It is from Philo, as Marcus noted, that we learn that Moses the king is Moses the god. The works of Philo, then—and specifically his *Life of Moses*—seem to be the best comparative

---

46. Fletcher-Louis's language is much stronger. In Ezekiel's *Exagoge*, as he puts it, Moses receives the symbols of cosmic rulership and deification ("Sacral Son," 250).

47. Marcus, *Way of the Lord*, 84–87.

48. Ibid., 91–92, emphasis added. Marcus also makes a point about the transfigured Jesus' glory and its implications for deity. In Mark 8:38, Jesus foretells the coming of the Son of Man in the "glory of his Father" (δόξῃ τοῦ πατρὸς αὐτοῦ). On the Mount of Transfiguration, the glory of "the son" is revealed (Mark 9:2-3). Marcus is favorable to the old understanding of δόξα offered by Gerhard Kittel in *TDNT*. When applied to a deity, it is a technical term signifying "the divine mode of being" (91).

49. Andrew Erskine, "Epilogue," in *The Gods of Ancient Greece*, 505–510 (508). Probably one should say that rulers were accorded divine status from Lysander to Constantine. The giving of divine honors to kings only becomes the norm after Alexander the Great (see further Litwa, *We Are Being Transformed*, 68–85).

50. H. W. Pleket, "Religious History as the History of Mentality," in *Faith, Hope and Worship: Aspects of Religious Mentality in the Ancient World*, ed. H. S. Versnel (Leiden: Brill, 1981), 171–83; Lane Fox, *Pagans and Christians*, 98; Henrichs, "What is a Greek God?" 36–37; Litwa, *We Are Being Transformed*, 46–55; David Levene, "Defining the Divine in Rome," *Transactions of the American Philological Association* 142 (2012): 41–82.

51. Litwa, *We Are Being Transformed*, 86–116.

texts by which to illumine both an epiphanic and Mosaic reading of the transfiguration.[52]

Moses Transfigured: A Philonic Readings of Moses' Sinaitic Experience

In a previous study, I argued that the immortalization Moses experienced at the end of his life constituted a form of deification.[53] There I had the opportunity to show that many scholars—even those who seem to oppose Moses' deification in Philo—remain open to the notion of deifying transformation *with the caveat* that the deified Moses does not threaten the position of Philo's high God, whom he calls "the Existent" (ὁ ὤν).[54] The deified Moses, that is, becomes a different sort of god than the Existent—namely, a *mediate* deity—and this mediate status goes some way toward explaining Philo's putative "wavering" on this issue.[55] That is, Philo asserts both the sole divinity of his high God *and* the mediate divinity of the "god" Moses who participates in the deity of the Existent through the Logos (the divine Mind). Instead of duplicating that research here, I wish to take it in new directions.

Becoming Mind

In his work *On the Creation*, Philo posited an iconic affinity between God and human beings (§69). The image of God, for Philo, is not the Existent, but the Logos (Philo's "second God" [QG 2.62]).[56] The human made "according to the Image" (Gen. 1:26-27) conforms to the Logos in that both are incorporeal and noetic (*Opif.*, 134-35).[57] To be conformed to God's Image, then, requires a "noetification" in which the human becomes pure νοῦς: immortal, intellectual reality that is of the same nature as the Logos.[58]

---

52. Note also some scattered rabbinic traditions indicating belief in a divine Moses (noted by Marcus, *Way of the Lord*, 90–92).

53. Litwa, *We Are Being Transformed*, 106–108; cf. 268–69. Fletcher-Louis, *Luke-Acts*, 173–84, has a fuller treatment of the Jewish sources, although he does not distinguish between deification and angelification.

54. Litwa, *We Are Being Transformed*, 107–108, n. 48.

55. According to Wayne Meeks, Philo "wavers," "now elevating him [Moses] virtually to a 'second god,' again restricting him to the sphere of the human" (*The Prophet-King: Moses Traditions and the Johannine Christology* (Leiden: Brill, 1967), 105). In this judgment, Meeks followed E. R. Goodenough, who saw Philo's presentation of Moses as both man and god as a Philonic "vacillation" (*By Light, Light: The Mystic Gospel of Hellenistic Judaism* [New Haven, CT: Yale University Press, 1935], 223).

56. Cf. *Spec.* 1.81; 3.83; 3.207; *Plant.* 17–20.

57. Cf. QG 2.56.

The process of noetification is best seen in Moses' ascent of Mount Sinai. For Moses, the path out of Plato's cave (this world) to the vision of the Good was the path up Sinai. On the mountain, Moses entered the "darkness where God was" (Exod. 20:21). For Philo, Moses did not enter a visible mass of condensed smoke. Rather his trip up Sinai was "an ethereal and heavenly journey" (QE 2.44) to enter the intelligible realm (Mut. 7; Post. 14; Plant. 27). He beheld the forms that are the truly real, though unseen, models and archetypes of earthly things. "See," God says to Moses, "that you make according to the pattern (τὸν τύπον) displayed to you on the mountain!" (Exod. 25:40 LXX). The τύπος for Philo is the model of all existing things: the Logos, or Mind of God.[59]

To enter God's incorporeal intelligible world, Moses had to temporarily become incorporeal. All his passions had to be stripped away. He had to fully step out of the impure body, and thus out of bodily needs (e.g., eating, drinking, and sexual intercourse) (Mos. 2.68). He had to transcend the limits of his mortal nature in order to come into his true, noetic nature. Philo himself calls this transformation a divinization. God's command to Moses, "Come up to me to the mountain and be there" (Exod. 24:12) signifies that Moses was "divinized by ascending not to the air or to the ether or to heaven higher than all but to (a region) above the heavens" (QE 2.40, emphasis added).[60]

The deifying transformation Moses underwent is described in an important passage in Questions on Exodus (2.46). Here Philo designates Moses' upward call to Sinai "a second birth better than the first." Moses' first birth, Philo says, was "mixed with a body and had corruptible parents." In Moses' second birth, the lawgiver becomes—in a phrase unfortunately garbled in the transfer from Greek to Armenian—"an unmixed and simple soul of the sovereign." In the Loeb edition to Philo, Ralph Marcus rightly understood the phrase to mean "an unmixed and simple sovereign part of the soul," meaning "mind."[61] In other

---

58. David Runia put it this way: "If man is part of the Logos (part-whole relation), and the Logos is only nominally separated from God, then (part of) man is part of God" ("God and Man in Philo of Alexandria," JTS 39 [1988]: 72). For the divinity of νοῦς, see Plato, Phaedo 80a4; Resp. 589d2; Tim. 41c7; 45a1; 51e5-6; 69d6; 73a7; 88b2; 90a2-b1; Alcib. 1.133c1-6. Cf. Aristotle, De an. 1.4 408b29; Part. an. 4.10 686a29; Gen. an. 2.3 736a28; Nic Eth. 10.7 1177a16, b28-30; 8.2 1248a27; Ps.-Arist. De mundo 1. 391a15; Iamb., Protr. 8; Cic., Tusc. 1.65; Porph., Vita Plot. 2.

59. Philo associates Moses' reception of the name "god" with his entrance into the intelligible world (Mos. 1.158). The connection is difficult to understand unless the intelligible world is the place where Moses was first promoted to deity.

60. The Armenian of "divinized" is astouacanal, a passive verb that probably renders the Greek θεοῦσθαι.

words, Moses—elsewhere called ὁ καθαρώτατος νοῦς (*Cong.* 132)—became pure mind.[62]

This interpretation is borne out by the context of *QE* 2.46. As mind, Philo says, Moses did not have a mother (a material progenitor), but only a father (an intellectual progenitor), whom Philo indentifies with God.[63] This "God," although Philo does not specify, is probably the divine Mind, or Logos.[64] Moses' second birth was a coming into being "without a body"—that is, his coming into being as pure, divine mind.[65] Moses' kinship with the divine (*QE* 2.29) is not just metaphorical, but ontological. When he is "changed into the divine" he is changed into the divine nature, namely pure νοῦς. In this respect, Moses conformed to the reality of the Logos, the Mind of God (*QE* 2.46).

There were two consequences to Moses' divinization: Moses, like the Logos, became simple and immutable. "Simple," in this context means not having multiple parts. By becoming pure mind, Moses became absolutely one. "For when the prophetic mind becomes divinely inspired and filled with God," Philo explains, "it becomes like the monad" (*QE* 2.29).[66] In this respect, Moses conformed to the purely noetic nature of the Logos, which is absolutely one (*QE* 2.46).

Moses' immutability is indicated by Deuteronomy 5:31, where God says to Moses: "But you, stand here with me!" Philo considers this verse to be "an oracle vouchsafed to the prophet: true stability and immutable repose (ἠρεμία) is that which we experience at the side of the immutable ever-standing God" (*Gig.* 49).[67] Repose is not only a moral quality (control of the passions) but a state

61. Note *g. ad loc.* For the mind as the "sovereign and ruling element" (τὸ ἀρχηγετικὸν καὶ τὸ ἡγεμονικόν), see *QG* 1.45; cf. 2.54: 'the mind is the sovereign and ruling part of the soul.'

62. Cf. *QE* 2.44.

63. For "father" as mind (νοῦς) and "mother" as "the matter of the body" (ἡ τοῦ σώματος ὕλη), see Philo, *Leg.* 2.51, 3.225.

64. Cf. *Mos.* 2.209-210; *Her.* 62.

65. The Armenian of this passage reads that Moses' coming into being was "from the aether and without a body." The Greek fragment reads only ἄνευ σώματος. Cf. *Somn.* 1.36: Μωυσῆν ἀσώματον γενόμενον ["Moses, having become incorporeal"]. Philo also finds Moses' bodilessness signified in Moses' pitching the Tent of Meeting "outside the camp" (Exod. 33:7, *Gig.* 54; cf. *Leg.* 2.54-55; 3.46-48; *Det.* 160; *Ebr.* 100, 124).

66. In the philosophy of Eudorus, the monad is the second-tier principle after the One, and is—like the Logos—a thinking intellect (Robert M. Berchman, "The Categories of Being in Middle Platonism: Philo, Clement, and Origen of Alexandria," in *The School of Moses: Studies in Philo and Hellenistic Religion*, ed. John Peter Kenney [Atlanta: Scholars, 1995], 98–140).

67. Philo also bases Moses' immutability on an allegorical interpretation of Num. 14:44, which reads, "Moses and the ark were not moved." For Philo, Moses signifies the "wise man," and the ark signifies

of being. God "makes the worthy man sharer of his own nature (τῆς ἑαυτοῦ φύσεως), which is repose (ἠρεμίας)" (*Post.* 28). In his transformation on Sinai, Moses thus shares the unmoving nature of God.[68]

When Moses beheld the Good (represented by the Logos; *Conf.* 95; *Ebr.* 152) in the intelligible world (i.e., Sinai) his initiation was complete (*Mos.* 2.71). At this point Moses came down out of the divine world, as Plato bids in the *Republic* (519d-520c), to help his fellow human beings. In Philo's allegory, Moses the deified mind reentered his body to continue to lead the Israelites on the road to virtue.

The body of Moses bore the marks of his deified mind.[69] In Exodus, Moses descends Mount Sinai with a radiant face (34:29-35). Philo interprets this radiance in terms of beauty: Moses was "far more beautiful (πολὺ καλλίων) with respect to his appearance [or face, ὄψιν] than when he had gone up [Mount Sinai]." Beauty was one of the trademarks of divinity in the ancient world. Diotima asks Socrates in Plato's *Symposium*, "Don't you say that all the gods are . . . beautiful (καλούς)?" (202c). The historian Charax says of Io that she was considered a goddess on account of her beauty (θεός ἐνομίσθη διὰ τό κάλλος).[70]

"virtue." Neither the wise man nor virtue, says Philo, are subject to change because both "are stayed on the firm foundation of right reason" (*Gig.* 48).

68. For more on Moses' immutability, see *Conf.* 30; Goodenough, *By Light, Light*, 228; Michael Williams, *The Immovable Race: A Gnostic Designation and the Theme of Stability in Late Antiquity* (Leiden: Brill, 1985), 14–15, 27, 43–45; Hywel Clifford, "Moses as Philosopher-Sage in Philo," in *Moses in Biblical and Extra-Biblical Traditions*, eds. Axel Graupner and Michael Wolter (Berlin: Walter de Gruyter, 2007), 151–68 (157–59).

69. Moses' body, Philo explains, dramatically increased in strength (ἰσχύς) and vigorous condition (εὐεξία) (*Mos.* 2.69). In his *Opponents of Paul in 2 Corinthians* (Philadelphia: Fortress Press, 1986), 255, Dieter Georgi asserted that such strength and vigor are not simply human qualities, but belong to the reality of the divine sphere. His conclusion is not immediately apparent, since Philo often depreciates external εὐεξία gained by athletes in favor of an internal εὐεξία gained by philosophers (Philo's allegorical athletes). The quality of strength (ἰσχύς), furthermore, is not used by Philo to characterize a divine figure. Nonetheless, when speaking of divine inspiration, Philo describes an inward transformation of the mind resulting in an outward εὐεξία. First, Isaac was endowed in his mind (τὴν διάνοιαν) (his most divine part [τὸ θειότατον]) with power (δυνάμει) and superior condition (εὐεξία) such that no one would contend with him (*Det.* 29). A similar description of Abraham does not use the word εὐεξία, but contains the concept. When Abraham became inspired, everything changed for the better: his eyes, complexion, size, deportment, movements, and voice were all heightened in various ways (*Virt.* 217). In the case of Moses—whose prophetic ecstasy is a kind of metamorphosis (μεταμορφούμενος; *Mos.* 1.57)—a similar event occurs. His strength and vigor thus suggest divine inspiration. For the relation of inspiration and deification, see below.

70. *FGH* 103 frag. 13, end. Cf. also Dion. Hal., *Rom. hist.* 6.13.1.

Beauty, furthermore, is often revealed through an epiphany. When Aphrodite reveals herself to Anchises in a Homeric hymn, "her head reached to the well-hewn crossbeams, and from her cheeks immortal beauty (κάλλος ἄμβροτον) shone forth" (*Hom. Hymn Aphr.* 5.173-75). When Demeter reveals herself to Metaneira in another hymn, "Beauty (κάλλος) breathed about her . . . a light beamed far out from the goddess's immortal skin . . . The well-built house flooded with radiance like lightning" (*Hom. Hymn Dem.* 276, 278, 280).[71] Here beauty and light are associated, as in the case of Moses.[72]

More specifically, the beauty of Moses was concentrated in a "sun-like splendor flashing like lightning" from his face (*Mos.* 2.70). Moses' sun-like splendor is reminiscent of his final transformation at death, where he is definitively made into "most sun-like mind (νοῦς)" (*Mos.* 2.288).

LIGHT

I noted above that brilliant light imagery is perhaps the most common sign of an epiphany in the ancient Mediterranean world. In a childhood epiphany of Heracles's divinity, for example, the house is flooded with light, and his parents "can see the walls as clearly as if it was bright dawn" (Theocr., *Idylls* 24.22, 38). In a dream epiphany to Aeneas, the divine Penates are "manifest in brilliant light" (*multo manifesti lumine*) (Virg., *Aen.* 3.151). Aeneas later tells Dido that he saw Mercury come to him *manifesto in lumine* ("in clear light") (4.358). Venus later appears to Aeneas "bright white amidst ethereal clouds" (*aetherios inter . . . candida nimbos*) (8.608).[73] The fact that Moses' splendor is "sun-like" in Philo (*Mos.* 2.70) also recalls texts in which the Jewish deity has "the appearance of the sun" (*1 En.* 14:20; cf. Rev. 1:16).[74]

---

71. N. J. Richardson, *The Homeric Hymn to Demeter* (Oxford: Clarendon, 1974), 252–54. This Homeric hymn is appealed to by both Yarbro Collins ("The Worship of Jesus and the Imperial Cult," in *The Jewish Roots of Christological Monotheism: Papers from the St. Andrews Conference on the Historical Origins of the Worship of Jesus*, ed. Carey C. Newman et al. [Leiden: Brill, 1999], 252), and Moss ("Transfiguration: An Exercise," 81–82). Moss rightly observes that this is the second epiphany of Demeter in *Hom. Hymn Cer.* The first occurred as a sort of premonition, which Moss likens to the premonition of Jesus' divinity when he walks upon the water in Mark 6:45-52 (82). In the hymn to Demeter by Callimachus, Demeter is again suddenly metamorphosed into her "goddess shape": "Her steps touched the earth, but her head reached unto Olympus." Those who see her become "half-dead" and rush suddenly away (*Hom. Hymn Cer.* 57–60; cf. *Gos. Pet.* 10.40).

72. Cf. *Hymn Aphr.* 174-75; *T. Job* 46.7-9.

73. Cf. Ovid, *Fasti* 1.94; Apoll. Rhod., *Arg.* 4.1701-1717.

74. For the light motif in biblical theophanies, see Albrecht Scriba, *Die Geschichte des Motivkomplexes Theophanie* (Göttingen: Vandenhoeck & Ruprecht, 1995), 21–28.

In the ancient world, some of the gods who shone so brightly were also human kings. On gold coins, Ptolemy III Euergetes (246–221 BCE), Ptolemy V Epiphanes (204–180 BCE), and Ptolemy VIII (144–116 BCE) are all depicted with sun-like crowns beaming with light. The Seleucid kings Antiochus IV Epiphanes (175–164 BCE), Antiochus VI Epiphanes Dionysus (145–42 BCE) and Tryphon Diodotus (142–139 BCE) portrayed themselves on coins with a nimbus of radiating light.[75] This *corona radiata* in the royal context "is clearly meant to indicate apotheosis."[76] For an ancient Mediterranean reader, a kingly Moses could also appear in a divine light.

TERROR

As in divine epiphanies, the brilliance of Moses' appearance caused a shock of consternation. Moses' kinsmen, when they caught sight of their ruler, were "amazed and panic-stricken and were not able to withstand with their eyes for any length of time the assault" of the rays launched from Moses' face (*Mos.* 2.70).[77] Similarly, Metaneira before the unveiled Demeter is seized with "reverence, awe and pale terror" (*Hom. Hymn Dem.* 2.188-190).[78] Enoch before "the Great Glory" lies "prostrate and trembling" (*1 En.* 14:24). When Anchises sees Aphrodite in her unveiled beauty "he turns his gaze away in terror, hides his face under the covers, and begs for mercy" (*Hom. Hymn Aphr.* 181-90). When Ezekiel sees the appearance of Yahweh, he falls on his face (Ezek. 1:28). John falls as though dead before the divine Christ (Rev. 1:17).[79] Before the god Janus, Ovid feels his hair "stiffen with fear," and his chest freeze with a sudden chill (*Fast.* 1.97-98).[80] The "bright burst of Phoebus" in the Homeric Hymn to

---

75. See these coins and more examples in Dominique Svenson, *Darstellungen hellenistischer Könige mit Götterattributen* (Frankfurt am Main: Peter Lang, 1995), 370–74, and especially Marianne Bergman, *Die Strahlen der Herrscher: Theomorphes Herrscherbild und politische Symbolik im Hellenismus und in der römischen Kaiserzeit* (Mainz: Philipp von Zabern, 1998).

76. William J. Fulco, "Response to Badian," in *The Deification of Alexander the Great* (Berkeley, CA: Center for Hermeneutical Studies, 1976), 38.

77. Abundant Greco-Roman parallels for fear in the face of theophany are provided by Pfister, "Epiphanie," col. 317–18. Cf. Linda Belleville, *Reflections of Glory: Paul's Polemical Use of the Moses-Doxa Tradition in 2 Corinthians 3.1-18*, JSNTSup 52 (Sheffield: Sheffield Academic Press, 1991), 33, 50, 66, n. 2. She points to the Samaritan texts Memar Markah. 2.12; *L.A.B.* 12.1; *Sifre Num.* 140; *Cant. Rab.* 3.7.5; *Pesiq. R.* 10.6; *Sifre Num.* 1 and *Midr Hagadol* כי תשא 30.

78. Richardson, *Homeric Hymn to Demeter*, 208–210; Richard Buxton, *Forms of Astonishment: Greek Myths of Metamorphosis* (Oxford: Oxford University Press, 2009), 164–65.

79. See further Christopher Rowland, "The Vision of the Risen Christ," *JTS* 31 (1980): 1–11.

80. Cf. Virg., *Aen.* 4.279-80.

Apollo throws "great awe (μέγα . . . δέος) into all" (446-447).[81] The comment of Jean-Pierre Vernant applies to both Jewish and Greek sources: "the body of the gods shines with such an intense brilliance that no human eye can bear it."[82]

Philo uses the language of overpowering light to describe the high God. In his treatise *On Flight and Finding*, he writes that the person who tries to gaze on the Supreme Essence "will be blinded by the rays that beam forth all around him" (§165). Humans cannot bear the beams of light that flow from God, even as their human eyes cannot directly view the sun (*Abr.* 76; *Praem.* 36-40; *Fug.* 165). The parallel between Moses' appearance on Sinai and that of "the Supreme Essence" is striking. Scott Hafemann concluded from comparing these texts that Moses, when he descended from the mountain, mediated the divine presence.[83] Philo's line of thought, I think, allows for a bolder interpretation. He depicts Moses descending from Sinai with the key trademarks of a divine epiphany (beauty, light, the response of awe). If Moses mediated divine reality on the mountain, it is because he was himself deified.

From Philo's Moses to Mark's Christ

Philo's "Mosaic epiphany" indicates that a Mosaic background to Mark's transfiguration confirms rather than rules out the revelation of Jesus' divinity. If Jesus' transformation on the mountain was Mosaic, it was also divine. Both authors use the same stock epiphanic conventions to put their hero in a divine light.[84]

Terror

For example, Mark depicts the stunned fear of the disciples before the transfigured Jesus in no uncertain terms: "they became terrified out of their minds" (ἔκφοβοι . . . ἐγένοντο, 9:5).[85] Interestingly, ten verses later, Mark has

---

81. Cf. further Hom., *Il.* 20.129-31; 24.170; *Od.* 16.177-79; 24.533; Virg., *Aen.* 4.279-80; Horace, *Carm.* 2.19.5-7.

82. Vernant, *Mortals and Immortals*, 44.

83. Scott Hafemann, *Paul, Moses, and the History of Israel* (Milton Keynes, UK: Paternoster, 2005), 292–93.

84. Due to limited space, I am unable to discuss the resonances of the verb μεταμορφόω in Mark 9:2. In the past, comparisons between Mark and Greco-Roman religious thought centered on this word. Very few substantive results were gained in part due to the fact that a single word can vary dramatically in meaning depending on context (See esp. Jonathan Z. Smith, *Drudgery Divine*, 54–84). Although in Greco-Roman texts the verb is associated with metamorphosis into godhood, it more often signals a change of a god to a human or animal form. See further P. M. C. Forbes-Irving, *Metamorphosis in Greek Myths* (Oxford: Clarendon, 1990), and esp. Buxton, *Forms of Astonishment*.

Jesus, just like Philo's Moses, descend the mountain and approach a crowd. Those in the crowd "were immediately overcome with awe (ἐξεθαμβήθησαν)" at Jesus' presence. This detail, unmotivated by anything in the immediate context, is reminiscent of the awe felt by the Israelites as they beheld Moses descend the mountain transfigured. In Exodus, they fear to approach him (ἐφοβήθησαν ἐγγίσαι αὐτοῦ) (Exod. 34:30). In Philo, the amazed and bewildered Israelites cannot hold their gaze on Moses (*Mos.* 2.70).[86]

The verb ἐξεθαμβήθησαν in Mark is built from the verb θαμβέω ("to be astonished") and ultimately from the noun θάμβος ("astonishment"/"amazement"). Both terms regularly expressed the human reaction to a god's epiphany.[87] When, for instance, the Argonauts behold the epiphany of Apollo, "helpless amazement (θάμβος) seized them as they looked; and no one dared to gaze face to face into the fair eyes of the god" (Apoll. Rhod., *Arg.* 2.681-82). Helen was amazed (θάμβησεν) when she recognized Aphrodite behind the form of an old woman (Hom., *Il.* 3.398), as was Telemachus when he knew the deity (ὄισατο γὰρ θεὸν εἶναι) of Athena (*Od.* 1.323). Similarly, amazement (θάμβος) took hold of the Trojans and Greeks as they beheld Athena descend from heaven like a shooting star (Hom., *Il.* 4.75-80).[88]

WORSHIP

On the Mount of Transfiguration, Peter and the disciples not only fear Jesus, they seek to worship him. This is another common response to a divine epiphany, as Moss points out:

> Often the recipient of the divine visitation offers to institute an altar or place of worship dedicated to the deity. An example of this is found in the *Homeric Hymn to Aphrodite* where the mortal onlooker offers to set up an altar to the goddess: "I will make you an altar

---

85. For ἔκφοβος as "fright enough to make one's hair stand up on end," see Timothy Dwyer, *The Motif of Wonder in the Gospel of Mark*, JSNTSup 128 (Sheffield: Sheffield Academic Press, 1996), 141–42.

86. Marcus, *Way of the Lord*, 82–83. Cf. Dwyer, *Motif of Wonder*, 147–49.

87. For θάμβος and epiphanies, see esp. Pfister, "Epiphanie," col. 317; Jenny Strauss Clay, *Wrath of Athena: Gods and Men in the Odyssey* (Lanham, MD: Rowman & Littlefield, 1997), 167–70; Donald Lateiner, *Sardonic Smile: Nonverbal Behaviour in Homeric Epic* (Ann Arbor: University of Michigan Press, 1995), 45–46.

88. Cf. also Hom. *Od.* 19.36; *Hom. Hymn Aphr.* 4.84; *Hom. Hymn Bacc.* 7.37. For the fear motif in Hebrew Bible theophanies, see George W. Savran, *Encountering the Divine: Theophany in Biblical Narrative* (London: T&T Clark, 2005), 93–119.

upon a high peak, in a far-seen place, and will sacrifice rich offerings to you at all seasons."This tradition offers an interesting background for Peter's surprising offer to make tabernacles for Jesus, Moses and Elijah. From these examples it seems that far from being unexpected, the disciples' dual response of fear and worship fit perfectly the standard response of mortals in epiphany stories.[89]

Supporting evidence for this thesis is ready to hand. After Demeter reveals herself in her Homeric *Hymn* (268-71), for instance, she commands that a temple and altar be built for her. In the classical version of Jason and the Argonauts by Apollonius Rhodius, Apollo appears to the distressed Argonauts with a fiery and incandescent bow. After he brings safety to the crew, they set up a sacred enclosure and an altar, founding the cult of Apollo "the Gleamer" (Αἰγλήτην) (*Arg.* 4.1710-16). Some epiphanic traditions in the Hebrew Bible are similar. Jacob, when Yahweh appears to him in a dream at Bethel, sets up a pillar, pours oil upon it, and makes a vow as an act of worship (Gen. 28:18).[90] Gideon set up an altar (מזבח; θυσιαστήριον) to Yahweh in response to a theophany, calling it "Yahweh of prosperity" (יהוה שלום) (Judg. 6:24).

Peter, for his part, offers Jesus—in addition to Moses and Elijah—a "tabernacle" (σκηνή), reminiscent of the Tent of Testimony (σκηνὴ τοῦ μαρτυρίου) in the Exodus narratives (40:34, *passim*). Such a tabernacle, argues Heil, provides a fitting location for a heavenly figure "to continue his glorious appearance and communicate divine instructions to the disciples on earth, analogous to the role of the tent as a place for divine communication in the Tent of Meeting."[91] On the Mount of Transfiguration, Peter assumes that the three luminous beings are divine and should receive some sort of cult. Interpreters might censure Peter for his mistaken view (only *one* of the luminous beings, we soon find out, is God's beloved son); nevertheless, his action represents a common and appropriate Mediterranean response to the divine.[92]

The tents, as is sometimes suggested, may also be linked to the Feast of Tabernacles, indicating the establishment of a festival.[93] Herodotus describes a number of occasions wherein festivals are linked to the appearance of a deity.

---

89. Moss, "Transfiguration: An Exercise," 81. Cf. MacDonald, *Homeric Epics*, 94–95.

90. See further Savran, *Encountering the Divine*, 178–82.

91. Heil, *Transfiguration of Jesus*, 314.

92. See further Gerd Theissen, *The Miracle Stories of the Early Christian Tradition* (Philadelphia: Fortress Press, 1983), 96–97.

93. For this argument see Harald Riesenfeld, *Jésus transfiguré: L'arrière-plan du récit évangelique de la transfiguration de notre-Seigneur*, ASNU 16 (Copenhagen: Munksgaard, 1947). His theory is "rehabilitated"

"There appeared in Egypt that Apis whom the Greeks call 'Epaphus'; at whose revelation (ἐπιφανέος) straightway the Egyptians donned their fairest garments and kept high festival" (*Hist.*, 3.27).[94]

LIGHT

Finally—and most importantly—Mark uses light as a signal for Jesus' divine status, and specifically the light of his clothing. Jesus' garments, to quote the text, become "dazzling, extremely white" (στίλβοντα λευκὰ λίαν) (Mark 9:3). When introducing this chapter, I provided several examples of divine beings wearing garments of light. Additional instances are not difficult to find. The "splendid fine-woven garment" of the god Helios, "shimmers about him" (*Hom. Hymn Sol.* 31.13). Selene, the goddess of the Moon, has "garments that gleam from afar (εἵματα … τηλαυγέα)" (*Hom. Hymn Lun.* 32.8). Yahweh is "wrapped in light as with a cloak" (ἀναβαλλόμενος φῶς ὡς ἱμάτιον) (Ps. 103:2 LXX).[95]

Kings who dressed in luminous garments were also associated with gods. Josephus offers the famous example of King Agrippa who entered the theater of Caesarea in a robe of silver (στολὴν ἐνδὺς ἐξ ἀργύρου). In the early morning rays, the silver wondrously beamed (θαυμασίως ἀπέστιλβε) and sparkled (μαρμαίρων) so as to create fright (τι φοβερόν) and a shudder (φρικῶδες) in those who gazed at it (*Ant.* 19.344). Instantly there were acclamations that Agrippa was a god (θεόν) and something higher than mortal nature (κρείττονα . . . θνητῆς φύσεως) (§345). In the political capital of Judea and directed to a Jewish king, such cries are revealing. Jews too, it seems, inhabited a culture where bright garments signaled divinity, and royalty bled into deity. Yarbro Collins observes, "To listeners familiar with such traditions, the account according to which Jesus, in the sight of the three disciples, was changed in appearance from an ordinary man to a being with white, shining clothing, would signify that he was a divine being walking the earth in a modest disguise."[96]

---

in Fletcher-Louis, "Sacral Son," 262–65. Cf. David Daube, *The New Testament and Rabbinic Judaism* (London: Athlone, 1956), 30–31.

94. Further examples in Yarbro Collins, *Mark*, 418–19, n. 28; John B. Weaver, *Plots of Epiphany* 51–56; 117–26; 233–56; 273–75.

95. As additional evidence, Zeller cites Eunapius (*Vit. Philos.* 458) who says that the divine manifests itself not only in the face but in the clothes ("Métamorphose," 184).

96. Yarbro Collins, "Son of God Among Greeks and Romans," 91. MacDonald points out that Exodus 24 "says nothing of the alteration of Moses' clothing" (*Homeric Epics*, 94), and takes this as evidence that Mark was more dependent on ancient epic, specifically the transformation of Odysseus before

SON OF GOD

In my reading of the transfiguration as a "Jewish epiphany," I cannot pass over the divine declaration sounding at the culmination of Mark's transfiguration story: "This is my beloved son!" (Mark 9:7). What actually are the implications of Jesus' divine sonship for his divinity?

First, I note that it is an epiphanic convention for a god or divine being to be verbally identified in some way. When the god Dionysus speaks in the first line of Euripides's *Bacchae*, he announces, "I have come, the son of Zeus" (Ἥκω Διὸς παῖς). The speech that follows narrates the god's epiphany to his Theban homeland.[97] In the Homeric *Hymn to Apollo*, the god manifests himself as a dolphin, as light, and finally as a human being. In this form, he identifies himself to the men who will become his priests: "I am the son of Zeus; I declare that I am Apollo" (εἰμὶ δ᾽ ἐγὼ Διὸς υἱός, Ἀπόλλων δ᾽ εὔχομαι εἶναι) (480).[98] When a maddened Ajax walks on the stage in the play bearing his name, he recognizes the goddess: "Hail Athena, Zeus-born child!" (ὦ χαῖρ᾽ Ἀθάνα, χαῖρε Διογενὲς τέκνον) (Soph., *Ajax* 91). In the Markan transfiguration, neither Jesus nor a devotee identifies him as God's son. Such a testimony comes from the Father-God himself. This higher source of revelation only amplifies the validity and power of the declaration: "This is my beloved son!" The evangelist thus employs an epiphanic convention but improves upon it—probably for competitive and apologetic purposes. Jesus is just as divine—or rather more divine—than others who claim to be offspring of the high God. Yarbro Collins rightly remarks, "From the point of view of traditional Greek religion, the identification of Jesus in this scene [the transfiguration] as God's son is equivalent to identifying him as a divine being."[99]

But citing Greek parallels is not enough. Both Mediterranean religious sensibilities and ancient Jewish traditions combined to define the nature of Jesus'

Telemachus in *Od.* 16.178-85. The fact that in Matthew Jesus' face shines like the sun (ἔλαμψεν τὸ πρόσωπον αὐτοῦ ὡς ὁ ἥλιος) (17:2) only serves to amplify the epiphanic revelation of his divinity (cf. *1 En.* 14:20; Rev. 1:16).

97. Anton Bierl notes that it is possible to read the whole *Bacchae* "as the performance of an epiphany of Dionysus" ("'Turn on the Light!' Epiphany, the God-Like Hero Odysseus, and the Golden Lamp of Athena in Homer's *Odyssey*," *ICS* 29 [2004]: 43–62 [45]).

98. Less similar is Plautus, *Amph.* 19: "My name is Mercury; I come at the command of Jove (*Iovis iussu venio, nomen Mercurio est mihi*)." Cf. Eur., *Ion* 1-4. The conventional language is made fun of in Aristoph., *Ran.* 22: "I am Dionysus, son of Wine-jar" (ἐγὼ μὲν ὢν Διόνυσος, υἱὸς Σταμνίου). See further Bremer, "Epiphanie des Gottes," 3–5; Gerald Mussies, "Identification and Self-identification of Gods," in *Knowledge of God in the Greco-Roman World*, ed. Roelof van den Broek et al. (Leiden: Brill, 1988), 1–18, esp. 12–15.

99. Yarbro Collins, "Son of God Among Greeks and Romans," 92.

divine sonship. As Marcus points out in his treatment of the Markan baptism, "You are my son" is not just a "legal adoption," but (due to the resonance of Ps. 2:7: "Today I have begotten you") represents a change—not just in Jesus' "office"—but in his "essence." "Jesus is the Son of God because he is granted substantial participation in God's holiness." As son, Jesus participated "in God's very power and being."[100]

Recently, Michael Peppard has fruitfully compared Mark's use of "son of god" with its use chiefly among Roman emperors (the cosmocrators of Mark's day).[101] Peppard emphasizes that Roman imperial sonship occurred through adoption, that is, the election of a grown man by the ruler producing a transfer of power (since the adopted one inherited the rule of his father). With Marcus,[102] Peppard views the formula "You are my beloved son" spoken at Jesus' baptism—and restated at the transfiguration—as a means of adopting him to divinity.[103] This is not a low christology. "To the contrary," Peppard observes, "adoption is how the most powerful man in the world gained his power."[104] This "most powerful man in the world"—the Roman emperor—was also a god. Peppard, in accord with new trends in conceiving of the emperor's divinity, concludes that "son of god"—when applied to the emperor—does not imply "absolute" divinity or an abstract divine essence.[105] (This notion of divinity, he rightly points out, is restricted to philosophical circles.) Rather, like the emperor, Jesus was divine in terms of his status: as Yahweh's declared son and heir, Jesus was now able to exercise Yahweh's power and benefaction.

For Peppard, Jesus' baptism is "the beginning of his reign as God's representative."[106] Virtually the same declaration ("This is my beloved son!") heard by the disciples at the transfiguration, Peppard observes, confirms Jesus' adoption as if it took place in a *comitia curiata* or "representative assembly" (practiced in Roman ceremonies of adoption).[107] In the transfiguration, Jesus'

---

100. Marcus, *Way of the Lord*, 71–72.

101. Michael Peppard, *The Son of God in the Roman World: Divine Sonship in its Social and Political Context* (Oxford: Oxford University Press, 2011). Peppard focuses on Mark's baptismal account, where Jesus is god's "beloved son" (Mark 1:11) but his conclusions apply equally well to the transfiguration, which contains nearly the same declaration (9:7).

102. Marcus, *Way of the Lord*, 70–71.

103. Peppard concludes that Mark was adoptionist in the sense that "Mark narratively characterizes Jesus in comparison with the adopted Roman emperor, the most powerful man-god in the universe" (*Son of God in the Roman World*, 95).

104. Ibid., 95.

105. Ibid., 9–11.

106. Ibid., 98.

107. Ibid., 130.

divine rule is proved to be more than a private vision. It is a revelation to faithful witnesses. Now the disciples know (or should know) that Jesus is Yahweh's divine son and thus ruler of the world. The rule of God, as Jesus said, has come in power (Mark 9:1).[108]

EXCURSUS: PHILO ON SON OF GOD

In accordance with my comparison above, it is appropriate to ask whether Philo's deified Moses is also a "son of God." In a general sense, Philo acknowledges that human beings can be sons of God. Those who "enjoy [or employ] the knowledge of the One (οἱ δὲ ἐπιστήμῃ κεχρημένοι τοῦ ἑνός)," he says, "are rightly called 'sons of god' (υἱοὶ θεοῦ)" (Conf. 145).[109] This sonship has to do with knowledge of the true God, and with virtue. They are sons of God who hold moral beauty to be the only good. In another passage, Philo remarks that the Logos is God, the Mind of the universe (τὸν . . . τῶν ὅλων νοῦν, τὸν θεόν), and the one who created the universe (Migr. 192-93). The mind of the individual (τὸν ὑμέτερον νοῦν), stripped of the body, sense perception, and speech can gradually change its place and arrive at the "father of piety and holiness" (apparently the Logos). If the Logos is depicted as a father here, the individual logoi, freed from their bodies, are evidently his "sons."

Support for this interpretation comes from the Confusion of Tongues 146-48. Here Philo writes that if people cannot be called God's sons (i.e., sons of the high God) they should strive to become sons of the eldest born (ὁ πρεσβύτατος) Logos.[110] Specifically, the sons of the divine Logos are the "souls immortalized (ψυχῶν . . . ἀπαθανατιζομένων) by virtues (ἀρεταῖς)" (149). This same verb, ἀπαθανατίζω, is used of Moses in The Life of Moses 2.288: "and having left behind mortal life (θνητὸν ἀπολιπὼν βίον) he [Moses] was immortalized (ἀπαθανατίζεσθαι)." Moses, for Philo, is nothing less than the paragon of virtue and the model of one immortalized by it. Due to his immortalization and transformation into pure mind, it would seem, Moses could be called "son" of the divine Logos.[111]

108. Lucien Legrand points out that the transfiguration is a proleptic realization of the promise in Mark 13:26: "Then they will see the Son of Man coming in clouds with great power and glory" (L'annonce a Marie (Lc 1,26-38): Une apocalypse aux origines de l'Évangile, LD 106 [Paris: Éditions du Cerf, 1981], 286).

109. For this point, Philo quotes three prooftexts: Deut. 14:1; 32:6, 18. Cf. Spec. 1.318.

110. Conf. 41, 63. This is Philo's interpretation of "sons of one man (= the Logos)" (Gen. 42:11).

111. Further support for Moses' divine sonship can be drawn from a text we have already treated. We recall in the case of Moses that his "calling above [i.e., his heavenly journey on Mount Sinai]" is a second birth, which Philo calls a "divine birth" (QE 2.46). It is not a birth from a mother, which produces the

For Philo as for the Roman emperors, adopted sonship is real sonship. In his treatise *On Sobriety*, Philo notes that the one who has God enrolled (ἐπιγράφω, cf. *Somn.* 2.273) as his Father has become the adoptive "only" son of god (εἰσποιητὸς αὐτῷ μόνος υἱός) (*Sobr.* 56). This adopted *and* unique son is the man who is the "intelligible good" (νοητός ἀγαθός), the wise man (ὁ σοφός) (55), the friend (φίλος) of God (56), who is also sole king (μόνος βασιλεύς) (57). Significantly, Philo uses almost all of the above Stoic designations to describe the dignity of Moses. In his *Life of Moses*, Moses is the model wise man (2.67; cf. *Gig.* 47-48), the friend of God (1.156), who is king not just over Israel, but over the cosmos (1.158), who becomes νοῦς (2.288). Thus even though Philo never calls Moses a "son of God," his construction of Moses as super-sage, model of virtue, king, and eventual recipient of noetification all indicate that Moses fulfilled the Philonic type of "son of God (the Logos)."[112]

Does Moses' (implied) divine sonship have any implications for Mark's title "son of God"? The differences are immediately clear. By "son of God," Mark does not mean son of the Logos. The Evangelist does not distinguish being son of (the high) God from being son of God's firstborn Logos. In terms of divinity, however, there is some conceptual overlap. In Philo, as in the ruler cult, being "son of God" implies a form of divinity. In the ruler cult, the divinity is conceived more in terms of status than essence. Philo, as a Platonist, is more comfortable with an ontological understanding of divinity. Mind (νοῦς) is divine, and he who *becomes* pure, immortalized mind is both son of the Logos and divine. Mark's understanding of Jesus as "son of God" is—as in emperor worship—less a matter of *being* than of *rank*: Jesus is the divine Messiah, empowered by God to inaugurate the kingdom.

CONCLUSION

The argument of this chapter is not predicated on literary borrowing but on historical analogy and comparison based on common cultural conceptions. Although Homer and Virgil were standard texts by the first century CE, Mark need not have read the luminous epiphanies in Virgil or the amazed reactions

mortal body, but a birth from the father and maker of the universe (the Logos). Based on this passage, it appears that Moses would rightly be called a "son of god the Logos." As one who becomes solely mind, Moses becomes a true offspring of the divine Mind.

112. According to Joachim Kügler, Philo sketches a distinctive form of royal theology: "The breakthrough of the sage to the knowledge of God enabled by the divine Logos mediates the royal worth of a son of God" ("Spüren ägyptisch-hellenistischer Königsideologie bei Philo von Alexandria," in *Ägypten und der östliche Mittelmeerraum im 1. Jahrtausend v. Chr.*, ed. Manfred Görg and Günther Hölbl [Wiesbaden: Harrassowitz, 2000], 231–50 [247]).

in the Homeric *Hymns* to employ similar and widely assumed literary tropes. He did not even have to read about the sun-like splendor of Philo's Moses. Mark needed only to have read his Bible in a culture where it was commonly recognized that supernatural light, combined with the response of awe and worship, signaled the presence of the divine.

I conclude that Mark's Mosaic (i.e., "Jewish") depiction of Jesus in the transfiguration is no hindrance to the view that Jesus' transfiguration manifested his divinity. Human participation in the divine nature was not an impossible thought in the Judaism of the first century. Philo shows us that an exceptional hero could attain (if only briefly) divine status during his lifetime. Admittedly, Philo's conception of Moses' divinity was thoroughly Platonic. Mark did not think that Jesus had been turned into νοῦς on the Mount of Transfiguration. Nonetheless, Philo's philosophical framework ought not to obscure what was common to both Greek and Jewish literature: divinity is revealed through the presence of an unearthly light that inspires worship and awe.

For both Mark and Philo, neither Moses nor Jesus were revealed as gods in and of themselves. Both figures, rather, were enveloped in the nimbus of a higher deity. Both received light as a reflection of the light of the Logos (for Philo) or God the Father (for Mark). Both participated, ultimately, in the unique and all-encompassing divinity of Yahweh. For Mark's Jesus, just as for Philo's Moses, there is only one divinity—Yahweh (the "Existent"); thus those who are divine share the divine reality of the Jewish high God. What makes Jesus greater than Moses—at least in the eyes of Mark—is that Jesus is announced to be Yahweh's "beloved [i.e., specially promoted] son" (cf. Heb. 3).

If there is one word summing up the event of transfiguration, it is light. Light is the expression of both beauty and power. In ancient Mediterranean culture, it is divinity made visible. Indeed, of all symbols for divinity in the Greco-Roman world, light is perhaps the clearest token of divine reality. In the daring words of Gregory of Nazianzus: "Light was that Godhead which was shown on the mountain to the disciples, too strong for their eyes."[113]

To be sure, appearances of angels and other heavenly beings are also characterized by light, and scholars may dispute whether they belong to the divine world as ancient Jews—in all their diversity—conceived of it. Nevertheless, Mark goes out of his way to show that for Jesus the case is not ambiguous. The Second Evangelist fuses the light emerging from Jesus' clothing (Mark 9:3) to the light from the luminous cloud representing the Father's divine presence, or *kabod* (v.7).[114] In the vision of the transfiguration,

---

113. Gregory of Nazianzus, *Or.* 40.6.

the light of the divine Father merges with the light of the beloved son so that the latter is unambiguously deified.

114. Matthew alone writes what the other Synoptic writers seem to assume, namely that the cloud was φωτεινή (shining with light) (17:5). For the cloud as God's *kabod*, note Exod. 16:10, 24:16; 40:34, 38; cf. Luke 9:31.

"We Worship One who Rose from His Tomb"

Resurrection and Deification

". . . for when he [Christ] was raised, then he was glorified as god"

—IRENAEUS, *DEM.* 61

"But when he [Jesus] had put off this flesh, perhaps he became a god? Then why not rather Asclepius, Dionysus, and Heracles?"

—CELSUS IN ORIGEN, *CELS.* 3.42

INTRODUCTION

In Plato's *Apology*, Socrates offers two views of death: "Either death is a state of nothingness and utter unconsciousness, or, in accord with what is told, there is a change (μεταβολή) and change of residence for the soul from this place to another" (40c). Only with the latter view can we speak of an "afterlife." Typically for people (both ancient and modern) who believe in an afterlife, death involves a transformation (a μεταβολή) leading to another state of existence.

For most ancient Greeks and hellenized peoples, it seems, death involved a sort of halfway, twilight existence in a netherworld. The insubstantiality of dead people, often imagined as phantoms or wraiths, is typically signaled by their paleness, muteness, and mist-like quality. The dead become (literally) a shadow of their former selves, or (to employ a phrase of Pindar) "a dream of a shadow" (*Pyth.* 8.95-96). They exist on another plane—a subterranean realm—where they flit about "without strength or substance, partaking of the cold nothingness of drifting air."[1] Although the dead continue to exist on some lower level, their human identities are somehow diminished. They are, in this sense, "subhuman."

A few dead persons, however, experience a different fate. Instead of becoming ghosts and shadows, they are transformed into transcendent states. They live in peace and light on a loftier plane of existence, often conceived of as a kind of paradise. Sometimes they have increased power and can exert influence on the living. Their lives are somehow perpetuated beyond the grave. These are the heroes, spirits, gods, and so on. Such beings, presumably, are who they were when they were alive—yet greater, stronger, and more vibrant. They have been transformed into a higher mode of existence. They are, consequently, "superhuman."

These two classes of the dead (sub- and superhuman) appear in both ancient Greek and Jewish eschatologies.[2] Many ancient Jews, for instance, appeared to conceive of their dead as wraiths (רפאים) living a twilight existence in a chthonic dungeon called "Sheol" (Gen. 37:35; 2 Sam. 22:6; Ps. 18:5; cf. *1 En.* 102:6-8, 11; 2 Bar. 10:6-12:4). There deceased humans cannot praise God as a living human should (Ps. 6:5; 30:9; 88:10b; 115:17; cf. Isa. 38:18; Eccl. 9:10), and cannot (with rare exceptions, 1 Sam. 28:13-14) interact with the living or exert influence.[3] Alternatively, some special humans such as Elijah, Enoch, and (later) some Jewish martyrs seemed to have escaped this halfway existence. According to Jewish traditions, God swept up Enoch after 365 years

---

1. Michael Clark, *Flesh and Spirit in the Songs of Homer: A Study of Words and Myths* (Oxford: Clarendon, 1990), 148.

2. Ionia and Israel (more broadly: the Greek world and the Levant) were not so far distant in the ancient world. Cultural and theological exchanges are treated by Walter Burkert, *The Orientalizing Revolution: Near Eastern Influence on Greek Culture in the Early Archaic Age* (Cambridge, MA: Harvard University Press, 1992); M. L. West, *The East Face of Helicon: West Asiatic Elements in Greek Poetry and Myth* (Oxford: Clarendon, 1997); Carolina López-Ruiz, *When the Gods were Born: Greek Cosmogonies and the Near East* (Cambridge, MA: Harvard University Press, 2010).

3. Note that in this passage Samuel is called אלהים, or "god" (1 Sam. 28:13).

(Gen. 5:23-24), snatched away Elijah in a fiery chariot (2 Kgs. 2:11-12), and glorified "the wise" (after their deaths) so that they "shine like the brightness of the firmament . . . like the stars forever and ever" (Dan. 12:3).[4]

Homeric eschatology likewise presents two fates for human beings. The *Iliad* and *Odyssey* place most people in Hades—a chthonic realm where the dead exist as lifeless shades (εἴδωλα). They flit about like shadows, and screech like bats (*Od.* 11.605; 24.5-9) until they drink blood (*Od.* 11.146-49, 153-54, 228-32, 390).[5] Some special heroes, however—usually akin to gods or demigods like Menelaus (*Od.* 4.561-69; cf. 6.42-46)—exist in immortal, joyful, peaceful states in idyllic paradises often called the "Isles of the Blessed," or the "Elysian Fields."[6] Others are snatched up to heaven to enjoy the immortal and ageless life of the gods. Ganymede, for instance, was caught up "for the sake of his beauty, so he might be among the immortals" (*Il.* 20.234-35). For the same reason, Cleitus son of Mantius was carried away by Eos the dawn goddess (*Od.* 15.250-51). Homer's Heracles, interestingly, had a sort of double existence after death. In our manuscripts of the *Odyssey*, he is said to be both a deity on Olympus with Hebe to wife, and to exist as a troubled shade in Hades (*Od.* 11.601-602)—at once ghost and god.[7]

If the usual postmortem destiny of human beings can be classified either as (in most cases) ghostlike or (rarely) godlike, where does the resurrected Jesus end up? It appears that his postmortem mode of existence—at least in the minds of early Christians—flutters much closer to god than ghost (Luke 24:39). In fact, Jesus might be taken as a paradigmatic example of a deceased individual who

4. For a revisionist account of Sheol, along with important exceptions to the rule that all the dead go to Sheol, see Jon D. Levenson, *Resurrection and the Restoration of Israel: The Ultimate Victory of the God of Life* (New Haven, CT: Yale University Press, 2006), 35–81.

5. For a humorous description of Hades showing the continued influence of Homer, see Lucian, *Luct.* 2-13.

6. For death and the afterlife in Homer, see Lars Albinus, *The House of Hades: Studies in Ancient Greek Eschatology* (Aarhus: Aarhus University Press, 2000), 21–97; Clarke, *Flesh and Spirit*, 129–215. Other helpful studies include Martin P. Nilsson, *The Minoan-Mycenaean Religion and its Survival in Greek Religion*, 2nd ed. (Lund: C. W. K. Gleerup, 1968), 619–33. For Hades and Elysium in particular, note Timothy Gantz, *Early Greek Myth: A Guide to Literary and Artistic Sources* (Baltimore: Johns Hopkins University Press, 1993), 123–35.

7. Ancient critics rejected the lines that speak of Heracles's apotheosis as a sixth-century BCE interpolation (Walter Burkert, *Greek Religion: Archaic and Classical*, trans. John Raffan [Oxford: Basil Blackwell, 1985], 210). For further commentary on this passage, see Walter Pötscher, *Hellas und Rom: Beiträge und kritische Auseinandersetzung mit der inzwischen erschienenen Literatur* (Hildesheim: Georg Olms, 1988), 171–72. Lucian humorously exposes the tension between Heracles as ghost and god in *Dial. mort.* 11.

became a god or godlike figure in his postmortem state (Rom. 1:4; Phil. 2:9-11). That said, Jesus was hardly alone in his postmortem metamorphosis from mortal human to immortal god. In fact, he fits a type of postmortem metamorphosis shared by not a few individuals in the ancient Mediterranean world.

To be sure, for Christians (ancient and modern), Jesus is a unique figure—and his resurrection (ἀνάστασις) constitutes a key element of that uniqueness. Moreover, Jesus' resurrection as part of a larger Jewish and Christian eschatology of cosmic redemption is distinctive.[8] On the other hand, the nature of Jesus' resurrection itself is not for this reason incomparable with the postmortem transformations of other Greek and Roman figures.

DEFINING RESURRECTION

Here I must define resurrection, and specifically its meaning for Jesus in early Christian stories. Put briefly, the resurrection of Jesus is the revivification of his own body after a genuine death to an immortal transformed state. It is not:

1. a return from a merely apparent death (*Scheintod*)
2. the release or renewal of his soul (such as in the Platonic teaching of the immortal soul).
3. the transmigration of his soul to another body
4. the experience of renewed life in an underworld (as in some Egyptian religious traditions and Greek mysteries)
5. the return of a ghost from the grave (since ghosts remain dead)

Lastly—and most importantly—Jesus' resurrection does not merely return him to a *normal human* life. Whatever story of Jesus' resurrection we read in early Christian literature, it is evident that the resurrected Jesus returns to a qualitatively different kind of life. "Death no longer has dominion over" him, writes our earliest witness, "the life he lives, he lives to God" (Rom. 6:9-10). The resurrected Jesus becomes the prince of life, a life-creating spirit (1 Cor. 15:45) who has defeated death and Hades, and now (after his ascension) lives in

---

8. The bibliography for resurrection in Jewish tradition is enormous. A worthy entrance point is the classic study by George W. Nickelsburg, *Resurrection, Immortality, and Eternal Life in Intertestamental Judaism and Early Christianity*, 2nd ed. (Cambridge, MA: Harvard University Press, 2006). For additional surveys, see Alan J. Avery-Peck and Jacob Neusner, eds. *Judaism in Late Antiquity Part 4: Death, Life-after-Death, & The World-to-Come in the Judaisms of Late Antiquity* (Leiden: Brill, 2000); Leila Bonner "The Resurrection Motif in the Hebrew Bible: Allusions or Illusions," *JBQ* 30 (2002): 143–54; Alan Segal, *Life After Death: A History of the Afterlife in the Religions of the West* (New York: Doubleday, 2004), 248–531; Philip S. Johnston, *Shades of Sheol: Death and Afterlife in the Old Testament* (Downers Grove, IL: IVP, 2007), 69–230.

a transcendent state in the upper reaches of the cosmos. Jesus' resurrection is no mere resuscitation, but an *immortalization* (Origen, *Cels.* 2.16). In being raised, Jesus enters a state in which it is *impossible* for him to die. In New Testament traditions, Jesus' immortalization is not just the immortalization of his spirit or soul, but of his body. Jesus can show his immortalized body to others; the same immortalized body can be touched—even handled—and later ascend to heaven. This, then, is the understanding of resurrection I employ for this chapter—namely resurrection as *"corporeal immortalization."* In the framework that I use here, all post-mortem transformations that involve a return to a mortal human life and subsequent (repeated) death are not resurrections at all, but resuscitations—and will be referred to as such.[9]

CORPOREAL IMMORTALIZATION IN ANCIENT JUDAISM

Although resurrection as corporeal immortalization eventually found a place in ancient Judaism, it does not appear to be a native idea (2 Sam. 12:23; Job 7:9-10; 10:21; 16:22; Ps. 88:13). One of the few resurrection stories we meet in the Hebrew Bible—Elisha raising the Shunammite woman's son (2 Kgs. 4:8-37; cf. 1 Kgs. 17:17-24)—is a resuscitation, not a resurrection. The boy who is raised in this Hebrew tale had died not long before. The prophet had hoped to raise him through an act of associative magic—the touch of a magic wand—to no avail (4:29-31). Elisha then attempts to transmit life through a kind of corporeal osmosis—"putting his mouth upon his mouth, his eyes upon his eyes, and his hands upon his hands" (4:34). His strategy works, but the life Elisha gives the child is a normal human life. The boy is destined to die twice.

Resurrection (i.e., postmortem immortalization) elsewhere in the Hebrew Bible proves tantalizing but elusive. Many of the texts do not speak of resurrection at all in their historical settings, and only later came to be interpreted as resurrection texts (mostly by Christians and in some cases by rabbis). Only in the second century BCE, in the prophecy of Daniel 12:2-3 (cf. *1 En.* 104:2, 4, 6) do we find an unambiguous Jewish vision of resurrection as immortalization. Here the righteous and wise are raised from the dust (or from the "Land of Dust") and are said to shine forever like the brightness of the firmament and the stars (cf. Wisd. 3:7). The language seems to reflect the hopes of astral immortality in Greek culture at the time.[10] Here resurrection—at least for the righteous—is an immortalization: a transformation into a higher,

---

9. The distinction between resurrection and resuscitation is ancient, appearing in Hyg., *Fab.* 224, 251.

10. For an introduction to astral immortality, see Alan Scott, *Origen and the Life of the Stars: A History of an Idea* (Oxford: Clarendon, 1991).

celestial, kind of life. Although resurrection as immortalization and astral transformation are not out of step with Israel's hope in a covenant-keeping God who promises life to the righteous,[11] it does not appear to be a Jewish invention. Rather, resurrection as (astral) immortalization appeared in the context of a new cultural situation in which Palestine had already been shaped by the institutions and ideas of the Hellenistic kingdoms. This is not to argue that Jews borrowed a "pagan" belief foreign to their religion, since Jews were more than capable of assimilating Hellenistic soteriology and making it part of their own tradition. In this period, resurrection as immortalization and astral transformation *became* Jewish, and retains a Jewish "local color." Specifically, the type of transformation imagined in Daniel 12 seems to be solely *eschatological* (i.e., occurring at the end of time) and *collective* (i.e., featuring groups of people, not an individual)—two features that accord well with the national and apocalyptic consciousness of Daniel's author.[12] This form of resurrection thus differs from the resurrection of Jesus, which is conceived of as *individual* and occurring *before* the general resurrection on the last day. To find a true analogue to the resurrection of Jesus, then, we would expect at least three elements: (1) resurrection as transformation into *immortal* life that (2) occurs to an *individual*, (3) *before* a mass resurrection at the end of the world.

Where do we find this analogue? Christian theologians (ancient and modern) have declared that it is not in Judaism. Jesus' *individual, historical* resurrection, they urge, is a complete *novum* in Jewish thought—a surprising and unheard-of act of God. As a result, such a resurrection legitimates the uniqueness of Christian revelation and truth.[13]

11. So Levenson, *Resurrection*, xiii, 200, *passim.*

12. We also find a good description of an eschatological, collective resurrection in *1 En.* 51 (cf. 61:5). Note the comments of George Nickelsburg, *1 Enoch 2: A Commentary on the Book of 1 Enoch Chapters 37–82*, Hermeneia (Minneapolis: Fortress Press, 2012), 50–51. I agree with Andrew Chester that even cases of individual resurrection in Jewish thought (post 164 BCE) often include a national component ("Resurrection and Transformation," in *Auferstehung-Resurrection: The Fourth Durham-Tübingen Research Symposium: Resurrection, Transfiguration and Exaltation in Old Testament, Ancient Judaism and Early Christianity*, ed. Friedrich Avemarie and Hermann Lichtenberger, WUNT 135 [Tübingen: Mohr Siebeck, 2001], 47–78).

13. The uniqueness of the resurrection is an insider claim with apologetic import: Christianity is superior because it brought a new and joyous message to a moribund pagan culture. Occasionally this argument still rises to the surface of modern scholarship. "The Christian gospel of resurrection," says Peter Bolt, "held out a strong and living hope to a dying world . . . for those who continued to live under the shadow of death, it presented the assurance that something had been done about human mortality" ("Life, Death, and the Afterlife in the Greco-Roman World," in *Life in the Face of Death: The Resurrection Message of the New Testament*, ed. Richard Longenecker [Grand Rapids, MI: Eerdmans, 1998], 78).

From an etic perspective, however, although *individual* corporeal immortalization may have been novel in Judaism, it was not distinctive in Hellenistic culture. Justin Martyr famously (or infamously) declared that "when we [Christians] say also that the Word [i.e., Christ] . . . was crucified and died and rose again (ἀναστάντα) and ascended into heaven (ἀνεληλυθέναι εἰς τὸν οὐρανόν), we propound *nothing new* (οὐ . . . καινόν τι) beyond [what you believe] concerning those whom you call sons of Zeus" (*1 Apol.* 21.1, emphasis added).[14] Here Justin—thoroughly Christian—declares that resurrection (ἀνάστασις) is not a uniquely Jewish or Christian category. It is in fact a well-known way in the Mediterranean world to describe the transition of some individuals to postmortem superhuman states. Resurrection, that is, can be conceived of as a *type* of postmortem immortalization. In this chapter, I will explore the meaning of this claim with a view to Jesus' divinity. I will argue, in short, that the Christian depiction of Jesus' corporeal immortalization adopts and adapts the discourse of deification in Mediterranean culture with the intent of asserting Jesus' unique deity.[15]

HISTORY OF RESEARCH

Before I argue this point, it is necessary to situate my discussion in a larger conversation. Scholarship on the resurrection is enormous, and I make no attempt to be comprehensive. The following history of research will only sample some of the most relevant and recent treatments that examine resurrection in light of Greco-Roman culture.

In a 1965 article, Walter Pötscher argued that the very forms of Greek thought—a cyclical view of time, a prioritizing of this world, and an emphasis on memory through fame—did not allow ancient Greeks to arrive at concepts of individual corporeal resurrection. There are some exceptions (among them, Heracles), which he characterizes as slight and trivial. After death, Pötscher concedes, Heracles was exalted to live with the gods in a "glorified body."[16] Nonetheless, Pötscher is hesitant to see Heracles as an example of individual resurrection in the flesh because Heracles is both a god and a hero (Herod., *Hist.* 2.44). He also points out, as noted above, that Heracles is both ghost

---

14. Justin adds that the similarities are due to devilish imitation here in §21, §54 and in *Dial.* 69.

15. This is not an argument for Jesus as a dying and rising god. In the ancient Mediterranean, dying and rising gods are rare, and possibly non-existent (see Jonathan Z. Smith, *Drudgery Divine* 116–43). Tryggve N. D. Mettinger offers the best historical inquiry into and (limited defense of) dying and rising gods (esp. Melqart) in *The Riddle of Resurrection: "Dying and Rising Gods" in the Ancient Near East* (Stockholm: Almqvist & Wiksell International, 2001).

16. Walter Pötscher, "Die 'Auferstehung' in der klassischen Antike," *Kairos* 7 (1965): 208–15 (209).

(in Hades) and god (in heaven) in *Odyssey* 11. These distinctions, however, do not preclude a fruitful comparison of Heracles and Jesus on the point of corporeal immortalization. In fact, the idea that Heracles became immortal (thus divine) *and* suffered a human fate (death and descent to Hades) fits well with early Christian conceptions of Jesus as both son of Mary (who makes a descent to Hades, 1 Pet. 3:19-20) and son of God (who ascends to heaven, Acts 1:9; Eph. 4:8-10). Secondly, as Pötscher himself points out, Homer has Heracles's shade (εἴδωλον) in Hades, while "he himself" (αὐτός) is on Olympus. The "he himself," as Pötscher rightly points out, refers to the *body* of Heracles (cf. *Il.* 1.4). It is the body that preserves Heracles's identity—even if his body has been transformed and immortalized so that it can exist in heaven. The real Heracles, then, is the god in heaven, also the place to which Jesus is said to ascend (Luke 24:51). Pötscher rightly concludes that Heracles shows how individual resurrection in a transformed body should be understood (as it was for Heracles) as a union of humanity with divinity.[17]

Another classicist, Glen Bowersock, boldly affirmed that there are "virtually no examples" of bodily resurrection in the entire Greek tradition prior to 50 CE.[18] Resurrection from apparent death in Greek novels only becomes a theme, Bowersock proposed, after the advent of Christianity—and, he added, *because of* Christianity.[19] Although interesting, Bowersock's thesis is impossible to verify because almost all Greek novels appear after the advent of Christianity. He argues (fallaciously) *post hoc ergo propter hoc* (after x, therefore because of x), and makes no attempt to justify any actual influence of Christianity on Greek novels. Most importantly, however, his point is about *resuscitation*, not resurrection. The claim that there are no resurrections (in the sense of corporeal immortalizations) prior to 50 CE is simply false (as will be shown below).

More recently, Adela Yarbro Collins has argued that Mark's account of the empty tomb (Mark 16:1-8), borrows from Greco-Roman stories of translation.[20] Collins reviews ancient accounts of translation and immortalization from the ancient Near East and the larger Mediterranean world. Especially important are traditions in which the hero's body disappears (e.g., Cleomedes of Astypalaea, and Josephus's account of Elijah).[21] In a 2009

17. Ibid., 210.

18. Glen Bowersock, *Fiction as History: Nero to Julian* (Berkeley: University of California Press, 1994), 102.

19. Ibid., 119.

20. Adela Yarbro Collins, "Apotheosis and Resurrection," in *The New Testament and Hellenistic Judaism*, eds. Peder Borgen and Søren Giversen (Aarhus: Aarhus University Press, 1995), 88–100 (99).

21. Ibid., 95.

study, Collins returns to this subject.[22] Here she depicts a basic structural similarity between Roman apotheosis and Mark's empty-tomb story. In the Roman tradition, emperors must die—as in the case of Jesus—before being deified. The disappearance of the bodies of Romulus and Numa, and the full melting of the wax body of the deified emperor—analogous to Christ's empty tomb—signify the reality of deification.

In a 1999 article, Stanley Porter argued that "the Greeks did have a significant tradition of bodily resurrection" and asserted that "Greek teaching suggested to the Jews, or to some of them, that the dead would be raised from Sheol to live again on the earth."[23] Porter has been faulted, however, for presenting little relevant evidence for this claim. He discussed the shades in Hades, pre-mortem translation, metempsychosis, the immortality of the soul, and Orphism—none of which seem to be particularly relevant to Christian understandings of resurrection.[24] More promising are the resurrections of Horus by Isis (Diod., *Bibl. hist.* 1.25.6, where the verb ἀνίστημι is used), and Euripides's depiction of a raised Alcestis.[25] The resurrection of Horus, however, is not a Greek tradition (even if recorded in a Greek source), and Porter himself noted the problem with Alcestis: she "was revivified, only to die again at some future time."[26]

Perhaps the most serious challenge to anyone who would dare make resurrection a matter of historical comparison is made by N. T. Wright. In his *The Resurrection of the Son of God*, Wright strongly affirms the uniqueness of Jesus' resurrection; it is something that happened to Jesus "which had happened to nobody else."[27] Wright's bold thesis, however, depends on how he defines resurrection. The "resurrection" that he has in mind is a bodily return to *"the same sort of life that humans presently experience."*[28] It is this sort of resurrection that Wright depicts as impossible in Greco-Roman thought. Characteristically,

---

22. Collins, "Ancient Notions of Transferal and Apotheosis in Relation to the Empty Tomb Story in Mark," in *Metamorphoses: Resurrection, Body, and Transformative Practices in Early Christianity*, eds. Turid Karlsen Seim and Jorunn Økland (Berlin: Walter de Gruyter, 2009), 41–58.

23. Stanley Porter, "Resurrection, the Greeks and the New Testament," in *Resurrection*, eds. Stanley Porter, Michael Hayes, and David Tombs, JSNTSup 186 (Sheffield: Sheffield Academic Press, 1999), 53, 68.

24. Ibid., 68–76.

25. For the afterlife in tragedy (including Euripides's *Alcestis*), see Helen F. North, "Death and Afterlife in Greek Tragedy and Plato," in *Death and Afterlife: Perspectives of World Religions*, ed. Hiroshi Obayashi (New York: Praeger, 1992), 49–57.

26. Porter, "Resurrection, the Greeks and the New Testament," 79.

27. N. T. Wright, *The Resurrection of the Son of God* (London: SPCK, 2003), 83.

28. Ibid., 33, emphasis added.

he states this conclusion in no uncertain terms. "Resurrection was not an option [in Greco-Roman culture],"[29] the "road to the underworld [for Greeks] ran only one way,"[30] and "Christianity was born into a [Greco-Roman] world where its central claim [about resurrection] was known to be false."[31] Wright's conclusion that Homer and the tragedians offered a "total denial of resurrection" is based on a set of proof texts (*Il.* 24.549-51; Aesch., *Eum.* 647; Soph., *El.* 137-39) that are then taken as representative—and virtually canonical—for all hellenized peoples over a millennium of history.[32] Perhaps one can grant Wright that these texts make implausible a worldview in which previously dead people return to "the same sort of life that humans presently experience"—*but this is not an accurate description of the resurrection of Jesus.* Thus the (at first glance) impressive list of texts Wright draws up against resurrection in the Mediterranean world mean little when we focus on a truly Christ-like resurrection, namely *one leading to a transformed, immortalized corporeality.* If Greeks (and here we can include the Corinthians in 1 Cor. 15) had an aversion to the resurrection of *corpses* (ἀνάστασις τῶν νεκρῶν) returning to "the same sort of life that humans presently experience," they did not discount the notion of postmortem transformation to *transcendent, immortal* forms of life (as will be indicated below).[33]

---

29. Ibid., 60.

30. Ibid., 81. Technically there were exceptions to this rule, such as Orpheus and Alcestis. Sons of Zeus like Heracles and (in some traditions) Dionysus come back from Hades for certain tasks (to bring out Cerberus and Semele, respectively).

31. Ibid., 35. Even on his own terms, Wright would seem to be mistaken, since according to early Christian apologists, there were analogues to Christian resurrection. I have already mentioned Justin above (*1 Apol.* 21.1). Theophilus of Antioch, in addition, remarks, "You ['Greeks'] believe that Heracles, who burned himself up, is alive and that Asclepius, struck by lightning, was raised (ἐγηγέρθαι)" (*Autol.* 1.13; cf. Lucian, *Philops.*, 26).

32. Wright, *Resurrection of the Son*, 64. Wright quotes these anti-resurrection texts as if they were dogmas and does not hesitate to call Homer the Bible (specifically, the "Old Testament"!) of the Greeks (32). In treating the material this way, Wright subtly distorts the non-dogmatic and predominantly non-textual nature of Greek (and Roman) religion. Marie-Françoise Baslez quotes Aesch., *Eum.* 6.647-48 in a more nuanced discussion, but to the same effect ("Le corps, l'âme et la survie: anthropologie et croyances dans les religions du monde gréco-romain," in *Résurrection: L'après-mort dans le monde ancient et le Nouveau Testament,* eds. Odette Mainville and Daniel Marguerat, *Le monde de la Bible* 45 [Montréal: Labor et Fides, 2001], 88–89). It is significant that multiple resurrections performed by Asclepius are recorded (evidence in Emma Edelstein and Ludwig Edelstein, *Asclepius: A Collection of Interpretation of the Testimonies,* 2 vols. [Baltimore: Johns Hopkins Press, 1945], 1.§§ 66-86). It is not that resurrection is impossible in Greek thought, it is that the gods disapprove of it.

33. See further Dale Martin, *Corinthian Body* (New Haven, CT: Yale University Press, 1995), 104–36.

Over and over again, Wright avoids speaking about the corporeal implications of postmortem transformation in Mediterranean culture—repeatedly stressing that Greeks and Romans envisioned a transformation of the *soul*, not the body. To make this move plausible, Wright effectively canonizes Plato, calling his writings the "New Testament" for the hellenized world.[34] As Dag Øistein Endsjø points out, however, making Plato's doctrine of the immortal soul staple fare for ancient Mediterranean peoples (in particular non-philosophers) is a distortion of the general climate of thought (esp. in the first century CE).[35] One has the lingering sense that Wright's account of Plato's cultural ubiquity is meant to reinforce his tendentious view that "pagans" emphasized *only* the immortality of the soul, leaving corporeal immortalization (i.e., the resurrection of the body) to Jews and Christians. Recent scholarship, in particular the work of Endsjø, has overturned this outdated notion.[36]

In the end, Wright's highly apologetic attempt to establish the uniqueness of Jesus' resurrection fails because of a superficial comparison. In general, we might grant him that hellenized peoples may not have believed in a return of the dead to ordinary (mortal) human life—but this is not what Jesus' resurrection is! Jesus' resurrection much more resembles the stories of deified men immortalized after their deaths. These men are not just immortalized in their souls, but in their bodies as well. It is this postmortem *corporeal* transformation that allows one to compare their stories with the resurrection of Jesus.[37]

34. Wright, *Resurrection of the Son*, 47–48, cf. 81. Only *among professed Platonists* did Plato's writings constitute a kind of *scripta divinitus* (Cicero, *Or. Brut.* 1.49; cf. 3.15; *Leg.* 1.15; 2.14; 3.1). An example of Wright's exaggerated claims for Platonism is his assertion that no one in the Greco-Roman world "in their right mind" would have desired a corporeal existence "or something like it" after death (*Resurrection of the Son*, 60), and that re-embodiment was a "problem" for the Greco-Roman mind (82). Such a conclusion can in fact be turned on its head. It is more likely that only a few in the Greco-Roman world (that is, Platonic philosophers) would conceive of postmortem existence as entirely disembodied. To most hellenized peoples, it seems, postmortem corporeality would have been welcome as long as it was a *transformed, immortalized* corporeality (such as that of an astral body or the aetherial Stoic soul).

35. Dag Øistein Endsjø, *Greek Resurrection Beliefs and the Success of Christianity* (New York: Palgrave Macmillan, 2009), 13. Self-identifying Platonists represented only a tiny cross-section of people in the ancient Mediterranean world. (As Cicero notes, "Philosophy . . . deliberately eschews the masses" [*Tusc.* 2.4].) Wright admits that "Plato did not sweep the board of subsequent opinion at either a popular or an intellectual level." This point undermines the general tendency of his argument that Plato's doctrine of the immortal soul was determinative for the whole Greco-Roman world (*Resurrection of the Son*, 52).

36. Wright is aware that the "old assumption that Greeks believed in immortality while Jews believed in resurrection is not merely historically inaccurate; it is conceptually muddled" (ibid., 162). Regrettably, his awareness of this point does not prevent him from employing a wrong-headed dichotomy between Greek immortality of the soul and Jewish resurrection of the body.

A 2007 article by Deborah Thompson Prince argues that Jesus' post-mortem appearance in Luke 24 "surpasses" all expected modes of post-mortem apparition by drawing upon and adapting them all.[38] The four types of "returnee" from the dead include the ghost, the "revenant" (a temporarily resuscitated individual), the hero, and the translated (i.e., deified) person. Although her argument rightly underscores the complexity of Luke's relationship to Greco-Roman models—and his subtlety in adapting these models—her understanding of deification is too rigid. She wrongly assumes that the death and burial of an individual prevent deification.[39] This is certainly not the case for Roman emperors, of whom she is aware. Consequently, Prince appears to assume that deification only involves the ascension of the body, and not its revivification and metamorphosis into immortal life. That this view is mistaken will be indicated below.

In a recent monograph, Paul M. Fullmer offers several examples of resurrection as a theme in Greco-Roman folk narratives.[40] His main *comparanda* are the resurrections in the Gospel of Mark and Chariton's novel *Chaereas and Callirhoe*.[41] This particular novel is an interesting choice, since it depicts no cases of real (as opposed to apparent) death leading to resurrection and immortal life. Still, Fullmer is happy to use resurrection language for figures who have clearly *not* died (such as Zalmoxis in Herodotus, *Hist.* 4.93-94, Sarpedon in Homer, *Il.* 5.628-37, 655-62, 692-703, and Andromache in *Il.* 22.437-515). His strikingly broad view of resurrection (which includes resuscitations from *Scheintod*), and the consequent failure to distinguish resuscitation from a true transformation into immortal life (as in the case of Jesus) make his comparisons regrettably shallow.[42]

---

37. For further criticism of Wright, see Stephen J. Bedard, "Hellenistic Influence on the Idea of Resurrection in Jewish Apocalyptic Literature," *JGRChJ* 5 (2008): 174–89. When dealing with Christian texts, Wright is much more nuanced in his views. He recognizes, for instance, that for Paul resurrection "is one *form* or type of 'immortality'"—specifically a corporeal version of immortality (*Resurrection of the Son*, 164).

38. Deborah Thompson Prince, "The 'Ghost' of Jesus: Luke 24 in Light of Ancient Narratives of Post-Mortem Apparitions," *JSNT* 29, no. 3 (2007): 287–301.

39. Ibid., 297–98

40. Paul M. Fullmer, *Resurrection in Mark's Literary-Historical Perspective*, LNTS 360 (London: T&T Clark, 2007). Two significant examples are Herodotus's story of Aristeas of Proconnesus (62–65), and Ovid's story of Hippolytus-Virbius (68–70).

41. Fullmer also includes a chapter on resurrection in Jewish literature (ibid., 136–170). Here he has the tendency to lean heavily on texts that do not depict any actual resurrections (like Esther in Add. Esth 15.6-16 [Addition D], and Tobias in Tob. 8:9-18).

To sum up: in contemporary comparative scholarship on Jesus' resurrection, we find two opposing trends: (1) methodologically problematic comparisons of Jesus' resurrection with putative Mediterranean analogues, and (2) an implicit or explicit apologetic tendency to emphasize the uniqueness of Jesus' resurrection. Both trends tend to oppose the very idea that there is a Hellenistic notion of bodily immortalization at all.

Although I agree that it is important to note the distinctive features of Jesus' resurrection, the assumption that his resurrection is unique (and thus incomparable) halts inquiry and aborts knowledge. Jesus' resurrection can be compared with his competitors if one does it in a sophisticated way. The major comparative problem is that when scholars hunt for Mediterranean resurrection traditions, they typically look for a type of transformation that is fundamentally *un*like that of Christ—namely a return to *normal human life* (as in the case of Alcestis and Protesilaus). This trend only reinforces the tendency to contrast the immortalization of Jesus with the "mere resuscitations" in the "Greek" tradition.

The recent study by Endsjø helps to overturn the long tradition of solely negative comparisons.[43] Indeed, Endsjø may overcompensate in his zeal to redescribe Greco-Roman traditions of postmortem transformation as types of resurrection.[44] I prefer to view resurrection as a Christian sub-type of corporeal immortalization, a broader category that can involve the additional phenomena of ascent, rapture, and disappearance. What makes resurrection a distinctive subtype is that it involves a genuine death of the mortal body—either at the instant of immortalization or at some time before.

In what follows, I will discuss examples of corporeal immortalization in both the Gospels and in a variety of Greco-Roman sources. At the outset of my comparison, however, I must note a scholarly imbalance. For centuries

---

42. Fullmer states that "Christian resurrection is not simply a return to normal life, but a progression to an eternal life comparable to the existence of 'angels in heaven' ([Mark] 12.25)" (93). Unfortunately, he does not apply this insight to his comparisons. The study of Christopher Bryan (*The Resurrection of the Messiah* [Oxford: Oxford University Press, 2011]) does not focus on immortalized individuals raised from the dead. When he does speak of such individuals, they are conflated with heroes and not seen as deified individuals (24). In his discussion of the Greco-Roman evidence, Bryan only treats accounts of resuscitation: Eurydice, Alcestis, and Protesilaus (29–30)—and wrongly implies that Asclepius raised from the dead dies again (31). As an interpreter, he tries to situate himself between N. T. Wright on the one hand and Porter and Fullmer on the other, who propose a Greek tradition of bodily resurrection (31). He convincingly disputes Wright's unjustified claim that Alcestis "made no dent in the ruling assumption" that death was final (31–34).

43. Endsjø, *Greek Resurrection Beliefs*, esp. 54–64.

44. Ibid., 52–99. His tendency to conflate resurrection with other types of immortalization threatens in-depth comparison.

in the West, the resurrection of Jesus has enjoyed privileged status among other Mediterranean stories of corporeal immortalization. Every jot and tittle of the canonical accounts have been exegeted at length.[45] Given this excess of familiarity, I will not offer a full-scale exegesis of Christian tales of resurrection. Instead, I will present the highlights of the resurrection story in its canonical variants, along with that of the Gospel of Peter. My primarily aim, at least initially, is to describe both the Christian and non-Christian accounts of corporeal immortalization. Analysis will follow in the comparative section that follows.

Jesus and Corporeal Immortalization

I begin *in medias res* during the episode of Jesus' violent and humiliating death in the Gospel of Mark. On that day from noon to 3 o'clock darkness covers the earth (Mark 15:33). Jesus utters a death cry and immediately the temple veil is rent (vv. 37-38). A centurion testifies that Jesus was a son of God (v. 39). Female witnesses to the crucifixion are listed (vv. 40-41), some of whom also witness his burial (v. 47). About a day later, some women come to anoint the body at daybreak (16:1-2). They encounter a young man in shining clothes who announces the resurrection (ἠγέρθη), and foretells an appearance in Galilee (vv. 5-7). The women rush away, terrified, and say nothing to anyone (v. 8).

In Matthew's rendition, the crucified Jesus similarly dies with a loud cry (Matt. 27:50). Suddenly there is an earthquake, the temple veil is torn, and rocks split (27:51-53). A Roman centurion attests Jesus' divine sonship (v. 54). Friendly witnesses to Jesus' death are noted (vv. 55-56). Jesus' burial is then described, again with a list of witnesses (vv. 57-61). Distinctively, Jesus' enemies go out of their way to seal and secure his tomb (vv. 62-66). In Matthew 28, women visit the tomb (28:1). A second earthquake occurs (v. 2). An angel rolls away the stone, and announces the resurrection (vv. 5-6). Jesus then appears to the women, who worship him, grabbing his feet (vv. 8-10). Regrouping, the enemies of Christ conspire to report that the disciples stole the body (vv. 11-15). Suddenly we switch scenes to a mountain in Galilee (v. 16). Here—even when Jesus is manifest—some doubt, but most adore him (v. 17). Jesus then commissions his disciples to found his church with a designated entrance rite and regulations (vv. 18-20).

In Luke's Gospel, a solar eclipse and the rending of the temple veil occur before Jesus' death cry—now formulated as a quotation from the book of

---

45. In addition to the standard commentaries, see Jerome Neyrey, *The Resurrection Stories* (Wilmington, DE: Michael Glazier, 1988); Wright, *Resurrection of the Son*, 401–449, 616–82.

Psalms (Luke 23:44-46). A Roman soldier confesses Jesus' innocence as opposed to divine sonship (vv. 47-48). The narrator mentions the witnesses to the crucifixion (v. 49), and describes the burial (vv. 50-56). In chapter 24, the women find the tomb empty (24:1-3). Two angels appear and announce the resurrection (vv. 4-8). In turn, the women proclaim it to skeptical disciples (vv. 9-11), and Peter inspects the tomb (v. 12). Meanwhile, Jesus makes a clandestine appearance to two unnamed disciples (vv. 13-35). The moment they recognize him, Jesus eerily disappears (v. 31). Later he reappears to the disciples in a corporeal form, denying that he is a πνεῦμα (or "spirit," vv. 36-43). He then explains the scriptures (vv. 44-47), commissions his disciples (vv. 48-49), and ascends from the Mount of Olives (vv. 50-53). In Acts, we learn that the ascent actually occurred forty days after the resurrection, and that Jesus was conveyed by a cloud (Acts 1:3-9).

In John's Gospel, the death cry is heard as a sovereign declaration: "It is finished!" (John 19:30). The author emphasizes that Jesus' body remained intact (vv. 31-37). About a day after the burial, Mary Magdalene visits the tomb alone (20:1). She reports to the disciples only that the stone has been moved (v. 2). Peter and the beloved disciple rush to the tomb, finding no body and no angels (vv. 3-10). Jesus then appears to Mary (vv. 11-16) but strangely resists her embrace ("I have not yet ascended to my Father," v. 17). She then reports the resurrection to the disciples (v. 18). Subsequently, Jesus appears to his followers, after passing through locked doors (vv. 19-23). A week later, he makes a second appearance to Thomas, displaying his wounds (vv. 24-29). As an appendix, the author records a lengthy Galilean appearance (ch. 21).

Finally, in the Gospel of Peter we learn of the standard elements: the darkness at noon (*Gos. Pet.* 5:15), Jesus' death cry (5:19), and the rending of the temple veil (5:20).[46] The earthquake occurs here at Jesus' burial (6:21). The tomb is guarded by soldiers and Jewish leaders (8:28—9:34). In the darkness of Sunday morning, the soldiers hear a loud voice from heaven. From there, two shining men come and enter the tomb (9:34-37). Shortly thereafter they exit supporting a third figure—Jesus himself—whose head overtops the heavens (10:39-40). A voice booms from above: "Have you preached to those who sleep?" A cross, which happens to be following Jesus, reports: "Yes" (10:41-42). In their subsequent debriefing before Pilate, the soldiers confess that Jesus is a son of God (11:45). At dawn, Mary Magdalene and other women visit the tomb (12:50-54). They see within a young man in shining clothes who announces

---

46. The edition of *Gos. Pet.* used here is that edited by Thomas J. Kraus und Tobias Nicklas, *Das Petrusevangelium und die Petrusapokalypse: die griechischen Fragmente mit deutscher und englischer Übersetzung* (Berlin: Walter de Gruyter, 2004).

the resurrection (13:56). As in Mark, the women flee (13:57). Peter and his companions then return (apparently to Galilee) to resume fishing, and the text breaks off (14:58-60).

MEDITERRANEAN TRADITIONS OF CORPOREAL IMMORTALIZATION

To execute my comparison, I will discuss the corporeal transformations of three popular figures: Asclepius, Heracles, and Romulus. In the first century CE, the stories of these men-made-gods were more widely known than the tales of Jesus (whose early obscurity is notorious). To the modern reader, however, the accounts of their deaths and post-mortem transformations are not familiar, and so merit a thicker description. Unlike the Christian tales of Jesus' resurrection, the stories of Asclepius, Heracles and Romulus have no canonical version(s). In light of this situation, I synoptically present a variety of sources, including Christian ones (which already contain comparisons with Jesus). The synoptic lens is meant to give an idea of the main structural features of the stories, not to collapse all differences between them, or hide the biases of their tradents.[47]

ASCLEPIUS

Asclepius (the Latin Aesculapius), son of Apollo and famous doctor, was killed by Zeus's thunderbolt for resuscitating people from the dead. "Jupiter aimed a thunderbolt at him," relates Ovid, "who used the resources of a too potent art" (*Fasti* 6.759-60).[48] He was buried, some say, in Cynosura (Cic., *Nat. d.* 3.22.57), though others pointed to Epidaurus (Ps. Clem., *Hom* 6.21; *Rec.* 10.24). But Zeus raised Asclepius from the dead.[49] The second-century Christian apologist Theophilus of Antioch affirms that Asclepius "was raised" (ἐγηγέρθαι—a word

---

47. The synoptic viewpoint necessarily streamlines texts of diverse age and provenance. To present a full account of the tradition regarding these figures, such streamlining is unavoidable. My citations and notes should be used to locate the different sources and re-contextualize a detail in an individual author's work. The genre of the works I use are for the most part poetic and anthological. Such sources, admittedly, would have been known and read mostly by the literate few. One should not conclude, however, that the stories of Heracles, Romulus, and Asclepius were known only by the elite. Their tales are arguably pan-Mediterranean and had a vibrant life in oral tradition. I cite traditions passed on by archaic poets (Homer, Hesiod) because it is likely that these poets were in the first century CE still the most widely read and recited authors.

48. Further testimonies in Edelstein and Edelstein, *Asclepius*, 1.§§105-115; Wendy Cotter, *Miracles in Greco-Roman Antiquity: A Sourcebook for the Study of New Testament Miracles* (London: Routledge, 1999), 24–29.

49. "But if Asclepius the god had died, he had to come to life again, he had to become immortal, for he was ever-present in his temples . . . the god was resurrected by the intervention of the gods" (Edelstein and Edelstein, *Asclepius* 2.75-76).

used for the resurrection of Jesus in Matt. 16:21; Mark 14:28; Luke 24:6; John 21:14) from the dead (*Autol.* 1.13). According to Hyginus's *Fables*, Asclepius returned from the underworld (*ab inferis*) by the permission of the Fates (*Fab.* 251.2).[50] He was one of those made immortal from mortal human beings (*ex mortalibus immortales*) (*Fab.* 224.5). Out of mercy (κατ' ἔλεον), says Lucian, Zeus raised Asclepius not just to a normal human life, but made him participate in immortality (ἀθανασίας μεταλαμβάνω) (*Dial. Mort.* 13.1).[51] Justin Martyr apparently understands Asclepius's resurrection to involve a simultaneous ascent to heaven (ἀνεληλυθέναι εἰς οὐρανόν) (*1 Apol.* 21.2).[52] In Pseudo-Eratosthenes, Zeus leads Asclepius up to the stars (εἰς τὰ ἄστρα ἀναγαγεῖν) and makes him a constellation (the serpent-bearer) (1.6; cf. Dan. 12:3).[53]

That Asclepius's resurrection/ascension was also a deification was widely understood. Ovid addresses Apollo: "Phoebus, you complained [about Asclepius's death]. But Aesculapius is a god (*deus est*); be reconciled to your parent [Zeus]" (*Fasti* 6.761-62). Both Minucius Felix (*Oct.* 23.7) and Cyprian (*Quod idola dii non sint* 2) describe Asclepius as rising to godhood (*in deum surgat*).[54]

After his death, Asclepius eventually received worship due to a god. Indeed, during the infancy of Christianity, Asclepius's cult was one of the most popular in the Greco-Roman world.[55] In his cult centers, he was said to appear in full bodily presence to his votaries (usually in dream visions). According to Celsus, for instance, "a great multitude of people, Greeks and barbarians alike, confess that they have often seen and still see not a mere apparition (οὐ φάσμα)

50. The attribution of the *Fables* to Gaius Iulius Hyginus (ca. 64 BCE – 17 CE), freedman of Augustus and librarian of the Palatine library, is in serious doubt. The work itself appears to be a school exercise, perhaps a second-century CE abbreviation of a longer, more sophisticated work by Hyginus (cf. *OCD*[4] 714, *s.v.* "Hyginus[3]"). In accord with scholarly practice, however, I will continue to refer to this author as "Hyginus."

51. Wright rightly notes, "When a hero such as . . . Asclepius died and was buried, and was then believed to have been translated to heaven, this is not the resurrection which Homer, Aeschylus and others denied" (*Resurrection of the Son*, 77). The resurrection of Asclepius, in other words, includes an immortalization and a transformed body, not a return to normal human life.

52. Endsjø also compares Semele who was apparently deified immediately after being struck by Zeus's lightning (Pind., *Ol.* 2.25). Others maintained that Dionysus brought up Semele from Hades (Paus., *Descr.* 2.31-32; 2.37.5) (*Greek Resurrection*, 58).

53. Text in Edelstein and Edelstein, *Asclepius* 1.§121, cf. §122.

54. Further testimonies in ibid. 1.§232-56.

55. "His worship spread everywhere; it became one of the most renowned among the many ancient cults; it outlasted most of them; it was the hated enemy and dreaded competitor of Christianity" (ibid., 2.108). For the cult, images, and sanctuaries of Asclepius, see ibid., 1.§§482-861.

but Asclepius himself, healing, doing good and predicting the future" (*Cels.* 3.24; cf. Luke 24:39). Maximus of Tyre claims that he saw Asclepius (as well as the Dioscuri and Heracles) and insists that it was not in a dream (*Or.* 9.7; cf. Luke 24:39).[56]

HERACLES

According to Yarbro Collins, Heracles provides "a striking analogy" to the suffering and exaltation of Jesus in Phil. 2:8-9: "a human being suffers for the good of humankind and is, therefore, given a divine nature and status."[57] According to Homer, Heracles's sufferings led to a genuine death. "Not even the mighty Heracles escaped death," says Achilles in the *Iliad*, "even though he was most dear to Zeus. . . . But fate overcame him, and the dread wrath of Hera" (18.117-119).[58] A scholiast to this passage rightly notes that "saying that he [Heracles] did not escape death does not indicate ignorance of his deification."[59] In fact, a fragment of Hesiod's *Catalogue of Women* says that Heracles "died (θάνε) and then went to the grievous house of Hades, but now he is a god (νῦν δ' ἤδη θεός ἐστι), released from all evils, and lives there among those who possess the palaces of Olympus, immortal and ageless (ἀθάνατος καὶ ἄγηρος)

56. In this way, Antiochus of Aegae also saw Asclepius (αὐτῷ ἐγρηγορότι ["while he was awake"], Philostr., *Vit. Soph.* 2.568), as well as Proclus—although he was "between . . . sleeping and waking" (μεταξὺ . . . ὕπνου καὶ ἐγρηγόρσεως; Marinus, *Vit. Procl.* 30.744-45. Cf. also Ox. Papyrus XI, 1381 col. 5.108 (οὔτ' ὄναρ οὔθ' ὕπνος) (in Edelstein and Edelstein, *Asclepius* 1.§331). The normal practice was to see Asclepius in a dream while incubating in his temple. See the discussion in Robin Lane Fox, *Pagans and Christians* (New York: Knopf, 1987), 151–53; 161–62. For the topic of seeing the gods, see Lane Fox, *Pagans and Christians*, ch. 4.

57. Yarbro Collins, "Worship of Jesus and the Imperial Cult," 247. Cf. Aune: "Jesus' exaltation is also described in Heb 2:9 as a reward for suffering: Jesus was 'crowned [ἐστεφανωμένον] with glory and honor because of the suffering of death [διὰ τὸ πάθημα τοῦ θανάτου].' The same sentiment is reflected in Heb 12:2, where Jesus' present status is the result of his endurance of suffering and death; he is described as 'the pioneer and perfecter of our faith, who for the joy that was set before him endured the cross, despising the shame and is seated at the right hand of the throne of God'" ("Heracles and Christ: Heracles Imagery in the Christology of Early Christianity," in *Greeks, Romans, and Christians: Essays in Honor of Abraham J. Malherbe*, ed. David L. Balch, Everett Ferguson, and Wayne Meeks [Minneapolis: Fortress Press, 1990], 3–19 [18–19]). For the death and apotheosis of Heracles, see H. A. Shapiro, "Hêrôs Theos: The Death and Apotheosis of Heracles," *CW* 77 (1983): 7–18; Philip Holt, "Herakles' Apotheosis in Lost Greek Literature and Art," *L'Antiquité classique* 61 (1992): 38–59; Gantz, *Early Greek Myth*, 460–63; Marek Winiarczyk, "La mort et l'apothéose d'Héraclès," *Wiener Studien* 113 (2000): 13–29.

58. According to common tradition (classically dramatized in Sophocles's *Women of Trachis*), Heracles was inadvertently poisoned through a tunic sent to him by his wife and so burnt himself on a pyre on Mount Oeta. On the death of Heracles, see Franz Stoessl, *Der Tod des Herakles* (Zürich: Rhein,1945).

59. W. Dindorf, *Scholia Graeca in Homeri Iliadem* (Oxford: Clarendon, 1875), 2.153.

(frag. 25.25-28, Merkelbach and West). Death, as we see, does not exclude deification.

The mode of Heracles's immortalization is explained in different ways. According to most accounts, Heracles somehow separates himself from his mortal nature (not necessarily identical with his body), allowing his divine nature (not necessarily identical with his soul) to ascend or be carted up to heaven.[60] According to Theocritus, for instance, "the Thracian pyre will hold all the mortal nature" (θνήτα πάντα) of Heracles, while Heracles himself joins the gods (*Idyll*. 24.83-84). Cyprian, likewise, affirms that Hercules divested himself of his human aspect (*hominem exuat*) before his ascent to heaven (*Quod idola dii non sint* 2).

But does the ascending Heracles go up (to adopt a phrase of Paul) "in the body or out of the body"? The question, it must be admitted, is not posed in Greco-Roman tradition. Nevertheless, important textual and material evidence seem to assume that it was indeed "in the body." A series of Attic and Apulian vases appearing from about 420 BCE show Heracles being bodily carried away to Olympus from his pyre (cf. Paus., *Descr.* 3.18.11; 3.19.3).[61] This tradition is reminiscent of Elijah being taken up bodily in a chariot of fire (2 Kgs. 2:11), and also suggests a transformed body of Heracles that ascends to heaven.[62] That Heracles was actually bodily removed from his pyre is also suggested by Diodorus of Sicily, who has Heracles's companions search for the bones of the hero after his cremation—to no avail (*Bibl. hist.* 4.38.5). Heracles's body is gone, because it has ascended to the divine realm, leaving no remainder (cf. Jesus' empty tomb). Bodily transformation and deification also appears in

60. Max Mühl calls Heracles's divine nature not his soul, but his "a second self" (*eines zweiten Ich*) ("Des Herakles Himmelfahrt," *Rheinisches Museum* 101 [1958]: 106–34 [107]).

61. For the images, see *LIMC* V.2 Nrs. 2916-2938; Frank Brommer, *Herakles II: Die unkanonischen Taten des Helden* (Darmstadt: Wissenschaftliche Buchgesellschaft, 1984), 94–95. The chariot is usually driven by Nike or Athena, but at least once by Hermes. For further commentary see *LIMC* V.1.131-32. See also the Attic pelike (Munich 2360, attributed to the Cadmus painter) showing Heracles bodily carried away on a chariot in Raimund Wünsche, *Herakles Herkules* (Munich: Staatliche Antikensammlungen, 2003), 282 (cf. 283–85), as well as the Attic bell-krater depicting a similar scene (with an empty suit of armor on the pyre) in Rainer Vollkommer, *Herakles in the Art of Classical Greece* (London: Oxford Committee for Archaeology, 1988), 35, fig. 45 (also 70, fig. 90). Vollkommer presents a more exhaustive list of works portraying Heracles's apotheosis on 32–37, with brief commentary on 36–37.

62. For a comparison of Heracles's and Elijah's ascent, see Mühl, "Des Herakles Himmelfahrt," 110–115. Yarbro Collins interprets Mark's resurrection account as a transformation of Jesus' earthly body and translation to heaven similar to Heracles (*Beginning of the Gospel: Probings of Mark in Context* [Minneapolis: Fortress Press, 1992], 146).

Callimachus, who says that the very "limbs" (γυῖα) of Heracles were deified (θεωθείς), and (humorously) that Heracles's deified stomach lost nothing of its appetite (*Dian.* 159-61; cf. Aristoph., *Av.* 1601-1604).[63]

For the philosophically minded Cicero, to be sure, Heracles's mortal human body was not taken up to heaven (*Rep.* 3.40 quoted by Augustine, *Civ.* 22.4). "Nature would not allow that which comes from the earth but to remain on earth." His comment, however, does not disallow a *transformation* of Heracles's body to become fit for heaven. As Paul knew, the earthly body could become "pneumatic," fit for a celestial existence (1 Cor. 15:45-49; cf. Orig., *Cels.* 3.41). When Heracles ascended on a chariot to Olympus, we are led to imagine the transformation of his body. This transformation is likely signified by his being consumed by fire. In ancient myth, being burnt in fire can signify deifying transformation (cf. *Hom. Hymn Dem.* 2.231-69; Apollonius, *Argon.*, 4.869-72; Ps.-Apollodorus, *Bibl.* 3.13.6; Plut., *Is. Os.* 16 [*Mor.* 357c]).

Later authors in fact deny that *only* Heracles's soul ascends. In Ovid's *Metamorphoses*, Jupiter boasts that it is only Hercules's *materna pars* (motherly part) that can be consumed; what he has from his father Jupiter (*a me quod traxit*) is eternal (*aeternum est*), not subject to death (*expers atque immune necis*) (*Met.* 9.251-55; cf. 264-65). Ovid never says that what Hercules has from Jupiter is his *soul* as opposed to his *body*. In fact, Ovid's language discourages a Platonic reading of Hercules's transformation (i.e., body separated from deified soul). Ovid writes that Hercules's deification involves an increase in *gravitas* (*Met.* 15.270), which has both a figurative ("dignity," "majesty"), and a literal meaning ("weight"). A literal meaning of the word is suggested by what Ovid says three lines after the above-cited passage.[64] When the deified Heracles enters the skies, "Atlas [who holds the heavens] felt his [Heracles's] weight (*pondus*)" (*Met.* 15.273). *Pondus* (although spoken tongue-in-cheek) refers to Hercules's well-known physical girth. When Hercules enters heaven, he was no weightless soul, but a transformed (characteristically heavy) body. Even when Ovid uses the image of the snake sloughing off its skin to describe the transformation of Hercules, he does not speak of the exit of Hercules's *soul*, but of the invigoration of his "better part" (*pars maior*), which becomes "larger and worthy of worship"

---

63. Cf. Mühl, "Des Herakles Himmelfahrt,"109–110. On the passage in Callimachus, see also Bernd Effe, "Der Held als Gott: Die Apotheose des Herakles in der alexandrinischen Dichtung," in *Gottmenschen: Konzepte existentieller Grenzüberschreitung im Altertum*, ed. Gerhard Binder et al. (Trier: Wissenschaftlicher, 2003), 34–36.

64. Karl Galinsky, *Ovid's Metamorphoses: An Introduction to the Basic Aspects* (Oxford: Blackwell, 1975), 257.

(9.266-70).[65] Ovid goes on to relate that Jupiter—similar to depictions on pottery—swooped down in a four-horse chariot to carry up Hercules "to the radiant stars" (*Met.* 9.271-72). This very physical image suggests that Hercules's *body* was transformed and taken up to heaven.[66]

Lucian's report of Heracles's immortalization is important to note because it is often misinterpreted. This second-century satirist says *not* that Heracles left his body behind on the pyre, but "whatever was human" (ὁπόσον ἀνθρώπειον). Likewise, it was not his soul that rose to heaven, but his divine part (τὸ θεῖον) (*Herm.* 7). To view Heracles's ascent as merely an ascent of the soul is thus misleading.[67] In his *Dialogue of the Gods*, Lucian has Asclepius say to Heracles: "Have you nothing to say of how I healed your burns, when you came up half-scorched the other day [i.e., after Heracles was burnt on the pyre]? Between the tunic and the fire after it, your body (τὸ σῶμα) was in a fine mess!" (15 §237 [Harmon, LCL]). The remark seemingly taunts popular belief about Heracles's postmortem *corporeal* ascent, while simultaneously revealing the content and pervasiveness of this belief: Heracles ascended to heaven *in his own burnt body* that had to be healed by a divine doctor.

In a famous story from the life of Heracles, the hero wrestled with Death and brought Alcestis back from the grave (Eur., *Alc.* 844-54).[68] On his funeral pyre, Heracles himself defeated death and became a god. In his ascent to heaven, says Ovid, he became "larger," even "venerable in august solemnity" (*Met.* 9.269-270). At this defining moment he "obtained immortality" (τυχὼν ἀθανασίας) (Ps.-Apoll., *Bibl.* 2.7.7) and so became divine (Diod., *Bibl. hist.* 4.38.5-4.39.4). On Olympus he married Hebe, the goddess of vibrant youth, and had children from her. Heracles's ability to marry and reproduce indicates that in his celestial form, he remains in some sense corporeal.[69]

---

65. For the apotheosis of Heracles in Ovid, see D. C. Feeney, *The Gods in Epic: Poets and Critics of the Classical Tradition* (Oxford: Clarendon, 1991), 205–07.

66. Like Ovid, Ps.-Seneca calls Hercules's divine self the *paterna pars*—the aspect of Hercules that he has from his father Zeus (*Herc. Oet.* 1968). Here again, although this Stoicizing author might have easily called the *paterna pars* the soul (*anima*), the term is avoided. In a similar fashion, Pliny the Elder has only Hercules's mortality burned away (*exusta mortalitate*) and not his body (*corpus*) (*Nat.* 35.139).

67. Wright, for instance, wrongly defines apotheosis as "the taking of the soul to the land of the immortal gods" (*Resurrection of the Son*, 57). Deification through ascent, one must be clear, is not necessarily Platonic.

68. On Heracles and the defeat of Death and Old Age, see Emma Stafford, *Herakles* (London: Routledge, 2012), 120.

69. I stress this point in opposition to Wright who claims that inferring a bodily Heracles from his heavenly marriage and progeny is "a category mistake." Wright's "categories," however, are the old

In the first-century play *Hercules Oetaeus*, Hercules appears to his weeping mother Alcmene after his transformation.[70] He gives her courage: "Now I have reached the realms of the starry sky and have finally been granted my place in heaven, why do you force me by your mourning to feel fate? Refrain! My virtue has made a path for me now to the stars (*astra*) and the very gods (*ipsos . . . superos*)" (1940-43). The deified Hercules then prophesies his mother's triumph over their sworn enemy Eurystheus (1972-74). Though she begs him to stay, Hercules ascends to heaven (*subire caelestem plagam*) (1975). Alcmene responds to his appearance with a mixture of wonder and confusion. Doubts assail her. "Am I deceived, or do my eyes believe that I saw my son? My wretched mind is incredulous" (1978-79). But doubt is replaced with worship: "You are a divine being (*numen*), and the heavens hold you forever. I believe in your triumphs [over death]" (1980-81). She then goes off to announce the good news: "I shall make for the kingdom of Thebes, and proclaim this new god that joins their temples" (*novumque templis aditum numen canam*) (1981-82 [Fitch, LCL]).

The themes of a resurrected individual appearing to a mourning woman to offer hope and encouragement is reminiscent of Jesus' encounter with Mary Magdalene (John 20:11-15).[71] After finally recognizing Jesus, Mary worships and proclaims him (vv. 15-18). Similarly, Alcmene declares Hercules a god and proclaims his new status in Thebes. Immediately afterwards, the chorus of Greeks worships Hercules, praying to him to "be with us!" as the "great conqueror of beasts and bringer of peace to the world" (1989-90).

The worship that Hercules receives in *Hercules Oetaeus* is a logical and proper response in Mediterranean culture. In the first century CE, Heracles/Hercules was worshiped by Greeks and hellenized peoples all across the Mediterranean.[72] According to Dionysius of Halicarnassus, "one could scarcely find any place in Italy in which the god [Hercules] was not honored" (*Rom.*

apologetic categories of pagan mythology versus Christian history. The deified Heracles, according to Wright, has "entered the realm of mythology" and thus apparently his immortal body cannot be real. Wright apparently expects his readers to affirm Jesus' immortalized body standing up in heaven (Acts 7:56; cf. 1:9-10) as gospel truth, while at the same time discounting Heracles's immortal body in heaven as "mythology." His observation that the heavenly Heracles cannot have a body "in any ordinary sense" is precisely the point: he has—like Jesus—an immortalized, transformed body (*Resurrection of the Son*, 57, n. 144).

70. Although attributed to Seneca, the authorship of this tragedy is disputed.

71. See further Florence Dupont "Apothéose et héroïzation dans Hercule sur l'Oeta de Sénèque," in *Entre hommes et dieux. Le convive, le héros, le prophète*, ed. Annie-France Laurens (Paris: Les Belles Lettres, 1989), 99–106.

72. Stafford, *Herakles*, 175–97. For maps of places with sanctuaries or altars of Heracles, see Maps 4–5 in Vollkommer, *Herakles in Art*, 103–05.

Ant. 1.40.5). In a report of Diodorus of Sicily, after his ascent on the pyre, Heracles was first sacrificed to as a hero, and then as a god (*Bibl. hist.* 4.39.1). In the Homeric *Hymn to Heracles*, the new god is prayed to as one who can bestow prosperity (ὄλβος) and virtue (ἀρετή). As one who suffered many evils himself, worshippers of Heracles often appealed to him as the "averter of evil" (ἀλεξίκακος).[73]

ROMULUS-QUIRINUS

The deification of Romulus, first king of Rome, is widely recounted in ancient literature. Livy gives the basic account: when Romulus was reviewing his troops on the Campus Martius, a storm suddenly arose with great peals of thunder and lightning. A sudden eclipse of the sun, together with a thick cloud hid the king from the sight of his soldiers.[74] When the storm passed, the king was no longer sitting on his tribunal. The common people (well-disposed to Romulus) came to believe that he had ascended to heaven. There arose a persistent rumor, however, that the senators had seized him and torn apart his body.[75] In Matthew, similarly, although Jesus' disciples preached his resurrection, there arose the insistent report that the disciples had stolen the body (28:11-15). Here, it is the authorities who promote the rumor. In Livy, by contrast, the senators publish abroad that Romulus had been raptured to heaven (*raptum*; ἀνηρπάσθαι) in order to exculpate themselves (Livy, *Hist.* 1.16; Dion. Hal., *Ant. Rom.* 2.56.2).[76]

---

73. Karl Galinsky, *The Herakles Theme: The Adaptations of the Hero in Literature from Homer to the Twentieth Century* (Totowa, NJ: Rowman and Littlefield, 1972), 19. Cf. Pindar, *Nem.* 7.94-97.

74. The eclipse is also reported by Dion. Hal., *Rom. Ant.* 2.56.6; Cic., *Rep.* 2.17; Ovid, *Fasti* 2.493; Plut., *Rom.* 27.6.

75. Appian and Dionysius of Halicarnassus remark that Romulus had become tyrannical and that the senators had just cause (App., *Bell. Civ.* 2.114; Dion. Hal., *Ant. Rom.* 2.56.3).

76. Gerhard Lohfink's attempt to depict rapture (*Entrückung*) as totally different (*ein völlig anderer Typ*) from heavenly ascent and as coming from an "entirely different worldview (*einem ganz verschiedenen Weltbild*)" is untenable (*Die Himmelfahrt Jesu: Untersuchungen zu den Himmelfahrts-und Erhöhungstexten bei Lukas* [Munich: Kösel, 1971], 37, 40). Rapture is a subtype of ascent and never rigorously distinguished from ascent as a separate "type" or "genre" in the ancient sources. I therefore disagree with A. W. Zwiep who states that "on the level of content" a distinction between non-death rapture and postmortem assumption can be "neatly drawn" ("Assumptus est in caelum: Rapture and Heavenly Exaltation in Early Judaism and Luke-Acts," in *Auferstehung-Resurrection: The Fourth Durham-Tübingen Research Symposium : Resurrection, Transfiguration and Exaltation in Old Testament, Ancient Judaism and Early Christianity*, eds. Friedrich Avemarie und Hermann Lichtenberger, WUNT 135 [Tübingen: Mohr Siebeck, 2001], 323–50 [332]).

But if Romulus was taken up, did he actually die? Accounts differ, but Arnobius's (Christian) retelling of Romulus's ascent emphasizes the fact that Romulus did indeed meet a violent death before his deification. Thus he is able to draw an explicit parallel with Jesus (*Contra Gentes* 6.1.41).[77] Other ancient authors show no aversion to the idea that Romulus could be both killed and deified. Dionysus of Halicarnassus, representing a rationalizing form of Greek historiography, thinks it plausible that Romulus was murdered (*Rom. Ant.* 2.56.3). Nevertheless, after Romulus's postmortem appearance, Dionysius implies that he was rightly honored as someone who became "greater than human nature" (κρείττονα γενόμενον ἤ κατὰ τὴν θνητὴν φύσιν) (2.63.3). Again, death does not disallow deification.

Whatever the case may be, Romulus departed from this mortal life and was transformed into an immortal, transcendent being. His metamorphosis was simultaneously an ascent to heaven (i.e., Romulus's body spent no time in a tomb).[78] Was this an ascension of Romulus's body or merely of his soul? Again, the story presents several conflicting variants.[79] Ancient authors agree, however, that Romulus's body did disappear. The mortal remains, for those who believed in his ascent, were taken up and transformed for celestial life. On this point, Tertullian explicitly compares Romulus and Jesus: both were "encompassed with a cloud and taken up to heaven" (*Apol.* 21.23; cf. Acts 1:9-11). For Tertullian's comparison to work, Romulus must have been taken up bodily, like Jesus.

During his lifetime, Romulus was viewed simply as a good king. It was only after his death—as in the case of Jesus—that his votaries realized his divinity. Livy relates the subsequent reaction: "Then at first a few, then all, joyfully declared Romulus, the king and father of the city of Rome, to be a god, the son of God. They asked him with prayers for peace; so that he would always be pleased to wish favor for his children" (*Hist.* 1.16). The declaration of divine sonship after death is reminiscent of the centurion's confession in Mark (13:39, par.), as well as the early Christian tradition that Jesus "was declared to be son of God with power . . . by resurrection from the dead" (Rom. 1:4).

---

77. In *Cam.* 32.7, by contrast, Plutarch merely says that Romulus disappeared (ἠφανίσθη), with no explicit death notice.

78. In the earliest account of Jesus' resurrection, exaltation/ascension to heaven also seems to follow immediately after death (Phil. 2:8-9; cf. Luke 23:43). Note the comments of Zwiep below.

79. Augustine notes that for Cicero, the bodies of Heracles and Romulus cannot be earthly anymore because they exist in a heavenly environment (*Civ.* 22.4). This remark should not be taken to imply that Cicero denied the corporeal nature of the deified Heracles and Romulus. In accord with Stoic thought, they would be equipped with different, ethereal bodies that would allow them to dwell in heaven.

For Cicero, Romulus's sudden disappearance (whether torn apart or translated or both) meant that he had been added to the number of the gods (*Rep.* 2.17). It was appropriate, given these circumstances, to worship and pray to Romulus as a god. In a melodramatic line of the poet Ennius, the people cry out: "O Romulus, divine Romulus, what a guardian of your country the Gods created in you! You led us forth within the shores of light, O father, O begetter, O blood born of the Gods!" (*Ann.* 111-114 [Skutsch] in Lactantius, *Inst.* 1.15.31).[80] This kind of exalted and spontaneous language is comparable to early Christian hymns sung in honor of Jesus, who was considered to be divine after his exaltation (e.g., Phil. 2:6-11; cf. Pliny Min., *Ep.* 10.96.7).

It is important that both Romulus and Jesus are said to have witnesses for their ascension. The author of *Acts* has all eleven disciples witness Jesus lifted into the air (1:9). The witness to Romulus's ascension is Proculus Julius, who was—according to Plutarch—"a trusted and intimate friend of Romulus himself" (*Rom.* 28.1).[81]

The reports of Romulus's postmortem manifestation do not all agree in detail, but neither do the reports of Jesus' postmortem appearances. The gist, at any rate, is clear. "Proculus," writes Plutarch, "took an oath that he had seen Romulus ascending to heaven in full armor" (*Num.* 11.3; cf. Dion. Hal., *Rom. Ant.* 2.63.2-2.64.1; Justin, *1 Apol.* 21). In Plutarch's expanded account, we learn that Proculus was traveling on the road when he saw "Romulus coming to meet him, beautiful (καλός) and large (μέγας) to the eye as never before, and arrayed in flashing and fiery armor (ὅπλοις . . . λαμπροῖς καὶ φλέγουσι)." Proculus was terrified, but still asked to know why Romulus had abandoned the Roman people (leaving the patricians prey to accusations). Romulus replied, "It was the pleasure of the Gods, Proculus, from whom I came, that I should be with humankind only a short time, and that after founding a city destined to be the greatest on earth for empire and glory, I should dwell again in heaven." "These things," Plutarch reports (with a somewhat jaundiced eye), "seemed to the Romans worthy of belief, from the character of the man who related them, and from the oath which he had taken. Moreover, something divine (δαιμόνιόν τι) also, akin to inspiration (ὅμοιον ἐνθουσιασμῷ), laid hold upon their emotions" (*Rom.* 28.2-3 [Perrin, LCL, adapted]).

In their *Hellenistic Commentary to the New Testament*, Eugene Boring, Carsten Colpe, and Klaus Berger note the following points in comparing this

---

80. For the deification of Romulus in Ennius, see Feeney, *Gods in Epic*, 122–23, 125–26.

81. For Cicero, Proculus is an "untutored peasant" in (*Rep.* 2.20), and Dionysius of Halicarnassus calls him a noble farmer with a blameless life (*Ant. Rom.* 2.63.3).

story with the New Testament Gospels. First, the "credibility of the witnesses is enhanced by pointing out that they had been friends with the exalted one during his earthly life." Second, the ἐνθουσιασμός that overtook the Romans is not unlike the possession of the Holy Spirit experienced by the disciples (Acts 1–2). Third, the followers of the hero learn that he is preexistent. Romulus came from the gods, is incarnated for a specific mission, and returns to heaven (cf. John 3:13; 20:17).[82] I add that the immortalized Romulus, like the resurrected Christ, appears in a transcendent form. Romulus is "beautiful," "massive," appearing in bright and shiny raiment. The dazzling garb is most reminiscent of the accounts of Jesus' transfiguration (Mark 9:3, par.). Ovid makes clear that Romulus's exalted state is a divine one: "a beautiful look came upon him, more worthy of the couches of the gods on high (*pulvinaribus altis / dignior*)" (*Met.* 14.827-28).[83]

Wendy Cotter helps deepen the comparison of Romulus and Jesus in her study "Greco-Roman Apotheosis Traditions and the Resurrection Appearances in Matthew."[84] Before his final ascent to be with the gods, she points out, Plutarch depicts Romulus as returning in order to transmit a divine commission to the entire Roman community as well as promising to be a constant presence for the Roman people. The tradition of commission is even more pronounced in Livy, where Proculus swears to the senators:

> Quirites [the designation for the Roman people], the father of this city, Romulus, descended suddenly from the sky at dawn this morning and appeared to me. Covered with confusion, I stood reverently before him, praying that it might be allowed to me to look upon his face without sin. "Go," said he, "and declare to the Romans the will of heaven that my Rome shall be the capital of the world; so let them cherish the art of war, and let them know and teach their children that no human strength can resist Roman arms." So saying, he [Proculus] concluded, "Romulus departed on high." (Livy, *Hist.* 1.16.2-8)

82. Eugene Boring, Carsten Colpe, and Klaus Berger, eds., *Hellenistic Commentary to the New Testament* (Nashville: Abingdon, 1995), 164.

83. Cf. Rev. 1:12-16. In the *Fasti* the transformed Romulus is said to be "beautiful and greater than human" (*pulcher et humano maior*) (2.503). For the apotheosis of Romulus in Ovid, see Feeney, *Gods in Epic*, 208.

84. Cotter, "Greco-Roman Apotheosis Traditions and the Resurrection Appearances in Matthew," in *The Gospel of Matthew in Current Study*, ed. David Aune (Grand Rapids, MI: Eerdmans, 2001), 127–53 [134].

Cotter points out that these elements are comparable to the appearance of Jesus especially in Matthew 28. The last paragraph in Matthew's Gospel reads,

> Now the eleven disciples went to Galilee, to the mountain to which Jesus ordered them. When they saw him, they worshiped him; but some doubted. And Jesus came and said to them, "All authority in heaven and on earth has been given to me. As you go, therefore, make disciples of all nations, baptizing them in the name of the Father and of the son and of the holy spirit, teaching them to maintain everything that I commanded you. And behold, I am with you for all the days, until the consummation of the age. (28:16-20)

"It is fair to say," Cotter remarks, that this scene "would be understood by a Greco-Roman audience, Jew or Gentile, as an *apotheosis* of Jesus." The resurrected Jesus appears (1) on a mountain, (2) in an apparently immortalized body, (3) witnessed and worshiped by his own disciples, (4) authorized with cosmic power, and (5) mandating the spread of his teachings to the whole world until the end of time. "His final message," Cotter adds, "is a reminder of his constant presence until the end time (v. 20b-d)."[85] Only a divine being could make such a claim.

Romulus, to be sure, does not claim to possess universal power. Instead, that power is granted to Romulus's children and heirs (the Romans). They will receive unbounded authority. Rome will, according to Livy, be the "capital of the world" (*caput orbis terrarum*) (*Hist.* 16.7). In Plutarch, the Romans will "reach the utmost heights of human power" (ἐπὶ πλεῖστον ἀνθρωπίνης . . . δυνάμεως) (*Rom.* 28.2). The phrase is reminiscent of the line in Virgil where Jupiter promises to give the Romans *imperium sine fine* ("empire without end"). The context, where Jove divines the fates, is worth quoting: "Then Romulus, proud in the tawny hide of the she-wolf, his nurse, shall take up the line, and found the walls of Mars and call the people Romans after his own name. For these I [Jupiter] set no bounds in space or time; but have given empire without end" (*Aen.* 1.275-279 [Fairclough, LCL]). In this case, the power associated with divinity is granted to all those who participate in Romulus's mission and name.[86]

---

85. Ibid., 149.

86. The bestowal of power on Christ's Christian heirs is not utterly foreign to the New Testament. In Acts, immediately before Jesus ascends, he promises his disciples, "But you will receive power (δύναμιν)," and specifically power to preach the gospel "even to the ends of the earth (ἕως ἐσχάτου τῆς γῆς)" (Acts 1:8; cf. 1 Cor. 3:21-23; Rom. 8:32).

Only after his death and resurrection does Romulus become the recipient of worship. In both Plutarch's *Life of Romulus* and Ovid's *Fasti*, Romulus announces his deity, and commands that he be honored under the new cult title "Quirinus" (*Rom.* 28; *Fasti* 2.500-509). Dionysius of Halicarnassus has the next king, Numa Pompilius, honor Romulus-Quirinus with the erection of a temple and by sacrifices throughout the year (ἱεροῦ κατασκευῇ καὶ θυσίαις διετησίοις) (*Ant. Rom.* 2.63.3). Cicero adds that the actual shrine was built on the Quirinal hill, a prominent site in Rome (*Rep.* 2.20; cf. Lact., *Inst.* 1.15.32-33). Ovid mentions that other *sacra paterna* (ancestral rites) were regularly observed as well (*Fasti* 2.511). Here again we find worship of an immortalized one who appeared back on earth to manifest his transcendent state.

RESULTS: RESURRECTION AND DEIFICATION

In this section, I turn to directly compare and contrast these Greco-Roman traditions with the stories of Jesus' corporeal immortalization. Here and there, I have already suggested several fruitful avenues of comparison. One could compare corporeal post-mortem appearances, (female) witnesses to the resurrection, empty tomb traditions (i.e., disappearance of the mortal body), the theme of violent death, portents immediately before death (e.g., eclipse, earthquake), the commission of the deified hero, or some combination (sequential or otherwise) of these motifs. For the purposes of this study, however, I will focus solely on the themes of corporeal immortalization, the response of worship, and ascension. These are the main themes, it seems to me, that carry implications for Jesus' deification in the Gospels.

CORPOREAL IMMORTALIZATION

In one of his essays, Dieter Zeller remarks that "the Greek or Roman listener must understand a definitive deliverance from death as a deification (*Gottwerden*)."[87] Those immortalized are those deified, since in Mediterranean culture, "immortality means nothing other than divinity."[88] All the stories treated above are arguably instances of corporeal immortalization: the bodies of individuals raised to immortal life. Insofar as the life received is immortal life, it is also a divine life.

---

87. Dieter Zeller, "Hellenistische Vorgaben für den Glauben an die Auferstehung Jesu?" in *Von Jesus zum Christus: Christologische Studien: Festgabe für Paul Hoffmann*, eds. Rudolf Hoppe and Ulrich Busse (Berlin: Walter de Gruyter, 1998), 71–92 (82).

88. Lohfink, *Himmelfahrt Jesu*, 46.

In the context of ancient Mediterranean culture, the phenomenon of corporeal immortalization as deification is important for understanding the meaning of Jesus' resurrection. As Origen says, if one thinks of Jesus as a god, one sees a human being; if one thinks of him as human, one beholds him "returning from the dead with spoils after vanquishing the kingdom of death" (*Princ.* 2.6.2). Christian accounts of Jesus' resurrection differ, but all seem to agree that his corpse was immortalized and transformed. Other texts of the New Testament inform us that Christ remains forever (Heb. 7:24). Jesus himself testifies in a vision to the prophet John: "I was dead, and see, I am alive forever and ever (ἰδοὺ ζῶν εἰμι εἰς τοὺς αἰῶνας τῶν αἰώνων)" (Rev. 1:18).

As an immortal being, it seems, the resurrected Jesus could no longer be viewed as *merely* human. His transformation is indicated by his ability to disappear (Luke 24:31), appear in a location miles away (24:36), and walk through walls (John 20:19). The fact that the immortalized Jesus can eat fish and display his wounds in Luke (24:40-43) and John (20:20, 27) indicates a continuity of identity between the pre- and post-resurrected Jesus, not that the resurrected Jesus is a "normal" human being raised to ordinary human life.[89] Jesus is no Lazarus raised but doomed to die twice (John 11:1-44).[90] He emerges from the tomb as an immortal, powerful being—in biblical language, a "son of God" (Rom. 1:4).

In Mediterranean mythology, the signs of deification are inscribed on the transformed, immortalized body. Romulus meets Proculus in a beautiful (καλός) and large (μέγας) form, arrayed in bright and fiery armor (ὅπλοις . . . λαμπροῖς καὶ φλέγουσι). Ovid describes the deified Romulus as "lovely and greater than human" (*pulcher et humano maior*) (*Fasti* 2.503).[91] In "The Praise of Asclepius-Imouthes," a devotee describes Asclepius as being superhumanly massive (ὑπερμήκης μὲν ἤ κατ' ἄνθρωπον), clothed in shining garments, and able to disappear suddenly (ἀφανὴς ἐγένετο; cf. Luke 24:31: ἄφαντος ἐγένετο).[92] Similarly, Ovid's deified Hercules becomes larger and worthy of

89. Similarly, Yahweh in anthropomorphic form shares a meal with Abraham in Gen. 18:8 (cf. Philo, *Abr.* 115-18; *T. Ab.* 4:9), and the angel Raphael eats with Tobias (Tob. 12:19). Cf. John Damascene (*Orth. Fid.* 4.1): "Even if he [Jesus] tasted food after his resurrection, this was not by a law of nature—for he did not hunger. By way of the economy, he verified the truth of the resurrection: that the flesh that suffered and was raised was the same."

90. Cf. Jairus's daughter (Mark 5:21-24, 35-43 par.), the widow of Nain's son (Luke 7:11-17), and the resurrection of Tabitha (Acts 9:36-41). Similar Greek cases of resuscitation include Glaucus (Ps.-Apollod., *Bibl.* 3.17.1-21; Hyg., *Fab.* 49.1; 136.7), Protesilaus (Hyg., *Fab.* 103) and Pelops (Ps.-Apollod., *Bibl.* 2.3; Hyg., *Fab.* 83).

91. Cf. the "historical" deification of Marcus Lucceius Nepos, who is described as "larger than the known form of his body" (*maior . . . nota corporis effigie*) (*CLE* 1109.12).

worship (*maiorque videri / coepit et augusta fieri gravitate verendus*) (*Met.* 9.269-70). The massive size of these deified men recalls the size of the resurrected Jesus in the *Gospel of Peter*, whose head surpasses the heavens (ὑπερβαίνουσαν τοὺς οὐρανούς) (10.40).[93] We read in Acts that the resurrected Jesus met Paul in a flash of overpowering light (9:3; 22:6; 26:13). The actual description of Jesus' features is spelled out in Revelation 1:13-16 where he appears with all the accoutrements of the divine: a shining face, an overwhelming voice, luminescent clothing, and so on. The resurrected body of Jesus is no ordinary body; it is an immortalized, divine body.

If there is a difference between Christian and non-Christian accounts of corporeal immortalization, it is that Luke and John emphasize a closer relation between the mortal and immortal bodies of the resurrected individual. The body that dies and the body that is raised are the same body. Jesus is not a pneuma (Luke 24:39) and he appears with his death wounds (John 20:27). The fact that Heracles's mortal parts are burned away, by contrast, indicates more discontinuity between his mortal and immortal states. But there are implications of somatic continuity even for Heracles. Recall that in Diodorus of Sicily, his bones cannot be found—since Heracles's actual body is in heaven (*Bibl. hist.* 4.38.5). Lucian, moreover, jokes that Heracles came to Olympus thoroughly seared and in need of medical attention. To the gods at least, Heracles could show off his scars.

Georges Devallet, following Florence Dupont, argues that the Romans distinguished between two bodies: the mortal part (*pars mortalis*) and the divine part (*pars optima*).[94] The mortal part could be destroyed, while the divine part could be translated to the gods (often through disappearance). This distinction is reflected in the Roman ritual of *consecratio*, where a wax image of the emperor (representing the mortal part) is burnt, while an eagle (representing the divine part) is released from the pyre.[95] The Gospel writers, who do not make this

---

92. Oxyrhynchus Papyrus XI, 1381, col. 4, lines 117-25 in Edelstein and Edelstein, *Asclepius*, 1.§331. F. W. Danker quotes an inscription where Asclepius is called "my god, more resplendent than earth in the springtide" (*Benefactor: Epigraphic Study of a Graeco-Roman and New Testament Semantic Field*. (St. Louis: Clayton Publishing House, 1982), 193). In iconography, Asclepius likewise appears massive while standing over his patients (images in *LIMC* V.2.638-43).

93. Cf. also Eris in Hom., *Il.* 4.443 and Demeter in Call., *Hymn Cer.* 57-60.

94. Georges Devallet, "Apothéoses romaines: Romulus à corps perdu," in *Entre hommes et dieux*, 107–123.

95. See further Simon Price, "From Noble Funerals to Divine Cult: The Consecration of the Roman Emperors," in *Rituals of Royalty: Power and Ceremonial in Traditional Societies*, eds. David Cannadine and Simon Price (Cambridge: Cambridge University Press, 1987), 56–105.

distinction, represent the mortal part of Jesus as itself becoming the divine (immortalized) self, which can disappear and ascend to heaven.

Perhaps a deeper point of difference is that Christian stories go out of their way to emphasize Jesus' burial. This tradition was part of the earliest Christian kerygma (1 Cor. 15:4). Although the burial story may have many other functions (e.g., the fulfillment of Scripture), it surely underscores that Jesus was truly dead.

Here again, however, difference does not amount to uniqueness. We are told of a burial of Asclepius (Cic., *Nat d.* 3.22.57; Ps. Clem., *Hom* 6.21; *Rec.* 10.24), and a return from Hades (Hyg., *Fab.* 251.2).[96] Plutarch also passes on the story of Alcmene (the mother of Heracles), who was buried in Haliartus in Boeotia. Much later, her tomb was reopened at the command of Agesilaus the Spartan king. Agesilaus had intended to remove her remains to Sparta, but no body was found. The excavators discovered only a stone, together with some personal effects of Alcmene: a bronze bracelet and two clay urns (Plut., *Gen. Soc.* 5 [*Mor.* 577e-f]). Just as Jesus' body wrappings and head covering indicate that he was once present (Luke 24:12; John 20:6-7), Alcmene's bracelet and the two urns show that she also at one time lay there.[97] In this story, it is evident both that Alcmene died and that she was immortalized. Like Jesus, she was transported to a transcendent realm (in this case, the Islands of the Blessed) (Pherecydes, *FGH* 3 F 84; cf. Anton. Lib., *Met.* 33).

On the other hand, there is some doubt as to whether Heracles and Romulus actually died. Above I have offered variants of their stories that speak of their deaths (e.g., Arnobius *Contra Gentes* 6.1.41; Hom., *Il.* 18.117-119). In most accounts, however, the deaths of both figures are not underscored. One can find accounts in which Romulus—like Enoch—was raptured alive, and Heracles—like Elijah—flew on a chariot to heaven.[98] It is due to this ambiguity that one should probably categorize the immortalizations of Heracles and Romulus as post-*mortal* rather than post-*mortem*. Whether or not they, properly speaking, "died," Heracles and Romulus were transformed *after their mortal lives had ended*. (Paul allowed an analogous transformation for believers

---

96. According to Edelstein and Edelstein, "the death of the hero is an essential feature of the Asclepius saga; it forms the climax of the legend" (*Asclepius* 2.93). "Time and time again the Apologists insist that to believe in the godhead of Jesus, who died the death of a mortal is by no means stranger than to acclaim the god Asclepius who suffered the same fate . . . They could hardly have made use of this analogy, had not the death of the god Asclepius been a fact commonly agreed upon" (2.75).

97. For another case of an empty tomb, see the story of Aspalis in Antoninus Liberalis, *Met.* 13.

98. But note Zwiep, who observes that "death terminology is used" regularly for raptured persons (references in "Assumptus," 332, n. 43).

still alive at the parousia [1 Thess. 4:17].) When their mortal lives came to a close, their mortal bodies presumably died and they assumed a new, immortal kind of life. The unambiguous death of Jesus, on the other hand, indicates that his corporeal immortalization was more surprising and dramatic. This does not mean, *pace* Wright, that Christian resurrection is unique, since it still falls under the general category of corporeal immortalization. It is nevertheless a distinctive form of corporeal immortalization—distinctive enough for early Christians to establish their own peculiar identity.[99]

WORSHIP

As we have seen, immortalized individuals often receive adoration. Numa Pompilius honors Romulus-Quirinus with the erection of a temple and sacrifices. Heracles received widespread cultic worship as both a hero and a god. Asclepius's cult centers dotted the Mediterranean world. When these gods appear, their votaries respond to them with gestures of worship, including proskynesis, prayer, and hymns (Livy, *Hist.* 1.16.2-8; Ennius, *Ann.* 111-114 [Skutsch]).

We see a similar response among Christians for their immortalized lord. The hymnic material preserved in the New Testament (e.g., Phil. 2:6-11; Col. 1:15-20; 1 Tim. 3:16; Rev. 5:9-14) is perhaps the earliest evidence of ancient Christians worshiping Jesus "as a god" (*quasi deo*; Plin. Min., *Ep.* 10.96.7).[100] In literary accounts, the resurrected Jesus receives worship as a kind of reflex. The women worship Jesus after they see him outside the tomb (προσεκύνησαν αὐτῷ, Matt. 28:9).[101] When the male disciples see him in Galilee, they worship him (προσεκύνησαν, Matt. 28:17). Once he recognizes the resurrected Jesus, Thomas falls down before him, and cries out, "My Lord and my god!" (John 20:28). After Jesus ascends in Luke, the disciples worship (προσκυνέω) him

---

99. Later Christian apologists would emphasize that the immortalized body of Jesus retained all its fleshly qualities (e.g., Theophilus, *Autol.* 1.13). This would probably have seemed a strange feature of deification to the cultural elite of the second CE. Paul's idea that Christ's resurrection body is a "body of glory" or "pneumatic body" not made of flesh (Phil. 3:20; 1 Cor. 15:45) would have been viewed as more acceptable.

100. The particle *quasi*, as A. N. Sherwin-White notes, "has no strong effect" (*The Letters of Pliny: A Historical and Social Commentary* [Oxford: Clarendon: 1966], 705). Christians truly believed that Christ was a god. He compares the language of 2 Clem. 2:1: φρονεῖν περὶ Ἰησοῦ . . . ὡς περὶ θεοῦ ("to think about Jesus as about God") (706).

101. Bryan notes that Matthew reserves προσκυνέω for true worship, not the false worship of demons or hostile soldiers (*Resurrection of the Messiah*, 295, n. 43). He adds, "Apparently Matthew considers that *this* worship, which was and is proper toward none but the God of Israel (Isa 45:21-24), was and is properly offered to Jesus" (ibid., cf. 95).

as a god (Luke 24:52).[102] In Revelation, John falls like a dead man before the resurrected Jesus (1:17). It seems likely that early Christians shared the widespread cultural assumption that a resurrected, immortalized being was worthy of worship and thus divine. By telling these stories, Christians represented the deity of Jesus to themselves and proclaimed it to others in the Mediterranean world.[103]

Nonetheless there is a difference in how early Christians understood the act of worship. Jesus, it appears, was never honored as an independent deity. Rather, he was always worshiped as Yahweh's subordinate. Naturally Heracles and Asclepius were Zeus's subordinates, but they were also members of a larger divine family. Jesus does not enter a pantheon but assumes a distinctive status as God's chief agent and plenipotentiary. It is this status that, to Christian insiders, placed Jesus in a category far above the likes of Heracles, Romulus, and Asclepius who were in turn demoted to the rank of δαίμονες. Etically and historically speaking, however, the Christian promotion of Jesus is a modification of a broader theme of deification in the ancient Mediterranean world. Again it is through the particular elements of their stories that Christians obtain a distinctive identity.

ASCENSION

Perhaps the strongest indication of deification in the ancient world was ascent.[104] As we have seen, corporeal immortalizations in Mediterranean mythology often include an ascent. Heracles, for instance, flew to heaven on a chariot, and Romulus was taken up in the midst of a storm.

In Christian stories, ascent and resurrection are also linked.[105] Psalm 110:1 ("Sit at my right hand!"), read christologically, implied a heavenly ascent for Jesus. Accordingly in early Christian texts we read that after Jesus' death, God "highly exalted" him (Phil. 2:8-9), and seated him "in the heavenly places"

---

102. Zwiep notes that in Greek sources προσκυνέω is a commonly used term for the veneration of gods (see *LSJ* 1518). Occasionally it occurs in Hellenistic rapture stories as an act whereby the worshipers acknowledge someone's divinity (Soph., *Oed. col.* 1654; Plut., *Rom.* 27.8; Luc., *Per.* 39) (*The Ascension of the Messiah in Lukan Christology*, NovTSup 87 [Leiden: Brill, 1997], 93).

103. For a full discussion of early Christian worship of Jesus, see Larry Hurtado, *Lord Jesus Christ: Jesus in Earliest Christian Devotion* (Grand Rapids, MI: Eerdmans, 2003), esp. 134–53.

104. For a short introduction and typology of ascents, see Adela Yarbro Collins, "Traveling Up and Away: Journeys to the Upper and Outer Regions of the World," in *Greco-Roman Culture and the New Testament: Studies Commemorating the Centennial of the Pontifical Biblical Institute*, eds. David Aune and Frederick Brenk (Leiden: Brill, 2012), 135–66.

105. For verbal and conceptual parallels between Jesus' ascent in Luke and other Greco-Roman stories, see Zwiep, "Assumptus," 333.

(Eph. 1:20) at the "right hand of God" (1 Pet. 3:21-22). In his monograph on Jesus' ascent, A. W. Zwiep comments that "the general conviction in the earliest Christian preaching" is that "as of the day of his resurrection Jesus was in heaven, seated at the right hand of God." This is assumed, notably, in Luke 23:43, where Jesus says to the thief: "Today you will be with me in paradise." Indeed, says Zwiep, resurrection and exaltation were regarded as two sides of the same coin; resurrection meant "resurrection to heaven."[106] Thus in the earliest Christian tradition, "resurrection and exaltation could be used almost interchangeably."[107]

The link between ascent and deification is widely acknowledged in scholarship. In the words of Gerhard Lohfink: "the one who goes up to heaven is made a divine being or a new god."[108] Lohfink illustrated this point with a text from Ovid (Met. 8.218-220) where a shepherd and plowman who see Daedalus and his son Icarus flying in the sky instinctively suppose that they are gods. Lohfink also points to the novel Chaereas and Callirhoe where Chaereas takes his wife (putatively) ascended from the grave to be a goddess (3.3).[109] Morton Smith pointed out that "Apollonius [of Tyana] is made to declare it [ascent to heaven] the true test of deification . . . and we find it [ascent] in the magical papyri as the means of immortalization."[110] In his study, Zwiep notes that the "proposition 'Romulus has gone to heaven' is materially identical with 'Romulus has become a god.'"[111]

---

106. Zwiep, Ascension, 130. Cf. Codex Bobbiensis (it[k]), where after Mark 16:4, we read that "angels descended from the heavens, and as [Jesus] was rising in the glory of the living God, at the same time they ascended with him."

107. Zwiep, Ascension, 143. In the modern Christian tradition (as well as the modern liturgical calendar), resurrection and ascension have been separated. Luke may have been the first to separate the two events by a significant time period (forty days according to Acts 1:3). For text critical issues on this passage, see Bart Ehrman, The Orthodox Corruption of Scripture (Oxford: Oxford University Press, 1993), 227–32. For comments on the apologetic function of the forty-day interval, see Zwiep, Ascension, 171–75. Cf. James Robinson, "From Easter to Valentinus (or to the Apostle's Creed)," JBL 101 (1982): 5–37 (esp. 7–10). In John's Gospel, the ascension is in some sense a process. "Go to my brothers and say to them, 'I am ascending (ἀναβαίνω) to my Father and your Father'" (20:17). Note also the comments of Bryan, Resurrection of the Messiah, 16.

108. Lohfink, Himmelfahrt Jesu, 46.

109. Ibid., 47.

110. Morton Smith, Jesus the Magician (San Francisco: Harper & Row, 1978), 124.

111. Zwiep, "Assumptus," 334. Cf. Alan Segal, who claims that "the entire Hellenistic world came to understand" the "immortalization process . . . as inherent in crossing the boundary between earth and heaven" ("Heavenly Ascent in Hellenistic Judaism, Early Christianity and their Environment," ANRW 23.2:1333–1394 [1382]).

In ancient literature, ascension language can be used metonymically to refer to deification. Valerius Maximus, for instance, referred to deification as an "ascent into heaven" (*ascensus in caelum*) (*Fact. dict. mem.* 8.15, *praef.*). Cicero described the deification of Hercules, Asclepius, and Liber as their being lifted up to heaven (*in caelum . . . tollerent*) (*Nat. d.* 2.62).[112] In Augustan poetry, deification is often described as a transfer to heaven. The aether "desires" Augustus (Ovid, *Trist.* 5.2.51), Iulus goes to the stars (Virg., *Aen.* 9.641),[113] Aeneas is sent to heaven (*caelo*, Tib. 2.5.44),[114] Heracles enters Olympus ([Tib.] 4.1.12),[115] and Augustus is placed among the constellations (*sidera*; Ovid, *Pont.* 4.9.129-f).[116] All these figures, in Roman tradition, were thought to be deified.

The very idea that an ascent to heaven is or implies deification is rooted in the logic of ancient cosmology. "People with any sense of their own intelligence," writes the Christian apologist Lactantius, "realize that a living and earthly body cannot exist in the sky" (*Inst.* 1.11.22). Heaven is the place of the gods (including Yahweh, Ps. 33:13, 103:19).[117] Since heaven has a different ecology than earth, it requires a different form of corporeal existence. The mortal, corruptible body cannot make the trek to—and beyond—the stars. To ascend there, one must be temporarily or permanently deified either by leaving the body or by undergoing some form of corporeal transformation.

The process of corporeal transformation is vividly illustrated in the early Christian text *The Ascension of Isaiah*.[118] The author of this text knows that flesh cannot exist in heaven. When the prophet Isaiah mounts to the highest heaven, the angel in charge of the praise of the sixth heaven cries out: "How far is he

112. Cf. *Tusc.* 4.50, where bravery lifts Hercules to heaven (*in caelum . . . sustulit*). Further references can be found in Pease, *De Natura*, 2.700. Christian Zgoll gives the nouns associated with deification in Augustan poetry, many having to do with the sky or astral phenomena. Deification is either described as a gift or as a change of place. The place is often heaven (also spoken of as the aether, the stars, Olympus, etc.) (*Die Phänomenologie der Metamorphose: Verwandlungen und Verwandtes in der augusteischen Dichtung* [Tübingen: Gunter Narr, 2004], 256–58). For catasterisms (also forms of deification) in Augustan poetry, see ibid., 269–78.

113. Cf. Ovid, *Pont.* 4.8.63.

114. Cf. Virg., *Aen.* 12.145; 7.210-11; 12.795; Ovid, *Fasti* 3.510; *Heroid* 18.169; *Fasti* 3.703; *Am.* 3.8.51; *Ars* 2.218; Prop., 3.17.8.

115. Cf. Virg., *Ecl.* 5.56; *Georg.* 4.562.

116. Cf. *Trist.* 5.2.52; 2.57; Virg., *Aen.* 12.795. Most of these texts are noted in the lexeme indexes of Zgoll, *Metamorphose*, 254–57.

117. For the divinity of the sky and stars in the ancient world, see M. David Litwa, *We Are Being Transformed*, BZNW 187 (Berlin: Walter de Gruyter, 2012), 152–61.

118. For recent research on this document as well as dating, see Jonathan Knight, "The Origin and Significance of the Angelomorphic Christology in the Ascension of Isaiah," *JTS* 63 (2012): 66–105

who dwells in the flesh to go up!?" (9:1).[119] To live in the celestial spheres, Isaiah's earthly robe must be stripped off, and a new celestial skin put on (6:10; 7:25). When Isaiah and all the righteous with him reach the seventh heaven, they are given a robe, and are made "equal to the angels who (are) in the seventh heaven" (8:14-15; 9:8-9). "[I]n reality," Enrico Norelli clarifies, "the just are superior to the angels, by being able to see God (9,37-38)."[120] When Jesus (in this text called the "Beloved") fulfills his mission, the righteous are crowned and made to sit upon thrones as if members of the divine council (9:18; cf. 24-26; 11:40).[121]

Jesus' own ascent to heaven in the *Ascension of Isaiah* appears similar. He mounts up in his fully divine (or glory-filled) form, and all the daimones and angels worship him (11:22-33; cf. 10:14-16). He then sits at the right hand of his Father as the vizier of God. Jesus in *The Ascension of Isaiah* is clearly a divine figure, and the luminous glory that he receives is indicative of his divine status. Philip Alexander pithily sums up Jesus' experience: "descent from heaven involved 'incarnation,' ascent from earth 'deification.'"[122]

Similarly in *The Book of Parables* (c. 40 bce – 70 ce), Enoch ascends to become a powerful angelic figure called the Son of Man (*1 En.* 71:14). "My spirit was taken away," he testifies, "and it ascended to heaven" (v. 1). He saw "the Head of Days . . . And I fell on my face, and all my flesh melted,

119. Enrico Norelli prefers the reading, "he who dwells among aliens." But Isaiah dwells among aliens "because of his fleshly garment" (*a causa della veste di carne*) (*Ascensio Isaiae: Commentarius* [Turnhout: Brepols, 1995], 451).

120. " . . . *in realtà i giusti sono superiori agli angeli, potendo vedere Dio (9,37-38)*" (ibid., 436).

121. Similarly in the *Apocalypse of Abraham*, when Abraham stands on the seventh firmament, he is transformed. When he finds himself back on the earth, he says to God, "I am no longer in the glory in which I was above" (30:1). Abraham's glorification occasioned by his ascent receives no additional development. It is an assumption: those who go to heaven must be made heavenly.

122. Philip Alexander, "From Son of Adam to Second God: Transformations of the Biblical Enoch," in *Biblical Figures Outside the Bible*, eds., M. E. Stone and T. A. Bergren (Harrisburg, PA: Trinity Press International, 1998), 103. If it is disputed that—unlike Christ—Isaiah and other glorified saints only become angels (and not gods), one must keep in mind that for the author of the *Ascension of Isaiah*, angels can be divine figures who share in divine prerogatives (i.e., priestly purity and royal rule as represented by robes, crowns, thrones, and glory). In *Asc. Isa.* 10:8-15, "princes," "angels," and "gods" seem to be used as synonymous terms. The Holy Spirit, moreover, is an angel (8:40-42). He is specifically the "second angel" (9:35), implying that the Son is actually the first angel (or emissary) of God superior to all the other angels (Loren Stuckenbruck, "The Holy Spirit in the *Ascension of Isaiah*," in *The Holy Spirit and Christian Origins*, eds. Graham N. Stanton et al. [Grand Rapids, MI: Eerdmans, 2004], 308-20 [309, n. 4]). Both the Son and Holy Spirit in *Asc. Isa.* are beings who have the prerogative of worship. The worship that they receive, the exceedingly bright glory that they have, and their proximity to the Most High God indicates that the category of angel blurs with that of divine beings.

and my spirit was transformed" (vv. 10-11).[123] In the *Parables*, the Son of Man is a Prime Mediator figure with clearly divine attributes and functions (e.g., preexistence, *1 En.* 48:2-6; eschatological rule and judgment, chs. 61–62). Assimilation or identification with such a figure qualifies, I think, as a Jewish form of deification.[124] The deification of Moses in Philo, furthermore, is also linked with an ascent. God's command to Moses, "Come up to me to the mountain and be there!" (Exod. 24:12) signifies that Moses was "divinized by ascending not to the air or to the ether or to heaven higher than all but to (a region) above the heavens. But beyond the heavens there is no place but God" (*QE* 2.40).[125]

I am aware that some scholars will argue that a different worldview prevented early Jews and Christians from too closely associating ascent and deification. At the end of his monograph on ascension, Zwiep states that the parallels between Jesus' ascent (Luke 24:50-51; Acts 1:9) and other ancient Mediterranean ascents are merely formal. For Zwiep, *Jewish* sources form the real background for Jesus' ascent, and Jewish sources, he believes, do not connect ascent and deification. In a later article, Zwiep directly attacks the idea of deifying ascent in Luke. Such an idea derives from a "polytheistic religiosity."[126] Turning to Jewish sources, he is willing to admit that figures of Israelite mythology could be elevated "even up to the status" of god (θεός or אל) as, for instance, in the writings of Philo and the Dead Sea Scrolls.[127] But because of Jewish "monotheism," this type of divinity (so Zwiep) was understood "in an attenuated, non-literal sense." Indeed, Zwiep remarks that a "literalistic conception [of deification] would be near to blasphemy to the Jewish mind."[128]

---

123. James VanderKam argues that Enoch is identified with the Son of Man and that *1 En.* 71 is an integral part of the *Parables* ("Righteous One, Messiah, Chosen One, and Son of Man in 1 Enoch 37–71," in *The Messiah: Developments in Earliest Judaism and Christianity*, ed., J. H. Charlesworth [Minneapolis: Fortress Press, 1992], 161–91 [182–85]; Nickelsburg, *1 Enoch 2*, 320–32). John and Adela Yarbro Collins leave open the possibility that these verses merely extol Enoch as a righteous human being (*King and Messiah as Son of God: Divine, Human, and Angelic Messianic Figures in Biblical and Related Literature* [Grand Rapids, MI: Eerdmans, 2008], 92–93).

124. Cf. also *2 En.* 22:8–10; *3 En.* (*Sefer Hekhalot*) 15:1.

125. See the argument in chapter 4 below.

126. Zwiep, "Assumptus," 335.

127. Zwiep, *Ascension*, 39–40.

128. Ibid. Ultimately Zwiep wants to maintain a strict boundary between the Greco-Roman world and "Jewish apocalyptic tradition" (195–96). I believe this to be a sophisticated reinstantiation of the Judaism/Hellenism divide.

Elsewhere I have argued for a different view of divinity, of ancient Jewish monotheism, and for a form of Jewish deification.[129] Here I simply point out that the very ascended Jesus whom Zwiep studies undercuts his argument. That is to say, early Christians viewed Jesus' ascension as an exaltation above his human state—above angels, principalities, powers, and every name that is named (Eph. 1:21; cf. Phil. 2:9-11). In accordance with Ps. 110:1, they described Jesus' ascent as a *sessio ad dexteram*, effectively making Christ the new cosmocrator, or lord of the universe.[130] It is common in scholarship to conclude that such language implies a divine status for the exalted Christ. Are we to say that such language implying Jesus' exaltation to godhead is not "literal" because it is too Jewish or Christian or monotheistic? Christian monotheism does not undermine the deity of the resurrected and ascended Jesus. The case may be different for Christians, but for Jesus, (the subject of this study), his ascension implies his divine status. Without it, a distinctive Christian identity could not be secured.

CONCLUSION

To be sure, Jews and Christians did not use the precise vocabulary of deification to speak of Jesus' corporeal immortalization, reception of worship, or ascent. But the lack of shared vocabulary does not undercut shared concepts. Surely Christians did describe these events in their literature to reinforce the divine identity of their lord. It is this process of depicting Jesus as a divine figure—that is, the *literary* depiction of a human as a god—that I am concerned with here. That the depiction of Jesus' immortalization, worship, and ascent amounted to his deification in Mediterranean culture was—to borrow a phrase from Cicero—"common custom" (*consuetudo communis*) (*Nat d.* 2.62). By depicting Jesus' final removal from this earth as an ascension, Christians tapped into the mythic consciousness of their time, making it possible for their audience—and themselves—to imagine Jesus as a deity.

Zwiep is perhaps correct that Christians would not have assumed that ascent implies deification as a general principle. The claim that Jesus' divinity is unique was (and is) necessary to maintain Christian identity (and superiority). Only for their hero, Jesus, does ascent indicate a divine status. Here again I acknowledge the apologetic pattern of one-upmanship prevalent in Christian

---

129. Litwa, *We Are Being Transformed*, 37–57 (the nature of divinity); 229–57 (Jewish monotheism); 86–116 (Jewish deification).

130. See further David Hay, *Glory at the Right Hand: Psalm 110 in Early Christianity* (Nashville: Abingdon, 1973).

sources. Nonetheless, the uniqueness of Jesus' deity emically conceived does not undermine my etic conclusion: As those trying to maintain the distinctiveness of their own tradition, Christians used the "deifying" implications of immortalization, worship, and ascent to reinforce their understanding of Jesus' unique deity.

This sort of competitive assimilation is perhaps the major factor that produces both similarity and difference when we compare Christian and non-Christian cases of corporeal immortalization. If early Christians would have denied that the corporeal immortalization and ascent of Romulus or Heracles indicated their divinity, they would not have thereby rejected the deifying resonances of corporeal immortalization and ascent for Jesus. Christians were adamant that Jesus took on a divine form and status in his resurrection-ascent (Rom. 1:4; Phil. 2:9-11). Exegesis of Jewish prophecy alone (esp. Ps. 110:1), I believe, was not the sole factor leading them to this conclusion. Early Christians read Scripture in a culture wherein corporeal immortalization and ascent were deeply linked to deification. Christians thus found themselves in a hermeneutic circle in which Scripture and culture were taken to support the same conclusion: the divine status of their lord. In the end, Christians did not, did not want to, and (practically speaking) *could* not pluck off all the "deifying" associations involved in their narratives of Jesus' corporeal transformation, worship, and ascent. Over and over again, they used these cultural associations (consciously and unconsciously) to achieve their own distinctive and powerful theological construction: the deification of Jesus Christ.

6

The Name Above Every Name

Jesus and Greco-Roman Theonymy

> *"Names usually get changed when the dead are deified, in case anyone should think they were human, I suppose. After his death Romulus became Quirinus, Leda became Nemesis, Circe Marica; after her plunge into the sea, Ino became Leucothea and also Mater Matuta, while her son Melicertes became Palaemon and Portunus."*
>
> —LACTANTIUS, *INST.* 1.21.22-23

INTRODUCTION

In the previous chapter, I touched on the implications of Jesus' ascent for his deification. The present essay zeroes in on a single divine honor that Jesus receives in his ascent/exaltation: the reception of a divine name. We learn of Jesus' reception of a divine name—what I will call "theonymy" (from θέος and ὄνομα)—in one of the oldest texts of the New Testament, Philippians 2:6-11.[1]

1. Recent scholarship seems to favor Paul as the author of Phil. 2:6-11 (Gordon Fee, *Paul's Letter to the Philippians*, NICNT [Grand Rapid, MI: Eerdmans, 1995], 43–46; Markus Bockmuehl, *A Commentary on the Epistle to the Philippians*, BNTC [London: A&C Black, 1997], 120; P. O'Brien, *The Epistle to the Philippians: A Commentary on the Greek Text* [Grand Rapids, MI: Eerdmans, 1991], 202). I am persuaded (1) by the passage's *hapax legomena* (e.g., ἁρπαγμός, κενόω, μορφή instead of εἰκών), and (2) by non-Pauline theological ideas (strong affirmation of preexistence, name reception, exaltation instead of

Much ink has been spilled on the first half of this passage (vv. 6-8) among scholars studying the incarnation.[2] In what follows, I will focus entirely on the latter half of the passage (vv. 9-11). In this section we learn that as a result of Jesus' obedience unto death:

[9] God super-exalted him
and bestowed on him the name
that is above every name

[10] so that at the name of Jesus
every knee might bow
of heavenly and earthly and subterranean beings

[11] and every tongue might confess
that Jesus Christ is Lord (κύριος)
to the glory of God the Father. (my trans.)

Here the divine name bestowed upon Jesus is called "the name above every name" (τὸ ὄνομα τὸ ὑπερ πᾶν ὄνομα) (v. 9).[3] Although this name might be

resurrection language) that Paul did not himself compose Phil. 2:6-11. (On these points, see R. P. Martin, *A Hymn of Christ: Philippians 2:5-11 in Recent Interpretation and In the Setting of Early Christian Worship* [Downers Grove, IL: IVP, 1997], 42–62). This passage was for centuries considered simply as part of Paul's epistolary prose. Its poetic character was first systematically demonstrated by Ernst Lohmeyer, who called it a "psalm" (*Kyrios Jesus: Eine Untersuchung zu Phil. 2,5-11*, 2nd ed. [Darmstadt: Wissenschaftliche Buchgesellschaft, 1961]). Its designation as a "hymn" became standard in the mid-twentieth century. (See Martin's justification of the term, *Hymn to Christ*, 24–30.) More recent interpreters prefer to read it as a piece of poetic prose (vocally, Fee, *Philippians*, 40–43), an encomium (J. Reumann, *Philippians: A New Translation with Introduction and Commentary*, AB 33B [New Haven, CT: Yale University Press, 2008], 339, 361), or a "prose hymn" (Adela Yarbro Collins, "Psalms, *Philippians* 2:6-11, and the Origins of Christology," *BibInt* 11 [2003]: 361–72). Although I recognize that the passage lacks poetic meter, I maintain the standard designation "hymn" since it is praise that was in all probability sung in honor of Jesus as a god (cf. Plin. Min. *Ep.* 10.96.7). For the ancient understanding of hymns, note Menander Rhetor, *Division of Epideictic Speeches* 1.

2. See esp. James D. G. Dunn, *Christology in the Making: A New Testament Inquiry into the Origins of the Doctrine of the Incarnation*, 2nd ed. (Grand Rapids, MI: Eerdmans, 1989), 114–21.

3. Clement and Origen, along with some "Western" and secondary Alexandrian MSS (D F G Ψ), eliminate the article before ὄνομα. In this reading, Jesus is given "*a* name" that is above all other names, thus distinguishing his name, it seems, from the name of the Father. Bart Ehrman understands the omission of the article as a "subordinationist" corruption (*The Orthodox Corruption of Scripture: The Effect*

"Jesus" itself,[4] the weight of the evidence points toward κύριος (v. 11). In context, κύριος is much more than a polite address ("sir") or a royal title ("lord"). By depicting the prostration of all creation to Jesus (v. 10), the author alludes to Isaiah 45:23 (LXX), where Yahweh proclaims, "To me every knee shall bow and every tongue confess."[5] Since every knee bows to Jesus (Phil. 2:10), the writer grants Jesus the cultic prerogatives specific to Yahweh. The author of Phil. 2:6-11 thus indicates the content of what is confessed, namely that Jesus is himself κύριος.

The name is significant, since as an act of reverence in their worship services, Greek-speaking Jews and Christians used κύριος to vocalize the name of Yahweh as it appeared in texts of the Hebrew Bible.[6] Given the fact that Jesus is granted worship due solely to Yahweh in Phil. 2:9-11, most interpreters are persuaded that κύριος in v. 11 represents the divine name Yahweh.[7] In short,

of Early Christological Controversies on the Text of the New Testament. [Oxford: Oxford University Press, 1993], 268).

4. C. F. D. Moule, "Further Reflexions on Phil. 2:5-11," in *Apostolic History and the Gospel*, ed. W. Gasque and R. P. Martin (Grand Rapids, MI: Eerdmans, 1970), 270. Other options can be found in Reumann, *Philippians*, 355.

5. For Yahweh as the speaker of this verse, see Isa. 45:18, 21. Cf. also Paul's citation of Isa. 45:23 in Rom. 14:11.

6. In written copies of the LXX, κύριος appears as the translation of "Yahweh," but not uniformly. Sometimes the Hebrew letters were written (יהוה), or replaced by the Greek ΠΙΠΙ. See on this point D. Capes, "YHWH Texts and Monotheism in Paul's Christology," in *Early Jewish and Christian Monotheism*, eds. L. Stuckenbruck and W. E. S. North (London: T&T Clark, 2004), 120–137 (esp. 120–24).

7. Martin provides a list of older commentators who support this interpretation (*Hymn to Christ*, 245). More recent interpreters who adhere to this view include Otfried Hofius, *Der Christushymnus Phil 2, 6-11*, 2nd ed. WUNT 17 (Tübingen: Mohr Siebeck, 1991), 27–29; 109–11; Jean-François Collange, *The Epistle of Saint Paul to the Philippians* (London: Epworth, 1979), 90, 107; T. Nagata, "A Case Study in the Contextual Shaping of Early Christology," (Ph.D. diss., Princeton Theological Seminary, 1981), 267, 269; G. F. Hawthorne, *Philippians*, WBC (Waco, TX: Word Books, 1983), 92; Richard Bauckham, "The Worship of Jesus in Philippians 2:9-11," in *Where Christology Began*, ed. R. P. Martin and Brian Dodd (Louisville: Westminster John Knox, 1998), 131; Morna Hooker, "The Letter to the Philippians," in *The New Interpreter's Bible* (Nashville: Abingdon, 2000), 510; N. T. Wright, "Jesus Christ Is Lord: Philippians 2.5-11," in *The Climax of the Covenant: Christ and the Law in Pauline Theology* (Minneapolis: Fortress Press, 1991), 56–98 (94); and J. D. G. Dunn, *The Partings of the Ways: Between Christianity and Judaism and their Significance for the Character of Christianity* (London: SCM, 1991), 249. Important exceptions to this interpretation include Oscar Cullmann, *The Christology of the New Testament*, trans. S. Guthrie and C. Hall (Philadelphia: Westminster, 1959), 180; cf. 218, 235–37, 307, 312; and Martin Rösel, *Adonaj—warum Gott 'Herr' genannt wird* (Tübingen: Mohr Siebeck, 2000), 225–26 (κύριος = אדני). See further Charles Gieschen, "The Divine Name in Ante-Nicene Christology," *VC* 57 (2003): 115–58 (116–18).

Jesus in Phil. 2:9-11 is "κύριος-Yahweh." It is this name, granted to an exalted human being, that is rightly "above every name."[8]

Scholars who study theonymy in this passage are usually interested in the question of Christian monotheism—namely how Jesus is integrated into Yahweh's divine identity.[9] This issue is important, but it skips over the preliminary question of what in the ancient world it meant for a person to receive a divine name—and in particular, the *proper* name of a deity. I will argue in this chapter that the literary depiction of Jesus as receiving a proper divine name in Mediterranean culture exhibits his deification.

The bulk of my discussion traces the historical context of Jesus' reception of the name "κύριος-Yahweh." Even though Isaiah 45:23 clearly stands in the background of Phil. 2:9-11, early Jewish sources, I will argue, provide no analogous tradition of a human being receiving the name of Yahweh. Rather, the meaning of theonymy in Phil. 2:9-11 is informed chiefly by contemporary Roman imperial practice. As with so many imperial traditions, however, Roman emperors adapted theonymy from the royal customs of the eastern Mediterranean world. The first part of this chapter, then, also discusses traditions of royal theonymy in ancient Egypt and Greece.

ANCIENT TRADITIONS OF THEONYMY

EGYPT

From the beginning of the first dynasty, Egyptian Pharaohs assumed the names of their gods [10]. In earliest times, pharaohs were invoked solely with the Horus name, a name "which designated the Pharaoh as the manifestation of the old sky god Horus."[11] By bearing this name, Pharaoh became "Horus in the palace," or Horus present on earth.[12]

---

8. Cf. later Christian texts where Jesus is given a "superior name" (διαφορώτερον ὄνομα) (Heb. 1:4), and a crown with a "name written which no one knows but himself" (ὄνομα γεγραμμένον ὃ οὐδεὶς οἶδεν εἰ μὴ αὐτός) (Rev. 19:12).

9. See in particular Larry Hurtado, *One Lord One God: Early Christian Devotion and Ancient Jewish Monotheism*, 2nd ed. (Edinburgh: T&T Clark, 1998), and Bauckham, *Jesus and the God of Israel: God Crucified and Other Studies on the New Testament's Christology of Divine Identity* (Grand Rapids: Eerdmans, 2008), 1–59.

10. For a general treatment of divine name-reception among rulers, see A.M. Hocart, *Kingship* (Oxford: Oxford University Press, 1927), 77, 80, 85, 89.

11. Erik Hornung, *Akhenaten and the Religion of Light*, trans. David Lorton (Ithaca, NY: Cornell University Press, 1999), 32.

Beginning with the fourth dynasty, however, pharaohs received a five-name royal titulary. In addition to the Horus name, the third name of the titulary was the "Golden Horus" name. The "Horus of Gold name expresses the nature of Horus. Horus is characterized by the imperishable brightness of gold. Gold is 'the flesh of the gods' and 'Re said at the beginning of his words: My skin is of pure gold.'"[13] The epithet following the Horus and Golden Horus name was different for each king and defined "the particular incarnation of Horus involved."[14]

A representative example of the fivefold titulary is that of Pharaoh Thutmoses III (1479–1425 BCE), who recounts how he received his titles on the walls of the temple of Amon-Re (the Egyptian high God and Creator) at Karnak.[15] Before the names are given, Thutmoses III describes his ascent to heaven (cf. Jesus' exaltation in Phil 2:9): "He [Re] opened for me the portals of heaven; he spread open for me the portals of its horizon. I flew up to the sky as a divine falcon, that I might see his mysterious form which is in heaven." In the celestial world, Thutmoses is endowed with the crowns of Re and outfitted with the ultimate symbol of power, the uraeus-serpent. He receives all of Re's "states of glory," along with the wisdom of the gods, and "the dignities of the God." Finally Amon-Re draws up Thutmoses's titulary. The names are apparently received in heaven and announced at his coronation. Thutmoses reports,

> He fixed my falcon upon the façade; he made me mighty as a mighty bull; he made me appear in the midst of Thebes in this my name of Horus: "the Mighty Bull, Appearing in Thebes"
>
> He made me wear the Two Goddesses; he made my kingship to endure like Re in heaven, in this my name of the Two Goddesses: "Enduring in Kingship like Re in Heaven"
>
> He fashioned me as a falcon of gold; he gave me his power and his strength; I was august in these his appearances, in this my name of Horus-of-Gold: "Powerful of Strength, August of Appearances"

12. Geraldine Pinch, *Egyptian Myth: A Very Short Introduction* (Oxford: Oxford University Press, 2004), 72.

13. Henri Frankfort, *Kingship and the Gods: A Study of Ancient Near Eastern Religion as the Integration of Society & Nature* (Chicago: University of Chicago Press, 1948), 46

14. Ibid., 46. In fact, all five titles of the Pharaoh include distinctive epithets that presage the program and policies of the king.

15. For a collection of royal names from all periods, see Jürgen von Beckerath, *Handbuch der ägyptischen Königsnamen*, Münchner ägyptologische Studien 20 (Munich: Deutscher Kunstverlag, 1984).

> He caused that I appear as King of Upper and Lower Egypt
> in the Two Lands; he established my forms like Re, in this my
> name of King of Upper and Lower Egypt, "Lord of the Two Lands:
> Menkheper-Re"[16]
>
> I am his son, who came forth out of him, perfect of birth like
> Him Who Presides over Hesret [Thoth]; he united all my beings, in
> this my name of the Son of Re: "Thutmose-United-of-Being, living
> forever and ever."[17]

Immediately after he lists his names, Thutmoses tells how Amon-Re made all peoples submit to his authority: "He made all foreign countries [come] bowing down to the fame of my majesty. Terror of me is in the hearts of the Nine Bows [i.e., the nine traditional enemies of Egypt]; all lands are under [my] sandals. He has given victory through the work of my hands, to extend [the frontiers of Egypt]."[18] Theonymy, as we see, leads to dominion and the prostration of enemies. Such a sequence recalls the events narrated in Phil. 2:9-11, where every knee bows to Christ the cosmocrator. Thutmoses inspires fear when he bears the names of his God(s); he has become Amon-Re's vice-regent on earth, wielding the God's power and authority.[19] By bearing his divine names—the most primitive symbols of divine power—Thutmoses can boast that his Father, Amon-Re, "made me divine."[20]

The reception of the five throne names in Egypt had not passed into oblivion by the Hellenistic and early Roman periods. We possess the following titles bestowed on Ptolemy VIII Euergetes II (182–116 BCE), which are characteristic of the later Ptolemaic period:

> *Horus*: The Youth in Whose Life there is Rejoicing, who is on
> the throne of his Father, sweet of occasions, sacred in his dazzling,
> together with the living Apis Bull.
> *Two Ladies*: Who Makes Content the Heart of the Two Lands.

16. Menkheper-Re means "Established in the Form of Re." Cf. the "form of God" (μόρφη θεοῦ) in Phil. 2:6.

17. Text adapted from J. B. Pritchard, ed., Ancient Near Eastern Texts Relating to the Old Testament 2nd ed. (Princeton, NJ: Princeton University Press, 1955), 446–47. Cf. Gerald P. Verbrugghe and John M. Wickersham, eds., Berossos and Manetho, Introduced and Translated: Native Traditions in Ancient Mesopotamia and Egypt (Ann Arbor: University of Michigan Press, 1996), 109–10.

18. Pritchard, *Ancient Near Eastern Texts*, 447.

19. "The names associated with Horus demonstrate that the king was powerful and all-conquering like the god Horus" (Pinch, *Egyptian Myth*, 72).

20. Pritchard, *Ancient Near Eastern Texts*, 447.

Golden Horus: Great of Strength, Possessor of *sed*-festivals like his Father Ptah-Tanen, the Father of the gods.

Dula King [king of Upper and Lower Egypt]: Heir of the God Who Goes Forth, whom Ptah chose, who performs the *ma'at* of Re, living image of Amun.

Son of Re: Ptolemy, may he live forever, beloved of Ptah; together with his wife, the Female Ruler, Lady of the Two Lands: Cleopatra; the Two Efficacious Gods.[21]

The phrase "the Two Efficacious Gods" is an Egyptian translation of the Greek Θεοί Εὐεργεταί ("Benefactor gods").[22] Ptolemaic kings were deified while still alive. Their reception of the fivefold titulary was a way to depict their divine status. As later pharaohs of Egypt, Roman emperors continued to use the fivefold titulary, though in an abbreviated form.[23]

ANCIENT ISRAEL AND JUDEA

Since the royal symbolism of ancient Egypt formed one context of ancient Israelite kingship, it is appropriate to ask whether Hebrew traditions attest the

21. H. Junker and E. Winter, *Das Geburtshaus des Tempels der Isis in Philä*, Philä II, Österreichische Akademie der Wissenschaften, Phil.-hist. Klasse, Denkschriften, Sonderband (Vienna: Böhlau, 1965), 5.

22. Ibid., 21.

23. Hornung, *Akhenaten*, 33; Friederike Herklotz, *Prinzeps und Pharao: Der Kult des Augustus in Ägypten* (Frankfurt am Main: Verlag Antike, 2007), 117–22. In Herklotz's Catalogue H (413–21), he lists all the variants of the Horus name given to the Roman pharaohs. They are referred to as "Horus-Re" throughout. The study of Ronald J. Leprohon (*The Great Name: Ancient Egyptian Royal Titulary*, Writings from the Ancient World 33, ed. Denise M. Doxey (Atlanta: SBL, 2013) came out too late to be used in this study. I take exception to his view that the Egyptian "king himself was not a divine figure" (13). See further on this point M. David Litwa, *Becoming Divine: An Introduction to Deification in Western Culture* (Eugene: Cascade, 2013), 9–25, esp. 11.

practice of royal theonymy. There have been various proposals.[24] For the sake of brevity, I will focus on only the most suggestive evidence.

Isaiah 9:5 (English translation 9:6) is perhaps the clearest indication for a king receiving a divine name.[25] Here four (possibly five[26]) names are, it seems, bestowed on a Davidic ruler through the prophet Isaiah. In a literal translation of the Masoretic text[27], we read,

> For a child was born for us
> A son was given to us
> The dominion came upon his shoulder
> He called forth his name—
> He Who Counsels Wonder,
> Warrior god (אל גבור),
> Father of Eternity (אביעד),
> Commander of Peace! (my trans.)[28]

24. In accordance with Egyptian royal ritual, Gerhard von Rad argued that "son of God" (Ps. 2:7) was a throne name like "son of Re" ("Das judäische Königsritual," *TLZ* 72 [1947]: 211–16). Although this theory received some support (cf. Sigmund Mowinckel, *Psalms in Israel's Worship*, 2 vols. [Oxford: Blackwell, 1962], 1:62; Roland de Vaux, *Ancient Israel: Its Life and Institutions* [New York: McGraw Hill, 1961], 103; Hans-Joachim Kraus, *Theology of the Psalms*, trans. K. Crim [Minneapolis: Augsburg, 1986], 113), it is now defunct. Equally obsolete are theories that propose that "David" was originally the name of an old Canaanite deity (A. H. Sayce, *The Modern Review* 5 [1844]: 159; S. Cook, "The Rise of Israel," in *The Cambridge Ancient History*, eds., J. B. Bury, S. A. Cook, and F. E. Adcock, 12 vols. [Cambridge: Cambridge University Press, 1923–39], 2:393–94; Ivan Engnell, *Studies in Divine Kingship in the Ancient Near East* [Uppsala: Almqvist & Wiksells, 1943], 176–77).

25. The meaning and (historical) context of the oracle in Isa. 8:23—9:6 (MT) remain unclear. Solving these issues is, however, unnecessary for an examination of theonymy in 9:5.

26. H. Wildberger ("Die Thronnamen Des Messias," *TLZ* 16 [1960]: 329) argued for a fifth throne name from Isa. 9:6a in accordance with Egyptian custom: מרבה המשרה, "He who makes his lordship great." K.-D. Schunck ("Der fünfte Thronname" *VT* 23 [1973]: 108–10) claimed that the lost fifth throne name is שפט עולם or "Eternal judge" (reconstructed from לל!). W. Zimmerli ("Vier oder fünf Thronnamen" *VT* 22 [1972]: 249–52) opted to maintain four throne names. For the Egyptian background to Isa. 9:5, see Klaus Seybold, *Das davidische Königtum im Zeugnis der Propheten* (Göttingen: Vandenhoeck & Ruprecht, 1972), 82–88; Wildberger, *Isaiah 1–12: A Commentary*, trans. Thomas H. Trapp (Minneapolis: Fortress Press, 1991), 402.

27. Here I follow the understanding of Wildberger, who sees this name in connection with Isa. 28:29: "he makes counsel wondrous" (הפליא עצה). Cf. also the two epithets of Horemhab (Eighteenth Dynasty Pharaoh): "Ready in Plans," "Great in Marvels" (*Isaiah 1–12*, 403).

28. Translations of Hebrew Bible texts that follow, unless otherwise noted, are my own.

The names are spoken in an oracle from Yahweh, and might thus be understood as given by Yahweh himself.[29] The names are extraordinary because they blend the functions and powers of the king and his divine patron. As Peter Miscall notes, in Isaiah the "Lord's counsel stands (7.3-9; 14.24-27); the Lord plans wonders (25.1; 28.29; 29.14). The Lord is Mighty God or Divine Warrior (10.21; 42.13). He is the people's father (63.16) and is forever (26.4; 45.17; 57.15). He brings peace (26.3, 12) and joy (55.12)."[30] All these attributes and associations are now combined in the human king.

Two names in Isa. 9:5 can be viewed as specifically divine: אל גבור and אביעד. The first, אל גבור, can be understood to mean "Warrior god" (as I have translated) or—as it is most often rendered—"mighty god" (NRSV, NASB, ESV). In the mid-twentieth century, Sigmund Mowinckel translated אל גבור as "Divine Hero,"[31] and commented, "the heroic power which the child will possess is characterized as divine. In form the name offers a precise parallel to the epithet applied to Aleyan-Baal in the Ugaritic texts: *'ilu gaziru*, 'the victorious or heroic god.'"[32] R. A. Carlson preferred to relate the title "Mighty God" to the Assyrian royal title *ilu qarrādu* ("Strong God").[33] Whatever its historical background, אל in Isaiah always refers to God,[34] and אל גבור is specifically applied to Yahweh in Isa. 10:21 (cf. also Jer. 32:18; Deut. 10:17; Jer. 32:18; Neh. 9:32; Ps. 24:8). Although this exalted language is often explained (away) by Hebrew Bible scholars with the idea that the Israelite king merely *represents* Yahweh on earth,[35] bearing Yahweh's name "Warrior God" seems to indicate a closer relation to Yahweh than mere representation.[36]

---

29. "He calls forth" is my rendering of the MT וַיִּקְרָא. The subject of the verb is unidentified. It is not inconceivable that it is Yahweh or Yahweh's prophet. Most translators avoid the problem by reading a Niphal form ("He will be called") following the LXX, Syr, Vulg. See further Joseph Blenkinsopp, *Isaiah 1–39: A New Translation with Introduction and Commentary*, AB 19 (New York: Doubleday, 2000), 246.

30. Peter Miscall, *Isaiah* (Sheffield: JSOT Press, 1993), 41.

31. W. McClellan, ("El Gibbor," *CBQ* 6 [1944]: 276–88) pointed out that the phrase could also mean "Heroic God," or "a God of a Hero." He agreed, however, that אל גבור is a divine name.

32. Mowinckel, *He that Cometh: The Messiah Concept in the Old Testament and Later Judaism*, trans. G.W. Anderson (Nashville: Abingdon, 1956; repr. Grand Rapids, MI: Eerdmans, 2005), 105; cf. Wildberger, "Die Thronnamen," 317.

33. R. A. Carlson, "The Anti-Assyrian Character of the Oracle in is IX:1-6," *VT* 24 (1974): 134.

34. Paul D. Wegner, *An Examination of Kingship and Messianic Expectation in Isaiah 1–35* (Lewiston, NY: Mellen, 1992), 187.

35. The idea is widespread. See, e.g., Werner H. Schmidt, *The Faith of the Old Testament: A History* (Oxford: Basil Blackwell, 1983), 182.

36. The offense of אל in Isa. 9:6 was eliminated by the LXX translation ἄγγελος (as in Job 20:15). It is disputed whether גבור is translated in the LXX or not. The reason for the strange rendering, notes J.

The name אביעד, also applied to the king in Isa. 9:5, most likely means "Father of eternity" (cf. "Father of Years," used of El at Ugarit, and "Ancient of Days" in Dan. 7:9). In the maximalist reading of Mowinckel, it indicates "the one who produces, directs, and is lord of the ever-changing years . . . who thus produces and directs 'eternity', the entire fullness of events and reality. It is evident that such a name really belongs to a god, and not just any god, but *the* god, 'the high god', 'the supreme god', 'the father of the gods.'" Thus the king, though a "mere man," in Mowinckel's reading, is described "as a divine being with divine titles and faculties."[37] Certain rabbis, H. Reventlow pointed out, went so far as to explain all the royal names of Isa. 9:5 (including אביעד) as epithets of Yahweh.[38] If Mowinckel's line of interpretation is correct, they had good reason.[39]

A less fulsome reading of אביעד emphasizes that the king, if not eternal like the high God, is at least granted a kind of immortality. Nearly a century ago, Hugo Gressmann already noted as parallels the Egyptian royal titles "prince of eternity," and "lord of unendingness."[40] The implication of the king's immortality seems to have been understood by the psalmist who hints that the king may live as long as the sun endures (Ps. 72:5). Similarly, in Psalm 21:4, the king asks for life and Yahweh gives it to him, "length of days forever and ever" (cf. Ps. 61:6).[41]

In 1978, W. L. Holladay rejected the idea that "Warrior god" and "Father of eternity" were divine titles. Although they are—or at least resemble—titles for Yahweh, when applied to the king, Holladay claimed, they are merely theophoric names (like Samuel which means "El hears").[42] Holladay gave no justification for this view beyond the preemptive argument that "it is inconceivable . . . that Isaiah would call the king 'God.'"[43] Based on the same theological presuppositions, John Goldingay has recently argued that the names

---

Lust, "probably lies in the special character of the royal names given to the child. Most likely the translator understood these as divine epithets and therefore altered the text by dropping some of them and ascribing others to God" (*Messianism and the Septuagint: Collected Essays* [Leuven: Peeters, 2004], 11, cf. 167). See further Rodrigo Franklin de Sousa, *Eschatology and Messianism in LXX Isaiah 1–12* (London: T&T Clark, 2010), 106–7.

37. Mowinckel, *He that Cometh*, 106–107.

38. H. Reventlow, "A Syncretistic Enthronement-Hymn in Is 9:1-6," *UF* 3 (1971): 324, n. 25.

39. Wildberger, "Die Thronnamen," 325.

40. Noted in Wildberger, *Isaiah 1–12*, 404.

41. There are intermediate positions. Wegner, for instance, reads אביעד as "My father [is] forever," thus implying that the bearer of this name is "a son of deity" (*Kingship and Messianic Expectation*, 188).

42. W. L. Holladay, *Isaiah, the Scroll of a Prophetic Heritage* (Grand Rapids, MI: Eerdmans, 1978), 107.

43. Ibid., 108.

refer to God and not the king, as with the name "Immanuel" in Isa. 7:14.[44] But Immanuel as a name of God in Isaiah is also the name of the expected child (cf. 8:8 MT).[45] Moreover, Mark Smith has pointed out that the "element גבור never goes into making Israelite proper names."[46] Other Hebrew Bible texts, furthermore, refer to human beings—including royal ones—as אלהים or "god" (Ps. 45:6[47]; 1 Sam. 28:13; cf. Gen. 3:5, 22). In short, one should not assume that ancient Israelite monotheism prevented a king from bearing a divine name.

Is there evidence that Israelite kings received the *proper* name of their god "Yahweh" (יהוה)? To be sure, many passages closely associate the Davidic king with Yahweh. Yahweh's name saved the king (Ps. 54:3 MT), exalted/protected him (Ps. 20:2 MT), and lifted up his horn (Ps. 89:25 MT). The king knew Yahweh's name (Ps. 91:14).[48] He spoke in the name of Yahweh, he came "in the name of Yahweh," and he cut down his enemies in the name of Yahweh (Ps. 118:10-12). In 1 Chron. 29:23-25, the account of Solomon's coronation, it is said that the king sat on the throne of Yahweh as king[49] (וישב...על-כסא יהוה למלך), received obedience from all Israel, was highly exalted, and received unparalleled glory.[50] In all these texts, however, it is never said that the king bears Yahweh's name.

44. John Goldingay, "The Compound Name in Isaiah 9:5 (6)" *CBQ* 61 (1999): 239–44. Cf. Paul D. Wegner, "A Re-Examination of Isa IX 1-6," *VT* 42 (1992): 103–112 (109–10).

45. Thus Blenkinsopp views "Mighty God" as a divine title, but also as parallel "to the same theophoric element in the name Immanue-el" (*Isaiah 1–39*, 250).

46. Mark Smith, *The Origins of Biblical Monotheism: Israel's Polytheistic Background and the Ugaritic Texts* (New York: Oxford University Press, 2001), 159–60

47. For recent discussion of Ps. 45:6, see Adela Yarbro and John Collins, *King and Messiah as Son of God*, 14, 56; Smith, *Origins of Biblical Monotheism*, 160–62. J. S. M. Mulder dates this psalm to the seventh-century BCE (*Studies on Psalm 45* [Oss: Offsetdrukkerij Witsiers, 1972], 158). He notes that the term אלהים in v. 7a, which refers to the king, has a good Egyptian parallel that occurs in the set phrase "the perfect (or beautiful) god." B. Couroyer uses this Egyptian expression as one of his arguments to demonstrate that אלהים is a vocative ("Dieu ou Roi," *Revue Biblique* 78 [1971]: 234–39). For the king of Tyre as "god," note Ezek. 28:14. The Egyptian king is also addressed by his vassals as "my god" in the El Amarna letters 157, 213, 215, 233, 241, 243, 270, 299, 301, 305, 306, 319, 363, 366) (noted by Mark Smith, *God in Translation: Deities in Cross-cultural Discourse in the Biblical World* [Tübingen: Mohr Siebeck, 2008], 14).

48. These references are taken from J. H. Eaton, *Kingship and the Psalms* (London: SCM, 1976), 155–56.

49. Margaret Barker proposes that this verse implicitly identifies Yahweh and the king ("Enthronement and Apotheosis: The Vision in Revelation 4–5," in *New Heaven and New Earth—Prophecy and the Millennium*, eds. P.J. Harland and C.T.R. Hayward [Leiden: Brill, 1999], 218–19).

50. In 1 Chron. 29:20, David is even venerated along with Yahweh. The word for "venerate" (hishtaphel חוה), though it most often means "worship [before a divine being]," can mean "to perform

Deeper resonances between Yahweh's name and the king can be heard in two stories of David. Several times he is compared to the מלאך (angel/ messenger) of God—an angel thought to represent Yahweh on earth (Gen. 31:11; Exod. 14:19; Judg. 13:6, 9, 20). In 2 Sam. 19:28, Mephibosheth says to David, "But my lord the king is as the angel of God (כמלאך האלהים)." Likewise in 2 Sam. 14:17, the wise woman of Tekoa compliments David: "for as the angel of God (כמלאך האלהים), so is my lord the king to discern good and bad" (cf. v. 20; Greek addition D to Esther [15:13-15]).[51] To understand these locutions as mere "courtly flattery"[52] denudes them of their historical significance. They assume a deeper relation between royalty and divinity. J. R. Porter, comparing 2 Sam. 14 and Gen. 3, concludes that David as (1) an angel and (2) a knower of good and evil is like Adam among the אלהים (Gen. 3:22).[53] Nonetheless, David *compared* with the angel of Yahweh does not signify an identification with the angel,[54] or that David assumed Yahweh's name.

In postexilic prophecy, the house of David is directly compared with the "angel of Yahweh" (מלאך יהוה):

> On that day Yahweh will shield the dweller of Jerusalem. It will happen that the one who stumbles on that day—he will be as David, and the house of David will be as God (כאלהים), like the angel of Yahweh before them (כמלאך יהוה לפניהם). (Zech. 12:8)

By a daring comparison, this oracle directly assimilates the Davidic house to the angel in Exod. 23:20-21 (called "the angel [of Yahweh] before your face," מלאך לפניך). Importantly, this angel in Exodus is said to bear (or contain) the divine name (23:21) (שמי בקרבו). Unfortunately, the divine name that the angel bears is never said to be Yahweh.[55] Perhaps one could argue that after

---

obeisance [to a king]." That god and king can share the same verb of veneration reveals the flexibility of the term and the kinship of kingship with deity.

51. Kraus also compares 2 Sam. 14:17, 20, where David's ability to judge makes him "like the angel of God" (Kraus, *Psalms 1–59: A Commentary* [Minneapolis: Augsburg, 1988], 455); cf. Tryggve Mettinger, *King and Messiah: The Civil and Sacral Legitimation of Israelite Kings* [Lund: Gleerup, 1976], 242–43).

52. A. A. Anderson, *2 Samuel*, WBC 11 (Dallas: Word Books, 1989), 238, cf. 189. See also P. Kyle McCarter, Jr., *II Samuel: A New Translation with Introduction, Notes, and Commentary*, AB 9 (New Haven, CT: Yale University Press, 1984), 347. He calls it "[r]outine flattery" on 422.

53. J. R. Porter, "Psalm XLV.7," *JTS* 12 (1961): 51. In 1 Sam. 29:9, David is compared to God's angel because he is "blameless."

54. John Emerton, "The Syntactical Problem of Ps 45:7," *JSS* 13 (1968): 58–63 (58).

55. This issue is somewhat resolved in the *Apocalypse of Abraham* 10:4, where "Yahoel" (i.e., "Yahweh-God") is the name of the angel who meets Abraham. Importantly, this angel is also assimilated to the

the exile, David's house comes to function as the name-bearing messenger of Yahweh.[56] Such a function does not imply, however, that that Davidic king or dynasty ever historically assumed Yahweh's name.

Psalm 110:1—"Declaration of Yahweh to my lord (יהוה לאדני), 'Sit at my right hand!'"—was another text where the name of the king (at least in the Septuagint) converged with the name of God. Although interpretations of this psalm are legion, it appears to present the enthronement of Yahweh's vice-regent.[57] Whether real or ideal, this vice-regent was probably viewed as a king, and perhaps a Davidic king.[58]

The Masoretic text of Ps. 110:1 distinguishes between the divine proper name (יהוה) and the human lord (אדני). Greek-speaking Christians using the

---

Hebrew God by his snow-like hair (cf. Dan. 7:7), and the rainbow around his head (Ezek. 1:28). The angel is also a royal figure: he wears a turban, a purple cloak, and carries a golden scepter. It would appear, then, that the one who bears Yahweh's name also shares Yahweh's rule. I do not deny the importance of such a tradition for understanding Phil. 2:10-11 (see further Christopher Rowland, *The Open Heaven: A Study of Apocalyptic in Judaism and Early Christianity* [London: SPCK, 1982], 101–13; Gieschen, *Angelomorphic Christology: Antecedents and Early Evidence* [Leiden: Brill, 1998], 70–76). The problem with this tradition, however, is that it is not a *human* (like Jesus) who bears the name of God, but an angel. Although one might argue that the author who attributed God's name to Jesus was adapting a tradition from Jewish angelology, for a true analogy we must secure a firm case of a *human* (not a principal angel) bearing the name of God. The case of Enoch/Metatron bearing the name of Yahweh (in *3 En.* 10.3, 12.5, actually "Yahweh Junior" [יהוה הקטון])—although made much of by Jarl Fossum (*The Name of God and the Angel of the Lord: Samaritan and Jewish Concepts of Intermediation and the Origin of Gnosticism*, WUNT 36 [Tübingen: Mohr Siebeck, 1985], 292–301, 307–21)—is simply too late (fourth-sixth century CE) to be decisive. Moreover, Dieter Zeller points out that Enoch in *3 En.* receives the name *as an angel* (an intermediate being), not as (a) god above all beings ("New Testament Christology in its Hellenistic Reception," *NTS* 46 [2001]: 317).

56. According to C. F. Whitley, Zech. 12:8 "may reflect . . . the background of a 'high' royal theology, which applied *elohim* to the monarch" ("Textual and Exegetical Observations on Ps 45:4-7" *ZAW* 98 [1986]: 282). Even if true, Zech. 12:8 does not suggest that the king bore the name of Yahweh.

57. Psalm 110 is usually categorized as a royal psalm. The best brief treatment of the psalm as an enthronement text probably remains Klaus Homburg, "Psalm 110:1 im Rahmen des judäischen Krönungszeremoniells" *ZAW* 84 (1972): 243–46. In a comprehensive study ("Sit at My Right Hand!" in *Studies in Early Christology* [Edinburgh: T&T Clark, 1995], 119–225), Hengel reviews the use of Ps. 110 in the New Testament (133–75), its background in the Hebrew Bible, Pseudepigrapha, Qumran, and Rabbinic texts (175–214), and its christological significance (220–25).

58. See the discussion in Kraus, *Theology of the Psalms*, 111–19; Frank-Lothar Hossfeld and Erich Zenger, *Psalms 3: A Commentary on Psalms 101–150*, ed. Klaus Baltzer, trans. Linda M. Maloney, Hermeneia (Minneapolis: Fortress Press, 2011), 144–46. Zenger writes that the psalm's epigraph לדוד "is intended . . . to link the psalm to the enthronement of the historical David or the Davidic kings . . . In the composition of Psalm 107, 108-110 . . . the issue is not only recollection of the historical David but also a new David figure (*David redivivus*) in the return of a renewed kingship" (ibid., 141, cf. 147).

LXX, however, heard the phrase "κύριος said to my κύριος" (εἶπεν ὁ κύριος τῷ κυρίῳ μου). In a christological reading of this phrase, then, the Messiah is called by the same name as his divine overlord (cf. Heb. 1:3-4, John 17:6, 11, 12, 26; 18:5-6; Rev. 19:12). The first κύριος signifies Yahweh. The second κύριος, or the king, shares Yahweh's title. Perhaps it is Ps. 110:1, then, that provided the basis for seeing Jesus as κύριος-Yahweh in Phil. 2:9-11.[59]

Although enticing, there are several problems with this theory. In the psalm, κύριος-Yahweh never says to the second (and subordinate) κύριος: "I *give* you the name κύριος." Admittedly, in the ritualized court speech of an enthronement, the fact that the king is called κύριος might be taken to mean either that (1) he was given the name κύριος *prior* to this event, or (2) that the very act of naming the king κύριος is itself a bestowal of a divine name. Strictly speaking, however, Ps. 110 does not present us with a name bestowal. Furthermore, the second κύριος in Ps. 110:1 technically does not represent Yahweh at all, but the generic title אָדוֹן. Thus although the κύριοι in Ps. 109:1 LXX could blend in the Christian imagination, we must assume, I think, that ancient readers were also able to distinguish multiple meanings in the homonymous title κύριος (i.e., the proper name of the Jewish god, and a title for a human king).[60] The κύριοι are distinguished, for instance, in Mark 12:35-36, where the second κύριος is taken to be David's "lord" (i.e., the Messiah), not Yahweh. That Yahweh and the king shared the same name in the LXX of Ps. 109:1 (i.e., κύριος) is certainly suggestive, but it does not allow us to conclude that the king historically or literarily ever assumed the name "Yahweh."

---

59. Barnabas Lindars, for instance, suggested that the psalm's phrase τῷ κυρίῳ μου is equivalent to the absolute κύριος title (representing Yahweh) that early Christians applied to the resurrected Jesus (*New Testament Apologetic* [London: SCM, 1961], 47).

60. See Hengel, "Sit at My Right Hand!" 223. The attempt to distinguish the meanings of the two κύριοι may be reflected by the LXX use of the definite article. In v. 1 both κύριοι receive the article: "*The* Lord (ὁ κύριος) said to *my* Lord (τῷ κυρίῳ μου)." But in Ps. 110:4 ("Yahweh swore . . .")—where no confusion of κύριοι was possible—the LXX translator reverted to the common practice of representing the divine name Yahweh with the anarthrous κύριος. Nevertheless, the quotation of Ps. 110:1 in Mark 12:36—which may represent an earlier text of the LXX —lacks the definite article. Symmachus avoided the confusion by translating אֲדֹנִי by τῷ δεσπότῃ μου (F. Field, ed., *Origenis Hexaplorum*, 2 vols. [Hildescheim: Georg Olms, 1964], 2.266). For further comments, see Miriam von Nordheim, *Geborn von der Morgenröte? Psalm 110 in Tradition, Redaktion und Rezeption* (Düsseldorf: Neukirchener Verlag, 2008), 174; C. Breytenbach, "Das Markusevangelium, Psalm 110,1 und 118,22f.: Folgetext und Prätext," in *The Scriptures in the Gospels*, ed. C. M. Tuckett (Leuven: Leuven University Press, 1997), 197–222 (209).

There are, finally, two important Jewish traditions set in the court of foreign kings. In Genesis, when Pharaoh makes Joseph his vice-regent, he gives him a new name: "Zaphenath-paneah" (41:45). According to G. Steindorff, the Egyptian form of this name means "The god NN speaks and he [the bearer of the name] lives."[61] The "god" (a generic title) in mind might have been a particular deity, such as Amun, Mut, Thoth, and so on—the text does not specify. Tantalizingly in *Jub.* 40:7, when Joseph rides Pharaoh's chariot, the people cry out *el, el wa abirer*, an Ethiopic corruption of the Hebrew (אל אל ואביר אל), "god, god, mighty one of God!"[62] In concert with receiving a divine name, Joseph is made lord of the whole land and receives proskynesis (Gen. 42:6; 43:26, 28). Unfortunately, as Kenneth Kitchen points out, the Egyptian name Steindorff reconstructed from "Zaphenath-paneah" (צפנת פענח) is theoretical and unattested. Kitchen himself prefers the reconstruction *djad-naf (I)pi-ankh*, which means "[Joseph,] the one called (I)pi-ankh."[63] If Kitchen is correct, the theory that Zaphenath-paneah includes a divine name—or even a theophoric element—falls to pieces.

The tradition of Joseph's exaltation and name-reception resembles the case of Daniel in the court of the Babylonian king. In the biblical account, Daniel relates and interprets the mysterious dream of Nebuchadnezzar (Dan. 2:1-45). In response, the king falls on his face and commands grain and incense offerings to be burned for Daniel (v. 46). Josephus, who retells this story for a Greek and Roman audience, makes clear that in sacrificing and bowing to Daniel, Nebuchadnezzar treats Daniel in the way that people worship God (ᾧ τρόπῳ τὸν θεὸν προσκυνοῦσι). Significantly, Nebuchadnezzar "gave Daniel the name of his own god" (τὴν προσηγορίαν αὐτῷ τοῦ ἰδίου θεοῦ θέμενος). Evidently, the ἰδίου refers to *Nebuchadnezzar's* god. This is, at least, Josephus's interpretation of Dan. 4:8 (Theodotion), where Nebuchadnezzar refers to "Daniel, whose name is Baltasar according to the name of my god" (Δανιηλ, οὗ τὸ ὄνομα Βαλτασαρ κατὰ τὸ ὄνομα τοῦ θεοῦ μου) (cf. 1:7). Daniel's reception of this name, significantly, coincides with an exalted status: he is made vice-regent of the kingdom (ἐπίτροπον τῆς βασιλείας) (*Ant.* 10.10.5).[64]

---

61. Georg Steindorff, "Der Name Josephs Saphenat-P 'neach, Genesis Kapitel 41, 45" *ZÄS* 27 (1889): 41–42; Steinjdorff, "Weiteres zu Gen 41, 45," *ZÄS* 30 (1892): 50–52.

62. I owe this reference to Crispin Fletcher-Louis, *All the Glory of Adam* (Leiden: Brill, 2002), 69. Cf. *Joseph and Asenath* 3:4; 4:7; 18:1; 21:21.

63. Kenneth Kitchen, "Genesis 12–50 in the Near Eastern World," in *He Swore an Oath: Biblical Themes from Genesis 12–50*, ed. Richard S. Hess et al. (Grand Rapids, MI: Baker Book House, 1994), 67–92 (80–84).

The tradition of Daniel (and possibly Joseph) receiving a divine name when promoted in a foreign court is important, but only loosely analogous to Phil. 2:9-11. Assuming that they do receive divine names, both Joseph and Daniel fail to receive the *proper* name of *their own* God. Assuming that Steindorff's reconstruction is correct, there is no indication that Jewish readers—even those acquainted with the meaning of Zaphenath-paneah—would take the generic term "god" to refer to *Joseph's* God Yahweh. This name (at least according to the final form of the Pentateuch) had not yet even been revealed to Israel (Exod. 3:13-16; 6:2-3).[65] In Josephus's *Antiquities*, moreover, Nebuchadnezzar does not call Daniel "Yahweh." Instead, Joseph and Daniel bear the names of generic or foreign gods—an ambiguous honor (to say the least) for faithful Jews.

In conclusion, the idea that Joseph, Daniel, David—or any other Israelite royal figure—would be called by the name of "Yahweh" seems to be absent in Jewish tradition. To some, perhaps, such a tradition would have been threatening and aversive. Ezekiel condemned Judahite kings for placing their threshold next to the temple of Yahweh (43:8). What would he say to kings who dared to be called by the name of Yahweh?[66] The stories of Joseph and Daniel indicate that royal theonymy was depicted as a distinctively foreign custom, not something practiced in Israel. In contrast, Jesus in Phil. 2:9-11 receives no generic divine title ("Warrior god"), or the proper name of a foreign deity ("Horus," "Amun," "Bel," and so on). Rather, he receives the specific name of his own god—κύριος-Yahweh—from the high God himself. If we are to find an analogous tradition of theonymy contemporary with that of Phil. 2:9-11, then, we must turn to Greek and Roman sources.

ANCIENT GREECE

One of the greatest military feats of the ancient world was the bridging of the Hellespont by the Persian emperor Xerxes (ruled 486–465 BCE)[67]. Herodotus,

---

64. See further B. A. Mastin, "Daniel 2.46 and the Hellenistic World," *ZAW* 85 (1973): 80–93; Christopher Begg and Paul Spilsbury, *Flavius Josephus: Translation and Commentary*, ed. Steve Mason, 10 vols. (Leiden: Brill, 2005), 5:285.

65. *Pace* Alan Schulman, "On the Egyptian Name of Joseph: A New Approach," *Studien zur altägyptischen Kultur*, Band 2 (Hamburg: Helmut Buske, 1975), 241.

66. Similarly, the description of the king as אלהים in Ezek. 28:14 may represent a polemic against this notion of the monarchy (Mettinger, *King and Messiah*, 271).

67. For Greek kings assuming the epithet "god" (θεός), see Appian, *Bell. civ.*, "Syrian Wars," 65, with the discussion in Christian Habicht, *Gottmenschentum und griechische Städte*, 2nd ed. (Munich: C.H. Beck, 1970), 99–105. Θεοί became a standard title for Ptolemaic kings and queens in the third century BCE.

who tells the story, has a man of the Hellespont approach the Persian ruler and cry out, "O Zeus, why have you taken the likeness of a Persian man and changed your name to Xerxes, leading the whole world with you to remove Hellas from its place?" (*Hist.* 7.56, Godley, LCL, modified). Although such praise might be brazen flattery, it seems to have been standard fare for the Persian king among Greeks. The Sophist Gorgias of Leontini (485–380 BCE) called Xerxes ὁ τῶν Περσῶν Ζεύς ("The Persian Zeus," in Longinus, *On the Sublime* 3.2).[68]

It is not clear whether calling *native* Greek rulers "Zeus" was ever official cult practice. The Roman writer Valerius Maximus gives the example of Pericles, who accepted the news of his sons' death with admirable equanimity. A soul of such strength (*tanti roboris animus*), says Maximus, won him the nickname of Olympian Jupiter (*Olympii Iovis cognomen*) (*Fact. dict. mem.* 5.10. ext. 1). The specific name and reason for it differs. Pliny the Elder associated the cognomen with Pericles's building projects (*Nat.* 34.19.74). Diodorus of Sicily links it with Pericles's forceful rhetoric (*Bibl. hist.* 12.40.5-6). Comic poets "spoke of him as 'thundering' (βροντᾶν) and 'lightening' (ἀστράπτειν) when he harangued his audience, and as 'wielding a dread thunderbolt in his tongue'" (Plut. *Per.* 8.3).[69] Plutarch, for his part, calls the cognomen "puerile and pompous (μειρακιώδη καὶ σοβαράν)." Only a "benevolent disposition" (εὐμενὲς ἦθος) and a "life pure and undefiled in the exercise of power" (βίον ἐν ἐξουσίᾳ καθαρὸν καὶ ἀμίαντον) is called 'Olympian' ('Ολύμπιον)" (39.2). But this, Plutarch concedes, is (generally speaking) the kind of life that Pericles led.

Note a key example in E. Bevan, *The House of Ptolemy: A History of Egypt Under the Ptolemaic Dynasty* (Chicago: Argonaut, 1968), 230–31. "God" as a cult title was apparently less appealing to Romans. That Domitian was later hailed *dominus deusque* in public addresses and documents is a blot on his rule (Suet. *Dom.* 13.2; cf. Mart., *Epigr.* 5.81; 7.34.8).

68. The divinity of the Persian emperor is touted *passim* in Aeschylus's play *Persians*. Significant also are the words put into the mouth of Alexander in the *Alexander Romance* (3d century CE) in a putative letter to Darius II: "For the names of the gods, in coming to men, do not bestow great power or wisdom on them. Rather they [kings] become all the more arrogant and insolent, for the names of the immortals are being harbored in corruptible bodies. And now you have this reproach from us too: you are able to do nothing against us, even though you are bolstered by the names of the gods and have taken upon yourself, on earth, their heavenly power" (*The Romance of Alexander the Great by Pseudo-Callisthenes: Translated from the Armenian Version*, trans. A. Mugrdich Wolohojian [New York: Columbia University Press, 1969], 60–61).

69. Because of his elongated head, comic poets called him "Heady Zeus" (Ζεῦ . . . καραιέ) (Plut. *Per.* 8.3), and "the squill-head Zeus" (ὁ σχινοκέφαλος Ζεύς) (13.6). His concubine Aspasia, furthermore, was called "Hera" (24.6).

Around 343 BCE, the people of Eresos (on Lesbos) honored Philip II (father of Alexander the Great) with an altar dedicated to Zeus Philippios (τῶ Διός τῶ Φιλιππίω).[70] Based on such an eponymous epithet, Christian Habicht asserted that Philip must have been taken as a "hypostasis" (*Hypostase*) of Zeus.[71] Ernst Badian disputed this position, arguing that "Zeus Philippios" merely designates Zeus as Philip's "protector."[72] Sylvie le Bohec-Bouhet offered a mediating interpretation: Zeus Philippios means "Zeus in the guise of Philip."[73] Whatever the interpretation, it was through Philip that Zeus acted and delivered his blessings.[74] Zeus's name was linked with Philip because Philip manifested Zeus's saving power.

In early 331, Philip's son Alexander entered Egypt without a fight and was crowned in Memphis as the new Pharaoh. At his coronation, he was probably given all the divine titles of the native Egyptian Pharaohs.[75] As founder of a dynasty, Alexander passed these names on to his heirs.[76] When Ptolemy I Soter became Pharaoh in Egypt, he assumed the Pharaonic throne names.[77] This practice was continued, as noted above, by later Ptolemies.[78] In an inscription

70. For text, translation, and bibliography, see Haritini Kotsidu, *TIMH KAI ΔΟΞΑ: Ehrungen für hellenistische Herrscher im griechischen Mutterland und in Kleinasien unter besonderer Berücksichtigung der archäologischen Denkmäler* (Berlin: Akademie, 2000), 461–62.

71. Habicht, *Gottmenschentum*, 14.

72. Ernst Badian, "The Deification of Alexander the Great" in *Ancient Macedonian Studies in Honor of Charles F. Edson*, ed. Harry J. Dell (Thessaloniki: Institute for Balkan Studies: 1981), 27–71, esp. 41. See further his "Alexander the Great Between Two Thrones and Heaven," in *Subject and Ruler: The Cult of Ruling Power in Classical Antiquity*, ed. Alastair Small (Ann Arbor, MI: Journal of Roman Archaeology, 1996), 11–26, 13. So also F. W. Walbank, "Monarchies and Monarchic Ideas," in *CAH* 7:1, 2nd ed. (1984), 90.

73. Sylvie le Bohec-Bouhet, "The Kings of Macedon and the Cult of Zeus in the Hellenistic Period," in *The Hellenic World: New Perspectives*, ed. Daniel Ogden (London: Duckworth, 2002), 41–58 (43).

74. J.B. Lott, "Philip II, Alexander and the two Tyrannies at Eresos of IG xii.2 526," *Phoenix* 50 (1996): 26–40 (31). Lott thinks it plausible that "the altars of Zeus Philippios at Eresos stood before a statue group of Zeus and Philip" (ibid.)

75. His coronation is referred to in *The Greek Alexander Romance*: "When he [Alexander] reached Memphis, the Egyptians put him on the throne of Hephaestus [the Egyptian Ptah] as king of Egypt" (1.34) (trans. R. Stoneman [London: Penguin, 1991], 68).

76. Alexander's short-lived son Alexander IV, for instance, was called "Horus, the youthful, the rich in strength, the Lord of diadems, loving the gods who gave him the dignity of his Father, the Horus of gold, Lord in the whole world, the king of Upper and Lower Egypt, the Lord of both lands, the Delight of the heart of Amun, chosen by the Sun" (Bevan, *House of Ptolemy*, 28).

77. Ibid., 32.

78. The evidence for Ptolemy V is inscribed on the Rosetta Stone, where the king is also called "the living image of Zeus" (ibid., 232, 263).

dated 42–41 BCE, we find a distinctive development. Here the high priest of Memphis Pshereni-Ptah calls Ptolemy XI, "the New Osiris, son of the Sun, Lord of Diadems . . . The king of Upper and Lower Egypt, the Master of two worlds, the Father-loving Sister-loving God, the New Osiris."[79] This striking name, "New [or Young] Osiris" is also given to Ptolemy XI on an inscription of the temple at Edfu in Upper Egypt.[80] Ptolemy XI was also given the surname "New [or Young, νέος] Dionysus."[81] Probably the two names are equivalent, since the Greeks had long identified Osiris with Dionysus (Herod., *Hist.* 2.42, 144).[82] The Greco-Egyptian queens also took on the divine names of Greek goddesses. Arsinoë, wife of Ptolemy II Philadelphus, had her own special temple at Alexandria in which she was called "Arsinoë Aphrodite."[83] Later, the most famous Cleopatra (lover of Caesar and Antony) was styled the "New [or Young] Isis."[84]

In Syria, Alexander's successor, Seleucus I (c. 358–281 BCE) took on the name Zeus Nicator in the Seleucid state cult.[85] The Seleucid assimilation to Zeus was continued by Antiochus IV Epiphanes. After his victory over Ptolemy VI in 169–68 BCE, he issued a coin replacing the standard depiction of his royal head with the head of Zeus. The reverse bore the image of "Zeus of victory" seated upon the throne. The legend read: "Of King Antiochus, God Manifest"

---

79. Ibid., 347.

80. Ibid., 354.

81. Ibid., 344.

82. See further on "New/Young Dionysus," M. David Litwa, *We Are Being Transformed*, BZNW 187 (Berlin: Walter de Gruyter, 2012), 80–84.

83. Ibid., 129. "The identification of Arsinoë with a whole series of goddesses is reflected in the nomenclature of the streets of Alexandria in the third century BC" (A. D. Nock, "Notes on Ruler Cult I–IV," in *Arthur Darby Nock: Essays on Religion in the Ancient World*, 2 vols. [Oxford: Clarendon, 1972], 1:147).

84. Bevan, *House of Ptolemy*, 377.

85. W. Dittenberger, ed. *Orientis Graeci Inscriptiones Selectae* (Lipsiae: Hirzel, 1903), §245.10-11, 34-35. This inscription is tentatively dated between 212 and 114 BCE. Cf. Appian, *Syr.* 63. In 1928, Nock drew attention to a Lydian inscription dated ca. 228 BCE dedicated to "Zeus Seleucus and the harvest-giving Nymphs." This Seleucid Zeus would, says Nock "almost certainly be regarded as patron of the Seleucid line, which associated itself closely with Zeus" and controlled Lydia at the time (*Essays on Religion*, 1:157).

(βασιλέως Ἀντίοχου θεοῦ Ἐπιφανοῦς).[86] The additional imagery of the coin may suggest that the God manifest in Antiochus was in fact Zeus.

Even minor potentates like Cleitus—general under Antipater (who ruled Macedonia)—assumed a divine name. In the Lamian war (323–22 BCE), Cleitus defeated the Athenian fleet in two naval battles (Diod. Sic., *Bibl. hist.* 18.15). Consequently, "he caused himself to be proclaimed Poseidon and carried a trident" (Ποσειδῶν ἀνηγορεύθη καὶ τρίαιναν ἐφόρει) (Plut., *Fort. Alex.* [*Mor.* 338a]).

Finally, Theophanes of Mytilene (*FGH* 188), contemporary and historian of Pompey the Great, was posthumously honored as "Zeus of Freedom" (Ζεύς Ἐλευθέριος).[87] He earned the name by his good diplomacy with Rome, by which he became the "savior," "benefactor," and "second founder" of his city.

ANCIENT ROME

Although the Greek tradition is helpful background, Phil. 2:6-11 was composed in the Roman period and recited (possibly sung) at a Roman colony (Philippi) where the founder Julius Caesar was worshiped as a god. Consequently, it is the Roman ruler cult that forms the immediate context for theonymy in Phil. 2:9-11.[88]

---

86. Elias Bickerman, *Institutions des Séleucides* (Paris: P. Geuthner, 1938), 239. For an example of this issue, see the gold stater published by C. Kraay and M. Hirmer, *Greek Coins* (New York: Harry N. Abrams, 1966), no. 749, pl. 206 (for commentary on the coin, see p. 374). Bikerman also mentions a series of coins struck in Antioch after Antiochus defeated Egypt that feature an eagle, the bird of Zeus, and the depiction of Zeus Amon (*Institutions*, 239).

87. *Syll*[3] 753 = *IG* XII.2.164-69. Cf. Tac., *Ann.* 6.18.2 (*caelestis honores*). Numismatic evidence of Theophanes's deification is discussed by Kostas Buraselis, "Two Notes on Theophanes' Descendents," in *The Greek East in the Roman Context*, ed. Olli Salomies (Helsinki: Vammalan Kirjapaino Oy, 2001), 64–65.

88. Among modern biblical scholars, the κύριος title in Phil. 2:9b is often explained by the fact that Roman emperors were also called κύριοι (see, e.g., W. Foerster and G. Quell, *Lord: Bible Key Words from Gerhard Kittel's Theologisches Wörterbuch zum Neuen Testament* [London: A&C Black, 1958], 27–35). This observation is somewhat problematic given that Augustus strictly and vigorously forbade anyone—even his closest relations—from calling him κύριος/*dominus* (Suet., *Aug.* 53.1-2). Like Augustus, Tiberius too explicitly rejected the κύριος title (Tac., *Ann.* 2.87.2; cf. Dio Cass., *Rom. Hist.* 57.8.2). To be sure, these emperors, in spite of their resistance, were called κύριοι throughout the east (Foerster, "κύριος," *TDNT* 3:1049, 1054). But κύριος only becomes an official imperial title with Nero (ruled 54–68 CE), and only common in the early second century with Trajan and Hadrian (ibid. 1054). More importantly, there is an essential difference between κύριος as an imperial title and κύριος as applied to Jesus in Phil. 2:9b. The former is a title that is often associated—but does not necessarily connote—divinity (Foerster and Quell, *Lord*, 30; Foerster, "κύριος," *TDNT* 3:1056). The latter, by contrast, represents a proper divine name (Yahweh).

As we saw in the last chapter, Romulus, after his ascension to heaven, was given the name "Quirinus" (Livy, *Hist.* 1.16).[89] Under the name "Quirinus," Romulus was worshiped with a proper name of a more ancient god. "Quirinus" does not, however, designate the high god of the Roman pantheon, but was (it seems) a sort of double of the god Mars.[90]

After the exile of Tarquinius Superbus (ruled 534–510 BCE), kingship died out in Rome, only to be functionally reestablished (without the name) in the person of Julius Caesar.[91] After the Battle of Munda in Spain (45 BCE), Caesar ended the civil war with Pompey's party and became the undisputed ruler of the Mediterranean world. He celebrated "triple triumphs" at Rome (Cass. Dio, *Rom. Hist.* 43.42.2) and was decreed permanent dictator. Some time before, Cicero had compared the power of a Roman dictator to that of Jupiter Optimus Maximus (*Rosc. Amer.* 131). When Caesar was declared permanent dictator (44 BCE) "the analogy became concrete political imagery."[92] In a play probably written by an imitator of Seneca, the emperor Nero is made to say of Julius: "unconquered in battle, leader of nations, equated with Jove (*Iovi aequatus*) through a continual series of the highest honors" ([Sen.], *Oct.* 500-501).

During Caesar's final days, the Roman Senate began to address him outright as "Jupiter Julius" (Δία τε αὐτὸν ἄντικρυς Ἰούλιον προσηγόρευσαν). This is the report of Cassius Dio (*Rom. Hist.* 44.6.4), a prominent senator in the early third century CE. The report has long been debated by classicists and historians.

In the mid-twentieth century, Fritz Taeger pointed out independent confirmation of Dio's report.[93] Antipater of Sidon (first century BCE) mentions in a poem about the coming Parthian campaign of Augustus that Augustus is

---

89. Cf. Plut., *Rom.* 28.3. For other authors identifying Romulus with Quirinus, see Pease, *De Natura*, 2:704. See further Walter Burkert, "Caesar und Romulus-Quirinus," *Historia* 11 (1962): 356–76.

90. Cf. the case of Hippolytus, who received the cult title "Virbius" as a sign of his deification (Ovid, *Met.* 15.544-45). In the Greek tradition, the boy Melicertes becomes the sea god Palaemon (Ps.-Apollod., *Bibl.* 3.4.3), and the deified girls Metioche and Menippe become "the Coronid Maidens" (Antoninus Liberalis, *Met.* 25). Several other examples are noted by Lact., *Inst.* 1.21.22-23 (quoted in the epigraph to this chapter).

91. For *royauté sans le nom* beginning in the time of Julius Caesar, see P. M. Martin, *L'idée de Royauté à Rome: Haine de la royauté et séductions monarchiques*, 2 vols. (Clermont-Ferrand: Adosa, 1994), 2.288–94, 310–15; 363–426. Note also on this point Gerhard Dobesch, *Caesars Apotheose zu Lebzeiten und sein Ringen um den Königstitle* (Wien: Selbstverlag, 1966), 71–142.

92. J. R. Fears, "Jupiter and Roman Imperial Ideology," *ANRW* 17.1:54.

93. Fritz Taeger, *Charisma: Studien zur Geschichte des Antiken Herrscherkultes* 2 vols. (Stuttgart: Kohlhammer, 1960), 2.70–71.

the "son of Zeus" (Ζηνὸς τέκος) (*Greek Anthology* 9.297.1).[94] In an epigram from Egypt, one Catilius writes in reference to Augustus: "To Zeus Caesar . . . who is from his father Zeus" (Καίσαρι . . . Ζανί, τῷ ἐκ Ζανὸς πατρός) (*CIG* 4923).[95] Taeger concluded from this evidence that Augustus's father, Julius Caesar, was called "Zeus."[96] Stefan Weinstock believed that the title "Jupiter Julius" was a possible cult title offered to Caesar, but that the title was experimental.[97] With this opinion concurred the great epigraphist Habicht.[98]

Dio's reliability was strongly criticized by J. A. North, who argued that no evidence requires that Caesar be identified with Jupiter. The only parallel evidence is Cicero's *Philippics*, where the orator lists the honors decreed for Caesar during his lifetime. "What greater honor," says Cicero, "had he [Julius Caesar] obtained than to have a couch on which a god is seated (*pulvinar*), an image (*simulacrum*), a pediment to his house (*fastigium*), a flamen [a priesthood devoted to a specific deity, in this case Caesar himself]" (2.110, cf. 111; 13.41, 47). But in this text the cult title given to Caesar is *divus* Iulius. North supposed that Dio's "Jupiter Julius" comes from this very passage, which Dio misunderstood.[99]

More recently, however, experts in ruler cult have been more hesitant to explain away Dio's testimony. Duncan Fishwick states that "Iuppiter Iulius" as a cult title is "entirely credible."[100] The designation does not, however, mean that Caesar was identified with Jupiter (just as κύριος-Jesus is not strictly identical to Yahweh). There remained, and would remain differences between the cult of Jupiter and the cult of Jupiter Julius.[101] The title meant, according to Fishwick,

---

94. The Greek Anthology refers primarily to the *Palatine Anthology* compiled probably by Constantine the Rhodian in 940 CE. It is mainly a collection of epigrams formed from three previous collections, one produced by Meleager ca. 100 BCE, another by Philippus of Thessalonica compiled under Nero, and a third compiled by Agathias around 567–68 CE (*OCD*[4] 98-99 *s.v.* "anthology (ἀνθολόγιον) Greek").

95. The epigram, found on the island of Philae on the Nile, is quoted fully in Foerster, "κύριος," *TDNT* 3:1056. In the inscription, Zeus-Caesar is distinguished from the high God Zeus, for it is the high God who caused Zeus-Caesar to "rise like the dawn" (ἀνέτειλε).

96. Dobesch, *Caesars Apotheose*, 18. Cf. Epict., *Diatr.* 1.3, who equates the man adopted by Caesar with "a son of Zeus."

97. Stefan Weinstock, *Divus Julius* (Oxford: Clarendon, 1971), 300–305.

98. J. A. North, "Die augusteische Zeit und das erste Jahrhundert nach Christi Geburt," in *Le culte des souverains dans l'empire romain* (ed. Bickerman; Vandoeuvres-Genève: Fondation Hardt, 1973), 39–99, esp. 52.

99. J. A. North, "Praesens Divus," *Journal of Roman Studies* 65 (1975): 171–77.

100. Duncan Fishwick, *The Imperial Cult in the Latin West: Studies in the Ruler Cult of the Western Provinces of the Roman Empire* (Leiden: Brill, 1987), 63.

101. Ibid., 64, 66.

that Jupiter was Julius's "protective deity." *Iuppiter Iulius* means "Julian Jupiter, that is Jupiter who operates in the sphere of Julius, a personalization and specialization of Jupiter's function."[102] Fishwick's reasoning, however, fails to explain why the cult title was given to *Caesar*, not to Jupiter himself as a protective deity.

Ittai Gradel also accepts Dio's testimony that Caesar was decreed the title *Iuppiter Iulius*. He believes, however, that this was one of the titles that Caesar did not accept. When he was alive, Gradel thinks, Caesar may have accepted the title *divus* as a substitute.[103] It is the title *divus* that became the standard cult title for deified emperors.[104]

If the name "Jupiter Julius" is historically reliable as a designation at least *offered* to Caesar, what was its context? Why would the Roman senate have bestowed such a name upon Caesar? Hellenistic kingship provided a precedent: Philip II as Zeus Philippios and Seleucus I as "Zeus Nicator" have already been noted. In the Roman context, *Iuppiter Iulius* may have been connected with Caesar's triumph. After his victory at Munda, the senate voted that Caesar "should always ride, even in the city itself, wearing the triumphal dress" (στολὴν τὴν ἐπινίκιον) (Cass. Dio, *Rom. Hist.* 44.4.2). According to Pliny the Elder, early triumphators painted their faces red, like the statue of Jupiter on the Capitoline temple (*Nat.* 35.157; 33.111).[105] They also bore the attributes of

---

102. Ibid., 66 citing P. M. Fraser, "Zeus Seleukeios," *CR* 63 (1949): 92–4 and Nock, *Essays on Religion*, 1.156–57. Cf. Badian's interpretation of "Zeus Philippios" above.

103. Ittai Gradel, *Emperor Worship and Roman Religion* (Oxford: Clarendon, 2002), 70–71.

104. Dobesch thinks that Caesar's common title among the people was *deus Caesar*, based on an honorary inscription from Nola (*CIL*² 1611 = X 1271): *M. Salvio Q. f/Venusto/decurioni/[be]nific. Dei Caesaris*. Another inscription (*CIL* VI 14211) calls Calpurnia the wife of the great god Caesar (. . . *magnifici coniunx Caesaris illa dei*). Dobesch dates this later inscription to Caesar's lifetime (*Caesars Apotheose*, 23). Thus by using the title *divus*, Caesar would have distanced himself from the other gods. We know that he was dissatisfied with the title "demigod" (ἡμίθεος), but accepted the title "unconquered god" (θεὸς ἀνίκητος). Dobesch dares to take *divus* as the substantive and *Iulius* as the adjective, producing "Julian Divus" (24). Drawing on Lily Ross Taylor (*The Divinity of the Roman Emperor* [Middletown, CT: American Philological Association, 1931], 70), he thinks that *divus* was closely connected to Jupiter, since *divus* according to Varro means "sky" (*Lingua Latina* 5.66). He concludes that *Iuppiter Iulius* and *divus Iulius* amount to the same thing (25), and that this was Caesar's own clandestine way of identifying himself with Jupiter (if only by implication) (27). Perhaps, Dobesch says, the senate's decree only mentioned the title *divus Julius*, but the designation allowed Caesar to be *acclaimed* "Jupiter Julius" in an informal, spontaneous sense (27–28).

105. Cf. Plut., *Quaest. rom.* 98.287d; Serv., *Commentary on Virgil's Eclogues* 10.27: "Jupiter is the aether. Therefore those who triumph, who have all the insignia of Jove . . . also smear their faces with red like the color of aether (*rubrica inlinunt instar coloris aetherii*)." From the same author in the Daniel Scholia 6.22

Jupiter: a scepter and a golden crown.[106] Thus on the day of his triumph, the triumphing general represented Jupiter.[107] It is possible that the senators attempted to transfer these associations to Julius Caesar in a more permanent sense.[108]

Admittedly, flatterers sometimes called their benefactors "Jupiter," as is evidenced in Latin comedy.[109] Moreover, Cicero's enemy Clodius had accused the orator of self-flattery, since he was wont to call himself "Jove" (*me dicere solere esse me Iovem*) (Cic., *de Domo sua* 92). It is true that Cicero wrote an epic poem about his deeds as consul. In the poem (which does not survive), it is not inconceivable that Cicero poetically likened himself to Jupiter in his capacity as ruler. In his formal speech delivered to the pontiffs, however, Cicero shied away from any such claim.

Caesar's reception of the name "Jupiter Julius" is of a different order. Caesar after his triumphs was much more than a Roman consul. Moreover, the Capitoline Jupiter was the national god of the Romans, "the pre-eminent god of the city, guarantor of Roman victory, expression of the city's identity to the citizens and to the outside world."[110] "Rome's destiny and function were represented by Jupiter Optimus Maximus, who had taken up residence in the Capitoline temple. It was for this reason that every year the new consuls, on entering office, went in procession to perform a sacrifice to him and that every year the first meeting of the Senate was held in his temple."[111] Cassius Dio

we read that "red is the color of the gods. Therefore both those who triumph have their faces painted red (*facie miniata*), and Jupiter on the Capitoline in his four-horse chariot is painted red (*Iuppiter . . . minatus*)."

106. Livy, *Hist.* 10.7.10; Juvenal, *Sat.* 10.38; Serv. *Ecl.* 10.27; Suet., *Aug.* 94.6.

107. Weinstock, *Divus Julius*, 302.

108. For Julius and Jupiter in Lucan, *Bellum Civile*, see D. C. Feeney, *The Gods in Epic: Poets and Critics of the Classical Tradition* (Oxford: Clarendon, 1991), 295–97. Mary Beard's *The Roman Triumph* (Cambridge, MA: Belknap, 2007) has called into question nearly every element of the Roman triumph—including the triumphator's attempt to "play god." I agree that sources often disagree, and that what applied to earlier triumphs does not apply to later ones, but I do not share her overall skepticism of the ancient sources.

109. "O, my earthly Jupiter! (*o mi iuppiter terrestris*)" (Plaut., *Pers.* 99; cf. *Asin.* 712-13); "Bring sacrifices, victims, and butchers, so that I can sacrifice to him as Jove Most High (*huic sacruficem summo Iovi*)! For now he is to me a much more powerful Jupiter than Jupiter" (*hic mihi nunc est multo potior Iuppiter quam Iuppiter*) (*Pseud.* 326); "Now *I* am for you Jupiter Most High (*ego nunc tibi sum summus Iuppiter*)" (*Capt.* 863). Plautus also jokes about the mortality of *humani Ioves* ("human Joves") in *Cas.* 333. Cf. a possible model in [Eur.], Rhesus 355: "You are to me Zeus manifest!" (σύ μοι Ζεὺς ὁ φαναῖος).

110. Feeney, *Gods in Epic*, 114–15.

111. R. M. Ogilvie, *The Romans and their Gods in the Age of Augustus* (London: Chatto & Windus, 1969), 16.

specifically says that the senate ordered a separate temple to be consecrated to Caesar and to his Clemency and appointed Marc Antony as the priest "like some *flamen Dialis* (i.e., special priest of Jupiter)" (*Rom. Hist.* 44.6.4). Caesar's statue, furthermore, was placed in the *cella* or inner sanctum of Jupiter Capitolinus. The statue featured Caesar in his triumphal chariot, with a globe under his feet (*Rom. Hist.* 43.14.6). Gerhard Dobesch interpreted the statue to mean that there was an "identification" (*Identifizierung*) between Julius and Jupiter.[112] Another of Caesar's statues—decked out in Jupiter's triumphal garb—was carried in the procession of the gods in the *pompa circensis* on a special carriage (the *tensa*) that only the Capitoline deities (Jupiter, Juno, and Minerva) possessed. Still another statue of Caesar was placed in the Circus next to the *pulvinar* (divine couch) of the Capitoline gods.[113] In these symbolic acts of state, writes J. R. Fears, "Caesar was equated with the Capitoline Triad, the pre-eminent divine patrons of the community."[114]

Such evidence also implies that Julius—at the time, ruler of the entire Mediterranean world—was recognized as Jupiter's vice-regent. The award of the *tensa*, Fears notes, "was a political statement of monarchy. It heralded the establishment of an earthly master of the Roman commonwealth, who would tend the mortal concerns of the state, assuming those functions which had been the sole preserve of Capitoline Jupiter."[115] Fears also points out that in the coinage of 44 BCE, Jupiter's head, so common on republican *denarii*, was replaced by Caesar's.[116] This evidence does not imply that Caesar replaced Jupiter. Rather, Caesar was thought to be Jupiter's *image* on earth—the man through whom the Roman high God reigned and revealed himself as ruler. Caesar as "Jupiter Julius" does not in fact require an identification between the Roman high God and the deified dictator. It means, rather, that Caesar was

112. Dobesch, *Caesars Apotheose*, 19, 42.

113. Weinstock adds that in the theater, Caesar's golden crown was exhibited on a golden throne apparently in the same manner as the crown of Jupiter (*Divus Julius*, 303).

114. Fears, "Jupiter and Roman Imperial Ideology," 54.

115. Ibid., 54–55.

116. Ibid., 55. Dobesch also thinks it significant that the decrees honoring Caesar, written with gold letters on silver plates, were attached to the pedestal of the statue of Jupiter Capitolinus (Cass. Dio, *Rom. Hist.* 44.7.1) (*Caesars Apotheose*, 19).

viewed as Jupiter's vice-regent.[117] This theology becomes more clear in the case of Caesar's adopted son, Octavian ("Augustus" after 27 BCE).[118]

Weinstock compactly presents the epigraphic evidence for Augustus being called "Zeus."[119] In the provinces, Augustus was "Zeus Aineiades, Zeus Sebastos Kronides, Zeus Eleutherios in Egypt,[120] Zeus Patröos in Asia,[121] Olympius at Athens[122] and in Asia,[123] Iuppiter Augustus at Cyrene[124] and in Dalmatia."[125] In Ovid's *Fasti* we hear that "he [Augustus] has a name that ranks with Jove supreme" (*hic socium summo cum Iove nomen habet*) (1.608, cf. 615). In fact, Ovid directly refers to Augustus as Jupiter: "Livia [Augustus's wife] is the only woman found worthy of the couch of great Jupiter (*magni . . . Iovis*)" (*Fasti* 1.650; cf. *Trist.* 1.4.26), and elsewhere prays directly to Augustus as Jupiter (*Trist.* 5.2.45–47).[126]

---

117. Caesar was connected with Jupiter even in death. The night before he was murdered, Suetonius says that Caesar dreamed that he was exalted above the clouds and clasped hands with Jupiter (*Jul.* 81.3; cf. Cass. Dio, *Rom. Hist.* 44.17.1). The handclasp may have signified that Caesar was fated to share Jove's rule. After Caesar perished, his followers demanded that his body be burned in the cella of Jupiter Capitolinus (Suet., *Jul.* 84.3; cf. Cass. Dio 44.50.2; Appian, *Bell. civ.* 2.615). It may also be significant that two years after Caesar's death, anyone who interfered with the cultic celebration of Caesar's birthday was put under the curse of both Julius and Jupiter (Cass. Dio, *Rom. Hist.* 47.18.5).

118. For acute comments on the relation of Augustus and Jupiter, see Feeney, *Gods in Epic*, 199, 214, 216–17, 219–24. The name "Augustus" itself, since it described "the most precious and sacred objects" (τὰ ἐντιμότατα καὶ τὰ ἱερώτατα) signified that the emperor was "more than human" (πλεῖον τι ἢ κατὰ ἀνθρώπους) (Cass. Dio, *Rom. Hist.* 53.16.8).

119. Weinstock, *Divus Julius*, 304–05.

120. See further Herklotz, *Prinzeps und Pharao*, 256–61.

121. V. Ehrenberg and A. H. M. Jones, *Documents Illustrating the Reigns of Augustus and Tiberius* (Oxford: Clarendon, 1955) §98a; *IGR* §4.1410; 1608; 522. See further W. H. Buckler, "Auguste, Zeus Patroos," *Revue de Philologie* 9 (1935): 177–88 (186). Also in Asia Minor, we possess a dedication dated to 52 CE under Claudius by Eratophanes, a Rhodian living at Cys in Caria. In the inscription, we learn that Eratophanes was the priest of the "god Augustus, Founder of the city, Zeus Eleutherios" (*OGIS* 2.457, p. 48). Simon Price notes that Augustus is given the title of Ancestral Zeus in Antioch, which may suggest an identification. The decree could date from Augustus's lifetime (*Rituals and Power: The Roman Imperial Cult in Asia Minor* [Cambridge: Cambridge University Press, 1984], 76, n. 89).

122. Suet., *Aug.* 60.

123. *IGR* §4.11; 72; 76; 95; *IG* 12; Suppl. 42; 59 (Mytilene); Jos. *BJ* 1.217.414 (Caesarea Philippi).

124. R. G. Goodchild and J. M. Reynolds, "The Temple of Zeus at Cyrene," *Papers of the British School at Rome* 26 (1958): 30–62.

125. H. Dessau, ed., *Inscriptiones Latinae Selectae* (Berlin: Wiedmanns, 1892–1916), 3088: *Iovi Augusto* ("to Augustus Jove"). For further discussion of Augustus as Jupiter, see Martin, *L'Idée de Royauté*, 432–34; and especially M. Ward, "The Association of Augustus with Jupiter," *Studi e Materiali di Storia delle Religioni* 9 (1933): 203–24 (esp. 216).

Despite the poetic exaggeration, Ovid clarifies that Augustus-as-Jupiter is in actuality Augustus as Jupiter's vice-regent. "Jupiter controls the heights of heaven and the kingdoms of the triformed universe," says Ovid, "but the earth is under Augustus's sway. Each is both sire and ruler" (*pater est et rector uterque*) (*Met.* 15.858-60; Miller, LCL).[127] Augustus's palace is Jupiter's house (*Pont.* 3.1.135-140). His marriage with Livia is parallel with that of Jupiter and Juno (*Fasti* 1.650; *Pont.* 3.1.117). Both share the name of Augustus and *pater* (*Fasti* 2.127-32). In his *Tristia* and *Epistula ex Ponto*, Ovid often compares Augustus's power with that of Jupiter. The poet's banishment by Augustus is likened to being struck by Jupiter's thunderbolt.[128]

Other Augustan poets, such as Propertius, Manilius (*Astron.* 1.799, 1.916), and Virgil also depict Augustus as Jupiter's vice-regent. Horace prays to Jupiter: "Father and protector of the human race, O son of Saturn, you have been entrusted by fate with the care of mighty Caesar; may you have Caesar as vice-regent of your kingdom" (*tu secundo Caesare regnes*) (*Od.* 1.12.49-57, Rudd, LCL; cf. 3.4.42-48). With Caesar as Jove's vice-regent, Augustus obtains command of the entire world: "Whether it be the Parthians (now a threat to Latium) that he [Augustus] conquers and leads in a justified triumph, or the Chinese and Indians who live close to the region of the rising sun," Horace sings, "he will rule in fairness over a happy world, so long as he is subordinate to you [Jupiter]" (*Od.* 1.12; cf. *Carm.*, 3.5.1). We possess an epigram attributed to Virgil, dated to just before the turn of the era: "O Caesar, you administer a common rule with Jove" (*commune imperium cum Iove, Caesar, agis*).[129]

126. Based on his reading of the evidence, in particular Ovid, Manfred Clauss calls Augustus "the human side" of a single divinity he calls "Jupiter-Augustus" (*Kaiser und Gott: Herrscherkult im römischen Reich* [Stuttgart: Teubner, 1999], 248).

127. The triformed universe (*mundi . . . triformis*) is particularly reminiscent of Phil 2:10. Cf. *Met.* 1.168; cf. *Fasti* 3.421; *Trist.* 2.33-40; 2.215-218; *Pont.* 1.1.63; 1.4.55

128. *Trist.* 1.1.81; 2.143; 2.179-81; 3.5.7; 4.5.5; 4.8.45; *Pont.* 1.7.49-50; 3.6.17. See further Kenneth Scott, "Emperor Worship in Ovid," *TAPA* 61 (1930): 53–57. To reduce this language to mere obsequiousness is to misunderstand the power of poetry to reflect popular piety and in turn to shape belief. On this point, note Hartwig Heckel, "Der Dichter und der Gott: Ovid über die Göttlichkeit des Augustus," in *Gottmenschen: Konzepte existentieller Grenzüberschreitung im Altertum* (Trier: Wissenschaflicher, 2003), 71–89.

129. Alexander Riese, F. Bueheler, and E. Lommatzsch, eds., *Anthologia Latina sive Poesis Latinae Supplementum*, 2 vols. (Lipsius: Teubner, 1869–1926), 1:179, no. 256. The epigram is cited in Ward who says that it was found on the island of Philae (on the Nile), and dated to ca. 7 BCE. She takes the epigram as evidence of an "identification" of Augustus "with the 'princeps' of the universe" ("Association," 208). For Augustus as Jupiter/Zeus in coins and art, see Fears, "Jupiter and Roman Imperial Ideology"; Paul Zanker, *The Power of Images in the Age of Augustus* (Ann Arbor: University of Michigan, 1988); J. Pollini,

The later emperor Gaius Caligula (ruled 41–37 BCE) stretched the limits of theonymy to the breaking point. Dio Cassius tells us that in the year 40 CE, Gaius began "to pretend that he was Jupiter" (*Rom. Hist.* 59.26.5). He was called "Jupiter" in official documents (γράμματα) (59.28.8; 59.30.1). He assumed Jupiter's most famous epithets, "Optimus Maximus" (Suet., *Calig.* 22.1; cf. Cic., *Rep.* 1.50; 3.23), "Olympius" (Dio Cass., *Rom. Hist.* 59.28.3) and "Jupiter Latiaris" (the protector of the Latin people; Suet., *Calig.* 22.2; Cass. Dio, *Rom. Hist.* 59.28.3). As Jupiter Latiaris, Caligula created for himself his own priesthood, with his uncle Claudius, his wife Caesonia—and himself—as priests (Cass. Dio, *Rom. Hist.* 59.28.5-6). He dressed himself in the guise of various gods (Philo, *Legat.* 93-114), including the one "with a golden beard, holding in his hand a thunderbolt" (Suet., *Calig.* 52.1) and in this guise would receive "supplications, prayers, and sacrifices" (Cass. Dio, *Rom. Hist.* 59.26.10). When Caesonia bore a daughter only a month after their marriage, Gaius said that this had come about through supernatural means. He took the girl up to the Capitol and placed her on the knees of Jupiter, thereby hinting that she was his child. Going beyond his great-grandfather Julius, Gaius even had "a sort of lodge" on the Capitoline, "so that, as he said, he might dwell with Jupiter" (Cass. Dio, *Rom. Hist.* 59.28.3). Nevertheless, he resented the fact that Jupiter occupied the Capitoline ahead of him, and so—according to Suetonius—built a temple to himself on the Palatine. For this temple, he ordered that the famous statue of Jupiter at Olympia be taken apart and reassembled with his own bust (Suet., *Calig.* 22.2). According to Philo (*Legat.* 346), he wished to call the temple in Jerusalem, the shrine "of Gaius, the New Zeus made Manifest" (Διὸς Ἐπιφανοῦς Νέου Γαΐου). In accordance with this plan, he "ordered a colossal statue of himself to be erected in the Holy of Holies, having his own name inscribed upon it with the title of Jupiter" (*Legat.* 188).[130] Here for the first time the imperial likeness to Jupiter and the bearing of his name bridges dangerously into identification.

The emperor Claudius (ruled 41–54 CE), although he deliberately resisted the bestowal of excessive divine honors, continued nonetheless to be called "Zeus." The name appears, for instance, on an inscription in the east, in Acmonia (Phrygia) where Claudius would have had less control of the honors bestowed upon him. It reads: "To Tiberius Claudius Caesar, [and] to

"Man or God: Divine Assimilation and Imitation in the Late Republic and Early Principate," in *Between Republic and Empire: Interpretations of Augustus and His Principate*, ed. Kurt A. Raaflaub, Mark Toher, and G. W. Bowersock (Berkeley: University of California Press, 1990), 334–63 (338).

130. Cf. Jos. *Ant.* 19.1.4; 19.2.11.

Britannicus [son of Claudius], son of the new Zeus (Διὸς νέου) Claudius Caesar Augustus."[131]

Thirteen years after Claudius's death (in November of 67 CE), Nero "liberated" Greece by granting the province of Achaia autonomy and freedom from taxation. Out of gratitude, the town of Acraephia in Boeotia erected an altar with the inscription: "TO NERO-ZEUS LIBERATOR ETERNALLY." Along with the altar, cult statues of "Nero-Zeus Liberator" and the divine Augusta (Nero's wife) were set up in the local temple of Apollo.[132] The assimilation of Nero to Zeus the Liberator also appears on an issue of copper coins struck in Greece.[133] Fears comments, "As Zeus Eleutherios had earlier delivered Greece from peril [in the time of the Persians], so his earthly counterpart Nero now had liberated Greece from her burdens."[134] The poet Calpurnius Siculus writes of Nero: "Whether you are now Jupiter himself (*Iuppiter ipse*) with changed appearance, Caesar, or another of the gods, unknown under a deceiving and mortal image (for you are a god); I pray you, rule this world; I pray you, rule these peoples forever! (*hunc precor, orbem, / hos, precor, aeternum populos rege*)" (*Ecl.* 4.142-45, my trans.). "This dual theme," Fears observes, "the emperor as vicegerent of Jupiter and Jupiter as protector of his vicegerent, were to form the two pillars of a Jovian theology of imperial power at Rome."[135]

Fears's comment is a good summary of the ideological context of the imperial reception of the name "Zeus/Jupiter." In Roman political theology, the emperors were viewed as Jupiter's viceregents.[136] As viceregents, Roman

---

131. E. Mary Smallwood, *Documents Illustrating the Principates of Gaius, Claudius, and Nero* (Cambridge: Cambridge University Press, 1967), 51 no. 138. Caterina Maderna notes that sculptures depicting the emperor as the standing Jupiter reach their acme in the reign of Claudius (*Iuppiter Diomedes und Merkur als Vorbilder für römische Bildnisstatuen: Untersuchungen zum Römischen statuarischen Idealporträt* [Heidelberg: Archäologie und Geschichte, 1988], 24. In her study, Maderna reviews Roman sculpture that conforms the emperor to Zeus in both a standing and an enthroned position (18–49), and gives a brief survey of previous Hellenistic traditions for the conformation of a ruler to Zeus (49–52) (for the art, see esp. plates 6–17). She emphasizes that the emperor depicted in the form of Jupiter is not a strict identification with the Roman high God, but an indication that the emperor served as Jove's representative and vice-regent. She errs, I think, when she denies that such conformation of the emperor to Jove is not a means of deification (38, 41, 43).

132. Smallwood, *Documents*, 35–37 (*ILS* 8794 = *Syll.*[3] 814).

133. Fears, "Jupiter and Roman Imperial Ideology," 71 n. 343.

134. Ibid., 71. Recall that the same name was given to Theophanes of Mytilene.

135. Ibid.

136. For the emperor as Zeus's vice-regent or "earthly counterpart," see ibid., 68–91. The idea that Zeus gave regency to his elect is an idea found as far back as Homer. Odysseus says to the Danaan troops:

emperors received the name of the king of gods in the Roman pantheon—Jupiter (the Greek Zeus).[137] Such a practice constituted a divine honor, and part of a series of honors that was part and parcel of the deification of emperors in the ancient Mediterranean world.[138]

RESULTS

What are the implications of these data for understanding the bestowal of the proper name of God on Jesus in Phil. 2:9b? Although Isa. 45:23 ("To me [Yahweh-κύριος] every knee shall bow, every tongue shall swear"), stands behind Phil. 2:9b, it cannot fully explain Jesus' reception of the divine name. Indeed, Isa. 45:23 does not speak of the bestowal of a divine name at all. Such a tradition was not native to Israelite and later Jewish culture. It seems likely, then, that the tradition of theonymy reflected in Phil. 2:9-10 was adapted from the imperial conventions of the larger (Mediterranean) culture contemporary with the author of the hymn.

Imperial theonymy was widespread in the ancient Mediterranean world. It was in Asia that Augustus Caesar was called "Zeus Patröos"; it was in Boeotia that Nero was called "Zeus Eleutherios"; and it was in Jerusalem that Gaius threatened to set up an image of himself as the "New Zeus made manifest." We even possess an inscription from Arabia in which the Nabataean King Obodas I (ruled c. 93–85 BCE) is called "Zeus Obodas" (in the vocative Ζεῦ ᾿Οβοδα).[139] Given the extent of the practice, we may presume that its meaning was widely understood in Greco-Roman culture.[140] The Philippians who lived in a Roman colony are even more likely to have been familiar with the custom and its significance.[141]

"The rule of the many is not well. One must be chief in war, and one the king, to whom the son of Cronus, crafty in counsel, the scepter gives" (*Il.* 2.204-06).

137. The fundamental idea that Jupiter grants ruling authority appears widely in Roman political writers throughout the first century CE. For Domitian as Zeus's plenipotentiary, see Statius, *Silv.*,1. *praef.*; 1.1.79-81; 1.6.39-50; 4.3.128; 4.4.58; Mart., *Epigr.* 4.8, 7.99. For Trajan, note esp. Pliny Min., *Pan.* 1.5; 5.2-9; 80.4-5; 94.4. Significantly, the Senate also bestowed on Trajan the title *Optimus* (Pliny, *Pan.* 2.7; 88.4), reminiscent of the title of Capitoline Jupiter (*Optimus Maximus*). Pliny draws this connection in *Pan.* 88.7-9,

138. For a similar practice in the late third century, see Roger Rees, "The Emperor's New Names: Diocletian Jovius and Maximian Herculius," in *Herakles and Hercules: Exploring a Graeco-Roman Divinity*, ed. Louis Rawlings and Hugh Bowden (Swansea: Classical Press of Wales, 2005), 223–39. Rees does not view "Diocletian Jovius" as the reception of a divine name, but a *signum*, "a name type of rather informal status" which allowed an association with Jupiter (224).

139. A. Negev et al., "Obodas the God," *IEJ* 36 (1986) 56–60 [esp. 59–60]. His cult continued until the third century CE.

The diffusion of the tradition, however, does not amount to a genetic relation. We cannot assume, that is, that the author of Phil. 2:6-11 borrowed from a *specific* instance of theonymy. Nor should we assume that the author of the hymn merely aped imperial convention in general. What we find in verses 9-11 is an instance of theonymy fully appropriated and organically part of a larger Christian story. This larger story, moreover, does not much resemble the content of imperial biographies. The emperors were not typically viewed as incarnations of a preexistent divinity. They never suffer on a cross (Phil. 2:6-8). Nor do they receive Zeus's name only after their death.

Apart from obvious differences between Christ and the Caesars, however, there remains a common meaning underlying the two traditions of theonymy. In the first century CE, hellenized peoples around the Mediterranean employed theonymy as a way to deify their emperor—that is, to integrate the emperor into the larger cult of Greco-Roman Gods (with Zeus generally acknowledged as the high God). I believe that a similar function underlies the use of theonymy in Phil. 2:9-11. In a culture featuring other deities and deified men, the author of this text did not need to invent out of whole cloth a new vocabulary to express Jesus' divinity and promotion to become God's vice-regent. The writer could employ the widespread encomiastic practice of theonymy, whose implications were widely understood. This time, however, the one deified was not Rome's supreme commander, but that "other emperor . . . Jesus" (βασιλέα ἕτερον . . . Ἰησοῦν) (Acts 17:7).

One might argue that Jesus' deification is unique because he does not become an independent god, but is integrated into the preexistent deity of Yahweh.[142] Nevertheless, the idea of being integrated into the deity of a pre-established god is precisely what Greco-Roman theonymy implies. In Greek ruler cult, Augustus (or any Roman emperor) is also not an independent god.[143]

140. The provenance of the hymn writer is unknown. If there was truly an Aramaic *Vorlage* behind the hymn (on which see J. A. Fitzmyer, "The Aramaic Background of Philippians 2:6-11," *CBQ* 50 [1988]: 470–83), a Syrian or Palestinian provenance seems to be the best guess.

141. "For the people in Philippi the most significant factor in life historically and socially was probably Roman rule and ordering of society" (Reumann, *Philippians*, 365).

142. Notes esp. Bauckham, *Jesus and the God of Israel*, 1–59.

143. The idea of deification by association with a pre-established god is widespread in the imperial cult. The idea is best exemplified by the practice of temple sharing. Emperors did not typically have their own temples, but were made "co-templar" (σύνναος) with another deity (often a local Greek deity). Such a practice expressed both the subordination of the emperor to the major deity and the emperor's deification. See further Price, *Rituals and Power*, 146–69; Maria Kantiréa, *Les dieux et les dieux augustes: Le culte impérial en Grèce sous les Julio-claudiens et les Flaviens* (Athens: Center for Hellenic and Roman Antiquity, 2007), 125–58.

Rather, he is integrated into the deity of the king God, Zeus. "For Zeus the son of Cronos has care over august kings," wrote Theocritus (*Idyll*. 17.73-74). Zeus's divine power was already universally lauded in the Greco-Roman world. If Roman emperors could share his name, they could also share his ruling power—the culminating expression of his divinity.[144]

The author of Phil. 2:6-11 knew, presumably, that those who bear a particular god's name also bear that god's status. Just as the emperors exercised world sovereignty as plenipotentiaries of Zeus, so the exalted Jesus obtained Yahweh's name as Yahweh's cosmic vice-regent.[145] Such vice-regency implies a divine status, and depicting Jesus in a divine status amounts to a deification. The living emperor who bore the name of Zeus was worshiped in a host of cities as he was integrated into the cults of local gods. Jesus who received the name of Yahweh was worshiped by all three tiers of the cosmos (Phil. 2:10-11). The three tiers may signify a touch of one-upmanship on the part of early Christians. The Roman emperor was lord only of those on earth. Yahweh-Jesus is thus revealed as the true deity.[146]

Despite the high status of Christ and his imperial competitors, in both traditions the ultimate glory is directed to the supreme God. Horace addressed his fellow citizens (notably Augustus): "You rule, Roman, because you keep yourself lesser than the Gods: with them all things begin, to them refer each outcome" (*Odes* 3.6.5-6). Despite all the bold adulation bestowed upon the emperor, Rome's kings remained Jupiter's vice-regents, integrated into a larger state cult presided over by Jupiter Optimus Maximus. Those emperors (such as Caligula) who did not play by the rules of this theology were assassinated and suffered *damnatio memoriae*.

144. Admittedly, Zeus is not a monotheistic God. But monotheism is not absolute, but relative (Litwa, *We Are Being Transformed*, 229–57). On monotheistic developments outside Judaism, note Polymnia Athanassiadi and Michael Frede, eds., *Pagan Monotheism in Late Antiquity* (Oxford: Clarendon, 1999); Stephen Mitchell and Peter van Nuffelen, eds., *One God: Pagan Monotheism in the Roman Empire* (Cambridge: Cambridge University Press, 2010).

145. Adela Yarbro Collins notes that one of "the most striking similarities between the worship of Jesus and the cult of the emperor is the way in which each, as a divine being, is closely associated with a full deity" ("Worship of Jesus and Imperial Cult," in *The Jewish Roots of Christological Monotheism: Papers from the St. Andrews Conference on the Historical Origins of the Worship of Jesus*, eds. Carey C. Newman, James R. Davila, and Gladys S. Lewis [Leiden: Brill, 1999], 249).

146. Cf. Ovid, *Met.* 15.858-60, cited above.

EXCURSUS: ANTI-IMPERIALISM?

Although the intentions of the original composer of Phil. 2:6-11 are buried in obscurity, some might speculate that Paul inserted this hymn into his letter with a distinctly anti-imperial motive. Today, anti-imperial readings of Matthew, Paul, Luke, and Revelation are much in vogue.[147] Thomas Phillips notes that "the theology in Paul's letters certainly competed with many of the empire's claims of ultimacy and that Paul himself probably viewed many of the empire's claims as blasphemous." Despite the theological conflicts, however, Phillips rightly asserts that "Paul's letters probably were not shaped in conscious opposition to the Roman Empire." Rather, his theology was "shaped with its own theological and ideological agendas in mind and should not be read primarily as a reaction to some external force or influence."[148] Moreover, Leif E. Vaage observes that since Paul's very language of opposition to empire was "derived from the discourse of empire, the long-term legacy of such speech could hardly be anything other than a recurrence of the same."[149] If Paul (who transmits Phil. 2:6-11) opposed imperial ideology, he also re-inscribed it in an attempt to exalt Jesus over the imperial gods of his day. Again, we see the same pattern emerge that we saw in other chapters: Christians compete with perceived cultural rivals, but in the very thick of that competition they assimilate and appropriate cultural ideas to promote the unique deity of their

---

147. See, e.g., Warren Carter, *Matthew and Empire: Initial Explorations* (Harrisburg, PA: Trinity Press International, 2001); Carter, *Matthew and the Margins* (Maryknoll, NY: Orbis Books, 2001); Carter, ed., *Paul and Empire* (Harrisburg, PA: Trinity Press International, 1997); Richard Horsley, ed., *Paul and Politics* (Harrisburg, PA: Trinity Press International, 2000); Horsley, ed., *Paul and the Roman Imperial Order* (Harrisburg, PA: Trinity Press International, 2004); Bradly S. Billings, "'At the Age of 12': The Boy Jesus in the Temple (Luke 2:41-52), the Emperor Augustus, and the Social Setting of the Third Gospel," *JTS* 60 (2009): 70–89; C. Kavin Rowe, "Luke-Acts and the Imperial Cult: A Way Through the Conundrum?" *JSNT* 27 (2005): 279–300; Seyoon Kim, *Christ and Caesar: The Gospel and the Roman Empire in the Writings of Paul and Luke* (Grand Rapids, MI: Eerdmans, 2008); Kazuhiko Yamazaki-Ransom, *The Roman Empire in Luke's Narrative*, LNTS 421 (New York: T&T Clark, 2010); Leonard L. Thompson, *The Book of Revelation: Apocalypse and Empire* (Oxford: Oxford University Press, 1990); and Steven Friesen, "Satan's Throne, Imperial Cults and the Social Settings of Revelation," *JSNT* 27 (2005): 351–73.

148. Thomas Phillips, "Why Did Mary Wrap the Newborn Jesus in 'Swaddling Clothes'? Luke 2.7 and 2.12 in the Context of Luke-Acts and First-century Jewish Literature," in *Reading Acts Today: Essays in Honour of Loveday C. A. Alexander*, ed. Steve Walton et al., LNTS 427 (London: T&T Clark, 2011), 29–42 (41); see further Phillips, *Paul, His Letters, and Acts* (Peabody, MA: Hendrickson), 97–104.

149. Vaage, "Why Christianity Succeeded (in) the Roman Empire," in *Religious Rivalries in the Early Roman Empire and the Rise of Christianity*, ed. Leif Vaage (Waterloo: Wilfrid Laurier University Press, 2006), 253–78 (278).

lord. In the judgment of Karl Galinsky, "Paul's message is not *anti*-imperial, but *supra*imperial: the emperor and the dispensations of empire go only so far. They are surpassed, in a far more perfect way, by God and the kingdom of heaven."[150]

CONCLUSION

The use of theonymy in Phil. 2:9-11 undercuts Hengel's claim that "the official-profane state religion was at best a negative offense [for early christology], not a model."[151] Offense versus model is a false opposition. Christians are all the more likely to competitively assimilate to a perceived contender in the "market" of deification—as indeed the emperor was. In the end, both Christ and the Caesars share the high God's power in perhaps the closest possible way—*by sharing his name*. "A name," writes Tryggve N. D. Mettinger, "establishes and manifests a person's identity."[152] If Augustus-Zeus and Yahweh-Jesus were not equivalent to the high God, they were, as God's vice-regents, made sharers of his divine status.

In the Greco-Roman world, the tradition of theonymy implied deification. The deifying implications of theonymy, I believe, were assumed and exploited by early Christians who exalted Jesus in their liturgy and literature. Jesus, by virtue of the name that he inherited, became far greater than the angels (Heb. 1:4). When he was resurrected, he received "all power in heaven and on earth" (Matt. 28:18). After his ascension, all beings on every tier of creation bowed the knee to him (Phil. 2:10-11). In the framework of Mediterranean culture—as well as the narrative frame of Phil. 2:9-11 itself—Jesus had become God's vice-regent and a god himself.

---

150. Karl Galinsky, "In the Shadow (or not) of the Imperial Cult: A Cooperative Agenda," in *Rome and Religion: A Cross-Disciplinary Dialogue on the Imperial Cult*, eds. Jeffrey Brodd and Jonathan L. Reed (Atlanta: Society of Biblical Literature, 2011), 215–25 (222).

151. Martin Hengel, *Der Sohn Gottes: Die Entstehung der Christologie und die jüdisch-hellenistische Religionsgeschichte*, 2nd ed (Tübingen: Mohr Siebeck, 1977), 50 ("*Die offiziell-profane Staatsreligion war bestenfalls negative Anstoss, nicht Vorbild.*")

152. Mettinger, *In Search of God: The Meaning and Message of the Everlasting Names*, trans. Frederick H. Cryer (Philadelphia: Fortress Press, 1987), 1. Wilhelm Heitmüller went much further: "The name is the source of power and destiny (*Kraft- und Geschicks-Quelle*) for its bearer. With the change of the name, one's essence and destiny also changes" (*Im Namen Jesu: Eine sprach-u.religionsgeschichtliche Untersuchung zum Neuen Testament* [Göttingen: Vandenhoeck & Ruprecht, 1903], 161; evidence on 160–76).

Conclusion

"[T]he Divine Sonship of Christ . . . in some sense or other . . . is the common property of the religious humanity of all ages; in general, therefore, it has its ultimate source in the depths of the religious consciousness, in mankind's natural surmise that we are of divine descent, a surmise which has been everywhere awakened by the observation of the extraordinary gifts and deeds of particular men, and therefore has at first been connected with those elect heroes of knowledge and power who stand as the representatives and sureties of the close relationship of our common human nature with the divine."

—OTTO PFLEIDERER[1]

In this study I have made the claim that early Christians imagined and depicted Jesus with some of the basic traits common to other Mediterranean divinities and deified men. In Mary's womb, Jesus is conceived from divine pneuma and power (ch. 1). As a child, he kills and punishes to defend his own honor (ch. 2). During his ministry, he proves himself to be the ultimate (moral) benefactor (ch. 3). In his transfiguration, he shines with the brilliance of deity (ch. 4). When he rises, his body is immortalized and ascends on a cloud (ch. 5). After his exaltation, he receives the name of the most high God (ch. 6). All these traditions are genuinely Christian, but all of them have analogues in the larger Mediterranean culture and to a great extent assume their meaning from that culture. What they indicate is that in Christian literature, the historical human being called Jesus of Nazareth received deification.

Throughout this study, I have not engaged in cross-cultural comparison, but in *intra*-cultural comparison. That is, I have focused on how early Christians employed and adapted ideas in the dominant (Hellenistic) culture for their construction of Jesus' deity. Ironically, the distance between Europe and Iran or America and Africa often seems less than that between Athens and Jerusalem. This is because for centuries Christians have constructed massive ideological bulwarks protecting their faith from the great, Protean "other" called

---

1. Otto Pfleiderer, *The Early Christian Conception of Christ: Its Significance and Value in the History of Religion* (London: Williams & Norgate, 1905), 156.

"paganism." In Late Antiquity, so-called "pagans" did the same when they claimed the heritage of "Hellenism" only for themselves. In scholarship, it has taken decades of labor to undermine and tear down these dividing walls, built from the brick and mortar of apologetics and—ultimately—threatened self-definition.

This study stands as a single brick in the ongoing project of constructing and reconstructing early christology. I do not claim to provide an omni-competent explanation for early Christian assertions of Jesus' deity. My aim has been more modest: to restore balance to scholarship by understanding the nature and meaning of Jesus' divinity firmly in its ancient Mediterranean context. Since the horrors of the Holocaust, Judaism has gradually attained a kind of privileged status as the primary *comparandum* for early Christianity.[2] Many scholars working today (including myself) welcome this development. Appreciating the value of Judaism, however, does not mean that the Jewish religious matrix should be exalted to become virtually the sole touchstone for understanding early christology (and Jesus' deity in particular). The dismantling of the Judaism/Hellenism divide calls for a new understanding of Judaism as part of a larger world, and for Jews as participants in a larger culture. The distinctives of Judaism and its daughter (or sister) Christianity must not only be valued, but understood as formed in dialogic contact with the many perceived (and sometimes invented) religious "others" of Mediterranean antiquity.

Regrettably, for some scholars, lack of full engagement with the broader Mediterranean world is due to a simplistic notion of historical influence. Such influence, it is often assumed, designates some type of genetic connection or borrowing. Christians, it is often contended, could not have borrowed from the "pagan other," whom Christian scholars (ancient and modern) find furtive and learned ways to deride and downplay. "It is as if," writes J. Z. Smith, "the only choices the comparativist has are to assert either identity or uniqueness, and that the only possibilities for utilizing comparisons are to make assertions regarding dependence.... The thought appears to be that, from a standpoint of protecting

---

2. For a brief review of the post-Holocaust change in sensibilities, see Bruce Chilton and Jacob Neusner, *Types of Authority in Formative Christianity and Judaism* (New York: Routledge, 1999), ix–x; Clark M. Williamson, *A Guest in the House of Israel: Post-Holocaust Church Theology* (Louisville: Westminster John Knox, 1993), esp. ch. 7 "Christology," 167–201. Martin Hengel in particular made clear that it was his experience growing up in Nazi Germany that fostered in him a counter-response to anti-Jewish scholarship. This counter-response, mixed with diligent study, led him to the conclusion that "early Christianity was almost wholly dependent on Jewish thought and tradition" and that the "fundamental teaching of the church was built on basically Jewish foundations" ("A Gentile in the Wilderness," in *Kleine Schriften VII*, 542).

the privileged position of early Christianity, it is only genealogical comparisons that are worthy of note, if only, typically, insistently to be denied."[3] It does not matter which sector of the Christian movement the scholar comes from—there remains a confessional pressure to argue that the forefathers of christology could only have adapted their theological raw materials from the Jews, who—in the early days at least—were not perceived as "other" and could thus provide a buffer to the "pagan" threat.

Given current levels of historical knowledge, "borrowing" (even if highly creative) cannot be viewed as the primary model of historical influence. Today scholars generally recognize that most genetic links between ideas are often impossible to trace (or test) due to the complexity of cultural interaction and the shear inventiveness of the human mind. The logic of influence ought instead to be rooted in a pervasive and assertive Hellenistic culture that tended to foster shared notions of divine traits in the minds of ancient Romans, Jews, Syrians, Phrygians, Samaritans, and the many other Hellenized ἔθνη.

Today, there continues to be a wariness about such comparison because of its past superficiality and lack of concrete specificity. Scholars of the (old) Religionsgeschichtliche Schule were known to blithely hop from text to text, displaying putative parallels, all the while paying scarce attention to either provenance or date. Comparisons were often based on "the co-occurrence of a single word or a single image, largely shorn of all context, be it historical or literary."[4] Every text and ritual was assumed to float in one gigantic river of tradition, and there was insufficient attention to socio-historical and conceptual difference. Such comparisons always appeared theologically problematic since even the scholars who valued the "Greek" tradition as the true heritage of Western civilization still depicted the confluence of Mediterranean religions and Christianity as the latter's pollution.[5] Such discourse reinstantiated old Protestant anti-Catholic charges about the paganization of Christianity after "the Apostolic Age" and the subsequent emergence of the monstrous product of syncretism early Protestants called "pagano-papism."[6]

---

3. Smith, *Drudgery Divine* (Chicago: Chicago University Press, 1990), 47–48.

4. Ibid., 25.

5. Ibid., 10–11.

6. Documented with bibliography in ibid., 13–35; cf. Smith, *To Take Place: Toward Theory in Ritual* (Chicago: University of Chicago Press, 1987), 96–101. Some Jewish scholars also argued that Christianity was paganized (Susannah Heschel, "Jewish Studies as Counterhistory," *Insider/Outsider: American Jewish & Multiculturalism*, ed. D. Biale et al. (Berkeley: University of California Press, 1998), 101–15 (102, 108).

To avoid superficial comparison, the studies contained in this book have focused on ideas about divinity that are fairly narrow in scope. They are drawn from a limited number of texts that are not wildly different in date and provenance. Also, care has been taken to ensure that the Greco-Roman texts employed do not date significantly later than the Christian *comparanda*. When a plethora of Greco-Roman texts are cited, it is meant to give a sense of the commonplace nature of an idea—not to indicate genetic links between texts. The whole point has been to provide in-depth and thoughtful comparisons with attention to similarities and due acknowledgement of differences.

If the focused nature of these comparisons leave me open to the charge of narrowness, I offer the sage words of F. J. P Poole: "Comparison does not deal with phenomena *in toto* or in the round, but only with an aspectual characteristic of them."[7] To allow the fullest level of magnification, ideas compared must be sliced thin enough to enclose in a cover slip and slide under a microscope. In this study, I have examined Greco-Roman and Christian conceptions of divinity based on fairly narrow themes and traditions: divine conception, the punitive protection of honor, superhuman benefaction, epiphanic manifestation, corporeal immortalization, and the reception of a proper divine name.

Historically speaking, the Christian application of these divine traits to Jesus in their literature can be redescribed as his "deification." Jesus' divinity may have existed before our world began—but (given our historical existence) the notion of his divinity had to be conceived and propagated by human communities. Early Christians, with both creativity and competitiveness, applied marks of divinity widely accepted in Mediterranean culture to Jesus. In this sense, then, Christians "constructed" his divinity for their communities. The early Christian writings I have discussed in this study are the artifacts of this construction.

If becoming a Christian in the ancient world cut one off from other Mediterranean cults, it did not cut one off from Mediterranean culture. Narrative traits like divine conception and epiphany would not, given widespread Hellenistic sensibilities, have been viewed as any more "pagan" than Christian. Christians did not eschew the notion of corporeal immortalization as something "other" and thus tainted. Although part of the broad tradition of Greco-Roman deification, corporeal immortalization was an appropriate way for them to depict the resurrection of their own lord. Similarly, Origen does not deny that superhuman benefaction is basic to godhood—he exploits it for his

---

7. F. J. P Poole, "Metaphors and Maps: Towards Comparison in the Anthropology of Religion," *JAAR* 54 (1986): 411–57 (414, cf. 420).

own apologetic ends. The author of Philippians 2:6-11 does not shun theonymy because it was associated with Roman emperor worship. He embraces it as an effective means of declaring the perceived unique divinity of his lord.[8]

Scholars have long argued that despite these analogies, Jesus' story nonetheless remains unique, and thus incomparable. In *Der Sohn Gottes*, for instance, Martin Hengel threw down the gauntlet and challenged any scholar to find a preexistent *Mittlergestalt* sent into the world to be crucified for human redemption. The very uniqueness of this Christian story (which Hengel subtly elided with *his*tory) is assumed to be the seal and guarantee of its truth. One can agree with Hengel that if one wishes to find a parallel to Jesus who is "identical with a divine being before all time, a mediator between God and his creation," one can fruitfully look to the figure of Wisdom in Hellenistic Judaism, or Jacob in the *Prayer of Joseph*.[9] The point of this study, however, is not to hunt for an exact narrative parallel matching Jesus' story from pre-incarnational form to post-ascension glory. In general, I have compared ideas of divinity, not *stories* of divinities.

Bracketing for the moment the immensely diverse ways in which Jesus' story was told, Hengel was surely correct to highlight its narrative singularity. No other Mediterranean narrative of a god or deified man corresponds point by point to the narrative sequence of Jesus' story (in all its variants). No amalgamation of Greco-Roman motifs, no motley patchwork of mythic fragments or bevy of type-scenes can be sewn together to give us a story, pre-Christian or post-Christian, of an incarnate and crucified Jewish savior, who now "sitteth at the right hand of God the Father."

One must understand, however, the kind of uniqueness that narrative uniqueness represents. In the words of J. Z. Smith:

> There is a quite ordinary sense in which the term 'unique' may be applied in disciplinary contexts. When the historian speaks of unique events, the taxonomist of the unique *differentium* that allows

---

8. Compare the conclusion of Hengel: "No matter how rigorously Judaism had marked off its veneration of God from 'alien worship' (especially since the time of the Maccabees), there could arise cult-motifs from alien spheres in Palestinian Judaism as well as in early Christianity. One need not necessarily have to speak of a pagan influence directly and consciously taken over, or of missionary adaptation" ("The Dionysiac Messiah," in *Studies in Early Christology* (Edinburgh: T&T Clark, 1995), 293–331 [331]).

9. Hengel, *Der Sohn Gottes*, 30–31. On deriving a parallel *Mittlervorstellung* from Judaism, see 137. Hengel treats the figure of Wisdom at some length (78–82) with some very brief observations on Jacob in the *Prayer of Joseph* (76–7).

the classification of this or that plant' or animal species, the geographer of the unique physiognomy of a particular place, or the linguist of each human utterance as unique, he or she is asserting a reciprocal notion which confers no special status . . . In such formulations 'uniqueness' is generic and commonplace rather than being some odd point of pride. In my language, I would prefer, in such instances, the term 'individual', which permits the affirmation of difference while insisting on the notion of belonging to a class.[10]

Following Smith's line of thought, the narrative uniqueness of Jesus is a factor of his individuality; it does not make him an unclassifiable *novum* in Mediterranean literature and culture. The adjective "unique" is equivocal: Jesus' narrative uniqueness (i.e., individuality) does not make him unique (i.e., religiously true or even historically special). The stories of Attis, of Socrates, and of Thomas Jefferson retold by their devotees all have their own unique qualities, events, and sequences of action. In themselves, their distinctive content speaks nothing of an in-breaking of divine revelation. Narrative individuality is indisputable but universal, and thus banal. A more interesting feature of Jesus' stories (and one must emphasize the plural) is how the welter of motifs, attitudes, and narrative elements that scholars now label "Greek," "Roman," and "Jewish" shaped the early Christian experience of Jesus, producing the literary depiction of a genuinely new and singular Mediterranean god: κύριος Ἰησοῦς Χριστός.[11]

It is not my intent to depict early Christians as mere *bricoleurs*, deifying Jesus by pasting together a pastiche of prefabricated ideas about divinity. I fully admit that their applied notions of divinity are threads in larger, distinctively Christian narrative tapestries. These distinctive narratives, I believe, were equally structured by early Christian experience of Jesus' perceived presence (physical and spiritual) after his death—experiences which in turn conditioned new readings of Jewish Scripture. Ultimately, however, both Christian experience of Jesus and Christian readings of Scripture were conditioned by cultural patterns of thought about the nature and character of divinity. Such is the hermeneutical circle.

10. Smith, *Drudgery Divine*, 36–7.

11. If the so-called "Christ event" is a matter of early Christian experience, one cannot dispute its uniqueness (in the sense of its superlative value) for early (and contemporary) Christians. One can show, however, how experience is culturally shaped by commonplace Mediterranean ideas of (in this case) the divine and how humans are deified. It is no doubt surprising that early Christians chose to depict a "crucified god." On the other hand, as Origen shows us, Jesus' death on the cross features nothing unworthy of a Greco-Roman god (see ch. 3).

Given the early and pervasive hellenization of Judaism, one can ask exactly how early Christians came to view Jesus as a deity. In older scholarship under the influence of Adolf von Harnack, it was assumed that Jesus' deification was a product of late hellenization, when the church became mostly Gentile.[12] Hengel showed that Christianity was hellenized from the womb and that Jesus was viewed as a deity within the first twenty years of the Christian movement.[13] Larry Hurtado has boldly reduced Hengel's figure of twenty years to three or four.[14] He is confident of this timeframe because he believes that Jesus' deification occurred in a solely Jewish thought world.[15] Interestingly, he places no emphasis on Hengel's other conclusion, that Jews (and thus Jewish Christians) had long been hellenized by the first century. If Hengel is right (as I believe), it was only hellenized Jews who became Christians who in turn began to worship Jesus. If hellenization occurred early, so did Jesus' deification.

To be sure, both "hellenization" and "deification" should always be recognized as etic terms of historical redescription. Ancient Jews would not admit to being hellenized (in our sense); much less would early Christians admit to deifying Jesus. When Christians applied the concepts and (to some degree) the language of deification to their lord, they imagined themselves as faithful to previous tradition as it had been developed and maintained by Jews.[16]

Although one might still appeal to increasing degrees of hellenization in Christianity, this point should not obscure the fact that traditions of deification were applied to Jesus from the very beginning. The practice of theonymy, so intertwined with imperial theology, was part of the earliest recoverable christology (Phil. 2:9-11). Mark's transfiguration story, composed in the mid-first century, presents Jesus with the key epiphanic earmarks of divinity (cf. 2

---

12. See further William Rowe, "Adolf von Harnack and the Concept of Hellenization," in *Hellenization Revisited: Shaping a Christian Response within the Greco-Roman World*, ed. Wendy E. Helleman (Lanham, MD: University Press of America, 1994), 69–98.

13. Hengel, *Der Sohn Gottes*, 11, cf. 92. See his earlier essay "Christologie und neutestamentliche Chronologie: Zu einer Aporie in der Geschichte des Urchristentums," in *Neues Testament und Geschichte: Historisches Geschehen und Deutung im Neuen Testament*, eds. Heinrich Baltensweiler and Bo Reicke (Zürich: Theologischer, 1972), 43–67.

14. Larry Hurtado, *How on Earth did Jesus Become a God? Historical Questions about Earliest Devotion to Jesus* (Grand Rapids, MI: Eerdmans, 2005), 33.

15. Hurtado, *Lord Jesus Christ: Jesus in Earliest Christian Devotion* (Grand Rapids, MI: Eerdmans, 2003), 3, 7, 135–7, *passim*.

16. Patristic writers later adopted and adapted the explicit language of deification—this time not in reference to Christ but to Christians (see Norman Russell, *The Doctrine of Deification in the Greek Patristic Tradition* [Oxford: Oxford University Press, 2004]). Even in light of these explicit doctrines of deification, however, patristic writers would have generally denied Greek ("pagan") influence.

Cor. 4:6; Acts 9:3-9; 22:6-16; 26:13-18). Luke depicts at some length both Jesus' divine conception and ascent to heaven. Both Luke and John underline Jesus' corporeal immortalization. The early (i.e., first century) deification of Jesus is sound history. It does not, however, undermine the fact that deification as a process occurred both early and late, over a long period of Christian history. Indeed, the process of depicting Jesus with the (ever evolving) nature and qualities of divinity continues in our time.

In *Der Sohn Gottes*, Hengel wished to tie together history and theology in the investigation of early christology. The historian, he said, misses the "essence" (*Wesen*) of christology when he does not understand its theological intents and "inner consequences."[17] I agree that scholars can fruitfully make use of theological understandings to deepen their historical investigations. Hengel's problem is not that he brings to bear theological insights, but that he leaves these insights behind when treating non-Christian materials. Over and over again in *Der Sohn Gottes*, he misses the meaning and potential of Greco-Roman theologies for shedding light on early Christian christologies. Although Hengel obviously sympathized with Christian theological sentiments, he had a tin ear for the theological intents and "inner consequences" of Greco-Roman traditions. By his zeal to protect Christianity from the "pagan" world, his attempts at comparison in *Der Sohn Gottes* lack sympathy, depth, and imagination. In the end, he uses an old apologetic tactic: compare in order to deny comparison.[18]

As a Christian historian, Hengel followed the lead of early Christian texts. Throughout this study I have observed how early Christians, in applying commonly accepted divine traits to Jesus, consistently played the game of apologetic one-upmanship. Hengel (and others) recognized the theological

---

17. Hengel, *Der Sohn Gottes*, 5, cf. 17. For Hengel the theologian, see Roland Deines, "Martin Hengel—a Life in the Service of Christology," *TynBul* 58 (2007): 25–42. Deines points out that Hengel "himself has made no secret of the fact" that though a historian, he "sees himself first and foremost as a theologian. Correspondingly, he views New Testament scholarship as a theological discipline. . . . In his works he was and is concerned not with one truth among many but with the one Truth, which makes the sinner into a righteous person and appoints the lost person to eternal life for Jesus Christ's sake" (30). Hengel himself argued that "our [New Testament] discipline should always also be understood as 'ecclesial studies'" ("A Young Theological Discipline in Crisis," in *Earliest Christian History: History, Literature, and Theology*, eds. Michael F. Bird and Jason Maston; WUNT 2/320; Tübingen: Mohr Siebeck, 2012], 459–72, esp. 471, emphasis his) and argues against "a non-binding religious pluralism" that removes theology from New Testament studies (463).

18. "The display of history of religions parallels," Hengel says, "ever heightens the consciousness of distance and the newness that broke out in early Christianity" (*Der Sohn Gottes*, 137) J. Z. Smith harshly calls this method of comparison "exorcism or purgation, not scholarship" (*Drudgery*, 143).

intent of his own literature (christological uniqueness), but mistook it for historical fact. Both Hengel and his theological ancestors had the same goal: to construct and maintain Christian identity on the church's sole foundation: a divine Jesus (1 Cor. 3:11).

It is sometimes stated or assumed that Christians eventually "won" the game of theological one-upmanship: the other gods died.[19] But the so-called "triumph" of the divine Jesus was at least partially a triumph of creative—and sometimes unconscious—assimilation. In Christian writings—indeed, in the person of Jesus himself—the theology of the Greeks and Romans did not die. In Christ, it rose again.

In closing, I recognize that comparison is no neutral instrument. In the hands of a Celsus, it can be used to de-legitimate a confessional portrait of Jesus—showing how he is just like any other Mediterranean deity. In the hands of Christian apologists, the very same comparative techniques can be shifted toward asserting the final difference of Jesus—exalting him far above contemporary competitors.[20] Both kinds of comparison, driven as they are by ideology and religious necessities, are often culpably selective and disappointingly shallow since they tell us more about contemporary "theo-politics" than about historical phenomena. Controlled by outside concerns and interreligious competition, comparison becomes either a sword cutting Jesus off from his environment or a cudgel beating down the proud head mouthing the "I am" of religious superiority.

As one of the many historians chastened by postmodernism, I know that I am not innocent of ideology. But as a confessed lover of Christian theology and a historical critic, I must acknowledge that I feel no conscious urge to "de-legitimate" Jesus (as if an academic study could aim so high). But neither do I feel the urge to celebrate his utter uniqueness and superiority. I frankly confess that it is the pitiless gadfly of curiosity that drives me on and gives me hope that genuine understanding can be generated out of comparisons at once honest and deep. I dare say that in contemporary scholarship many of our comparative

---

19. Note the interesting but dangerously simplistic study of Rodney Stark, *The Triumph of Christianity: How the Jesus Movement Became the World's Largest Religion* (New York: HarperOne, 2011).

20. Gerald Seelig's *Religionsgeschichtliche Methode* tells the story not of the *Religionsgeschichtliche Schule* as a whole, but how what one might call its conservative wing (represented by Georg Heinrici, Wilhelm Heitmüller, Ernst von Dobschütz, and Adolf Deissmann) sought for Greco-Roman parallels to early Christianity in order to show the superiority of the latter. Hengel's *Der Sohn Gottes* firmly belongs to this tradition of comparison.

swords have already been beaten into plowshares, with the result that we now have the appropriate frame of mind to cultivate the soil of ancient texts and artifacts in order to produce that succulent (if dangerous) fruit of knowledge with all the fairness and empathy to which human nature can attain.

Bibliography

PRIMARY SOURCES

Aelian. Translated by Nigel G. Wilson et al. 5 vols. Loeb Classical Library. Cambridge, MA: Harvard University Press, 1949–1997.

Apollonius Rhodius. *Argonautica*. Translated by William H. Race. Loeb Classical Library. Cambridge, MA: Harvard University Press, 2009.

Appian. *Roman History*. Translated by Horace White. 3 vols. Loeb Classical Library.

Apuleius. *Apulei Platonici Madaurensis Opera Quae Supersunt*. Edited by C. Moreschini. 3 vols. Vol. 3, *De Philosophia Libri*. Bibliotheca scriptorum Graecorum et Romanorum Teubneriana. Stuttgart: Teubner, 1991.

———. *Rhetorical Works*. Translated by Stephen Harrison, John Hilton, and Vincent Hunink. Oxford: Oxford University Press, 2001.

Aristophanes. Translated by Jeffrey Henderson. Loeb Classical Library. Cambridge, MA: Harvard University Press, 1936–2008.

Aristotle. Translated by H. Rackham et al. 23 vols. Loeb Classical Library. Cambridge, MA: Harvard University Press, 1926–2011.

Arnobius of Sicca. *The Case Against the Pagans*. Translated by George E. McCracken. 2 vols. Ancient Christian Writers 7–8. Westminster, MS: Newman, 1949.

———. *Contre les Gentils. Livre I*. Edited by Henri Le Bonniec. Paris. Les Belles Lettres, 1982.

Arrian. Translated by P. A. Brunt. 2 vols. Loeb Classical Library. Cambridge, MA: Harvard University Press, 1976.

Athenaeus. *The Learned Banqueters*. Edited and translated by S. Douglas Olson. 4 vols. Loeb Classical Library. Cambridge, MA: Harvard University Press, 2006.

Augustine. *The City of God*. Translated by Marcus Dods. New York: Modern Library, 1994.

Boeckhio, Augusto, and Ioannes Franzius, eds. *Corpus Inscriptionum Graecarum*. 4 vols. Berlin: Officina Academica, 1853.

Bormann, Eugene, William Henzen, and Christian Hvelsen, eds. *Corpus Inscriptionum Latinarum: Inscriptiones Urbis Romae Latinae*. Vol. 6. 3rd part. Berlin: George Reimerum, 1886.

Buecheler, Francis, and E. Lommatzsch, eds. *Carmina Latina Epigraphica.* 3 vols. Teubner: Leipzig, 1895–1926.

Burke, Tony, ed. *De Infantia Iesu: Evangelium Thomae Graece.* Corpus Christianorum Series Apocryphorum 17. Turnhout: Brepols, 2010.

Callimachus. Translated by A. W. Mair et al. 2 vols. Loeb Classical Library. Cambridge, MA: Harvard University Press, 1921–1973.

Cassius Dio Cocceianus. *Roman History.* Translated by Earnest Cary. 9 vols. Loeb Classical Library. Cambridge, MA: Harvard University Press, 1914–27.

Charlesworth, James H., ed. *The Old Testament Pseudepigrapha.* 2 vols. New York: Doubleday, 1983.

Cicero. Translated by L. H. G. Greenwood et al. 28 vols. Loeb Classical Library. Cambridge, MA: Harvard University Press, 1913–2010.

Clement of Alexandria. *Le Protreptique.* Translated by Claude Mondésert. 2nd ed. Sources chrétiennes 2. Paris: Editions du Cerf, 1961.

———. *Les Stromates.* Translated by Marcel Caster. 7 vols. Sources chrétiennes 30, 38, 278–279, 428, 446. Paris: Editions du Cerf, 1951–2001.

Cyprian. *Quod idola dii non sint.* Pages 19–31 in *Corpus Scriptorum Ecclesiasticorum Latinorum.* Edited by Guilelmus Hartel. 3 vols. Vol. 1. Vienna: C. Gerold, 1868.

Dessau, H., ed. *Inscriptiones Latinae Selectae.* Berlin: Weidmanns, 1892–1916.

Dindorf, W. *Scholia Graeca in Homeri Iliadem.* 6 vols. Oxford: Clarendon, 1875–88.

Dio Chrysostom. Translated by J. W. Cohoon et al. 5 vols. Loeb Classical Library. Cambridge, MA: Harvard University Press, 1932–1951.

Diodorus of Sicily. Translated by Charles Henry Oldfather. 12 vols. Loeb Classical Library. London: Heinemann, 1933–1967.

Diogenes Laertius. Translated by R. D. Hicks. 2 vols. Loeb Classical Library. Cambridge, MA: Harvard University Press, 1925.

Dionysius of Halicarnassus. Translated by Earnest Cary et al. 9 vols. Loeb Classical Library. Cambridge, MA: Harvard University Press, 1937–1985.

Dittenberger, W., ed. *Orientis Graeci Inscriptiones Selectae.* Leipzig: Hirzel, 1903.

Edelstein, Emma J., and Ludwig Edelstein. *Asclepius: A Collection of Interpretation of the Testimonies.* 2 vols. Baltimore, MD: Johns Hopkins University Press, 1945.

Ehrenberg, V., and A. H. M. Jones. *Documents Illustrating the Reigns of Augustus and Tiberius.* Oxford: Clarendon, 1955.

Epictetus. *The Discourses as Reported by Arrian, the Manual, and Fragments.* Translated by W. A. Oldfather. 2 vols. Loeb Classical Library. Cambridge, MA: Harvard University Press, 1926–28.

Euripides. Translated by David Kovacs et al. 8 vols. Loeb Classical Library. Cambridge, MA: Harvard University Press, 1994–2009.

Eusebius of Caesarea. *Preparation for the Gospel.* Translated by Edwin Hamilton Gifford. 2 vols. Grand Rapids, MI: Baker Book House, 1981.

———. *The Proof of the Gospel.* Edited and translated by W. J. Ferrar. 2 vols. London: SPCK, 1920.

Paton, W. R., ed. and trans. *The Greek Anthology.* 5 vols. Loeb Classical Library. Cambridge, MA: Harvard University Press, 1916–18.

Gregory of Nazianzus. *Festal Orations.* Translated by Nonna Verna Harrison. Crestwood, NY: St. Vladimir's Seminary Press, 2008.

Gregory Palamas. *The Triads.* Edited by John Meyendorff. Translated by Nicholas Gendle. The Classics of Western Spirituality. Mahwah, NJ: Paulist, 1983.

Heraclitus. *Homeric Problems.* Edited and translated by Donald A. Russell and David Konstan. Writings from the Greco-Roman World 14. Atlanta: Society of Biblical Literature, 2005.

Herodotus. Translated by A. D. Godley. 4 vols. Loeb Classical Library. Cambridge, MA: Harvard University Press, 1926–38.

Hesiod. Translated by Glenn W. Most. 2 vols. Loeb Classical Library. Cambridge, MA: Harvard University Press, 2007.

Homer. Translated by A. T. Murray. 4 vols. Loeb Classical Library. Cambridge, MA: Harvard University Press, 1919–1925.

Horace. *Odes and Epodes.* Translated by Niall Rudd. Loeb Classical Library. Cambridge, MA: Harvard University Press, 2004.

Hyginus. *Fabulae.* Edited by P. K. Marshall. Stuttgart: Teubner, 1993.

Irenaeus. *Contre les hérésies.* Edited and translated by Adelin Rousseau and Louis Doutreleau. 5 vols. Sources chrétiennes 100, 150, 152–153, 210–211. Paris: Editions du Cerf, 1965–1982.

Jacoby, Felix, ed. *Die Fragmente der griechischen Historiker.* Leiden: Brill, 1923–1958.

John Damascene. *La Foi Orthodoxe.* Edited by P. Ledrux. Sources Chrétiennes 535 and 540. 2 vols. Paris: Éditions du Cerf, 2011.

Josephus. Translated by H. St J. Thackeray et al. 10 vols. Loeb Classical Library. Cambridge, MA: Harvard University Press, 1926–1965.

Justin Martyr. *Apologie pour les chrétiens: Introduction, traduction et commentaire.* Edited by Charles Munier. Paris: Éditions du Cerf, 2006.

———. *Justin, Philosopher and Martyr, Apologies.* Edited by Denis Minns and Paul Parvis. Oxford: Oxford University Press, 2009.

Kotsidu, Haritini. *TIMH KAI ΔOΞA. Ehrungen für hellenistische Herrscher im griechischen Mutterland und in Kleinasien unter besonderer Berücksichtigung der archäologischen Denkmäler.* Berlin: Akademie, 2000.

Kraus, Thomas J., and Tobias Nicklas, eds. *Das Petrusevangelium und die Petrusapokalypse. Die griechischen Fragmente mit deutscher und englischer Übersetzung.* Berlin: Walter de Gruyter, 2004.

Lactantius. *Divine Institutes.* Translated by Anthony Bowen and Peter Garnsey. Liverpool: Liverpool University Press, 2003.

Lauterbach, Jacob Z. *Mekilta de-Rabbi Ishmael.* 3 vols. Philadelphia: Jewish Publication Society, 1933.

Livy. Translated by B. O. Foster. 14 vols. Loeb Classical Library. Cambridge, MA: Harvard University Press, 1919–1959.

Lucan: the Civil War (Pharsalia). Translated by J. D. Duff. Loeb Classical Library. Cambridge, MA: Harvard University Press, 1943.

Lucian. Translated by A. M. Harmon. 8 vols. Loeb Classical Library. Cambridge, MA: Harvard University Press, 1913–1967.

Manilius. *Astronomica.* Translated by G. P. Goold. Loeb Classical Library. Cambridge, MA: Harvard University Press, 1977.

Masullo, Rita. *Vita di Proclo. Testo critic, introduzione, traduzione e commentario.* Napoli: M. D'Auria Editore, 1985.

Maximus of Tyre. *The Philosophical Orations.* Translated by Michael B. Trapp. Oxford: Clarendon, 1997.

Menander Rhetor. Edited by D. A. Russell and N. G. Wilson. Oxford: Clarendon, 1981.

Merkelbach, R., and M. L. West, eds. *Fragmenta Hesiodea.* Oxford: Clarendon, 1967.

Migne, J.-P., ed. *Patrologiae Cursus Completus: Series Graecae.* 218 vols. Paris: Garnier Editories, 1912.

Musurillo, H. *The Acts of the Christian Martyrs.* Oxford: Clarendon, 1972.

Origen. *On First Principles, Being Koetschau's Text of the De principiis.* Translated by G. W. Butterworth. Gloucester, MA: P. Smith, 1973.

———. *Contra Celsum, Gegen Celsus.* Edited by Michael Fiedrowicz. Translated by Claudia Barthold. Fontes Christiani Band 50/1. 3 vols. Freiburg: Herder, 2011.

———. *Contra Celsum.* Translated by Henry Chadwick. Cambridge: Cambridge University Press, 1953.

Ovid. Loeb Classical Library. Translated by Frank Justus Miller et al. 6 vols. Cambridge, MA: Harvard University Press, 1914–1989.

———. *Metamorphoses.* Translated by A. D. Melville. Oxford: Oxford University Press, 1986.

Page, D. L., ed. *Greek Literary Papyri.* 2 vols. Cambridge, MA: Harvard University Press, 1942–.

Pausanias. Translated by W. H. S. Jones et al. 5 vols. Loeb Classical Library. Cambridge, MA: Harvard University Press, 1918–1935.

Philo of Byblos. *The Phoenician History.* Edited by Harold Attridge and Robert Oden. Washington, DC: Catholic Biblical Association of America, 1981.

Philo. Translated by F. H. Colson et al. 12 vols. Loeb Classical Library. Cambridge, MA: Harvard University Press, 1929–1962.

Philostratus. Translated by Christopher P. Jones. 6 vols. Loeb Classical Library. Cambridge, MA: Harvard University Press, 1921–2006.

Pindar. Translated by William H. Race. 2 vols. Loeb Classical Library. Cambridge, MA: Harvard University Press, 1997.

Plato. *Complete Works.* Edited by John M. Cooper. Indianapolis: Hackett, 1997.

Plautus. Translated by Paul Nixon. 5 vols. Loeb Classical Library. Cambridge, MA: Harvard University Press, 1916–38.

Pliny the Elder. *Natural History.* Translated by H. Rackham. 10 vols. Loeb Classical Library. Cambridge, MA: Harvard University Press, 1938–63.

Pliny the Younger. *Letters and Panegyricus.* Translated by Betty Radice. 2 vols. Loeb Classical Library. Cambridge, MA: Harvard University Press, 1969.

Plutarch. *Oeuvres Morales Tome IX 3d part Books VII-IX.* Edited and translated by Françoise Frazier and Jean Sirinelli. Paris: Les Belles Lettres, 1996.

———. *Lives.* Translated by Bernadotte Perrin. 11 vols. Loeb Classical Library. Cambridge, MA: Harvard University Press, 1914–1926.

Polybius. Translated by W. R. Paton. 6 vols. Loeb Classical Library. Cambridge, MA: Harvard University Press, 1926–2011.

Pritchard, James B., ed. *Ancient Near Eastern Texts Relating to the Old Testament.* 2nd ed. Princeton, NJ: Princeton University Press, 1955.

Propertius. Translated by G. P. Goold. Loeb Classical Library. Cambridge, MA: Harvard University Press, 1990.

Pseudo-Apollodorus. *Apollodori bibliotheca. Pediasimi libellus de duodecim Herculis laboribus.* Edited by R. Wagner. *Mythographi Graeci* 1. Leipzig: Teubner, 1894.

Pseudo-Callisthenes. *The Greek Alexander Romance.* Translated by Richard Stoneman. London: Penguin, 1991.

———. *The Romance of Alexander the Great by Pseudo-Callisthenes: Translated from the Armenian Version.* Translated by Albert Mugrdich Wolohojian. New York: Columbia University Press, 1969.

Quintus Curtius. *History of Alexander.* Translated by J. C. Rolfe. 2 vols. Loeb Classical Library. Cambridge, MA: Harvard University Press, 1962.

Rahlfs, Alfred, and Robert Hanhart. *Septuaginta, id est Vetus Testamentum graece iuxta LXX interpretes.* 2nd ed. Stuttgart: Deutsche Bibelgesellschaft, 2006.

Rehm, Bernhard, and Franz Paschke, eds. *Die Pseudoklmentinen I: Homilien.* 2nd ed. Die griechischen christlichen Schriftsteller der ersten Jahrhunderte 42. Berlin: Akademie, 1969.

Richardson, Nicholas, ed. *Three Homeric Hymns: To Apollo, Hermes and Aphrodite.* Cambridge: Cambridge University Press, 2010.

Riese, Alexander, F. Bueheler, and E. Lommatzsch, eds. *Anthologia Latina sive Poesis Latinae Supplementum.* 2 vols. Lipsius: Teubner, 1869–1926.

Schneemelcher, Wilhelm, ed. *New Testament Apocrypha.* Translated by R. McL. Wilson. 2 vols. 2nd ed. Louisville: Westminster John Knox, 1991.

Seneca. Translated by John W. Basore et al. 13 vols. Loeb Classical Library. Cambridge, MA: Harvard University Press, 1913–2004.

Shakespeare, William. *The Complete Works of Shakespeare.* Edited by W. J. Craig. New York: Oxford University Press, 1936.

Skutsch, O., ed. *The Annals of Ennius.* Oxford: Clarendon, 1985.

Smallwood, E. Mary. *Documents Illustrating the Principates of Gaius, Claudius, and Nero.* Cambridge: Cambridge University Press, 1967.

Sophocles. Translated by Hugh Lloyd-Jones. 3 vols. Loeb Classical Library. Cambridge, MA: Harvard University Press, 1994–1996.

Strabo. *The Geography of Strabo.* Translated by Horace Leonard Jones. 8 vols. Loeb Classical Library. Cambridge, MA: Harvard University Press, 1960–70.

Strutwolf, Holger, et al., eds. *Nestle-Aland Novum Testamentum Graece.* 28th ed. Stuttgart: Deutsche Bibelgesellschaft, 2012.

Suetonius. Translated by J. C. Rolfe. 2 vols. Loeb Classical Library. Cambridge, MA: Harvard University Press, 1997.

Tacitus. Translated by John Jackson et al. 5 vols. Loeb Classical Library. Cambridge, MA: Harvard University Press, 1914–1937.

Tertullian. Translated by T. R. Glover et al. Loeb Classical Library. Cambridge, MA: Harvard University Press, 1931.

Theocritus. *The Idylls of Theocritus.* Translated by Robert Wells. Manchester: Carcanet, 1988.

Theophilus of Antioch. *Ad Autolycum.* Translated by Robert M. Grant. Oxford: Clarendon, 1970.

Valerius Maximus. Translated by D. R. Shackleton Bailey. 2 vols. Loeb Classical Library. Cambridge, MA: Harvard University Press, 2000.

Virgil. Translated by H. Rushton Fairclough et al. 2 vols. Loeb Classical Library. Cambridge, MA: Harvard University Press, 1999.

Xenophanes of Colophon. *Fragments.* Edited by J. H. Lesher. Toronto: University of Toronto Press, 1992.

Xenophon. *Memorabilia.* Translated by Amy L. Bonnette. Ithaca, NY: Cornell University Press, 1994.

DICTIONARIES

Ackermann, Hans Christoph, and Jean-Robert Gisler, eds. *Lexicon Iconographicum Mythologiae Classicae (LIMC).* Zürich: Artemis, 1981–.

Becking, B., K. van der Toorn, and P.W. van der Horst, eds. *The Dictionary of Deities and Demons of the Bible.* 2nd ed. Leiden: Brill, 1999.

Botterweck, G. Johannes, and Helmer Ringren, eds. *Theological Dictionary of the Old Testament.* 15 vols. Grand Rapids, MI: Eerdmans, 1986.

Brown, Francis, et al. *Brown-Driver-Briggs Hebrew and English Lexicon With an Appendix Continuing the Biblical Aramaic.* Boston: Houghton Mifflin, 1906.

Danker, Frederick William, ed. *A Greek-English Lexicon of the New Testament and Other Early Christian Literature.* 3rd edition. Chicago: University of Chicago Press, 2000.

Freedman, David Noel, ed. *The Anchor Bible Dictionary.* 6 vols. New York: Doubleday, 1992.

Hornblower, Simon, and Anthony Spawforth, eds. *The Oxford Classical Dictionary.* 4th ed. Oxford: Oxford University Press, 2012.

Kittel, Gerhard, and Gerhard Friedrich, eds. *Theological Dictionary of the New Testament.* Translated by Geoffrey W. Bromiley. 10 vols. Grand Rapids, MI: Eerdmans, 1964–1976.

Kluser, Theodor. *Reallexikon für Antike und Christentum: Sachwörterbuch zur Auseinandersetzung des Christentums mit der antiken Welt.* 25 vols. Stuttgart: Anton Hiersemann, 1950–.

Landfester, Manfred, Hubert Cancik, and Helmuth Schneider, eds. *Brill's New Pauly: Encyclopedia of the Ancient World.* 5 vols. Leiden: Brill, 2006–.

Liddell, Henry George, and Robert Scott, eds. *A Greek-English Lexicon* with Revised Supplemented edited by P.G.W. Glare. Oxford: Clarendon, 1996.

Lust, J., E. Eynikel and K. Hauspie, eds. *A Greek-English Lexicon of the Septuagint.* Stuttgart: Deutsche Bibelgesellschaft, 1992.

Spicq, Ceslas. *Theological Lexicon of the New Testament.* Translated and edited by James D. Ernest. 3 vols. Peabody, MA: Hendrickson, 1994.

SECONDARY SOURCES

Aasgaard, Reidar. *The Childhood of Jesus: Decoding the Apocryphal Infancy Gospel of Thomas.* Eugene, OR: Cascade Books, 2009.

Albinus, Lars. *The House of Hades: Studies in Ancient Greek Eschatology.* Aarhus: Aarhus University Press, 2000.

Alexander, Philip. "From Son of Adam to Second God: Transformations of the Biblical Enoch." Pages 87–122 in *Biblical Figures Outside the Bible.* Edited by M. E. Stone and T. A. Bergren. Harrisburg, PA: Trinity Press International, 1998.

Algra, Keimpe. "Stoic Theology." Pages 153–78 in *The Cambridge Companion to Stoicism.* Edited by Brad Inwood. New York: Cambridge University Press, 2003.

Allison, Dale. *The New Moses: A Matthean Typology.* Minneapolis: Fortress Press, 1993.

Anderson, A. A. *2 Samuel.* Word Biblical Commentary 11. Dallas: Word Books, 1989.

Aune, David E. "Heracles and Christ: Heracles Imagery in the Christology of Early Christianity." Pages 3–19 in *Greeks, Romans, and Christians: Essays in Honor of Abraham J. Malherbe.* Edited by David L. Balch, Everett Ferguson, and Wayne Meeks. Minneapolis: Fortress Press, 1990.

Avery-Peck, Alan J., and Jacob Neusner, eds. *Judaism in Late Antiquity. Part 4: Death, Life-after-Death, and the World-to-Come in the Judaisms of Late Antiquity.* Leiden: Brill, 2000.

Badian, Ernst. "Alexander the Great Between Two Thrones and Heaven: Variations on an Old Theme." Pages 11–26 in *Subject and Ruler: The Cult of the Ruling Power in Classical Antiquity.* Edited by A. Small. Ann Arbor, MI: Journal of Roman Archaeology, 1996.

———. "The Deification of Alexander the Great." Pages 27–71 in *Ancient Macedonian Studies in Honor of Charles F. Edson.* Edited by Harry J. Dell. Thessaloniki: Institute for Balkan Studies, 1981.

Baines, J. "Ancient Egyptian Kingship: Official Forms, Rhetoric, Context." Pages 16–53 in *King and Messiah in Israel and the Ancient Near East*. Edited by John Day. Sheffield: Sheffield Academic Press, 1998.

Baird, William. *History of New Testament Research*. Vol. 2, *From Jonathan Edwards to Rudolf Bultmann*. Minneapolis: Fortress Press, 2003.

Bakhos, C. *Ancient Judaism in its Hellenistic Context*. Leiden: Brill, 2005.

Balsdon, John Percy Vyvian Darce. *The Emperor Gaius*. Oxford: Clarendon, 1934.

Barclay, John. *Jews in the Mediterranean Diaspora: From Alexander to Trajan (323 BCE–117CE)*. Berkeley: University of California, 1999.

———. *Negotiating Diaspora: Jewish Strategies in the Roman Empire*. Edinburgh: T&T Clark, 2004.

Barker, Margaret. "Enthronement and Apotheosis: The Vision in Revelation 4–5." Pages 217–27 in *New Heaven and New Earth—Prophecy and the Millennium*. Edited by P. J. Harland and C. T. R. Hayward. Leiden: Brill, 1999.

Barret, J. C. "Romanization: A Critical Comment." Pages 51–64 in *Dialogues in Roman Imperialism: Power, Discourse, and Discrepant Experience in the Roman Empire*. Edited by D. J. Mattingly. Portsmouth, RI: Journal of Roman Archaeology, 1997.

Barrett, C. K. *The Holy Spirit and the Gospel Tradition*. London: SPCK, 1966.

Baslez, Marie-Françoise. "Le corps, l'âme et la survie: anthropologie et croyances dans les religions du monde gréco-romain." Pages 73–89 in *Résurrection: L'après-mort dans le monde ancient et le Nouveau Testament*. Edited by Odette Mainville and Daniel Marguerat. *Le monde de la Bible* 45. Montréal: Labor et Fides, 2001.

Bateman, Herbert. "Psalm 110:1 and the New Testament." *Bibliotheca Sacra* 149 (1992): 438–53.

Bauckham, Richard. *Jesus and the God of Israel: God Crucified and Other Studies on the New Testament's Christology of Divine Identity*. Grand Rapids, MI: Eerdmans, 2008.

———. "The Worship of Jesus in Philippians 2:9-11." Pages 128–39 in *Where Christology Began: Essays on Philippians 2*. Edited by Ralph Martin and Brian Dodd. Louisville: Westminster John Knox, 1998.

Baumgarten A. I. "Euhemerus' Eternal Gods: or, How Not To Be Embarrassed by Greek Mythology." Pages 91–103 in *Classical Studies in Honor of D. Sohlberg*. Edited by Ranon Katzoff et al. Ramat Gan: Bar-Ilan University Press, 1996.

Beard, Mary. *The Roman Triumph.* Cambridge, MA: Belknap, 2007.

Beaumont, Leslie. "Mythological Childhood: A Male Preserve? An Interpretation of Classical Athenian Iconography in its Socio-historical Context." *Annual of the British School at Athens* 90 (1995): 339–361.

Becker, Adam H., and Annette Yoshiko Reed, eds. *The Ways that Never Parted: Jews and Christians in Late Antiquity and the Early Middle Ages.* Texts and Studies in Ancient Judaism 95. Tübingen: Mohr Siebeck, 2003.

Bedard, Stephen J. "Hellenistic Influence on the Idea of Resurrection in Jewish Apocalyptic Literature." *Journal of Greco-Roman Christianity and Judaism* 5 (2008): 174–89.

Begg, Christopher, and Paul Spilsbury. *Flavius Josephus: Translation and Commentary.* Edited by Steve Mason. 10 vols. Leiden: Brill, 2005.

Belleville, Linda. *Reflections of Glory: Paul's Polemical Use of the Moses-Doxa Tradition in 2 Corinthians 3.1-18.* Journal for the Study of the New Testament Supplement Series 52. Sheffield: Sheffield Academic Press, 1991.

Berchman, Robert M. "The Categories of Being in Middle Platonism: Philo, Clement, and Origen of Alexandria." Pages 98–140 in *The School of Moses: Studies in Philo and Hellenistic Religion.* Edited by John Peter Kenney. Atlanta: Scholars, 1995.

Berger, Peter L., and Thomas Luckmann. *The Social Construction of Reality: A Treatise in the Sociology of Knowledge.* New York: Doubleday, 1966.

Bergman, Marianne. *Die Strahlen der Herrscher: Theomorphes Herrscherbild und politische Symbolik im Hellenismus und in der römischen Kaiserzeit.* Mainz: Philipp von Zabern, 1998.

Bernett, Monika. *Der Kaiserkult in Judäa unter den Herodiern und Römern.* Wissenschaftliche Untersuchung zum Neuen Testament 203. Tübingen: Mohr Siebeck, 2007.

Betz, Hans Dieter. "Credibility and Credulity in Plutarch's Life of Numa Pompilius." Pages 39–55 in *Reading Religions in the Ancient World: Essays Presented to Robert McQueen Grant on his 90th Birthday.* Edited by David Aune and Robin Darling Young. Leiden: Brill, 2007.

Bevan, Edwyn Robert. *The House of Ptolemy: A History of Egypt under the Ptolemaic Dynasty.* Chicago: Argonaut, 1968.

Bickerman, Elias. "Die Römische Kaiserapotheose." *Archiv für Religionswissenschaft* 27 (1929): 1–31.

———. *Institutions des Séleucides.* Paris: P. Geuthner, 1938.

Bieler, Ludwig. ΘΕΙΟΣ ANHP. *Das Bild des 'Göttlichen Menschen' in Spätantike und Frühchristentum.* 2 vols. Darmstadt: Wissenschaftliche Buchgesellschaft, 1967.

Bierl, Anton. "'Turn on the Light!' Epiphany, the God-Like Hero Odysseus, and the Golden Lamp of Athena in Homer's *Odyssey.*" *Illinois Classical Studies* 29 (2004): 43–62.

Billings, Bradly S. "'At the Age of 12': The Boy Jesus in the Temple (Luke 2:41-52), the Emperor Augustus, and the Social Setting of the Third Gospel." *Journal of Theological Studies* 60 (2009): 70–89.

Black, Matthew. "All Powers Will Be Subject to Him." Pages 74–82 in *Paul and Paulinism.* London: SPCK, 1982.

Blackburn, Barry. *Theios Anēr and the Markan Miracle Traditions: A Critique of the theios Anēr Concept as an Interpretive Background of the Miracle Traditions Used by Mark.* Wissenschaftliche Untersuchungen zum Neuen Testament 2/ 40. Tübingen: Mohr Siebeck, 1991.

Blenkinsopp, Joseph. *Isaiah 1–39: A New Translation with Introduction and Commentary.* Anchor Bible 19. New York: Doubleday, 2000.

Boatwright, Mary T. *Peoples of the Roman World.* Cambridge: Cambridge University Press, 2012.

Bockmuehl, Markus. *A Commentary on the Epistle to the Philippians.* Black's New Testament Commentaries. London: A&C Black, 1997.

Bodéüs, Richard. *Aristotle and the Theology of the Living Immortals.* Translated by Jan Edward Garrett. Albany: State University of New York Press, 2000.

Bohak, Gideon. *Ancient Jewish Magic: A History.* Cambridge: Cambridge University Press, 2008.

Böhme Hartmut, ed. *Transformation: Ein Konzept zur Erforschung kulturellen Wandels.* Munich: Wilhelm Fink, 2011.

Bolt, Peter G. "Life, Death, and the afterlife in the Greco-Roman World." Pages 51–79 in *Life in the Face of Death: The Resurrection message of the New Testament.* Edited by Richard N. Longenecker. Grand Rapids, MI: Eerdmans, 1998.

Bömer, Franz. *P. Ovidius Naso Metamorphosen Kommentar.* 7 vols. Heidelberg: Carl Winter, 1969.

Bonner, Leila. "The Resurrection Motif in the Hebrew Bible: Allusions or Illusions." *Jewish Bible Quarterly* 30 (2002): 143–54.

Borg, Marcus, and N. T. Wright. *The Meaning of Jesus: Two Visions.* New York: HarperSanFrancisco, 1999.

Boring, Eugene. "Markan Christology: God-language for Jesus?" *New Testament Studies* 45 (1999): 451–71.

Boring, Eugene, Carsten Colpe, and Klaus Berger, eds. *Hellenistic Commentary to the New Testament*. Nashville: Abingdon, 1995.

Bornkamm, Günther. "Zum Verständnis des Christus-Hymnus Phil. 2,5-11." Pages 177–87 in *Studien zu Antike und Urchristentum*. Munich: Kaiser Verlag, 1959.

Bousset, Wilhelm. *Kyrios Christos: Geschichte des Christusglaubens von den Anfängen des Christentums bis Irenaeus*. Göttingen: Vandenhoeck & Ruprecht, 1921.

———. *Kyrios Christos: A History of the Belief in Christ from the Beginnings to Irenaeus*. Translated by John Steely. Nashville: Abingdon, 1970.

Bovon, François. "The First Christologies: From Exaltation to Incarnation, Or From Easter to Christmas." Pages 27–43 in *Jesus Christ Today: Studies of Christology in Various Contexts*. Edited by Stuart George Hall. Berlin: Walter de Gruyter, 2009.

———. *Luke 1: A Commentary on the Gospel of Luke 1:1—9:50*. Edited by Helmut Koester. Translated by Christine M. Thomas. Hermeneia. Minneapolis: Fortress Press, 2002.

Bow, Beverly Ann. "The Story of Jesus' Birth: A Pagan and Jewish Affair." PhD diss. University of Iowa, 1995.

Bowersock, Glen W. *Fiction as History: Nero to Julian*. Berkeley: University of California Press, 1994.

———. *Hellenism in Late Antiquity*. Ann Arbor: University of Michigan Press, 1990.

Bowman Robert M., and J. Ed Komoszewski. *Putting Jesus in His Place: The Case for the Deity of Christ*. Grand Rapids, MI: Kregel, 2007.

Box, G. H. "Gospel Narratives of the Nativity and the Alleged Influence of Heathen Ideas." *Zeitschrift für die Neutestamentliche Wissenschaft* 6 (1905): 80–101.

Bremer, Dieter. "Die Epiphanie des Gottes in den homerische Hymnen und Platons Gottesbegriff." *Zeitschrift für Religions- und Gestesgeschichte* 27 (1975): 1–21.

Bremmer, Jan. "Close Encounters of the Third Kind: Heliodorus in the Temple and Paul on the Road to Damascus." Pages 215–33 in *Greek Religion and Culture, the Bible and the Ancient Near East*. Edited by Jan Bremmer. Jerusalem Studies in Religion and Culture. Leiden: Brill, 2008.

Brenk, F. E. "Greek Epiphanies and Paul on the Road to Damaskos." Pages 415–24 in *The Notion of 'Religion' in Comparative Research*. Edited by U. Bianchi. Rome: "L'Erma" di Bretschneider, 1994.

Breytenbach, C. "Das Markusevangelium, Psalm 110,1 und 118,22f.: Folgetext und Prätext." Pages 197–222 in *The Scriptures in the Gospels*. Edited by C. M. Tuckett. Leuven: Leuven University Press, 1997.

Brisson, Luc. *How Philosophers Saved Myths: Allegorical Interpretation and Classical Mythology*. Translated by Catherin Tihanyi. Chicago: University of Chicago, 2004.

Brodd, Jeffrey, and Jonathan L. Reed, eds. *Rome and Religion: A Cross-Disciplinary Dialogue on the Imperial Cult*. Atlanta: Society of Biblical Literature, 2011.

Brommer Frank. *Herakles II: Die unkanonischen Taten des Helden*. Darmstadt: Wissenschaftliche Buchgesellschaft, 1984.

Brown, Raymond. *The Gospel According to John i-xii*. 2 vols. Anchor Bible 29. Garden City, NY: Doubleday, 1966.

———. *The Virginal Conception and Bodily Resurrection of Jesus*. New York: Paulist, 1973.

———. *The Birth of the Messiah: A Commentary on the Infancy Narratives in Matthew and Luke*. Garden City, NY: Doubleday, 1977.

———, ed. *Mary in the New Testament*. Philadelphia: Fortress Press, 1978.

Brownlee, W. H. "Psalms 1–2 as a Coronation Liturgy." *Biblica* 52 (1971): 321–36.

Brucker, R. *'Christushymnen' Oder 'Epideiktische Passagen'?* Forschungen zur Religion und Literatur des Alten und Neuen Testaments 176. Göttingen: Vandenhoek & Ruprecht, 1997.

Bryan, Christopher. *The Resurrection of the Messiah*. Oxford: Oxford University Press, 2011.

Buckler W. H. "Auguste, Zeus Patroos." *Revue de Philologie* 9 (1935): 177–88.

Bultmann, Rudolf. *History of the Synoptic Tradition*. Revised edition. Translated by John Marsh. New York: Harper & Row, 1968.

———. *Theology of the New Testament*. 2 vols. New York: Scribner, 1951–1955.

Buraselis, Kostas. "Two Notes on Theophanes' Descendents." Pages 61–70 in *The Greek East in the Roman Context: Proceedings of a Colloquium Organised by the Finnish Institute at Athens May 21 and 22, 1999*. Edited by Olli Salomies. Helsinki: Vammalan Kirjapaino Oy, 2001.

Burke, Peter. *Cultural Hybridity*. Cambridge: Polity, 2009.

Burke, Tony. "The Infancy Gospel of Thomas: The Text, its Origins, and its Transmission." PhD diss., University of Toronto, 2001.

Burkert, Walter. "Caesar und Romulus-Quirinus." *Historia* 11 (1962): 356–76.

———. *Greek Religion: Archaic and Classical.* Translated by John Raffan. Oxford: Blackwell, 1985.

———. *The Orientalizing Revolution: Near Eastern Influence on Greek Culture in the Early Archaic Age.* Cambridge, MA: Harvard University Press, 1992.

———. "From Epiphany to Cult Statue." Pages 15–30 in *What is a God? Studies in the Nature of Greek Divinity.* Edited by Alan B. Lloyd. Swansea: Classical Press of Wales, 1997.

Buxton, Richard. *Forms of Astonishment: Greek Myths of Metamorphosis.* Oxford: Oxford University Press, 2009.

———. "Metamorphoses of Gods into Animals and Humans." Pages 81–91 in *The Gods of Ancient Greece: Identities and Transformations.* Edited by Jan N. Bremmer and Andrew Erskine. Edinburgh: Edinburgh University Press, 2010.

Capes, David. "YHWH Texts and Monotheism in Paul's Christology." Pages 120–37 in *Early Jewish and Christian Monotheism.* Edited by L. Stuckenbruck and W. E. S. North. London: T&T Clark, 2004.

Carter, Warren, ed. *Paul and Empire.* Harrisburg, PA: Trinity Press International, 1997.

———. *Matthew and the Margins.* Maryknoll, NY: Orbis Books, 2001.

———, *Matthew and Empire: Initial Explorations.* Harrisburg, PA: Trinity Press International, 2001.

Casey, Maurice. *From Jewish Prophet to Gentile God: The Origins and Development of New Testament Christology.* Louisville: Westminster John Knox, 1991.

Castellani, Victor. "Two Divine Scandals: Ovid Met. 2.680ff and 4.171ff and His Sources." *Transactions of the American Philological Association* 110 (1980): 37–50.

Chester, Andrew. "Resurrection and Transformation." Pages 47–78 in *Auferstehung-Resurrection: The Fourth Durham-Tübingen Research Symposium: Resurrection, Transfiguration and Exaltation in Old Testament, Ancient Judaism and Early Christianity.* Edited by Friedrich Avemarie and Hermann Lichtenberger. Wissenschaftliche Untersuchungen zum Neuen Testament 135. Tübingen: Mohr Siebeck, 2001.

———. *Messiah and Exaltation: Jewish Messianic and Visionary Traditions and New Testament Christology.* Tübingen: Mohr Siebeck, 2007.

Chilton, Bruce, and Jacob Neusner. *Types of Authority in Formative Christianity and Judaism.* London: Routledge, 1999.

Clark, Gillian. *Christianity and Roman Society.* Cambridge: Cambridge University Press, 2004.

Clarke, Michael. *Flesh and Spirit in the Songs of Homer: A Study of Words and Myths.* Oxford: Clarendon, 1990.

Clauss, Manfred. *Kaiser und Gott: Herrscherkult im römischen Reich.* Stuttgart: Teubner, 1999.

Clay, Jenny Strauss. *Wrath of Athena: Gods and Men in the Odyssey.* Lanham, MD: Rowman & Littlefield, 1997.

———. *The Politics of Olympus: Form and Meaning in the Major Homeric Hymns.* 2nd edition. London: Bristol, 2006.

Clifford, Hywel. "Moses as Philosopher-Sage in Philo." Pages 151–68 in *Moses in Biblical and Extra-Biblical Traditions.* Edited by Axel Graupner and Michael Wolter. Berlin: Walter de Gruyter, 2007.

Cohen, Shaye. "Alexander the Great and Jaddus the High Priest According to Josephus." *Annual of Jewish Studies* 7–8 (1982): 41–68.

Collins, Adela Yarbro. "Apotheosis and Resurrection." Pages 88–100 in *The New Testament and Hellenistic Judaism.* Edited by Peder Borgen and Soren Giversen. Aarhus: Aarhus University Press, 1995.

———. "Mark and His Readers: The Son of God Among Jews." *Harvard Theological Review* 92, no. 4 (1999): 393–408.

———. "The Worship of Jesus and the Imperial Cult." Pages 234–57 in *The Jewish Roots of Christological Monotheism: Papers from the St. Andrews Conference on the Historical Origins of the Worship of Jesus.* Edited by Carey C. Newman, James R. Davila, and Gladys S. Lewis. Leiden: Brill, 1999.

———. "Psalms, *Philippians* 2:6-11, and the Origins of Christology," *Biblical Interpretation* 11 (2003): 361–72.

———. "'How on Earth did Jesus Become a God?': A Reply." Pages 55–66 in *Israel's God and Rebecca's Children: Christology and Community in Early Judaism and Christianity: Essays in Honor of Larry W. Hurtado and Alan F. Segal.* Edited by David B. Capes, Larry W. Hurtado, and Alan F. Segal. Waco, TX: Baylor University Press, 2007.

———. *Mark: A Commentary.* Hermeneia. Minneapolis: Fortress Press, 2007.

————. "Ancient Notions of Transferal and Apotheosis in Relation to the Empty Tomb Story in Mark." Pages 41–58 in *Metamorphoses Resurrection, Body, and Transformative Practices in Early Christianity*. Edited by Turid Karlsen Seim and Jorunn Økland. Berlin: Walter de Gruyter, 2009.

————. "Traveling Up and Away: Journeys to the Upper and Outer Regions of the World." Pages 135–66 in *Greco-Roman Culture and the New Testament: Studies Commemorating the Centennial of the Pontifical Biblical Institute*. Edited by David Aune and Frederick Brenk. Leiden: Brill, 2012.

Collins, John J. "A Throne in the Heavens: Apotheosis in Pre-Christian Judaism." Pages 41–56 in *Death, Ecstasy, and Other Worldly Journeys*. Edited by John J. Collins and Michael Fishbane. Albany: State University of New York Press, 1995.

————. *Between Athens and Jerusalem: Jewish Identity in the Hellenistic Diaspora*. 2nd ed. Grand Rapids, MI: Eerdmans, 2000.

————. "The Sons of God and the Daughters of Men." Pages 259–274 in *Sacred Marriages: The Divine-Human Sexual Metaphor from Sumer to Early Christianity*. Edited by Martti Nissinen and Risto Uro. Winona Lake, IN: Eisenbrauns, 2008.

Collins, John J., and Adela Yarbro Collins. *King and Messiah as Son of God: Divine, Human, and Angelic Messianic Figures in Biblical and Related Literature*. Grand Rapids, MI: Eerdmans, 2008.

Collins, John J., and Gregory Sterling. *Hellenism in the Land of Israel*. Notre Dame, IN: University of Notre Dame Press, 2001.

Colpe, Carsten. *Die religionsgeschichtliche Schule: Darstellung und Kritik ihres Bildes vom gnostischen Erlösermythus*. Göttingen: Vandenhoeck & Ruprecht, 1961.

Conrady, Ludwig. "Das Thomasevangelium: Ein wissenschaftlicher Versuch." *Theologische Studien und Kritiken* 76 (1903): 377–459.

Cook, John Granger. *The Interpretation of the New Testament in Greco-Roman Paganism*. Studien und Texte zu Antike und Christentum. Tübingen: Mohr Siebeck, 2000.

Cook, S. A. "The Rise of Israel." Pages 352–406 in vol. 2 of *The Cambridge Ancient History*. Edited by J. B. Bury, S. A. Cook, and F. E. Adcock. 12 vols. Cambridge: Cambridge University Press, 1923–39.

Cotter, Wendy. "Greco-Roman Apotheosis Traditions and the Resurrection Appearances in Matthew." Pages 127–153 in *The Gospel of Matthew in Current Study: Studies in Memory of William G. Thompson, S. J.* Edited by David Aune. Grand Rapids, MI: Eerdmans, 2001.

———. *Miracles in Greco-Roman Antiquity: A Sourcebook for the Study of New Testament Miracles.* London: Routledge, 1999.

Couroyer, B. "Dieu Ou Roi." *Revue Biblique* 78 (1971): 234–39.

Craffert, Pieter F. *The Life of a Galilean Shaman: Jesus of Nazareth in Anthropological-Historical Perspective.* Eugene, OR: Cascade Books, 2008.

Cribiore, Raffaella. *Gymnastics of the Mind: Greek Education in Hellenistic and Roman Egypt.* Oxford: Oxford University Press, 2001.

Cranfield, C. E. B. "Some Reflections on the Subject of the Virgin Birth." *Scottish Journal of Theology* 41 (1988): 177–89.

Crossan, John Dominic, "The Infancy and Youth of the Messiah." Pages 59–81 in *The Search for Jesus.* Edited by Hershel Shanks. Washington, DC: Biblical Archaeology Society, 1994.

———. *The Birth of Christianity: Discovering What Happened in the Years Immediately After the Execution of Jesus.* New York: HarperSanFrancisco, 1998.

Cullmann, Oscar. *The Christology of the New Testament.* Translated by S. Guthrie and C. Hall. Philadelphia: Westminster, 1959.

Cuss, Dominique. *Imperial Cult and Honorary Terms in the New Testament.* Fribourg: University Press of Fribourg, 1974.

Danker, F. W. *Benefactor: Epigraphic Study of a Graeco-Roman and New Testament Semantic Field.* St. Louis: Clayton Publishing House, 1982.

———. "Graeco-Roman Cultural Accommodation in the Christology of Luke-Acts." Pages 391–414 in *SBL Seminar Papers 1983.* Edited by Kent Harold Richards. Chico, CA: Scholars, 1983.

———. *Jesus and the New Age: A Commentary on St. Luke's Gospel.* Revised edition. Philadelphia: Fortress Press, 1988.

Daube, David. *The New Testament and Rabbinic Judaism.* London: Athlone, 1956.

de Savignac, Jean. "Essai d'interpretation du Psaume CX a l'aide de la literature Egyptienne." *Oudtestamentische Studien* 9 (1951): 107–35.

de Sousa, Rodrigo Franklin. *Eschatology and Messianism in LXX Isaiah 1–12.* London: T&T Clark, 2010.

de Vaux, Roland. *The Bible and the Ancient Near East.* Garden City, NY: Doubleday, 1971.

———. *Ancient Israel: Its Life and Institutions.* Translated by J. McHugh. Grand Rapids, MI: Eerdmans, 1997.

Dearman, Andrew J. "Theophany, Anthropomorphism, and the *Imago Dei*: Some Observations about the Incarnation in the Light of the Old Testament." Pages 31–46 in *The Incarnation: An Interdisciplinary Symposium on the Incarnation of the Son of God.* Edited by Stephen T. Davis et al. Oxford: Oxford University Press, 2002.

Deines, Roland. "Martin Hengel—a Life in the Service of Christology." *TynBul* 58 (2007): 25–42

del Agua, Agustín. "The Narrative of the Transfiguration as a Derashic Scenification of a Faith Confession (Mark 9.2-8 PAR)." *New Testament Studies* 39 (1993): 340–54.

Devallet, Georges. "Apothéoses romaines: Romulus à corps perdu." Pages 107–123 in *Entre hommes et dieux. Le convive, le héros, le prophète.* Edited by Annie-France Laurens. Paris: Les Belles Lettres, 1989.

Dibelius, Martin. "Jungfrauensohn und Krippenkind. Untersuchungen zur Geburtsgeschichte Jesu im Lukas-Evangelium." Pages 1–78 in *Botschaft und Geschichte: Gesammelte Aufsätze von Martin Dibelius.* Tübingen: Mohr Siebeck, 1932.

Dixon, Edward. "Descending Spirit and Descending Gods: A 'Greek' Interpretation of the Spirit's 'Descent as a Dove' in Mark 1:10." *Journal of Biblical Literature* 128 (2009): 759–80.

Dobesche, Gerhard. *Caesars Apotheose zu Lebzeiten und sein Ringen um den Königstitle.* Wien: Selbstverlag, 1966.

Dodd, C. H. *According to the Scriptures.* London: Nisbet, 1952.

———. "The Appearances of the Risen Christ: An Essay in Form-Criticism of the Gospels." Pages 9–35 in *Studies in the Gospel: Essays in Memory of F. L. H. Lightfoot.* Edited by D. Nineham. Oxford: Basil Blackwell, 1955.

Doriani, Daniel M. "The Deity of Christ in the Synoptic Gospels." *Journal of the Evangelical Theological Society* 37 (1994): 333–350.

du Toit, David S. *Theios Anthropos: Zur Verwendung von θεῖος ἄνθρωπος und sinnverwandten Ausdrücken in der Literatur der Kaiserzeit.* Wissenschaftliche Untersuchungen zum Neuen Testament 2/91. Tübingen: Mohr Siebeck, 1997.

Dunn, James D. G. *Romans 1–8.* Word Biblical Commentary 38a. Nashville: Thomas Nelson, 1988.

———. *Christology in the Making: A New Testament Inquiry into the Origins of the Doctrine of the Incarnation.* 2nd ed. Grand Rapids, MI: Eerdmans, 1989.

———. *The Partings of the Ways: Between Christianity and Judaism and their Significance for the Character of Christianity.* London: SCM, 1991.

———. "Christ, Adam, and Preexistence." Pages 74–83 in *Where Christology Began: Essays on Philippians 2.* Louisville: Westminster John Knox, 1998.

Dupont, Florence. "Apothéose et héroïzation dans Hercule sur l'Oeta de Sénèque." Pages 99–106 in *Entre hommes et dieux. Le convive, le héros, le prophète.* Edited by Annie-France Laurens. Paris: Les Belles Lettres, 1989.

Dwyer, Timothy. *The Motif of Wonder in the Gospel of Mark.* Journal for the Study of the New Testament Supplement Series 128. Sheffield: Sheffield Academic Press, 1996.

Eaton, J. H. *Kingship and the Psalms.* London: SCM, 1976.

Eck, Werner. "An Emperor Is Made: Senatorial Politics and Trajan's Adoption." Pages 211–28 in *Philosophy and Power in the Graeco-Roman World: Essays in Honour of Miriam Griffin.* Edited by Gillian Clark and Tessa Rajak. Oxford: Oxford University Press, 2002.

Effe, Bernd. "Der Held als Gott: Die Apotheose des Herakles in der alexandrinischen Dichtung." Pages 27–44 in *Gottmenschen: Konzepte existentieller Grenzüberschreitung im Altertum.* Edited by Gerhard Binde, Bernd Effe, and Reinhold Glei. Trier: Wissenschaflicher, 2003.

Ehrman, Bart D. *The Orthodox Corruption of Scripture: The Effect of Early Christological Controversies on the Text of the New Testament.* Oxford: Oxford University Press, 1993.

Ehrman, Bart D., and Zlatko Pleše, eds. *The Apocryphal Gospels: Texts and Translations.* Oxford: Oxford University Press, 2011.

Elliot, J. K. *The Apocryphal New Testament.* Oxford: Clarendon, 1993.

Endsjø, Dag Øistein. *Greek Resurrection Beliefs and the Success of Christianity.* New York: Palgrave Macmillan, 2009.

Engberg-Pedersen, Troels. *Paul Beyond the Judaism/Hellenism Divide.* Louisville: Westminster John Knox, 2001.

———. ed. *Cosmology and the Self: The Material Spirit.* Oxford: Oxford University Press, 2010.

Engnell, Ivan. *Studies in Divine Kingship in the Ancient Near East.* Uppsala: Almqvist & Wiksells, 1943.

Erskine, Andrew. "Epilogue." Pages 505–10 in *The Gods of Ancient Greece: Identities and Transformations.* Edited by Jan N. Bremmer and Andrew Erskine. Edinburgh: Edinburgh University Press, 2010.

Evans, Donald. "Academic Scepticism, Spiritual Reality and Transfiguration." Pages 175–86 in *The Glory of Christ in the New Testament.* Edited by L. D. Hurst and N. T. Wright. Oxford: Clarendon, 1987.

Evans, John K. *War, Women and Children in Ancient Rome.* London: Routledge, 1991.

Fears, J. R. "Nero as the Vicegerent of the Gods in Seneca's *De Clementia*." *Hermes* 103 (1975): 486–96.

———. "Jupiter and Roman Imperial Ideology." *ANRW* 17.1: 3–141. Part 1, *Heidentum*, 17.1. Edited by Wolfgang Haase. Berlin: Walter de Gruyter, 1981.

Fédou, Michel. *Christianisme et religions païennes dans le* Contra Celse *d'Origène*. Théologie Historique 81. Paris: Beauchesne, 1988.

Fee, Gordon. *Paul's Letter to the Philippians*. New International Commentary on the New Testament. Grand Rapids, MI: Eerdmans, 1995.

Feeney, D. C. *The Gods in Epic: Poets and Critics of the Classical Tradition*. Oxford: Clarendon, 1991.

Field, F., ed. *Origenis Hexaplorum*. 2 vols. Hildescheim: Georg Olms, 1964.

Fishwick, Duncan. "The Name of the Demi-God." *Historia* 24 (1975): 624–28.

———. *The Imperial Cult in the Latin West: Studies in the Ruler Cult of the Western Provinces of the Roman Empire*. Leiden: Brill, 1987.

Fitzmeyer, Joseph. "Virginal Conception of Jesus in the New Testament." *Theological Studies* 34 (1973): 541–75.

———. *The Gospel According to Luke: Introduction, Translation and Notes*. 2 vols. Anchor Bible 28–28a. Garden City, NY: Doubleday, 1981–85.

———. "The Aramaic Background of Philippians 2:6-11." *Catholic Biblical Quarterly* 50 (1988): 470–83.

Fletcher-Louis, Crispin H. T. *Luke-Acts: Angels, Christology and Soteriology*. Tübingen: Mohr Siebeck, 1997.

———. "The Revelation of the Sacral Son of Man: The Genre, History of Religions Context and the Meaning of the Transfiguration." Pages 247–300 in *Auferstehung-Resurrection*. Edited by Friedrich Avemarie and Hermann Lichtenberger. Wissenschaftliche Untersuchungen der Neuen Testament 135. Tübingen: Mohr Siebeck, 2001.

———. *All the Glory of Adam*. Leiden: Brill, 2002.

———. "Alexander the Great's Worship of the High Priest." Pages 71–102 in *Early Jewish and Christian Monotheism*. Edited by Loren Stuckenbruck and Wendy North. London & New York: T&T Clark, 2004.

Foerster, Werner, and G. Quell. *Bible Key Words from Gerhard Kittel's Theologisches Wörterbuch zum Neuen Testament*. London: A&C Black, 1958.

Forbes-Irving, P. M. C. *Metamorphosis in Greek Myths*. Oxford: Clarendon, 1990

Foskett, Mary. *A Virgin Conceived: Mary and Classical Representations of Virginity.* Bloomington: Indiana University Press, 2002.

Fossum, Jarl. *The Name of God and the Angel of the Lord: Samaritan and Jewish Concepts of Intermediation and the Origin of Gnosticism.* Wissenschaftliche Untersuchungen zum Neuen Testament 36. Tübingen: Mohr Siebeck, 1985.

———. "Kyrios Jesus as the Angel of the Lord in Jude 5-7." *New Testament Studies* 33 (1987): 226–43.

———. "The New Religionsgeschichtliche Schule: The Quest for Jewish Christology." Pages 638–46 in *SBL Seminar Papers 1991.* Edited by Eugene H. Lovering. Atlanta: Scholars, 1991.

———. *The Image of the Invisible God: Essays on the Influence of Jewish Mysticism on Early Christology.* Göttingen: Vandenhoeck & Ruprecht, 1995.

France, R. T. *The Gospel of Mark: A Commentary on the Greek Text.* Grand Rapids, MI: Eerdmans, 2002.

Frankfort, Henri. *Kingship and the Gods: A Study of Ancient Near Eastern Religion as the Integration of Society & Nature.* Chicago: University of Chicago Press, 1948.

Frede, Michael. "Celsus philosophus Platonicus." *ANRW* 36.7:5183–5213. Part 2, *Principat,* 36.7. Edited by Wolfgang Haase. Berlin: Walter de Gruyter, 1994.

Fredriksen, Paula. "Lord Jesus Christ: Devotion to Jesus in Earliest Christianity." *Journal of Early Christian Studies* 12 (2004): 539–41.

Frenschkowski, Marco. *Offenbarung und Epiphanie: Die verborgene Epiphanie in Spätantike und frühem Christentum.* Wissenschaftliche Untersuchungen zum Neuen Testament 2/80. 2 vols. Tübingen: Mohr Siebeck, 1997.

Friesen, Steven. "Satan's Throne, Imperial Cults and the Social Settings of Revelation." *Journal for the Study of the New Testament* 27 (2005): 351–73.

Frontisi-Ducroux, Françoise. *L'homme-cerf et la femme-araignée: Figures grecques de la métamorphose.* Paris: Gallimard, 2003.

Fulco, William J. "Response to Badian." Pages 37–42 in *The Deification of Alexander the Great.* Berkeley, CA: Center for Hermeneutical Studies, 1976.

Fullmer, Paul M. *Resurrection in Mark's Literary-Historical Perspective.* Library of New Testament Studies 360. London: T&T Clark, 2007.

Funk, Robert, ed. *The Acts of Jesus: The Search for the Authentic Deeds of Jesus.* New York: HarperSanFrancisco, 1998.

Gager, John G. *Kingdom and Community: The Social World of Early Christianity.* Englewood Cliffs, NJ: Prentice-Hall, 1975.

Galinsky, Karl. *The Herakles Theme.* Oxford: Basil Blackwell, 1972.

————. *Ovid's Metamorphoses: An Introduction to the Basic Aspects.* Oxford: Blackwell, 1975.

Gallagher, Eugene. *Divine Man or Magician?* Atlanta: Scholars, 1982.

Gamble, Harry Y. "Euhemerism and Christology in Origen: *Contra Celsum* 3,22–43." *Vigiliae Christianae* 33 (1979): 12–29.

Gantz, Timothy. *Early Greek Myth: A Guide to Literary and Artistic Sources.* Baltimore, MD: Johns Hopkins University Press, 1993.

Gathercole, Simon J. *The Pre-existent Son: Recovering the Christologies of Matthew, Mark, and Luke.* Grand Rapids, MI: Eerdmans, 2006.

Gauthier, P. *Les cités grecques et leur bienfaiteurs.* Athens: Ecole française d'Athènes, 1985.

Geber, Wolfgang. "Metamorphose." *Theologische Zeitschrift* 23 (1967): 385–95.

Geerlings, Wilhelm. "Die θεῖος ἀνήρ-Vorstellung der 'Religionsgeschichtlichen Schule' und ihre Kritik." Pages 121–132 in *Gottmenschen: Konzepte existentieller Grenzüberschreitung im Altertum.* Edited by Gerhard Binder et al. Trier: Wissenschaftlicher, 2003.

Georgi, Dieter. "Der Vorpaulinische Hymnus Phil. 2:6–11." Pages 263–93 in *Zeit und Geschichte: Dankesgabe an Rudolf Bultmann Zum 80.Geburtstag.* Edited by Erich Dinkler. Tübingen: Mohr Siebeck, 1964.

————. *Opponents of Paul in 2 Corinthians.* Philadelphia: Fortress Press, 1986.

Gesche, Helga. *Die Vergottung Caesars.* Regensburg: Michael Lassleben, 1968.

Gieschen, Charles. *Angelomorphic Christology: Antecedents and Early Evidence.* Leiden: Brill, 1998.

————. "The Divine Name in Ante-Nicene Christology." *Vigiliae Christianae* 57 (2003): 115–58.

Gillingham, S. E. "The Messiah in the Psalms: A Question of Reception History and the Psalter." Pages 209–37 in *King and Messiah in Israel and the Ancient near East.* Edited by John Day. Sheffield: Sheffield Academic, 1998.

Glawe, Walther. *Die Hellenisierung des Christentums in der Geschichte der Theologie von Luther bis auf die Gegenwart.* Berlin: Trowitzsch & Sohn, 1912.

Gnilka, Joachim. *Das Evangelium nach Markus: 2 Teilband Mk 8,27–16,20.* 2 vols. Evangelisch-Katholischer Kommentar. Zürich: Benziger, 1979.

Golden, Mark. *Children and Childhood in Classical Athens.* Baltimore, MD: Johns Hopkins University Press, 1990.

Goldstein, Jonathan A. *Semites, Iranians, Greeks, and Romans: Studies in their Interactions.* Atlanta: Scholars, 1990.

Goodchild, R. G., and J. M. Reynolds. "The Temple of Zeus at Cyrene." *Papers of the British School at Rome* 26 (1958): 30–62.

Goodenough, E. R. "Kingship in Early Israel." *Journal of Biblical Literature* 48 (1929): 169–205.

———. *By Light, Light: The Mystic Gospel of Hellenistic Judaism.* New Haven, CT: Yale University Press, 1935.

Gradel, Ittai. *Emperor Worship and Roman Religion.* Oxford: Clarendon, 2002.

Graf, Fritz. *Magic in the Ancient World.* Cambridge, MA: Harvard University Press, 1997.

Graf-Reventlow, Henning. "A Syncretistic Enthronement Hymn in Is 9,1-6." *Ugarit-Forschungen* 3 (1971): 321–5.

Gray, J. "Canaanite Kingship in Theory and Practice." *Vetus Testamentum* 2 (1952): 193–220.

Green, Joel B. *The Gospel of Luke.* New International Commentary on the New Testament. Grand Rapids, MI: Eerdmans, 1997.

Green, Peter. *Alexander to Actium: The Historical Evolution of the Hellenistic Age.* Berkeley: University of California Press, 1990.

Greenberg, Moshe. *Ezekiel 21–37: A New Translation with Introduction and Commentary.* Anchor Bible 22A. New York: Doubleday, 1997.

Griffith, G.T., ed. *Alexander the Great: The Main Problems.* Cambridge: Barnes & Noble, 1966.

Grindheim, Sigurd. *Christology in the Synoptic Gospels: God or God's Servant?* London: T&T Clark, 2012.

Gromacki, Robert. *The Virgin Birth: A Biblical Study of the Deity of Jesus Christ.* 2nd ed. Grand Rapids, MI: Kregal, 2002.

Gruen, Erich S. *Heritage and Hellenism: The Reinvention of Jewish Tradition.* Berkeley: University of California Press, 1998.

———. *Diaspora: Jews Amidst Greeks and Romans.* Cambridge: Harvard University Press, 2002.

———. "Greeks and non Greeks." Pages 295–314 in *The Cambridge Companion to the Hellenistic World.* Edited by Glenn R. Bugh. Cambridge: Cambridge University Press, 2006.

———. "Hebraism and Hellenism." Pages 129–139 in *The Oxford Handbook of Hellenic Studies.* Edited by George Boys-Stones et al. Oxford: Oxford University Press, 2009.

Grusec, Joan E., and Paul D. Hastings, eds. *Handbook of Socialization: Theory and Research.* New York: Guilford, 2006.

Guthrie, W. K. C. *A History of Greek Philosophy*. 6 vols. Cambridge: University of Cambridge Press, 1962.

Habermann, Jürgen. *Präexistenzaussagen im Neuen Testament*. Frankfurt am Main: Bern, 1990.

Habicht, Christian. *Gottmenschentum und griechische Städte*. 2nd ed. Munich: C. H. Beck, 1970.

———. "Die augusteische Zeit und das erste Jahrhundert nach Christi Geburt." Pages 39–99 in *Le culte des souverains dans l'empire romain*. Edited by E. J. Bickerman. Vandoeuvres-Genève: Fondation Hardt, 1973.

Haenchen, Ernst. *John 1: A Commentary on the Gospel of John Chapters 1–6*. Edited by Robert Funk and Ulrich Busse. Translated by Robert Funk. Hermeneia. Philadelphia: Fortress Press, 1984.

Hafemann, Scott. *Paul, Moses, and the History of Israel*. Milton Keynes, UK: Paternoster, 2005.

Hahn, Ferdinand. *The Titles of Jesus in Christology*. Translated by Harold Knight and George Ogg. New York: World Publishing, 1969.

Hall, Jonathan M. *Hellenicity: Between Ethnicity and Culture*. Chicago: University of Chicago, 2002.

Hallo, William. *Early Mesopotamian Royal Titles: A Philologic and Historical Analysis*. New Haven, CT: American Oriental Society, 1957.

Halpern, Baruch. *The Constitution of the Monarchy in Israel*. Harvard Semitic Monographs. Chico, CA: Scholars, 1981.

Hamerton-Kelly, R. G. *Pre-existence, Wisdom, and the Son of Man: A Study of the Idea of Pre-existence in the New Testament*. Cambridge: Cambridge University Press, 1973.

Hamilton, J. R. "Alexander and His So-Called Father." *Classical Quarterly* 3 (1953): 151–57.

Hamori, Esther. *"When Gods Were Men": The Embodied God in Biblical and Near Eastern Literature*. Berlin: Walter de Gruyter, 2008.

Hannah, Darrell. *Michael and Christ: Michael Traditions and Angel Christology in Early Christianity*. Wissenschaftliche Untersuchungen zum Neuen Testament. 2/109. Tübingen: Mohr Siebeck, 1999.

———. "The Throne of His Glory: The Divine Throne and Heavenly Mediators in Revelation and the Similitudes of Enoch." *Zeitschrift für Neutestamentliche Wissenschaft* 94 (2003): 68–96.

Hardie, P. R. "Plutarch and the Interpretation of Myth." *ANRW* 33.6: 4743–4787. Part 2, *Principat*, 33.6. Edited by Wolfgang Haase. Berlin: Walter de Gruyter, 1992.

Hardy, Edward. "The Date of Psalm 110." *Journal of Biblical Literature* 64 (1945): 385–93.

Hargis, Jeffrey W. *Against the Christians: The Rise of Early Anti-Christian Polemic.* New York: Peter Lang, 1999.

Harnack, Adolf. "Die Verklärungsgeschichte Jesus, der Bericht des Paulus (1 Kor. 15,3ff) und die beiden Christusvisionen des Petrus." *Sitzungsberichte der Preussischen Akademie der Wissenschaften* 34 (1922): 62–80.

Harris, Murray J. *Jesus as God: The New Testament Use of Theos in Reference to Jesus.* Grand Rapids, MI: Baker Book House, 1992.

Hasenfuss, Josef. "Die Jungfrauengeburt in der Religionsgeschichte." Pages 11–23 in *Jungfrauengeburt gestern und heute.* Edited by Hermann Josef Brosch and Josef Hasenfuss. Essen: Verlag Hans Driewer, 1969.

Hay, David M. *Glory at the Right Hand: Psalm 110 in Early Christianity.* Society of Biblical Literature Monograph Series 18. Nashville: Abingdon, 1973.

Hayes, John H. "Resurrection as Enthronement and the Earliest Church Christology." *Interpretation* 22 (1968): 33–45.

Hayward, C. T. R. "The Holy Name of the God of Moses and the Prologue of St John's Gospel." *New Testament Studies* 25 (1978): 16–32.

Heckel, Hartwig. "Der Dichter und der Gott: Ovid über die Göttlichkeit des Augustus." Pages 67–96 in *Gottmenschen: Konzepte existentieller Grenzüberschreitung im Altertum.* Trier: Wissenschaflicher, 2003.

Heil, John Paul. *The Transfiguration of Jesus: Narrative Meaning and Function of Mark 9:2-8, Matt 17:1-8 and Luke 9:28-36.* Analecta Biblica 144. Rome: Pontifical Institute, 2000.

Heitmüller, Wilhelm. *Im Namen Jesu: Eine sprach-u.religionsgescihtliche Untersuchung zum Neuen Testament.* Göttingen: Vandenhoeck & Ruprecht, 1903.

Heller, Jan. "Namengebung und Namendeutung: Grundzüge der alttestamentlichen Onomatologie und ihre Folgen für die biblische Hermeneutik." *Evangelische Theologie* 27 (1967): 255–66.

Hengel, Martin. "Christologie und neutestamentliche Chronologie: Zu einer Aporie in der Geschichte des Urchristentums." Pages 43–67 in *Neues Testament und Geschichte: Historisches Geschehen und Deutung im Neuen Testament.* Edited by Heinrich Baltensweiler and Bo Reicke. Zürich: Theologischer, 1972.

———. *Der Sohn Gottes: Die Entstehung der Christologie und die jüdisch-hellenistische Religionsgeschichte.* 2nd ed; Tübingen: Mohr Siebeck, 1977.

———. *Judentum und Hellenismus: Studien zu ihrer Begegnung unter besonderer Berücksichtigung Palästinas bis zur Mitte des 2.Jh. v.Chr.* Wissenschaftliche Untersuchungen zum Neuen Testament 10. 3d edition. Tübingen: Mohr Siebeck, 1988.

———. *The 'Hellenization' of Judaea in the First Century after Christ.* London: SCM, 1989.

———. *Studies in Early Christology.* Edinburgh: T&T Clark, 1995.

———. *Theologische, historische, und biographische Skizzen. Kleine Schriften VII.* Edited by Claus-Jürgen Thornton. WUNT 253. Tübingen: Mohr Siebeck, 2010.

———. "A Young Theological Discipline in Crisis." Pages 459–72 in *Earliest Christian History: History, Literature, and Theology.* Edited by Michael F. Bird and Jason Maston. Wissenschaftliche Untersuchungen zum Neuen Testament 2/320. Tübingen: Mohr Siebeck, 2012.

Henrichs, Albert."Two Doxographical Notes: Democritus and Prodicus on Religion." *HSCP* 79 (1975): 93–123.

———. "Gods in Action: The Poetics of Divine Performance in the *Hymns* of Callimachus." Pages 127–48 in *Callimachus.* Edited by M. A. Harder et al. Groningen: Egbert Forsten, 1993.

———. "What is a Greek God?" Pages 19–39 in *The Gods of Ancient Greece: Identities and Transformations.* Edited by Jan N. Bremmer and Andrew Erskine. Edinburgh: Edinburgh University Press, 2010.

Herklotz, Friederike. *Prinzeps und Pharao: Der Kult des Augustus in Ägypten.* Frankfurt am Main: Verlag Antike, 2007.

Heschel, Susannah. "Jewish Studies as Counterhistory." Pages 101–15 in *Insider/ Outsider: American Jewish & Multiculturalism.* Edited by D. Biale et al. Berkeley: University of California Press, 1998.

Hocart, A. M. *Kingship.* Oxford: Oxford University Press, 1927.

Hock, R. F. *The Infancy Gospels of James and Thomas.* Santa Rosa, CA: Polebridge, 1995.

Hofius, Otfried. *Der Christushymnus Phil 2,6-11.* 2nd ed. Wissenschaftliche Untersuchungen zum Neuen Testament 17. Tübingen: Mohr Siebeck, 1991.

Hoïstad, Ragnar. *Cynic Hero and Cynic King: Studies in the Cynic Conception of Man.* Lund: C. Bloms Boktryckeri, 1948.

Holladay, Carl. *Theios Aner in Hellenistic-Judaism: A Critique of the Use of This Category in New Testament Christology.* Missoula, MT: Scholars, 1977.

Holladay, William L. *Isaiah, the Scroll of a Prophetic Heritage.* Grand Rapids, MI: Eerdmans, 1978.

Holt, Philip. "Herakles' Apotheosis in Lost Greek Literature and Art." *L'Antiquité classique* 61 (1992): 38–59.

Homburg, Klaus. "Psalm 110,1 Im Rahmen des judaischen Kronungzeremoniells." *Zeitschrift für die Alttestmentliche Wissenchaft* 84 (1972): 243–46.

Honeyman, Alexander Mackie. "The Evidence for Regnal Names Among the Hebrews." *Journal of Biblical Literature* 67 (1948): 13–25.

Hooker, Morna. "The Letter to the Philippians." Pages 467–550 in vol. 11 of the *The New Interpreter's Bible*. Edited by Leander Keck. 12 vols. Nashville: Abingdon, 2000.

Horbury, William. *Jewish Messianism and the Cult of Christ*. London: SCM, 1998.

———. "Lord Jesus Christ: Devotion to Jesus in Earliest Christianity." *Journal of Theological Studies* 56 (2005): 537–38.

Hornung, Erik. *Akhenaten and the Religion of Light*. Translated by David Lorton. Ithaca, NY: Cornell University Press, 1999.

Horsley, Richard, ed. *Paul and Politics*. Harrisburg, PA: Trinity Press International, 2000.

———, ed. *Paul and the Roman Imperial Order*. Harrisburg, PA: Trinity Press International, 2004.

Hossfeld, Frank-Lothar, and Erich Zenger. *Psalms 3: A Commentary on Psalms 101–150*. Edited by Klaus Baltzer. Translated by Linda M. Maloney. Hermeneia. Minneapolis: Fortress Press, 2011.

Howard, G. "The Tetragramm and the New Testament." *Journal of Biblical Literature* 96 (1977): 63–83.

Huie-Jolly, Mary. "Threats Answered by Enthronement: Death/Resurrection and the Divine Warrior Myth in John 5:17-29, Psalm 2 and Daniel 7." Pages 191–217 in *Early Christian Interpretation of the Scriptures of Israel*. Edited by Craig Evans and James Sanders. Sheffield: Sheffield Academic Press, 1997.

Hunter, Richard. *Theocritus: Encomium of Ptolemy Philadelphus*. Berkeley: University of California, 2003.

Hurst, L. D. "Christ, Adam, and Preexistence Revisited." Pages 84–95 in *Where Christology Began: Essays on Philippians 2*. Edited by Ralph P. Martin and Brian J. Dodd. Louisville: Westminster John Knox, 1998.

Hurtado, Larry. "New Testament Christology: A Critique of Bousset's Influence." *Theological Studies* 40 (1979): 306–17.

———. "New Testament Christology: Retrospect and Prospect." *Semeia* 30 (1985): 15–28.

————. *One God, One Lord: Early Christian Devotion and Ancient Jewish Monotheism.* 2nd ed. Edinburgh: T&T Clark, 1998.

————."The Binitarian Shape of Early Christian Worship." Pages 187–213 in *Jewish Roots of Christological Monotheism. Papers from the St. Andrews Conference on the Historical Origins of the Worship of Jesus.* Edited by Carey C. Newman, James R. Davila, and Gladys S. Lewis. Leiden: Brill, 1999.

————. *Lord Jesus Christ: Jesus in Earliest Christian Devotion.* Grand Rapids, MI: Eerdmans, 2003.

————. *How on Earth Did Jesus Become a God?: Historical Questions about Earliest Devotion to Jesus.* Grand Rapids, MI: Eerdmans, 2005.

————. "'Jesus' as God's Name, and Jesus as God's Embodied Name in Justin Martyr." Pages 128–36 in *Justin Martyr and His Worlds.* Edited by S. Parvis and P. Foster. Minneapolis: Fortress Press, 2007.

Huskinson, Janet, ed. *Experiencing Rome: Culture, Identity, and Power in the Roman Empire.* London: Routledge, 2000.

Jacobsen, Thorkild. "The Investiture and Anointing of Adapa in Heaven." *American Journal of Semitic Languages and Literatures* 46 (1930): 201–03.

Jaillard, Dominique. *Configurations d'Hermès. Une "théogonie hermaïque."* Kernos Supplément 17. Liège: Centre International d'Étude de la Religion Grecque Antique, 2007.

Janowitz, Naomi. *Magic in the Roman World: Pagans, Jews and Christians.* London: Routledge, 2001.

Johnson, Aaron P. *Ethnicity and Argument in Eusebius'* Praepartio Evangelica. Oxford: Oxford University Press, 2006.

Johnson, Aubrey. "The Role of the King in the Jerusalem Cultus." Pages 71–112 in *The Labyrinth: Further Studies in the Relation Between Myth and Ritual in the Ancient World.* Edited by S. H. Hooke. London: Society for Promoting Christian Knowledge, 1935.

————. "Divine Kingship and the Old Testament." *Expository Times* 62 (1950): 36–42.

————. "Hebrew Conceptions of Kingship." Pages 204–35 in *Myth, Ritual and Kingship: Essays on the Theory and Practice of Kingship in the Ancient Near East and in Israel.* Edited by S. H. Hooke. Oxford: Clarendon, 1958.

————. *Sacral Kingship in Ancient Israel.* Cardiff: University of Wales Press, 1967.

Johnson, Luke Timothy. *Religious Experience in Early Christianity: A Missing Dimension in New Testament Studies.* Minneapolis: Fortress Press, 1998.

————. *Among the Gentiles: Greco-Roman Religion and Christianity*. New Haven, CT: Yale University Press, 2009.

Johnston, Philip S. *Shades of Sheol: Death and Afterlife in the Old Testament*. Downers Grove, IL: IVP, 2007.

Jones, C. P. *Plutarch and Rome*. Oxford: Clarendon, 1971.

Junker, H., and E. Winter. *Das Geburtshaus des Tempels der Isis in Philä*. Philä II, Österreichische Akademie der Wissenschaften, Phil.-hist. Klasse, Denkschriften, Sonderband. Vienna: Böhlau, 1965.

Kaldellis, Anthony. *Hellenism in Byzantium: The Transformations of Greek Identity and the Reception of the Classical Tradition*. Cambridge: Cambridge University Press, 2007.

Kantiréa, Maria. *Les dieux et les dieux augustes: Le culte impérial en Grèce sous les Julio-claudiens et les Flaviens*. Athens: Center for Hellenic and Roman Antiquity, 2007.

Kee, Howard Clark. "The Transfiguration in Mark: Epiphany or Apocalyptic Vision?" Pages 135–52 in *Understanding the Sacred Text: Essays in Honor of Morton S. Enslin on the Hebrew Bible and Christian Beginnings*. Edited by John Reumann. Valley Forge, PA: Judson, 1972.

————. *Miracle in the Early Christian World: A Study in Sociohistorical Method*. New Haven, CT: Yale University Press, 1983.

Keith, A. M. *The Play of Fictions: Studies in Ovid's* Metamorphoses *Book 2*. Ann Arbor: University of Michigan, 1992.

Kienast, Dietmar. "Augustus und Alexander." *Gymnasium* 76 (1969): 430–56.

Kim, Seyoon. *The Origin of Paul's Gospel*. 2nd ed. Wissenschaftliche Untersuchungen zum Neuen Testament 2/4. Tübingen: J. C. B. Mohr, 1984.

————. *Christ and Caesar: The Gospel and the Roman Empire in the Writings of Paul and Luke*. Grand Rapids, MI: Eerdmans, 2008.

Kitchen, Kenneth. "Genesis 12–50 in the Near Eastern World." Pages 67–92 in *He Swore an Oath: Biblical Themes from Genesis 12–50*. Edited by Richard S. Hess et al. Grand Rapids, MI: Baker Book House, 1994.

Klauck, Hans-Josef. *Apocryphal Gospels: An Introduction*. Translated by Brian McNeil. London: T&T Clark, 2003.

Klotz, Frieda, and Katerina Oikonomopoulou, eds. *The Philosopher's Banquet: Plutarch's* Table Talk *in the Intellectual Culture of the Roman Empire*. Oxford: Oxford University Press, 2011.

Klutz, Todd. "The Value of Being Virginal: Mary and Anna in the Lukan Infancy Prologue." Pages 71–88 in *The Birth of Jesus: Biblical and Theological Reflections*. Edited by George J. Brooke. Edinburgh: T&T Clark, 2000.

Knight, Jonathan. "The Origin and Significance of the Angelomorphic Christology in the Ascension of Isaiah." *Journal of Theological Studies* 63 (2012): 66–105.

Knox, Wilfred L. "The 'Divine Hero' Christology in the New Testament." *Harvard Theological Review* 41 (1948): 229–249.

Kohler, Kaufmann. "The Tetragrammaton (Shem Ham-M'forash) and Its Uses." *Journal of Jewish Lore and Philosophy* 1 (1919): 19–32.

Korpel, Marjo Christina Annette. *A Rift in the Clouds: Ugarit and Hebrew Descriptions of the Divine*. Münster: Ugarit-Verlag, 1990.

Koskenniemi, Erkki. "Apollonius of Tyana: A Typical Θεῖος Ἀνήρ?" *Journal of Biblical Literature* 117 (1998): 455–67.

Kraay C., and M. Hirmer. *Greek Coins*. New York: Harry N. Abrams, 1966.

Kramer, W. *Christ, Lord, Son of God*. London: SCM, 1966.

Kraus, Hans-Joachim. *Theology of the Psalms*. Translated by Keith Crim. Minneapolis: Augsburg, 1986.

———. *Psalms 1–59: A Commentary*. Minneapolis: Augsburg, 1988.

Kreitzer, Larry J. *Striking New Images: Roman Imperial Coinage and the New Testament World*. Sheffield: Sheffield Academic Press, 1996.

Kügler, Joachim. "Spüren ägyptisch-hellenistischer Königsideologie bei Philo von Alexandrien." Pages 231–50 in *Ägypten und der östliche Mittelmeerraum im 1. Jahrtausend v. Chr.* Edited by Manfred Görg and Günther Hölbl. Wiesbaden: Harrassowitz, 2000.

Kuschel, Karl-Josef. *Born Before All Time? The Dispute over Christ's Origen*. Translated by John Bowden. New York: Crossroad, 1992.

Kyrtatas, Dimitris. "Epiphany: Concept Ambiguous, Experience Elusive." *Illinois Classical Studies* 29 (2004): 227–34.

Lamberton, Robert. *Plutarch*. New Haven, CT: Yale University Press, 2001.

Landry, David T. "Narrative Logic in the Annunciation to Mary (Luke 1:26–38)." *Journal of Biblical Literature* 114 (1995): 65–79.

Lane Fox, Robin. *Pagans and Christians*. New York: Knopf, 1987.

Lang, Bernhard. "Der vergöttlichte König im Polytheistischen Israel." Pages 37–59 in *Menschwerdung Gottes-Vergöttlichung Von Menschen*. Edited by Dieter Zeller. Freiburg: Vandenhoeck & Ruprecht, 1988.

Lanzillotta, Lautaro Roig. "Christian Apologists and Greek Gods." Pages 442–64 in *The Gods of Ancient Greece: Identities and Transformations*. Edited by Jan N. Bremmer and Andrew Erskine. Edinburgh: Edinburgh University Press, 2010.

Lateiner, Donald. *Sardonic Smile: Nonverbal Behavior in Homeric Epic.* Ann Arbor: University of Michigan Press, 1995.

Lau, Andrew Y. *Manifest in Flesh: The Epiphany Christology of the Pastoral Epistles.* Wissenschaftliche Untersuchungen zum Neuen Testament 2/86. Tübingen: Mohr Siebeck, 1996.

Laurence, Ray, and Joanne Berry, eds. *Cultural Identity in the Roman Empire.* London: Routledge, 1998.

Le Bohec-Bouhet, Sylvie. "The Kings of Macedon and the Cult of Zeus in the Hellenistic Period." Pages 41–58 in *The Hellenic World: New Perspectives.* Edited by Daniel Ogden. London: Duckworth, 2002.

Le Boulluec, Alain. "Hellenism and Christianity." Pages 858–69 in *Greek Thought: A Guide to Classical Knowledge.* Edited by Jacque Brunschwig and Geoffrey E. R. Lloyd. Cambridge: Belknap, 2000.

Le Déaut, R. "ΦΙΛΑΝΘΡΩΠΙΑ *dans* la littérature grecques jusqu'au Nouveau Testament." Pages 255–94 in vol. 1 of *Mélanges Eugène Tisserant.* Edited by E. Tisserant. 7 vols. Vatican City: Biblioteca Apostolica Vatican, 1964.

Lee, Dorothy. *Transfiguration: New Century Theology.* London: Continuum, 2004.

Lee, Simon. *Jesus' Transfiguration and the Believer's Transformation: A Study of the Transfiguration and Its Development in Early Christian Writings.* Wissenschaftliche Untersuchungen zum Neuen Testament 2/265. Tübingen: Mohr Siebeck, 2009.

Legrand, Lucien. *L'annonce a Marie (Lc 1,26-38): Une apocalypse aux origines de l'Évangile.* Lectio Divina 106. Paris: Éditions du Cerf, 1981.

Lehmann, Thomas, ed., *Wunderheilungen in der Antike: Von Asklepios zu Felix Medicus.* Oberhausen: Athena, 2006.

Lehmkühler, Karsten. *Kultus und Theologie: Dogmatik und Exegese in der religionsgeschichtliche Schule.* Göttingen: Vandenhoeck & Ruprecht, 1996.

Leprohon, Ronald J. *The Great Name: Ancient Egyptian Royal Titulary,* Writings from the Ancient World 33. Edited by Denise M. Doxey. Atlanta: SBL, 2013.

Leisegang, Hans. *Pneuma hagion: der Ursprung des Geistbegriffs der synoptischen Evangelien aus der griechischen Mystik.* Leipzig: Hinrichs, 1922.

Lett, J. W. *The Human Enterprise: A Critical Introduction to Anthropological Theory.* Boulder, CO: Westview, 1987.

Levene, D. S. "Defining the Divine in Rome." *Transactions of the American Philological Association* 142 (2012): 41–82.

Levenson, Jon D. *Resurrection and the Restoration of Israel: The Ultimate Victory of the God of Life*. New Haven, CT: Yale University Press, 2006.

Levine, Lee I. *Judaism and Hellenism in Antiquity: Conflict or Confluence?* Seattle: University of Washington Press, 1998.

Liebeschuetz, J. H. W. G. *Continuity and Change in Roman Religion*. Oxford: Clarendon, 1979.

Lieu, Judith M. *Christian Identity in the Jewish and Graeco-Roman World*. Oxford: Oxford University Press, 2004.

———. *Neither Jew Nor Greek? Constructing Early Christian Identity*. London: T&T Clark, 2002.

Lincoln, Andrew T. "'Born of the Virgin Mary': Creedal Affirmation and Critical Reading." Pages 84–103 in *Christology and Scripture: Interdisciplinary Perspectives*. Edited by Lincoln and Angus Paddison. London: T&T Clark, 2007.

Lindars, Barnabas. *New Testament Apologetic*. London: SCM, 1961.

Litwa, M. David. *We Are Being Transformed*. Beihefte zum Zeitschrift für neue testamentliche Wissenschaft 187. Berlin: Walter de Gruyter, 2012.

———. *Becoming Divine: An Introduction to Deification in Western Culture*. Eugene: Cascade, 2013.

Loader, W. R. G. "Christ at the Right Hand-Ps. CX in the New Testament." *New Testament Studies* 24 (1978): 199–217.

Lods, A. "La Divinisation du roi dans l'orient méditerranéen et ses répercussions dans l'ancien Israel." *Revue d'Histoire et de Philosophie Religieuses* 10 (1930): 209–27.

Lohfink, Gerhard. "Meinen Namen zu tragen (Apg 9:15)." *Biblische Zeitschrift* 10 (1966): 108–15.

———. *Die Himmelfahrt Jesu: Untersuchungen zu den Himmelsfahrts-und Erhöhungstexten bei Lukas*. Munich: Kösel, 1971.

Lohmeher, Ernst. "Die Verklärung Jesu nach dem Markus-Evangelium." *Zeitschrift für Neutestamentliche Wissenschaft* 21 (1922): 185–215.

———. *Kyrios Jesus: Eine Untersuchung Zu Phil. 2,5-11*. 2nd ed. Sitzungberichte Der Heidelberger Akademie Der Wissenschaften, Philsophisch-Historische Klasse, Jahrgang 1927/1928, 4. Abhandlung. Heidelberg: Carl Winter Universitätsverlag, 1961.

———. *Das Evangelium des Markus*. Meyer Commentary 2. Göttingen: Vandenhoeck & Ruprecht, 1967.

Lona, Horacio E. *Die 'wahre Lehre' des Kelsos.* Freiburg: Herder, 2005.

Long, A. A. *Hellenistic Philosophy: Stoics, Epicureans, Sceptics.* 2nd ed. Berkeley: University of California, 1986.

López-Ruiz, Carolina. *When the Gods Were Born: Greek Cosmogonies and the Near East.* Cambridge, MA: Harvard University Press, 2010.

Lorsch, Robin S. "Augustus' Conception and the Heroic Tradition." *Latomus* 56 (1997): 790–99.

Lösch, Stephan. *Deitas Jesu und antike Apotheose: Ein Beitrag zur Exegese und Religionsgeschichte.* Rottenburg: Bader'sche Verlagsbuchhandlung, 1933.

Lott, J. B. "Philip II, Alexander and the Two Tyrannies at Eresos of IG xii.2 526." *Phoenix* 50 (1996): 26–40.

Lüdemann, Gerd. "Die 'Religionsgeschichtliche Schule' und die Neutestamentliche Wissenschaft." Pages 9–22 in *Die "Religionsgeschichtliche Schule": Facetten eines theologischen Umbruchs.* Edited by Gerd Lüdemann. Frankfurt am Main: Peter Lang, 1996.

———. *Virgin Birth? The Real Story of Mary and Her Son Jesus.* Translated by John Bowden. Harrisburg, PA: Trinity Press International, 1998.

Lüdemann, Gerd, and Martin Schröder. *Die religionsgeschichtliche Schule in Göttingen: Eine Dokumentation.* Göttingen: Vandenhoeck & Ruprecht, 1987.

Lührmann, Dieter. "Epiphaneia. Zur Bedeutungsgeschichte eine griechischen Wortes." Pages 185–99 in *Tradition und Glaube.* Edited by G. Jeremias et al. Göttingen: Vandenhoeck & Ruprecht, 1971.

Lust, J. *Messianism and the Septuagint: Collected Essays.* Leuven: Peeters, 2004.

Lutz-Bachmann, Matthias. "Hellenisierung des Christentums?" Pages 77–98 in *Spätantike und Christentum: Beiträge zur Religions- und Geistesgeschichte der griechisch-römischen Kultur und Zivilisation der Kaiserzeit.* Edited by Carsten Colpe et al. Berlin: Akademie, 1992.

MacDonald, Dennis. *Christianizing Homer:* The Odyssey, *Plato, and* The Acts of Andrew. Oxford: Oxford University Press, 1994.

———. *The Homeric Epics and the Gospel of Mark.* New Haven, CT: Yale University Press, 2000.

Mach, Michael. "Christus Mutans. Zur Bedeutung der 'Verklärung Jesu' im Wechsel von jüdischer Messianität zur neutestamentlichen Christologie." Pages 177–98 in *Messiah and Christos: Studies in the Jewish Origins of Christianity.* Edited by Ithamar Gruenwald et al. Tübingen: Mohr Siebeck, 1992.

MacMullen, Ramsay. *Paganism in the Roman Empire.* New Haven, CT: Yale University Press, 1981.

————. *Christianizing the Roman Empire.* New Haven, CT: Yale University Press, 1984.

Maderna, Caterina. *Iuppiter, Diomedes und Merkur als Vorbilder für römische Bildnisstatuen: Untersuchungen zum Römischen statuarischen Idealporträt.* Archäologie und Geschichte 1. Heidelberg: Archäologie und Geschichte, 1988.

Marcus, Joel. *The Way of the Lord: Christological Exegesis of the Old Testament in the Gospel of Mark.* Louisville: Westminster John Knox, 1992.

————. *Mark 8–16.* 2 vols. Anchor Yale Bible 27–27a. New York: Doubleday, 2000–09.

Marshall, I. H. "The Christ-Hymn in Philippians 2.5-11." *Tyndale Bulletin* 19 (1968): 104–27.

Martin, Dale. *The Corinthian Body.* New Haven, CT: Yale University Press, 1995.

Martin, P. M. *L'idée De Royauté à Rome: Haine de la royauté et séductions monarchiques.* 2 vols. Adosa: Clermont-Ferrand, 1994.

Martin, Ralph. "New Testament Hymns: Background and Development." *Expository Times* 94 (1983): 132–36.

————. *A Hymn of Christ: Philippians 2:5-11 in Recent Interpretation and In the Setting of Early Christian Worship.* Downers Grove, IL: IVP, 1997.

Mastin, B. A. "Daniel 2.46 and the Hellenistic World." *Zeitschrift für alttestementliche Wissenschaft* 85 (1973): 80–93.

Mattingly, D. "Vulgar and Weak 'Romanization,' or Time for a Paradigm Shift?" *Journal of Roman Archaeology* 15 (2002): 536–40.

McCarter, P. Kyle. *II Samuel: A New Translation with Introduction, Notes, and Commentary.* Anchor Yale Bible 9. New Haven, CT: Yale University Press, 1984.

McClellan, W. "El Gibbor." *Catholic Biblical Quarterly* 6 (1944): 276–88.

McDonough, Sean M. *YHWH at Patmos: Rev 1:4 in Its Hellenistic and Early Jewish Setting* Wissenschaftliche Untersuchungen zum Neuen Testament 107. Tübingen: Mohr Siebeck, 1999.

McEwan, C. W. *The Oriental Origin of Hellenistic Kingship.* Chicago Studies in Ancient Oriental Civilization. Chicago: University of Chicago Press, 1934.

McGuckin, John. *The Transfiguration of Christ in Scripture and Tradition.* Lewiston, NY: Mellen, 1986.

McHugh, John F. *A Critical and Exegetical Commentary on John 1–4.* Edited by Graham Stanton. London: T&T Clark, 2009.

Meeks, Wayne. *The Prophet-King: Moses Traditions and the Johannine Christology.* Leiden: Brill, 1967.

Meier, John. *A Marginal Jew: Rethinking the Historical Jesus.* Vol. 1, *The Roots of the Problem and the Person.* New York: Doubleday, 1991.

Menken, Maarten J. J. "'Born of God' or 'Begotten by God'? A Translation Problem in the Johannine Writings." *Novum Testamentum* 51 (2009): 352–68.

Menzies, Robert. *The Development of Early Christian Pneumatology with Special Reference to Luke-Acts.* Sheffield: Sheffield Academic, 1991.

Mettinger, Tryggve N. D. *King and Messiah: The Civil and Sacral Legitimation of the Israelite Kings.* Lund: Gleerup 1971.

——. *In Search of God: The Meaning and Message of the Everlasting Names.* Translated by Frederick H. Cryer. Philadelphia: Fortress Press, 1987.

——. *The Riddle of Resurrection: "Dying and Rising Gods" in the Ancient Near East.* Stockholm: Almqvist & Wiksell, 2001.

Meyer, Eduard. *Ursprung und Anfänge des Christentums.* 5th ed. Stuttgart: J. G. Cotta, 1921–23.

Meyers, Carol, and Eric Meyers. *Haggai; Zechariah 1–8: A New Translation with Introduction and Commentary.* Anchor Bible 25B. Garden City, NY: Doubleday, 1987.

Michel, Otto, and Otto Betz. "Von Gott gezeugt." Pages 3–23 in *Judentum, Urchristentum, Kirche: Festschrift für Joachim Jeremias.* Edited by Walther Eltester. Berlin: Alfred Töpelmann, 1964.

Mikalson, Jon. *Honor Thy Gods: Popular Religion in Greek Tragedy.* Chapel Hill: University of North Carolina, 1991.

——. *Greek Popular Religion in Greek Philosophy.* Oxford: Oxford University Press, 2010.

Miller, Robert J. "Historicizing the Transhistorical: The Transfiguration Narrative (Mark 9:2-8; Matt 17:1-8; Luke 9:28-36)." *Forum* 10 (1994): 219–48.

——. *Born Divine: The Births of Jesus and Other Sons of God.* Santa Rosa, CA: Polebridge, 2003.

Mirecki, Paul, and Marvin Meyer, eds. *Magic and Ritual in the Ancient World.* Leiden: Brill, 2002.

Miscall, Peter. *Isaiah.* Sheffield: JSOT, 1993.

Mitchell, Margaret. "Epiphanic Evolutions in Earliest Christianity." *Illinois Classical Studies* 29 (2004): 183–204.

————. "Origen, Celsus and Lucian on the 'Dénouement of the Drama' of the Gospels." Pages 215–36 in *Reading Religions in the Ancient World: Essays Presented to Robert Mcqueen Grant on His 90th Birthday*. Leiden: Brill, 2007.

Momigliano, Arnold. *Alien Wisdom: The Limits of Hellenization*. Cambridge: Cambridge University Press, 1975.

Moore, Carey. *Daniel, Esther and Jeremiah: The Additions*. Anchor Bible 44. New York: Doubleday, 1977.

Morawiecki, L. "The Power Conception of Alexander the Great and of Gaius Julius Caesar in Light of the Numismatic Sources." *Eos* 63 (1975): 99–127.

Morenz, S. "Ägyptische und Davidische Königstitulatur." *Zeitschrift für die Ägyptische Sprach und Altertumskunde* 79 (1954): 73–74.

Morgenstern, J. "The King-God among the Western Semites and the Meaning of Epiphanes." *Vetus Testamentum* 10 (1960): 138–97.

Moss, Candida R. "The Transfiguration: An Exercise in Markan Accommodation." *Biblical Interpretation* 12 (2004): 69–89.

Moule, C. F. D. "Further Reflections on Phil. 2:5–11." Pages 264–76 in *Apostolic History and the Gospel*. Edited by W. Gasque and R. P. Martin. Grand Rapids, MI: Eerdmans, 1970.

Mowinckel, Sigmund. *He That Cometh: The Messiah Concept in the Old Testament and Later Judaism*. Translated by G. W. Anderson. Nashville: Abingdon, 1956. Reprint, Grand Rapids, MI: Eerdmans, 2005.

Mühl, Max. "Des Herakles Himmelfahrt." *Rheinische Museum* 101 (1958): 106–34.

Mulder, J. S. M. *Studies on Psalm 45*. Oss: Offsetdrukkerij Witsiers, 1972.

Müller, Hans-Peter. "Die Verklärung Jesu: Eine motivgeschichtliche Studie." *Zeitschrift für neutestamentliche Wissenschaft* 51 (1960): 56–64.

Murphy-O'Connor, Jerome. "Christological Anthropology in Phil 2:6–11." *Revue Biblique* 83 (1976): 25–50.

————. "What Really Happened at the Transfiguration?" *Bible Review* 3 (1987): 8–21.

Mussies, Gerald. "Identification and Self-identification of Gods." Pages 1–18 in *Knowledge of God in the Greco-Roman World*. Edited by Roelof van den Broek et al. Leiden: Brill, 1988.

————. "Joseph's Dream (Matt 1,18–23) and Comparable Stories." Pages 177–86 in *Text and Testimony: Essays on New Testament and Apocryphal Literature in Honour of A. F. Klijn*. Kampen: J. H. Kok, 1988.

Nagata, Takeshi. "Philippians 2:5–11: A Case Study in the Contextual Shaping of Early Christology," PhD Dissertation, Princeton Seminary, 1981.

Negev, A. "Obodas the God." *Israel Exploration Journal* 36 (1986): 56–60

Nestle, W. *Vom Mythos zum Logos: die Selbstentfaltung des griechischen Denkens von Homer bis auf die Sophistik und Sokrates.* 2nd ed. Stuttgart: A. Kröner, 1975.

Neyrey, Jerome. *The Resurrection Stories.* Wilmington, DE: Michael Glazier, 1988.

Nickelsburg, George W. *Resurrection, Immortality, and Eternal Life in Intertestamental Judaism and Early Christianity.* 2nd ed. Cambridge, MA: Harvard University Press, 2006.

Nickelsburg, George W. E., and James C VanderKam. *1 Enoch 2: A Commentary on the Book of 1 Enoch Chapters 37–82.* Hermeneia. Minneapolis: Fortress Press, 2012.

Nicklin, T. "The Angel of God, or God the King?" *Expository Times* 33 (1921–22): 378–79.

Nilsson, Martin P. *The Minoan-Mycenaean Religion and its Survival in Greek Religion.* 2nd ed. Lund: Gleerup, 1968.

Nock, A. D. *Conversion: The Old and the New in Religion from Alexander the Great to Augustine of Hippo.* Oxford: Oxford University Press, 1933.

———. *Early Gentile Christianity.* New York: Harper & Row, 1964.

Nolland, John. *Luke 1–9:20.* Word Biblical Commentary 35a. Dallas: Word Books, 1989.

Norden, Eduard. *Die Geburt des Kindes: Geschichte einer religiösen Idee.* 3rd printing. Darmstadt: Wissenschaftliche Buchgesellschaft, 1958.

Norelli, Enrico. *Ascensio Isaiae: Commentarius.* Corpus Christianorum Series Apocryphorum 8. Turnhout: Brepols, 1995.

North, Helen F. "Death and Afterlife in Greek Tragedy and Plato." Pages 49–64 in *Death and Afterlife: Perspectives of World Religions.* Edited by Hiroshi Obayashi. New York: Praeger, 1992.

North, J. A. "Praesens Divus." *Journal of Roman Studies* 65 (1975): 171–77.

O'Brien, Peter T. *The Epistle to the Philippians.* Edited by I. H. Marshall and W. Ward Gasque. The New International Greek Testament Commentary. Grand Rapids, MI: Eerdmans, 1991.

Ogilvie, R. M. *The Romans and their Gods in the Age of Augustus.* London: Chatto & Windus, 1969.

Ostenfeld, Erik Nis. *Greek Romans and Roman Greeks: Studies on Cultural Interaction.* Aarhus: Aarhus University Press, 2002.

Pache, Corinne Ondine. *Baby and Child Heroes in Ancient Greece.* Urbana: University of Illinois, 2004.

Parpola, S. *Letters from Assyrian and Babylonian Scholars.* State Archives of Assyria 10. Helsinki: Helsinki University Press, 1993.

Patai, Raphael. "Hebrew Installation Rites: A Contribution to the Study of Ancient near Eastern-African Culture Contact." *Hebrew Union College Annual* 20 (1957): 143–225.

Paulissen, Lucie. "Jésus enfant divin: Processus de reconnaissance dans L'Évangile de l'Enfance selon Thomas." *Revue de Philosophie Ancienne* 22 (2004): 17–28.

Paulsen, Henning. "Synkretismus im Urchristentum und im Neuen Testament." Pages 301–9 in *Zur Literatur und Geschichte des frühem Christentums: Gesammelte Aufsätze.* Edited by Ute E. Eisen. Wissenschaftliche Untersuchungen zum Neuen Testament 99. Tübingen: Mohr Siebeck, 1997.

Paulsen, Thomas. "Verherrlichung und Verspottung. Die Gestalt des 'Gottmenschen' bei Philostrat und Lukian." Pages 97–120 in *Gottmenschen: Konzepte existentieller Grenzüberschreitung im Altertum.* Edited by Gerhard Binder et al. Trier: Wissenschaftlicher, 2003.

Pax, Elpidius. *ΕΠΙΦΑΝΕΙΑ. Eine religionsgeschichtliche Beitrag zur biblischen Theologie.* Munich: Karl Zink, 1955.

Pease, Arthur Stanley. *M. Tulli Ciceronis: De Natura Deorum.* Latin Texts and Commentaries. 2 vols. New York: Arno, 1979.

Pelling, Christopher. *Plutarch and History: Eighteen Studies.* Swansea: Classical Press of Wales, 2002.

Penner, Erwin. "The Enthronement of Christ in Ephesians." *Direction* 12 (1983): 12–19.

Pépin, Jean. "Christian Judgments on the Analogies between Christianity and Pagan Mythology." Pages 655–656 in vol. 2 of *Mythologies.* Edited by Yves Bonnefoy and Wendy Doniger. 2 vols. Chicago: University of Chicago Press, 1991.

Peppard, Michael. *The Son of God in the Roman World: Divine Sonship in Its Social and Political Context.* Oxford: Oxford University Press, 2011.

Perkins, Pheme. *Resurrection: New Testament Witness and Contemporary Reflection.* Garden City, NY: Doubleday, 1984.

———. "Christology and the Resurrection." Pages 173–81 in *Christology in Dialogue.* Edited by R. F. Berkey and S. A. Edwards. Cleveland: Pilgrim, 1993.

Petersen, Allan. *The Royal God: Enthronement Festivals in Ancient Israel and Ugarit?* Journal for the Study of the Old Testament Supplement Series. Sheffield: Sheffield Academic Press, 1998.

Pfister, Friedrich. "Epiphanie." Columns 277–323 in *Paulys Realencyclopädie der Classischen Altertumswissenschaft.* Edited by Georg Wissowa and Wilhelm Kroll. Supplementband 4. Stuttgart: Aldfred Druckenmüller, 1924.

———. "Herakles und Christus." *Archiv für Religionswissenschaft* 34 (1937): 42–60.

Pfleiderer, Otto. *The Early Christian Conception of Christ: Its Significance and Value in the History of Religion.* London: Williams & Norgate, 1905.

———. *Das Urchristentum seine Schriften und Lehren im geschichtlichen Zusammenhang.* Berlin: G. Reimer, 1887; 2nd edition, 1907.

Phillips, Thomas. *Paul, His Letters, and Acts.* Peabody, MA: Hendrickson, 2009.

———. "Why Did Mary Wrap the Newborn Jesus in 'Swaddling Clothes'? Luke 2.7 and 2.12 in the Context of Luke-Acts and First-century Jewish Literature." Pages 29–42 in *Reading Acts Today: Essays in Honour of Loveday C. A. Alexander.* Edited by Steve Walton et al. Library of New Testament Studies 427. London: T&T Clark, 2011.

Pickard-Cambridge, A. W. *Dithyramb Tragedy and Comedy.* Oxford: Clarendon, 1962.

Pilch, John. *Flights of the Soul: Visions, Heavenly Journeys, and Peak Experiences in the Biblical World.* Grand Rapids, MI: Eerdmans, 2011.

Pilgaard, Aage. "The Hellenistic *Theios Aner*—A model for Early Christian Christology?" Pages 101–22 in *The New Testament and Hellenistic Judaism.* Edited by P. Borgen and S. Giversen. Aahrus: Aahrus University Press, 1995.

Pinch, Geraldine. *Egyptian Myth: A Very Short Introduction.* Oxford: Oxford University Press, 2004.

Platt, Verity. *Facing the Gods: Epiphany and Representation in Graeco-Roman Art, Literature and Religion.* Cambridge: Cambridge University Press, 2011.

Pleket, H. W. "Religious History as the History of Mentality." Pages 171–83 in *Faith, Hope and Worship: Aspects of Religious Mentality in the Ancient World.* Edited by H. S. Versnel. Leiden: Brill, 1981.

Pollini, J. "Man or God: Divine Assimilation and Imitation in the Late Republic and Early Principate." Pages 334–63 in *Between Republic and Empire: Interpretations of Augustus and His Principate.* Edited by Kurt A. Raaflaub, Mark Toher, and G. W. Bowersock. Berkeley: University of California Press, 1990.

Poole, F. J. P. "Metaphors and Maps: Towards Comparison in the Anthropology of Religion." *Journal of the American Academy of Religion* 54 (1986): 411–57.

Porter, James I. "Hellenism and Modernity." Pages 7–18 in *The Oxford Handbook of Hellenic Studies*. Edited by George Boys-Stones et al. Oxford: Oxford University Press, 2009.

Porter, Stanley E. "Resurrection, the Greeks and the New Testament." Pages 52–81 in *Resurrection*. Edited by Stanley Porter, Michael Hayes, and David Tombs. Journal for the Study of the New Testament Supplement Series 186. Sheffield: Sheffield Academic Press, 1999.

Pötscher, Walter. "Die 'Auferstehung in der klassischen Antike." *Kairos* 7 (1965): 208–15.

———. *Hellas und Rom: Beiträge und kritische Auseinandersetzung mit der inzwischen erschienenen Literatur*. Hildesheim: Georg Olms, 1988.

Price, Simon. "Gods and Emperors: The Greek Language of the Roman Imperial Cult." *Journal of Hellenic Studies* 54 (1984): 79–95.

———. *Rituals and Power: The Roman Imperial Cult in Asia Minor*. Cambridge: Cambridge University Press, 1984.

———. "From Noble Funerals to Divine Cult: The Consecration of the Roman Emperors." Pages 56–105 in *Rituals of Royalty: Power and Ceremonial in Traditional Societies*. Edited by David Cannadine and Simon Price. Cambridge: Cambridge University Press, 1987.

———. *Religions of the Ancient Greeks*. Cambridge: Cambridge University Press, 1999.

Prince, Deborah Thompson. "The 'Ghost' of Jesus: Luke 24 in Light of Ancient Narratives of Post-Mortem Apparitions." *Journal for the Study of the New Testament* 29, no. 3 (2007): 287–301.

Prümm, Karl. "Herrscherkult und Neues Testament." *Biblica* 9 (1928): 3–25; 129–42; 289–301.

Puig i Tàrrech, Armand. "The Glory on the Mountain: The Episode of the Transfiguration of Jesus." *New Testament Studies* 58 (2012): 151–72.

Radl, Walter. *Der Ursprung Jesu: Traditionsgeschichtliche Untersuchungen zu Lukas 1–2*. Herders Biblische Studien 7. Freiburg: Herder, 1996.

Rainbow, Paul. "Jewish Monotheism as the Matrix for New Testament Christology." *Novum Testamentum* 33 (1991): 78–91.

Räisänen, Heikki. "Begotten by the Holy Spirit." Pages 321–41 in *Sacred Marriages: The Divine-Human Sexual Metaphor from Sumer to Early*

Christianity. Edited by Martti Nissinen and Risto Uro. Winona Lake, IN: Eisenbrauns, 2008.

Rajak, Tessa. *The Jewish Dialogue with Greece and Rome: Studies in Cultural and Social Interaction*. Leiden: Brill, 2001.

Rankin, H. D. *Antisthenes Sokratikos*. Amsterdam: Adolf M. Hakkert, 1986.

Rapp, Claudia. "Hellenic Identity, *Romanitas*, and Christianity in Byzantium." Pages 127–47 in *Hellenisms: Culture, Identity, and Ethnicity from Antiquity to Modernity*. Edited by Katerina Zacharia. Hampshire: Ashgate, 2008.

Rawson, Beryl. *Children and Childhood in Roman Italy*. Oxford: Oxford University Press, 2003.

Reed, Annette Yoshiko. "The Trickery of the Fallen Angels and the Demonic Mimesis of the Divine: Aetiology, Demonology, and Polemics in the Writings of Justin Martyr." *Journal of Early Christian Studies* 12 (2004): 141–71.

Reemts, Christiana. *Vernunftgemässer Glaube: Die Begründung des Christentums in der Schrift des Origenes gegen Celsus*. Bonn: Borengässer, 1998.

Rees, Roger. "The Emperor's New Names: Diocletian Jovius and Maximian Herculius." Pages 223–39 in *Herakles and Hercules: Exploring a Graeco-Roman Divinity*. Edited by Louis Rawlings and Hugh Bowden. Swansea: Classical Press of Wales, 2005.

Rehm, Martin. *Der Königliche Messias im Licht der Immanuel-Weissagungen des Buches Jesaja*. Kevelaer: Butzon u. Bercker, 1968.

Reimer, Andy. "A Biography of a Motif: The Empty Tomb." Pages 297–316 in *Ancient Fiction: The Matrix of Early Christian and Jewish Narrative*. Edited by Jo-Ann Brant et al. Atlanta: Society of Biblical Literature, 2005.

Remus, Harold. *Pagan-Christian Conflict over Miracle in the Second Century*. Cambridge, MA: Philadelphia Patristic Foundation, 1983.

Rengstorf, K. H. "Old and New Testament Traces of a Formula of the Judaean Royal Ritual." *Novum Testamentum* 5 (1962): 229–44.

Reumann, John. *Philippians: A New Translation with Introduction and Commentary*. Anchor Yale Bible 33B. New Haven, CT: Yale University Press, 2008.

Riesenfeld, Harald. *Jésus transfiguré: L'arrière-plan du récit évangelique de la transfiguration de Notre-Seigneur*. Copenhagen: Munksgaard, 1947.

Riginos, Alice Swift. *Platonica: The Anecdotes Concerning the Life and Writings of Plato*. Leiden: Brill, 1976.

Riley, Gregory J. *The River of God: A New History of Christian Origins*. New York: HarperSanFrancisco, 2001.

Rissi, Mathias. "Der Christushymnus in Phil 2,6–11." *ANRW* 33.17:3314–26. Part 2, *Principat*, 33.17. Edited by Wolfgang Haase. Berlin: Walter de Gruyter, 1987.

Roberts, J. J. M. "The Enthronement of YHWH and David: The Abiding Theological Significance of the Kingship Language of the Psalms." *Catholic Biblical Quarterly* 64 (2002): 675–86.

Robinson, James. "From Easter to Valentinus (or to the Apostle's Creed)." *Journal of Biblical Literature* 101 (1982): 5–37.

Rogers, G. M. "Demosthenes of Oenoanda and Models of Euergetism." *Journal of Roman Studies* 81 (1991): 91–100.

Rohde, Erwin. *Psyche: The Cult of Souls and Belief in Immortality among the Greeks.* Translated by W. B. Hillis from the 8th ed. New York: Arno, 1972.

Rooke, Deborah. "Kingship as Priesthood: The Relationship Between the High Priesthood and the Monarchy." Pages 187–208 in *King and Messiah in Israel and the Ancient Near East.* Edited by John Day. Sheffield: Sheffield Academic, 1998.

Roscoe, Paul. "The Comparative Method." Pages 25–46 in *The Blackwell Companion to the Study of Religion.* Edited by Robert A. Segal. Oxford: Blackwell, 2006.

Rose, H. J. "Herakles and the Gospels." *Harvard Theological Review* 31 (1938): 113–142.

Rösel, Martin. *Adonaj—warum Gott 'Herr' genannt wird.* Tübingen: Mohr Siebeck, 2000.

Rosenthal, E. I. J. "Some Aspects of the Hebrew Monarchy." *Journal of Jewish Studies* 9 (1958): 1–18.

Rowe, C. Kavin. "Luke-Acts and the Imperial Cult: A Way Through the Conundrum?" *Journal for the Study of the New Testament* 27 (2005): 279–300.

Rowe, William. "Adolf von Harnack and the Concept of Hellenization." Pages 69–98 in *Hellenization Revisited: Shaping a Christian Response within the Greco-Roman World.* Edited by Wendy E. Helleman. Lanham, MD: University Press of America, 1994.

Rowland, Christopher. "The Vision of the Risen Christ." *Journal of Theological Studies* 31 (1980): 1–11.

———. *The Open Heaven: A Study of Apocalyptic in Judaism and Early Christianity.* London: SPCK, 1982.

———. *Christian Origins: An Account of the Setting and Character of the most Important Messianic Sect of Judaism.* 2nd ed. London: SPCK, 2002.

Rubincam, Catherine. "The Nomenclature of Julius Caesar and the Later Augustus in the Triumviral Period." *Historia* 41 (1992): 88–103.

Ruck-Schröder, Adelheid. *Der Name Gottes und Der Name Jesus: Eine Neutestamentliche Studie.* Neukirchen: Neukirchener, 1999.

Runia, David T. "God and Man in Philo of Alexandria." *Journal of Theological Studies* 39 (1988): 48–75.

Rusam, Dietrich. *Die Gemeinschaft der Kinder Gottes: Das Motiv der Gotteskindschaft und die Gemeinden der johanneischen Briefe.* Stuttgart: Kohlhammer, 1993.

Russell, Norman. *The Doctrine of Deification in the Greek Patristic Tradition.* Oxford: Oxford University Press, 2004.

Sacks, Kenneth S. *Diodorus Siculus and the First Century.* Princeton, NJ: Princeton University Press, 1990.

Saller, Richard. "Corporal Punishment, Authority, and Obedience in the Roman Household." Pages 144–165 in *Marriage, Divorce, and Children in Ancient Rome.* Edited by Beryl Rawson. Oxford: Clarendon, 1991.

Sanders, Jack T. *The New Testament Christological Hymns: Their Historical Religious Background.* Study for the New Testament Monograph Series 15. New York: Cambridge University Press, 1971.

———. "Social Distance Between Christians and Both Jews and Pagans." Pages 361–84 in *Handbook of Early Christianity: Social Science Approaches.* Edited by Anthony J. Blasi et al. Lanham, MD: Altamira, 2002.

Sandmel, Samuel. "Parallelomania." *Journal of Biblical Literature* 81 (1962): 1–13.

Sauren, Herbert. "L'intronisation du roi en Israel a la lumière d'une lettre de Mari." *Orientalia Lovaniensia Periodica* 2 (1971): 5–12.

Savran, George W. *Encountering the Divine: Theophany in Biblical Narrative.* London: T&T Clark, 2005.

Sayce, A. H. *Lectures on the Origin and Growth of Religion as Illustrated by the Religion of the Ancient Babylonians.* 3rd ed. London: Williams & Norgate, 1891.

Schaberg, Jane. *The Illegitimacy of Jesus: A Feminist Theological Interpretation of the Infancy Narratives.* Expanded edition. Sheffield: Sheffield Phoenix Press, 2006.

Schenk, Wolfgang. *Die Philipperbriefe Paulus.* Stuttgart: Kohlhammer, 1984.

Schmidt, Werner H. *The Faith of the Old Testament: A History.* Oxford: Basil Blackwell, 1983.

Schulman, Alan. "On the Egyptian Name of Joseph: A New Approach." *Studien zur Altägyptischen Kultur* 2 (1975): 236–43.

Scott, Alan. *Origen and the Life of the Stars: A History of an Idea.* Oxford: Clarendon, 1991.

Scott, Kenneth. "Emperor Worship in Ovid." *Transactions of the American Philological Association* 61 (1930): 53–57.

———. "Tiberius' Refusal of the Title 'Augustus.'" *Classical Philology* 27 (1932): 43–50.

Scott, Ian W. "Is Philo's Moses a Divine Man?" *Studia Philonica Annual* 14 (2002): 87–111.

Scriba, Albrecht. *Die Geschichte des Motivkomplexes Theophanie.* Göttingen: Vandenhoeck & Ruprecht, 1995.

Seelig, Gerald. *Religionsgeschichtliche Methode in Vergangenheit und Gegenwart: Studien zur Geschichte und Methode des religionsgeschichtlichen Vergleichs in der neutestamentlichen Wissenschaft.* Leipzig: Evangelische Verlagsanstalt, 2001.

Segal, Alan. "Heavenly Ascent in Hellenistic Judaism, Early Christianity and their Environment." *ANRW* 23.2:1333–1394. Part 2, *Principat,* 23.2. Edited by Wolfgang Haase. Berlin: Walter de Gruyter, 1980.

———. *Rebecca's Children: Judaism and Christianity in the Roman World.* Cambridge, MA: Harvard University Press, 1986.

———. *Life After Death: A History of the Afterlife in the Religions of the West.* New York: Doubleday, 2004.

Serrano, Andrés García. *The Presentation in the Temple: The Narrative Function of Lk 2:22-39 in Luke-Acts.* Analecta Biblica 197. Rome: Gregorian & Biblical Press, 2012.

Seybold, Klaus. *Das davidische Königtum im Zeugnis der Propheten.* Göttingen: Vandenhoeck & Ruprecht, 1972.

Shapiro, H. A. "Hêrôs Theos: The Death and Apotheosis of Heracles." *Classical World* 77 (1983): 7–18.

Shavit, Yaacov. *Athens in Jerusalem: Classical Antiquity and Hellenism in the Making of the Modern Secular Jew.* Translated by Chaya Naor and Niki Werner. London: Littman Library of Jewish Civilization, 1997.

Sheppard, Beth M. *The Craft of History and the Study of the New Testament.* Atlanta: Society of Biblical Literature, 2012.

Sherwin-White, A. N. *The Letters of Pliny: A Historical and Social Commentary.* Oxford: Clarendon, 1966.

Sherwin-White, Susan, and Amélie Kuhrt. *From Samarkhand to Sardis: A New Approach to the Seleucid Empire.* Berkeley: University of California, 1993.

Simmons, Michael. *Arnobius of Sicca: Religious Conflict and Competition in the Age of Diocletian.* Oxford: Clarendon, 1995.

Simon, Marcel. *Hercule et le Christianisme.* Strasbourg: University of Strasbourg, 1955.

Simpson, C. J. "The Early Name of the Emperor Claudius." *Acta Antiqua: Academiae Scientiarum Hungaricae* 29 (1981): 363–68.

Sissa, Giulia. *Greek Virginity.* Cambridge, MA: Harvard University Press, 1990.

Smid, H. R. *Protoevangelium Iacobi: A Commentary.* Assen: Van Gorcum, 1956.

Smith, Jonathan Z. *Map is Not Territory: Studies in the History of Religion.* Chicago: University of Chicago Press, 1978.

———. *Imagining Religion: From Babylon to Jonestown.* Chicago: University of Chicago Press, 1982.

———. *To Take Place: Toward Theory in Ritual.* Chicago: University of Chicago Press, 1987.

———. *Drudgery Divine.* Chicago: Chicago University Press, 1990.

———. "Epilogue: The 'End' of Comparison: Redescription and Rectification." Pages 237–41 in *A Magic Still Dwells: Comparative Religion in the Postmodern Age.* Edited by Kimberley C. Patton and Benjamin C. Ray. Berkeley: University of California Press, 2000.

———. *Relating Religion: Essays in the Study of Religion.* Chicago: University of Chicago Press, 2004.

———. *God in Translation: Deities in Cross-cultural Discourse in the Biblical World.* Tübingen: Mohr Siebeck, 2008.

Smith, Mark S. *The Origins of Biblical Monotheism: Israel's Polytheistic Background and the Ugaritic Texts.* New York: Oxford University Press, 2001.

Smith, Morton. *Clement of Alexandria and a Secret Gospel of Mark.* Cambridge, MA: Harvard University Press, 1973.

———. *Jesus the Magician.* San Francisco: Harper & Row, 1978.

———. "Ascent to the Heavens and Deification in 4QM." Pages 181–88 in *Archaeology and History in the Dead Sea Scrolls: The New York University Conference in Memory of Yigael Yadin.* Edited by Laurence Schiffman. Sheffield: JSOT, 1990.

Sorek, Susan. *Remembered for Good: A Jewish Benefaction System in Ancient Palestine.* Sheffield: Sheffield Phoenix Press, 2010.

Spicq, C. "La philanthropie hellénistique, vertu divine et royale." *Studia Theologica* 12 (1958): 169–91.

Stafford, Emma. "Vice or Virtue? Herakles and the Art of Allegory." Pages 71–96 in *Herakles and Hercules: Exploring a Graeco-Roman Divinity.* Edited by Louis Rawlings and Hugh Bowden. Swansea: Classical Press of Wales, 2005.

———. "Herakles Between Gods and Heroes." Pages 228–44 in *The Gods of Ancient Greece: Identities and Transformations.* Edited by Jan N. Bremmer and Andrew Erskine. Edinburgh: Edinburgh University Press, 2010.

———. *Herakles.* London: Routledge, 2012.

Stamm, Johann Jakob. "Der Name Des Königs David." Leiden: Brill, 1960.

Stark, Rodney. "Economics of Religion." Pages 47–67 in *The Blackwell Companion to the Study of Religion.* Edited by Robert A. Segal. Malden, MA: Blackwell, 2006.

———. *The Triumph of Christianity: How the Jesus Movement Became the World's Largest Religion.* New York: HarperOne, 2011.

Stein, Robert. "Is the Transfiguration (Mark 9:2-8) a Misplaced Resurrection-Account?" *Journal of Biblical Literature* 95 (1976): 79–96.

Steindorff, Georg. "Der Name Josephs Saphenat-P 'neach, Genesis Kapitel 41, 45." *Zeitschrift für Ägyptische Sprache und Altertumskunde* 27 (1889): 41–42.

———. "Weiteres zu Gen 41, 45." *Zeitschrift für Ägyptische Sprache und Altertumskunde* 30 (1892): 50–52.

Steinmann, Alphons. *Die Jungfrauengeburt und die vergleichende Religionsgeschichte.* Paderborn: Ferdinand Schöningh, 1919.

Steinthal, Hermann. "Platons anthropologische Theologie—aus der Ferne betrachtet." Pages 233–50 in *Geschichte-Tradition-Reflexion: Festschrift für Martin Hengel.* Edited by Hubert Cancik. 3 vols. Tübingen: Mohr Siebeck, 1996.

Stephens, Susan. "Hellenistic Culture." Pages 86–97 in *The Oxford Handbook of Hellenic Studies.* Edited by George Boys-Stones et al. Oxford: Oxford University Press, 2009.

Stevens, Alexander. "Telling Presences. Narrating Divine Epiphany in Homer and Beyond." PhD diss., University of Cambridge, 2002.

Stewart, Z., ed. *Arthur Darby Nock: Essays on Religion in the Ancient World.* 2 vols. Oxford: Clarendon, 1972.

Steyn, Gert Jacobus. "Reflections on *to Onoma tou Kyriou* in 1 Corinthians." Pages 479–90 in *The Corinthian Correspondence.* Edited by Raymond Bieringer. Leuven: Leuven University Press, 1996.

Stietencron, Heinrich von, ed. *Der Name Gottes.* Düsseldorf: Patmos-Verlag, 1975.

Stoessl, Franz. *Der Tod des Herakles.* Zürich: Rhein-Verlag, 1945.

Stroumsa, Guy. "Celsus, Origen, and the Nature of Religion." Pages 81–96 in *Discorsi di Verita: Paganesimo, Giudaismo e Cristianesimo a confronto nel Contro Celso di Origene.* Edited by Lorenzo Perrone. Rome: Institutum Patristicum Augustinianum, 1998.

Stuckenbruck, Loren T. *Angel Veneration and Christology: A Study in Early Judaism and in the Christology of the Apocalypse of John.* Tübingen: Mohr Siebeck, 1995.

———. "The Holy Spirit in the *Ascension of Isaiah.*" Pages 308–20 in *The Holy Spirit and Christian Origins.* Edited by Graham N. Stanton et al. Grand Rapids, MI: Eerdmans, 2004.

Svenson, Dominique. *Darstellungen hellenistischer Könige mit Götterattributen.* Frankfurt am Main: Peter Lang, 1995.

Syme, R. "Imperator Caesar: A Study in Nomenclature." Pages 361–77 in *Roman Papers.* Edited by E. Badian. Oxford: Clarendon, 1979.

Taeger, Fritz. "Alexander der Grosse und die Anfänge des hellenistischen Herrscherkults." *Historische Zeitschrift* 172 (1951): 225–44.

———. *Charisma: Studien Zur Geschichte Des Antiken Herrscherkultes.* 2 vols. Stuttgart: Kohlhammer, 1960.

Talbert, Charles. "The Concept of the Immortals in Mediterranean Antiquity." *Journal of Biblical Literature* 94 (1975): 419–36.

———. *What is a Gospel? The Genre of the Canonical Gospels.* Philadelphia: Fortress Press, 1977.

———. "Jesus' Birth in Luke and the Nature of Religious Language." Pages 79–90 in *Reading Luke-Acts in its Mediterranean Milieu.* Leiden: Brill, 2003.

Tanner, Kathryn. *Theories of Culture: A New Agenda for Theology.* Minneapolis: Fortress Press, 1997.

Theissen, Gerd. *The Miracle Stories of the Early Christian Tradition.* Edited by John Riches. Translated by Francis McDonagh. Philadelphia: Fortress Press, 1983.

———. *A Theory of Primitive Christian Religion.* London: SCM, 1999.

Thompson, Leonard L. *The Book of Revelation: Apocalypse and Empire.* Oxford: Oxford University Press, 1990.

Tilling, Chris. *Paul's Divine Christology.* Wissenschaftliche Untersuchungen zum Neuen Testament 2/323. Tübingen: Mohr Siebeck, 2012.

Tondriau, J. "Rois Lagides comparés ou identifés à des divinités." *Chronique d'Égypte* 45–46 (1948): 127–46.

Toynbee, Arnold. *A Study of History.* 12 vols. London: Oxford University Press, 1939.

Trumbower, Jeffrey A. *Born from Above: The Anthropology of the Gospel of John.* Tübingen: Mohr Siebeck, 1992.

Tzaneteas, Peter. "The Symbolic Heracles in Dio Chrysostom's Orations 'On Kingship.'" PhD diss., Columbia University, 1972.

Tzifopoulos, Y. Z. "Hermes and Apollo at Onchestos in the *Homeric Hymn to Hermes:* the Poetics and Performance of Proverbial Communication." *Mnemosyne* 53 (2000): 148–63.

Ulrichsen, Jarl Henning. "*Diaphorōteron Onoma* in Hebr. 1,4: Christus als Träger des Gottesnamens." *Studia Theologica* 38 (1984): 65–75.

Urbaniak-Walczak, Katarzyna. *Die "conceptio per aurem": Untersuchungen zum Marienbild in Ägypten unter besonderer Berücksichtigung der Malereien in El-Bagawat.* Altenberge: Oros, 1992.

Vaage, Leif E. "Why Christianity Succeeded (in) the Roman Empire." Pages 253–78 in *Religious Rivalries in the Early Roman Empire and the Rise of Christianity.* Edited by Leif Vaage. Waterloo, Ont: Wilfrid Laurier University Press, 2006.

van Camp, Jean, and Paul Canart. *Le Sens Du Mot Theios Chez Platon.* Louvain: University of Louvain, 1956.

van der Horst, Pieter W. *Hellenism-Judaism-Christianity: Essays on Their Interaction.* Kampen: Kok Pharos, 1994.

van der Watt, Jan G. *Family of the King: Dynamics of Metaphor in the Gospel According to John.* Leiden: Brill, 2000.

van Kooten, George H. "Christianity in the Graeco-Roman World: Socio-political, Philosophical, and Religious Interactions Up to the Edict of Milan." Pages 3–37 in *The Routledge Companion to Early Christian Thought.* Edited by D. Jeffrey Bingham. London: Routledge, 2010.

———. "Pagan, Jewish and Christian Philanthropy in Antiquity: A Pseudo-Clementine Keyword in Context." Pages 36–58 in *The Pseudo-Clementines.* Edited by Jan Bremmer. Leuven: Peeters, 2010.

van Nuffelen, Peter. *Rethinking the Gods: Philosophical Readings of Religion in the Post-Hellenistic Period.* Cambridge: Cambridge University Press, 2011.

van Tilborg, Sjef, and Patrick Chatelion Counet. *Jesus' Appearances and Disappearances in Luke 24.* Leiden: Brill, 2000.

VanderKam, James. "Righteous One, Messiah, Chosen One, and Son of Man in 1 Enoch 37–71." Pages 161–91 in *The Messiah: Developments in Earliest Judaism and Christianity.* Edited by J. H. Charlesworth. Minneapolis: Fortress Press, 1992.

Vergados, Athanassios. *The Homeric Hymn to Hermes: Introduction, Text, and Commentary*. Texte und Kommentare 41. Berlin: Walter de Gruyter, 2012.

Vernant, Jean-Pierre. *Mortals and Immortals*. Princeton, NJ: Princeton University Press, 1991.

Versnel, H. S., ed. *Faith, Hope and Worship: Aspects of Religious Mentality in the Ancient World*. Leiden: Brill, 1981.

———. "What Did Ancient Man See When He Saw a God? Some Reflections on Greco-Roman Epiphany." Pages 42–55 in *Effigies Dei: Essays on the History of Religions*. Ed. D. van der Plas. Leiden: Brill, 1987.

Veyne, Paul. *Bread and Circuses: Historical Sociology and Political Pluralism*. Edited by Oswyn Murray and Brian Pearce. London: Penguin, 1990.

Vielhauer, Philipp. *Geschichte der urchristlichen Literatur: Einleitung in das Neue Testament, die Apokryphen und die Apostolischen Väter*. Berlin: Walter de Gruyter, 1975.

Vischer, W. *Die Immanuel-Botschaft Im Zeichen Des Königlichen Zionsfestes*. Edited by Karl Barth. Heft 45 Theologische Studien. Zürich: Evangelischer Verlag, 1955.

Vogt, Spira. "Zum Herrscherkult Bei Julius Caesar." Pages 1138–46 in *Studies Presented to David Moore Robinson on his Seventieth Birthday*. 2 vols. Edited by George Emmanuel Mylonas. Saint Louis: Washington University, 1953.

Vollenweider, Samuel. "'Der Name, der über jedem anderen Namen ist': Jesus als Träger des Gottesnames im Neuen Testament." Pages 173–88 in *Gott Nennen: Gottes Namen Und Gott Als Name*. Edited by Ingolf U. Dalferth and Phillip Stoellger. Tübingen: Mohr Siebeck, 2008.

Vollkommer, Rainer. *Herakles in the Art of Classical Greece*. Oxford University Committee for Archaeology Monograph 25. London: Oxford Committee for Archaeology, 1988.

von Beckerath, Jürgen. *Handbuch der ägyptischen Königsnamen*. Münchner ägyptologische Studien 20. Munich: Deutscher Kunstverlag, 1984.

von Nordheim, Miriam. *Geborn von der Morgenröte? Psalm 110 in Tradition, Redaktion und Rezeption*. Düsseldorf: Neukirchener, 2008.

von Pákozdy, L. M. "Elhanan Der Frühere Name Davids?" *Zeitschrift für Alttestmentliche Wissenschaft* 68 (1956): 257–59.

von Rad, Gerhard. "Das Judaische Königsritual." *Theologische Literaturzeitung* 72 (1947): 211–16.

Walbank, F. W. "Monarchies and Monarchic Ideas." Pages 62–100 in vol. 7.1 of *Cambridge Ancient History*. 2nd ed. 14 vols. Cambridge: Cambridge University Press, 1984.

Wallace-Hadrill, Andrew. *Rome's Cultural Revolution.* Cambridge: Cambridge University Press, 2008.

Ward, Margaret. "The Association of Augustus with Jupiter." *Studi e Materiali di Storia delle Religioni* 9 (1933): 203–24.

Warner, Marina. *Alone of All Her Sex: The Myth and the Cult of the Virgin Mary.* New York: Knopf, 1976.

Weaver, John B. *Plots of Epiphany: Prison-Escape in Acts of the Apostles.* Beihefte zum Zeitschrift für neuetestamentliche Wissenschaft 131. Berlin: Walter de Gruyter, 2004.

Wegner, Paul D. *An Examination of Kingship and Messianic Expectation in Isaiah 1–35.* Lewiston, NY: Mellen, 1992.

Weinreich, Otto. *Antike Heilungswunder: Untersuchungen z. Wunderglauben d. Griechen u. Römer.* Giessen: Töpelmann, 1909.

———. *Neue Urkunden zur Sarapisreligion.* Tübingen: Mohr Siebeck, 1919.

Weinstock, Stefan. *Divus Julius.* Oxford: Clarendon, 1971.

Welburn, Andrew. *Myth of the Nativity: The Virgin Birth Re-examined.* Edinburgh: Floris Books, 2006.

Wendland, Paul. *Die hellenistische-römische Kultur in ihren Beziehungen zum Judentum und Christentum.* Handbuch zum Neuen Testament I/2. 2nd ed. Tübingen: Mohr Siebeck, 1912.

Wengst, Klaus. *Christologische Formeln und Lieder des Urchristentums.* Gütersloh: Gütersloh Verlagshaus, 1973.

West, M. L. *The East Face of Helicon: West Asiatic Elements in Greek Poetry and Myth.* Oxford: Clarendon, 1997.

White, Michael L., and John T. Fitzgerald. "Quod est Comparandum: The Problem of Parallels." Pages 13–40 in *Early Christianity and Classical Culture: Comparative Studies in Honor of Abraham J. Malherbe.* Edited by John T. Fitzgerald, Thomas H. Olbricht, and L. Michael White. Leiden: Brill, 2003.

Whitmarsh, Tim. "Greece and Rome." Pages 114–28 in *The Oxford Handbook of Hellenic Studies.* Edited by George Boys-Stones et al. Oxford: Oxford University Press, 2009.

———. "Hellenism." Pages 728–47 in *The Oxford Handbook of Roman Studies.* Edited by Alessandro Barchiesi and Walter Scheidel. Oxford: Oxford University Press, 2009.

Widengren, Geo. *Sakrales Königtum Im Alten Testament und Im Judentum.* Stuttgart: Kohlhammer, 1955.

———. "Psalm 110 und Das Sakrale Königtum in Israel." Pages 185–216 in *Zur neueren Psalmenforschung*. Edited by Peter H. A. Neumann. Darmstadt: Wissenschaftliche Buchgesellschaft, 1976.

Wiedemann, Thomas. *Adults and Children in the Roman Empire*. London: Routledge, 1989.

Wildberg, Christian. *Hyperesie und Epiphanie: Ein Versuch über die Bedeutung der Götter in den Dramen des Euripides*. Munich: C. H. Beck, 2002.

Wildberger, Hans "Die Thronnamen Des Messias." *Theologische Literaturzeitung* 16 (1960): 314–32.

———. *Isaiah 1–12: A Commentary*. Translated by Thomas H. Trapp. Minneapolis: Fortress Press, 1991.

Wildung, Dietrich. *Egyptian Saints: Deification in Pharaonic Egypt*. New York: New York University Press, 1977.

Williams, Margaret. "Jews and Jewish communities in the Roman Empire." Pages 305–33 in *Experiencing Rome: Culture, Identity and Power in the Roman Empire*. Edited by Janet Huskinson. London: Routledge, 2000.

Williams, Michael. *The Immovable Race: A Gnostic Designation and the Theme of Stability in Late Antiquity*. Leiden: Brill, 1985.

Williamson, Clark M. *A Guest in the House of Israel: Post-Holocaust Church Theology*. Louisville: Westminster John Knox, 1993.

Winiarczyk, Marek. *Euhemeri Messenii Reliquae*. Stuttgart: Teubner, 1991.

———. *Bibliographie zum antiken Atheismus*. Bonn: R. Habelt, 1994.

———. "La mort et l'apothéose d'Héraclès." *Wiener Studien* 113 (2000): 13–29.

———. *Euhemeros von Messene: Leben, Werk und Nachwirkung*. Munich: Saur, 2002.

Winkler, J., and F. I. Zeitlin, eds. *Nothing to Do with Dionysus: Athenian Drama in its Social Setting*. Princeton, NJ: Princeton University Press, 1990.

Winston, David. *Logos and Mystical Theology in Philo of Alexandria*. Cincinnati: Hebrew Union College Press, 1985.

Winterling, Aloys. *Caligula: Eine Biographie*. Munich. C. H. Beck, 2003.

Wolff, Gustav. *Porphyrii de philosophia ex oraculis haurienda*. Hildesheim: Georg Olms, 1962.

Wolmarans, Johannes L. P. "Asclepius and Jesus of Nazareth." *Acta Patristica et Byzantina* 7 (1996): 117–27.

Wright, N. T. "Jesus Christ Is Lord: Philippians 2.5-11." Pages 56–98 in *The Climax of the Covenant: Christ and the Law in Pauline Theology*. Minneapolis: Fortress Press, 1991.

————. *The Resurrection of Son of God*. Vol. 3 of *Christian Origins and the Question of God*. London: SPCK, 2003.

Wünsche, Raimund. *Herakles Herkules*. Munich: Staatliche Antikensammlungen, 2003.

Yamauchi, Edwin M. *Pre-Christian Gnosticism: A Survey of Proposed Evidences*. Grand Rapids, MI: Eerdmans, 1973.

Yamazaki-Ransom, Kazuhiko. *The Roman Empire in Luke's Narrative*. Library of New Testament Studies 421. New York: T&T Clark, 2010,

Zanker, Paul. *The Power of Images in the Age of Augustus*. Ann Arbor: University of Michigan, 1988.

Zeller, Dieter. "La métamorphose de Jésus comme épiphanie (Mc 9, 2-8)." Pages 167–86 in *L'Évangile Exploré: Mélanges offerts à Simon Légasse*. Edited by Alain Marchadour. Paris: Éditions du Cerf, 1996.

————. "Hellenistische Vorgaben für den Glauben an die Auferstehung Jesu?" Pages 71–92 in *Von Jesus zum Christus: Christologische Studien: Festgabe für Paul Hoffmann*. Edited by Rudolf Hoppe and Ulrich Busse. Berlin: Walter de Gruyter, 1998.

————. "New Testament Christology in its Hellenistic Reception." *New Testament Studies* 46 (2001): 312–33.

————. "The θεῖα φύσις of Hippocrates and Other 'Divine Men.'" Pages 49–70 in *Early Christianity and Classical Culture: Comparative Studies in Honor of Abraham J. Malherbe*. Edited by John T. Fitzgerald, Thomas H. Olbricht, and L. Michael White. Leiden, Brill, 2003.

————. "Religionsgeschichtliche Erwägungen zum 'Sohn Gottes' in den Kindheitsgeschichten." Pages 83–94 in *Neues Testament und hellenistische Umwelt*. Bonner Biblische Beiträge 150. Hamburg: Philo, 2006.

Zgoll, Christian. *Die Phänomenologie der Metamorphose: Verwandlungen und Verwandtes in der augusteischen Dichtung*. Tübingen: Gunter Narr, 2004.

Zimmerli, Walther. "Vier oder Fünf Thronnamen des messianischen Herrschers von Jes. IX.5b.6." *Vetus Testamentum* 22 (1972): 249–52.

Zirkle, Conway. "Animals Impregnated by the Wind." *Isis* 25 (1936): 95–130.

Zsigmond, Ritoók. "Die Götter und der Ruhm." Pages 51–6 in *Religio Graeco-Romana: Festschrift für Walter Pötscher*. Edited by Joachim Dalfen, Gerhard Petersmann, and Franz Ferdinand Schwarz. Graz: F. Berger & Söhne, 1993.

Zwiep, A. W. *The Ascension of the Messiah in Lukan Christology*. Supplements to Novum Testamentum 87. Leiden: Brill, 1997.

————. "Assumptus est in caelum: Rapture and Heavenly Exaltation in Early Judaism and Luke-Acts." Pages 323–50 in *Auferstehung-Resurrection: The*

Fourth Durham-Tübingen Research Symposium : Resurrection, Transfiguration and Exaltation in Old Testament, Ancient Judaism and Early Christianity. Edited by Friedrich Avemarie and Hermann Lichtenberger. Wissenschaftliche Untersuchungen zum Neuen Testament 135. Tübingen: Mohr Siebeck, 2001.

Index

CPSIA information can be obtained
at www.ICGtesting.com
Printed in the USA
FFOW05n0005230414

9 781451 473032